The Divine Name(s) and the Holy Trinity

VOLUME ONE

Distinguishing the Voices

R. Kendall Soulen

First edition
Published by Westminster John Knox Press
Louisville, Kentucky

11 12 13 14 15 16 17 18 19 20—10 9 8 7 6 5 4 3 2 1

Book design by Sharon Adams
Cover design by Night & Day Design

Library of Congress Cataloging-in-Publication Data

Soulen, R. Kendall, 1959–
The divine name(s) and the Holy Trinity / R. Kendall Soulen.—1st ed.
p. cm.
Includes index.
ISBN 978-0-664-23414-0 (alk. paper)
1. Trinity. 2. God (Christianity—Name. I. Title. II. Title: Divine name and the Holy Trinity. III. Title: Divine names and the Holy Trinity.
BT111.3.S855 2011
231'.044—dc23
2011023741

PRINTED IN THE UNITED STATES OF AMERICA

♾ The paper used in this publication meets the minimum requirements of the American National Standard for Information Sciences—Permanence of Paper for Printed Library Materials, ANSI Z39.48-1992.

Westminster John Knox Press advocates the responsible use of our natural resources. The text paper of this book is made from 30% postconsumer waste.

For Allison

What my Eunomos sings is not the measure of Terpander, nor that of Capito, nor the Phrygian, nor Lydian, nor Dorian, but the immortal measure of the new harmony which bears God's name—the new, the Levitical song.

—*Clement of Alexandria*[1]

Contents

Part Two Distinguishing the Voices: The Name of the Trinity in the Scriptures of the Old and New Testaments

Abstract

The Divine Name(s) and the Holy Trinity explores the doctrine of the Trinity through an analysis of names. It asks, "What is the most appropriate way of naming the persons of the Trinity?" and proposes that there are in fact three such ways, each of which is most appropriate by virtue of its special affinity with one person of the Trinity in particular. The work develops this thesis in four parts. Part 1, "A Threefold Cord," explores the thesis in a historical context, showing how the three patterns of trinitarian naming have functioned in the history of Christian thought. Part 2, "Distinguishing the Voices," shows how the thesis emerges out of a theological reading of the church's canon of Old and New Testaments. Part 3, "Voices in Counterpoint," explores the value of the thesis in relationship to a series of contested issues in contemporary theology. Part 4, "Triple Fugue," concludes the work by drawing implications for the understanding of the immanent Trinity. Parts 1 and 2 appear in the present volume, *Distinguishing the Voices*, which gets its title from part 2. Parts 3 and 4 will appear together in a subsequent volume, *Voices in Counterpoint.*

The phrase "The Divine Name(s)" is intended to evoke two different understandings of the term "name," one shaped by the Scriptures' restrictive application of the term to the Tetragrammaton (the divine name), and the other by Christian antiquity's more generous application of the term to common nouns generally (the divine names). How these senses of the word "name" relate to each other—and to the kinship vocabulary of Father, Son, and Holy Spirit—in the context of the doctrine of the Trinity is a large part of the problem that the book seeks to address. The book argues that a right understanding of this relationship depends upon restoring the divine name to its proper place in the infinite economy of trinitarian names.

Acknowledgments

Adequately thanking those who have helped me write this book is as pleasant to attempt as it is impossible to do. My teachers Hans Frei, George Lindbeck, and David Kelsey kindled my first passion for the themes addressed here. Wallace Alston and Robert Jenson created an ideal setting for the book's early incubation during their tenures as Director and Senior Scholar for Research at The Center of Theological Inquiry, Princeton, NJ. Elizabeth Johnson and again Robert Jenson responded generously and insightfully to my discussion of their work in the following pages. Many people commented wisely on substantial portions of the manuscript, including Richard N. Soulen, Allison Rutland Soulen, Mandy Sayers, Patrick Miller, Mark Kinzer, Rusty Reno, Matthew Levering, Daniel Migliore, William Young III, Tarmo Toom, Matt Marston, and Marianne Blickenstaff. Mandy Sayers also provided invaluable assistance with research and the notes, as did Jean Dudek, Cynthia Burkert, Matt Tapie, and Nelson Long. Many others provided various forms of encouragement, direction, and support along the way, including Margaret Ann Soulen, M. Douglas Meeks, Bruce Birch, Amy Oden, David Tracy, Markus Bockmuehl, Reinhard Huetter, Gerhard Sauter, Heinrich Assel, Robert Herrera, Armand Maurer, Joe Mangina, Richard Bauckham, Jeremy Begbie, Ann Astell, Peter Ochs, Berthold Klappert, Mark Heim, Walt Lowe, Vigen Guroian, Nicholas Baechle, Sathianathan Clarke, Shaun Casey, Sharon Ringe, Stanley Hauerwas, Kathi Morley, Clint Stretch, Beth Norcross, Roy Howard, Jason Luttrell, Francine Samuelson, Wayne and Angela Valis, and Jason Sexton. I also profited greatly from colleagues, too many to name, who offered thoughtful responses to early versions of this work as presented at meetings of the Resident Members of the Center of Theological Inquiry, the Christian Scholars Group, the Duodecim Theological Society, the American

Theological Society, the University of Bonn, the Center for Catholic and Evangelical Theology, and the Systematic Theology working group of the Washington Theological Consortium. My work was generously supported by grants from the Pew Evangelical Scholars Program and the Center of Theological Inquiry. I also wish to acknowledge invaluable grant support from the Louisville Institute, which made it possible for me to complete this work while a Visiting Scholar at the University of St. Andrews. Finally, I treasure the memory of teaching this book for the first time in Seoul, South Korea, to a lively group of pastors and seminary leaders from South Korea, Vietnam, Myanmar, and Bangladesh, under the auspices of Wesley Theological Seminary and Kwanglim Methodist Church (Seoul). To all these people and institutions, I am more grateful than I can say.

Introduction

A Deep and Mysterious Subject

> Though our lips can only stammer, we yet chant the high things of God.
>
> —*Gregory the Great*[1]

Names are curious things. We use them so easily that they seem to be weightless, as insubstantial as a breath of air or mark on a page. Juliet, it seems, is simply right when she says, "A rose by any other name would smell as sweet."[2] Yet just when we start to ignore names altogether, we bark our shin against one. We mispronounce a name, or forget it, or mix it up with someone else's (a high school sweetheart!). Poor Romeo and Juliet die because of names.

Goethe famously proclaimed the nullity of names in his poem *Faust*:

> Name it then as you will!
> Name it Chance! Heart! Love! God!
> I have no name for it.
> Feeling is everything;
> The name is just Noise and Smoke.[3]

But Goethe sang a different tune when a contemporary made a pun on the poet's own name:

> It really was not very nice that he let himself make a joke with my name. For a person's proper name is not like a cape that merely hangs about him, and that one can just tug about this way and that, but it's like perfectly fitting clothes, or better like a person's very skin, which one can't scrape or mistreat without injuring the person himself.[4]

A name, it seems, is like a Möbius strip, a ring with two sides but—mysteriously—only one surface. Names are light and transparent on one side, heavy and opaque on the other, but each side leads endlessly to the other. Mere scraps of sound, the plaything of punsters, names still share somehow in the reality of what they signify.

The mystery of names intensifies when we consider divine names, names for God. It seems obvious that there is all the difference in the world between God's being and God's name. Surely, we think, it is God's being that matters. The name of God is just a noisy convention that falls infinitely short of its goal, like a campfire spark beneath the vault of heaven. This was the view of the ancient pagan author Celsus. Exasperated by what he took to be an obsession with names among Jews and Christians, Celsus exclaimed: "It makes no difference whether one calls the supreme God by the name used among the Greeks, or by that, for example, used among the Indians or by that among the Egyptians."[5]

Yet the Christian theologian Origen felt obliged to disagree. The nature of names, he observed, is "a deep and mysterious subject," far more intricate than Celsus seemed to be aware. Far from being interchangeable, divine names often bring with them associations that other names do not (for instance, the name "Zeus" brings with it the association "husband of Hera"). Origen went on:

> We . . . defend the fact that Christians strive to the point of death to avoid calling God Zeus or naming him in any other language. For either they use the ordinary name "God" without qualification, or with the addition of the words "the Creator of the universe, the Maker of heaven and earth, who sent down to the human race such and such wise men."[6]

Origen's defense of martyrdom on behalf of a name was not a rhetorical flourish. His own father was beheaded by "tolerant" paganism for professing the name of Christ, and Origen himself would die of injuries sustained while being tortured for his faith.

Few readers of this book are likely to risk martyrdom for their allegiance to a divine name. Still, many have some such allegiance. Celsus was right to think that this calls for an explanation. God is utterly unique, a member of no class or genus. No generic label is adequate to God. "I am who I am!" But humans have no language except generic language, a net of words too coarse to catch the glorious uniqueness of even mundane things, such as the shape of a tree leaf or the smell of lilac in spring. Therefore, no human speech is adequate to convey the uniqueness of God. Except—and this is what Celsus did not know or could not believe—God can take what is inadequate in itself and speak through it, thereby making it proportional to God, even in the midst of its still greater disproportion. "Say to them, 'I am sent me to you'" (Exod. 3:14). Then, but only then, the vain, upwardly rising sparks of human language can become descending tongues of flame.

The name of God is the linguistic token that signifies the uniqueness of God. To be sure, divine names are as inadequate as any other such token, as common as bread and water and even less substantial. Yet somehow in the context of Scripture, worship, proclamation, and prayer, the Spirit speaks through them, imbuing them with a spiritual density that is almost physical in heft, as heavy and flavorful as sacramental wine. The sacramental analogy is helpful, too, because it clarifies what divine names are not. The name of God is not magic, any more than is baptism or the laying on of hands. But neither is the name of God just an arbitrary tag or empty label. Ordinary and awesome at once, the name of God is something like an audible sacrament. In the name, the bearer of the name is present. "Blessed is the one who comes in the name of the Lord!" (Ps. 118:26; Matt. 21:9).

It would be impossible to draw a circle around all the names important to Christian faith. Even agreeing on the chief of these would be difficult. Christ? Certainly. Mary? Yes. Bright morning star? Well, . . . Bartholomew? Probably not. But it would not be hard to agree on the names that belong at the center of the circle.

The first of these is the name of Jesus. While the central figure of Christian faith is called many things (Christ, Good Shepherd, Prince of Peace, and so on) this particular name has special significance for Christians for a simple reason. It is its bearer's personal proper name, and indeed, his only proper name. A personal proper name is a very humble form of speech. Unlike other kinds of names (common nouns, titles, epithets, and so forth), the ordinary grammatical role of a proper name is not to describe but simply to point: this one and not another. Yet the very humility of personal proper names is also the source of a distinct advantage. For whereas other kinds of names derive their meaning from the general class of things to which they refer (King, Shepherd, Friend), a personal proper name acquires its sense from the person and history of the one who bears it, from his character, actions, and fate. So it is with the name Jesus. The name has logical priority over other names because it specifies who Christians mean when they speak of Christ, Son of God, and so on. These other names acquire their sacred sense precisely insofar as they are assimilated to the contours of the one who bears the name Jesus, even as they in turn expound the infinite riches of the name Jesus by repeating these contours in other terms.

The other name that belongs at the center of the Christian life is the name of the Trinity. That name is the particular concern of this book. Down through the centuries, the name of the Trinity has played a role in Christian life unequalled by any name other than the name of Jesus. And indeed, the two names are intimately linked. "Jesus" signifies the human being whose personhood is eternally caught up in relation with God and the Spirit. The name of the Trinity signifies the eternal bond of tripersonal love revealed in the man Jesus. Christians know, as deeply as they know anything, that God without Christ and the Spirit is remote and unavailing, that Christ without God and the Spirit is a martyred saint, that the Spirit without God and Christ is power bereft of form and direction. Faith lives from the interconnection of the three. A hymn ascribed to St. Patrick and put into popular form by Frances Alexander in 1875 expresses this sense well:

> I bind unto myself today
> the strong name of the Trinity,
> By invocation of the same,
> the Three in One, the One in Three.[7]

For Alexander and many others, the name of the Trinity is more than a linguistic token. It participates in the mystery of the Trinity itself. It is the audible sacrament that reveals in time the endless pattern of eternal love.

Still, a curiosity lurks in Alexander's opening stanza. She evokes the name of the Trinity but does not tell us what it is. What is "the strong name of the Trinity" to which the poet refers? Or is the question out of order, a sign of pedantic literal-mindedness or unseemly speculation?

Another hymnist did not think so. In a lyric of 1743, Charles Wesley wrote:

> Thee, great tremendous Deity,
> Whom Three in One, and One in Three
>   I to the world proclaim,
> Inspire with purity and peace,
> And add me to thy witnesses
>   By telling me thy name.[8]

Wesley asked, "Tell me thy name," not out of a spirit of hubris, but because he wanted to testify more credibly of the Trinity to the world. In this, he was following the precedent of Moses, who asked a similar question for a similar reason at the edge of a burning bush:

> But Moses said to God, "If I come to the Israelites and say to them, 'The God of your ancestors has sent me to you,' and they ask me, 'What is his name?' what shall I say to them?" (Exod. 3:13)

Moses knew that slaves do not ask, "What is his name?" in a spirit of idle curiosity. It is the most fundamental question they *can* ask. Before putting his own life on the line, and asking others to do the same, Moses wanted to know the name of the one who backed up the promise of freedom. Christians, too, have received a promise of freedom, summed up for them in the name Jesus. And like Moses and the Israelites, they want to know the name that backs up this promise, in time and eternity. The question "What is the name of the Trinity?" is not out of order, pedantic, or unseemly. It is the most fundamental question Christians *can* ask.

1

Who Shall I Say Sent Me?

> The doctrine of the Trinity has helped to divide Eastern from Western Christianity. Nowadays within the West itself a further divisive issue has arisen: the naming of the three persons.
>
> —*Gerald O'Collins*[1]

"What is the name of the Trinity?" is a fundamental question, but it is not always an urgent one. Most of the time, Christians invoke the persons of the Trinity confident that they know well enough how this is done. This is as it should be, for without a measure of such confidence, Christians would scarcely dare to call upon the Trinity at all. To put it another way, Christians do not ordinarily live as though they stand at the edge of the burning bush, with Moses' question still hanging in the air. They live, rather, from the fund of names *already* given to them by God, Christ, and the Spirit, at the burning bush, on the mountain in Galilee, on the morning of Pentecost, and on other occasions of sacred memory as well.

From time to time, though, Christians encounter some new question, experience, or problem that interrupts the self-evidence of familiar names. They then find it necessary to step back from the daily language of faith in order to explore its logic, weigh its justification, and ponder its significance. On such occasions, Christians may indeed feel as though they stand again in the heat of the burning bush, straining with every fiber to hear God's voice anew. What Christians seek in such instances is *not* a new revelation, nor even some new name, but a deepening, purification, and renewal of old names and patterns of naming, in order that they may more faithfully meet the needs of the day.

Many Christians experience the present as a season of the second kind. Like others before them, they have found it necessary to inquire more deeply into the names that they customarily use to invoke the persons of the Trinity. What is distinctive about the present, perhaps, is the number and variety of issues that are prompting people to do this. In what follows, we will examine three such issues, each of which intersects the church's trinitarian language at a somewhat different point.

CONTEMPORARY QUESTIONS ABOUT THE CHURCH'S ECONOMY OF TRINITARIAN NAMES

The three issues we will explore are the emancipation of women, the church's exponential growth in Africa and Asia, and the church's renewed relationship with the Jewish people. Each of these exciting and welcome developments raises issues that touch on the whole economy of names that Christians use to express their faith in the Trinity; yet each does so at a particular point, which we can signal with reference to three sites of sacred memory in the Christian tradition: the burning bush, the unnamed mountain in Galilee where the risen Christ appeared to the disciples, and the morning of Pentecost.

We begin our survey with the church's renewed relationship to the Jewish people. While this is not the most familiar or pressing issue for many Christians, it is a fitting place to start; because of all the developments we will consider, it is the one most directly connected with the names and patterns of naming connected with the burning bush.

NAME(S) FROM THE BURNING BUSH AND THE CHURCH'S RENEWED RELATION TO THE JEWISH PEOPLE

The traditions known today as Judaism and Christianity were born from the same earthly mother, the Second Temple Judaism of the early Common Era. United by exclusive worship of one God, the deity who spoke to Moses at the burning bush, the two communities parted ways by the second century, due to the Christian confession of Jesus as Messiah and Lord, the influx of Gentiles into the church, and divergent stances toward the Mosaic law. Much bitterness accompanied the divorce on both sides. For centuries thereafter, the church maintained that it alone was the heir of God's promises to Abraham, that God's covenant with the patriarchs' natural descendants (if it ever existed) was void, and that the continued practice of the Mosaic law was odious to God.

In the second half of the twentieth century, however, many churches stopped to reassess this teaching, stunned by the almost total destruction of

Jewry in the heart of modern Christian Europe. After careful study, many concluded that the teaching was rooted more in bitterness and a false sense of superiority than in Scripture and sound theology. Since then, scores of churches have gone on record articulating a new and more faithful understanding of the church's relationship to Judaism. In virtually every instance, the churches officially affirm in some fashion the continued status of the Jews as the covenant partner of God, in keeping with the teaching of the apostle Paul that "as regards election they are beloved, for the sake of their ancestors; for the gifts and calling of God are irrevocable" (Rom. 11:28–29).[2]

While the new chapter in the history of Christians and Jews has still barely begun, it has already witnessed extraordinary events. One of these was the pilgrimage made by Pope John Paul II in the year 2000 to the Western Wall of the Temple Mount in Jerusalem, the most sacred site of Judaism. "With 86 shuffling steps," the pope approached the wall, "reached out a trembling hand to touch its cool stone, and, as is the custom of Jewish visitors, tucked into a crevice a note to God."[3] The note read:

> God of our fathers, you chose Abraham and his descendants to bring your name to the nations. We are deeply saddened by the behavior of those who in the course of history have caused these children of yours to suffer. And asking your forgiveness, we wish to commit ourselves to genuine brotherhood with the people of the covenant. Jerusalem, 26.3.2000. Johannes Paulus II[4]

Better than any document of comparable length, John Paul II's prayer epitomizes the sea change that has taken place in the church's understanding of God's relation to Israel. God's choice of "Abraham and his descendants" defines the contours of salvation history not only in the past but also in the present: the Jews remain "these children of yours" and "the people of the covenant."

At the same time, the pope's prayer, and the extraordinary way in which he offered it up, provides occasion for Christians to reflect on the implications of these new developments for other dimensions of Christian faith. Consider, for example, the statement that God chose Abraham's descendants "to bring your name to the nations." While the note does not explicitly say so, the context suggests that the pope was thinking of the name that God revealed to Moses at the burning bush.[5] This is the name that unites Jews and Christians, if they are united at all, and that makes it possible for the pope to begin a prayer in Jerusalem with the words "God of *our* fathers." Yet one may ask, with trepidation, but also with Mosaic boldness, What *is* this name? And how, precisely, does it relate to the church's language of trinitarian faith?

The church's traditional economy of trinitarian language supplies ready answers to these questions. The name pronounced at the burning bush is "I am," as recorded in Exodus 3:14.

> God said to Moses, "I am who I am." He said further, "Thus you shall say to the Israelites, 'I am has sent me to you.'"[6]

"I am" (or *qui est*, "He Who Is," in the Latin translation of Exod. 3:14b influential in the West) relates to the church's trinitarian faith by signifying the one divine essence common to the three persons of the Trinity. It refers to what the three persons are or have in common, rather than to what distinguishes them. At the same time, "I am" is really a "nameless name," a sign of the incomprehensible mystery of God. It describes God's deity more aptly than any other name or description, yet even it does not define God's nature, which is essentially uncircumscribable.

It would be foolish to ignore the lasting value of this answer, which distills the wisdom of centuries. Still, it would be equally foolish to ignore what it leaves out, at least when evaluated in light of the church's new relationship to the Jewish people. What the answer omits is the sacred Tetragrammaton, *the* divine name par excellence. The Tetragrammaton (from Gk. *tetragrammaton*, lit., "having four letters") is so called because it consists of four Hebrew characters: י (*yod*), ה (*he*), ו (*waw*), and ה (*he*), spelled right to left in Hebrew יהוה, and transliterated left to right as "YHWH" in English. These four letters are typically represented in English Bible by the capitalized Lord, a word which, following ancient precedent, is neither a translation of the Tetragrammaton, nor a transliteration of it, but a *surrogate* used in its place, in token of reverence for the name itself. The Tetragrammaton appears not in Exodus 3:14, but in the following verse, which contains *the rest* of God's reply to Moses.

> God also said to Moses, "Thus you shall say to the Israelites, 'The Lord [יהוה], the God of your ancestors, the God of Abraham, the God of Isaac, and the God of Jacob, has sent me to you': This is my name forever, and this my title for all generations." (Exod. 3:15)

Congruent with God's words in Exodus 3:15, the Tetragrammaton is the most sacred name for God in Jewish tradition, and the most common name for God in the Old Testament, where it appears more than twice as often as all other divine names combined (some 6,000 times in all). The Tetragrammaton is the name that God actually commissioned Israel to "bring to the nations," and for the sake of which the temple in Jerusalem was built (cf. 1 Kings 8). For well over two millennia, Jews have marked out the unique status of this name by avoiding its pronunciation, and by employing some surrogate in its stead, a practice scrupulously followed by Jesus, the apostles, and the writers of the New Testament.

For much of the church's history, the Tetragrammaton has played little explicit role in the way in which the church thinks about the name and mystery of the Trinity. But it was not always so. In recent years, writers such as Richard Bauckham and Larry Hurtado have shown that reverence for the Tetragrammaton is something like the matrix out of which the church's trinitarian faith emerges.[7] Early Christians, who were Jews themselves, conformed to the Jewish practice of avoiding direct use of the divine name and employing surrogates in its stead, while at the same time putting this practice to use to express their understanding of God, Christ, the Spirit and the mutual relations among them. That is, they used indirect reference to the Tetragrammaton as a mode of *trinitarian* naming, to identify the persons of the Trinity.

Consider, for example, a passage from Paul's Letter to the Philippians, one of the earliest writings in the New Testament:

> 5Let the same mind be in you that was in Christ Jesus,
>
> 6Who, though he was in the form of God,
> did not regard equality with God as something to be exploited,
> 7but emptied himself, taking the form of a slave, being born in human likeness.
> And being found in human form,
> 8he humbled himself and became obedient to the point of death—even death on a cross.
> 9Therefore God also highly exalted him
> and gave him the name that is above every name,
> 10so that at the name of Jesus every knee should bend,
> in heaven and on earth and under the earth,
> 11and every tongue should confess that Jesus Christ is Lord,
> to the glory of God the Father.
>
> (Phil. 2:5–11)

Over the centuries, Christians have interpreted Paul's reference to "the name above every name" (v. 9) in different ways. Some have held that it refers to God's namelessness; others, the word "Lord"; and still others, the name "Jesus." When one takes into account the passage's Jewish context, however, a more likely possibility suggests itself. "The name above every name" refers to the Tetragrammaton, the name that first-century Jews—whether Christian or not—referred to *obliquely*, by means of phrases such as this one. If this interpretation is correct, then Paul in Philippians 2 uses oblique reference to the Tetragrammaton to identify all three persons of the Trinity. He identifies the first person as the one who gives the divine name, the second person as the one who receives it, and the third person as the one who awakens its acknowledgment, in the second person to the glory of the first. True, our text does not explicitly mention the Holy Spirit, but its activity is implied by the cosmic acclamation of Jesus as "Lord" (another conventional surrogate for the divine name), a cry that Paul says elsewhere is possible only as a work of the Spirit (1 Cor. 12:3).

The references to the Tetragrammaton in Philippians 2:5–11 are far from unique. By one estimate, the New Testament contains well over two thousand forms of speech shaped in one way or another by the practice of avoiding the direct use of the Tetragrammaton.[8] Allowing for differences of length, this means that the density of allusion to the Tetragrammaton is about the same in the New Testament as in the Old, if not greater still. Even so, Christians gradually lost touch with this particular divine name, due in large part to the parting of ways between Judaism and Christianity over the first several centuries of the Common Era. The result was a marked impoverishment of the church's treasury of trinitarian names and patterns of naming.

Still, when we consider the Tetragrammaton, one may ask with Juliet, what's in a name? Perhaps it is only to be expected that Christians should have lost touch with this particular pattern of naming the persons of the Trinity, which is so deeply connected with a Jewish context. This need not be a problem, so long as Christians continue to express their faith in the Trinity by means of other, more generally accessible names, such as "Father, Son, and Holy Spirit," and, of course, the awesome "I am." Does it really matter, then, that Christians lost track of this particular pattern of trinitarian naming, centered in the unspoken Tetragrammaton?

Yes, it does matter. For one thing, when Christians eventually did recover knowledge of the Tetragrammaton (chiefly after the 12th century), they interpreted it through the lens of their existing doctrines of Israel, which had already been formulated in ways that churches in recent decades have judged to be inadequate. That is, Christians often made their understanding of the Tetragrammaton conform to a prior supersessionist understanding of God's relationship to the Jewish people, which maintained the obsolescence of God's covenant with Israel.[9] A discussion from the 1950s illustrates this point:

> Why then, we must ask, do [Christians] not say "Yahweh"? The only possible answer is that the name Yahweh belongs to the old covenant. . . . It does not occur in the NT. . . . Just as Christ is the goal and thus the "end" of the law, the name Yahweh attains its goal and its "end" in him. . . . The name Yahweh belongs as a name to the unfulfilled law, to the promise, to the old covenant. . . . If the Church still wanted to say "Yahweh" or (perhaps) "Jehovah," then it would be denying what God has done.[10]

The author (German theologian Otto Weber) simply applies to the Tetragrammaton the same pattern of reasoning that Christians had previously applied to other aspects of Jewish faith and practice, such as circumcision and dietary law, according to which Christ's coming had rendered the continued observance of such practices otiose and abhorrent to God. Obviously, a name that is obsolete can scarcely be the center of a pattern of naming the Trinity that is of continuing importance for the church. But surely Weber's view stands reality on its head. If Christians have not traditionally said "Yahweh" in their worship of the Trinity, it is not because the name is obsolete, but rather because they follow the precedent of the New Testament (whether knowingly or not), which always refers to the name obliquely, in keeping with Jewish oral law. Far from testifying to the wholesale obsolescence of the Old Covenant, the nonpronunciation of the Tetragrammaton in Christian worship testifies to the continuing presence and influence of Jewish practice at the heart of the church's liturgical life.

The other reason the Tetragrammaton matters for the doctrine of the Trinity, however, is still more important. Although Christians have more than one pattern of naming the persons of the Trinity, they have only one that revolves around a personal proper name. For like the name Jesus, the Tetragrammaton is indeed a personal proper name, which acquires its meaning not from any inherent sense of the word, but from the being and action of its bearer. In this respect, the Tetragrammaton is yet more primordial even than the name Jesus, for while the etymological sense of "Jesus" is "YHWH is Salvation," the Tetragrammaton itself has no certain semantic meaning at all. It figures in biblical testimony as a "pure" proper name, whose revealed "sense" derives wholly from the being and history of its bearer. The Tetragrammaton, although devoid of conventional semantic meaning, fills the pages of the Old Testament with its connotation the way the glory of the LORD filled the tabernacle of old (Exod. 40:34). The divine name encompasses within its cloud of connotation the truth of God's eternal being and the ontological distinction between Creator and creation (cf. Gen. 21:23; Isa. 40:28; Pss. 90, 103, 145; etc.). Yet it also encompasses in a quite particular way the truth of God's free and gracious condescension toward "these children of yours" (Pope John Paul II), Abraham and his chosen descendants:

> [35]Thus says the Lord, who gives the sun for light by day and the fixed order of the moon and the stars for light by night, who stirs up the sea so that its waves roar—the Lord of hosts is his name: [36]If this fixed order were ever to cease from my presence, says the Lord, then also the offspring of Israel would cease to be a nation before me forever. (Jer. 31:35–36)

As we just noted, the writers of the New Testament employ a plethora of buffer words and phrases to allude to the Tetragrammaton, so that the connotations of the divine name fill the New Testament as intensely as they do the Old—at least "for those with ears to hear." When, for example, Paul declares that "the gifts and the calling of God are irrevocable" (Rom. 11:29), it comes after an extended reflection in which he cites numerous Old Testament passages that contain or allude to the Tetragrammaton (Rom. 9–11). It is in part the pressure of *this* name—*the* divine name—that pushes Paul to affirm the irrevocability of God's gifts and calling.

In sum, the church's renewed relationship with the Jewish people provides an occasion for Christians to think again about how they name the persons of the Trinity. It does so both with respect to how they should estimate the significance of a long-neglected pattern of naming centered in the unspoken Tetragrammaton, and with respect to how this rediscovered pattern relates to other, more familiar forms of trinitarian speech.

NAMES FROM THE MORNING OF PENTECOST AND THE EMERGENCE OF WORLD CHRISTIANITY

The church's renewed relationship to "the people of the covenant" is one reason Christians are seeking a deepened understanding of their trinitarian language, but it is not the only one. Another is Christianity's explosive growth outside its traditional sphere of influence in the West. In 1900, four out of every five Christians lived in Europe or North America. Today the overwhelming majority of Christians live in the global south and east. Yesterday theologians expounded the mystery of the Trinity in categories drawn from Western culture and philosophy, such as "Primordial Being, Expressive Being, and Unitive Being" (John Macquarrie) and "Revealer, Revelation, and Revealedness" (Karl Barth). Tomorrow they may do so more often in the categories of Hindu philosophy (*Sat*, *Chit*, *Ananda*) or Daoism (*Dao/Tao*, *De*, *Qi*), as indeed some have already done.[11] This development, too, raises challenging questions about the logic of names that Christians use to invoke the persons of the Trinity, in this case from the primary vantage point of the Holy Spirit and the morning of Pentecost. Consider the following story.

In 1991, Chung Hyun-Kyung, a Korean professor of theology, delivered the keynote address at the Seventh General Assembly of the World Council of Churches in Canberra, Australia. Her theme was "Come, Holy Spirit—Renew the Whole Creation." In the course of her address, Chung interpreted the life and work of the Trinity by means of a number of non-Western concepts, such as *Han* (Korean for anger, resentment, and the raw energy for struggle); *Ina* (Tagalog for mother, also denoting the great goddess from whom all life comes); *ki* (a Northeast Asian concept denoting life energy and harmonious interconnection [236]); and *kwan in* (an East Asian divine personification of compassion and wisdom). Chung also characterized the persons of the Trinity, in tones reminiscent of Western feminist and liberation theology, as "the compassionate God who weeps with us," "the Liberator . . . tortured and killed on the cross" (232), and the "Fire of Life" (233). In what was perhaps the speech's most controversial section, Chung urged her listeners to hear "the cries of the Spirit" within "the cries of creation." She then invoked the spirits of departed victims of violence, including "women burnt at the 'witch trials,'" "indigenous people of the earth," "victims of genocide during the time of colonialism," "Korean women in the Japanese 'prostitution army,'" "jelly babies from the Pacific nuclear test zone," and others. "Without hearing the cries of these spirits," she admonished, "we cannot hear the voice of the Holy Spirit" (232).[12]

The address caused a sensation. Many delegates were deeply distressed. In a written response representatives of Orthodox churches warned of a tendency they detected in Chung's speech "to substitute a 'private' spirit, the spirit of the world or other spirits for the Holy Spirit who proceeds from the Father and rests in the Son."[13] Others, however, heartily welcomed Chung's words. They saw them as a demonstration that Christians from the global east and south could invoke the Trinity by names and categories not previously sanctioned by the West. In this, they saw the necessary continuation of the work begun on the morning of Pentecost, when the Holy Spirit enabled the apostles to preach so that "each one heard them speaking in the native language of each" (Acts 2:6).

The deeply divided reaction to Chung's speech reflected real and valid disagreements about its theological merits. But it also reflected another tender spot in Christianity's traditional economy of trinitarian names. Christians, it seems, have seldom if ever invoked the persons of the Trinity by using language drawn exclusively from the Bible; instead, they have always supplemented it with ternaries, names, and concepts originating from the church's host culture. But the status of this language has not always been entirely clear. Must such language always occupy a place inferior to that of biblically attested names, or can it possess an equal dignity?

The question is a very ancient one. We just saw how early Christian Jews used oblique reference to the Tetragrammaton to identify the persons of the Trinity, as the giver, receiver, and glorifier of the divine name. Yet the same Jewish leaders also extended the right hand of fellowship to Gentile Christians without demanding that they take on all the obligations of Jewish life (cf. Acts 15). They thereby opened the door to Gentile Christianity, which quickly devised its own ways of naming the persons of the Trinity by drawing on the cultural resources of their own pagan context. The rhetorician Tertullian compared the persons of the Trinity to various triads known from common experience: Root-Tree-Fruit, Sun-Ray-Apex, Fountain-River-Stream.[14] Basil the Great evoked the parlance of Neoplatonism to speak of the persons of the Trinity as "Archetype, Image, Purifying Sun."[15] Augustine followed his own restless heart as much or more than the letter of Scripture when he designated the Trinity as the Lover, the Beloved, and Love.

Indeed, Gentile Christians did more than enlarge the church's stock of trinitarian names. They expanded and transformed the very conception of what counts as God's "name" by assimilating it to the contours of their own cultural context. Within a biblical frame of reference, God's name (*shem*) refers exclusively to the Tetragrammaton, God's personal proper name. When Matthew, for example, writes of "the name of the Father and of the Son and the Holy Spirit" (Matt. 28:19), it is quite possible that he refers to the name that the Father gives to the Son and glorifies by the Spirit: the sacred Tetragrammaton.[16] Christians of late antiquity, in contrast, commonly understood the term "name" to encompass many words predicated of God, including common nouns, adjectives, participles, and even infinitives; thus for them, God had many names.[17] Gentile Christians also transformed the theory and practice of pious reserve and negation connected with God's name. In place of the Jewish practice of not pronouncing the divine name, Gentile Christians increasingly emphasized the final inadequacy of all the divine names predicated of God. Pseudo-Dionysius's *The Divine Names*, the most influential Christian treatise on the subject ever written, silently assumes the expanded definition of God's names and the doctrine of God's ineffability. Even so—and this is the key point—it purports to do nothing but expound sacred Scriptures' own teaching, a claim heartily endorsed by subsequent tradition.

All of this shows that when Chung took the liberty of naming the persons of the Trinity in language drawn from her own native cultural context, she was following an ancient precedent. What was new was the specific cultural context she invoked. Some wondered whether Chung's Orthodox critics would have felt the same need to admonish her if she had interpreted the Trinity in terms of the ternary of Archetype, Image, and Burning Sun, or Dionysius's celebration of the nameless God of many names. The need arose, the same persons suspected, at least in part because Chung interpreted the Trinity by means of ternaries drawn from an East Asian rather than ancient Mediterranean context.

In fairness to Chung's critics, however, it must be said that Western Christians have never endorsed the idea that Christians can rightly name the persons of the Trinity by invoking any existing ternary at hand. Quite the contrary. In the fourth century, Arians proposed that God, Christ, and the Spirit could be named (among other things) "Creator," "product," and "product of product." Arguably, this proposal did an excellent job of translating the gospel into terms comprehensible to late antiquity, which was accustomed to thinking about plural deities of descending rank. Nevertheless, the bishops who gathered at the Councils of Nicaea and Constantinople rejected the Arian "translation" on the grounds that it fatally compromised Christian worship of Christ Jesus as "Immanuel," God with us. It was along these lines that Chung's critics understood their objections to her lecture in Canberra. They did not fault her for attempting to express the gospel in non-Western terms, but for failing to distinguish the Spirit of God from the spirits of the world.

Indeed, Chung's critics were mild in comparison with some Western critics of the West's own trinitarian tradition. In the 1930s, the Swiss theologian Karl Barth denounced the venerable practice of seeking nonscriptural analogies of the Trinity in culture and common experience as a betrayal of the faith, expressly identifying Augustine himself as a chief source of the error. Such efforts, he maintained, inevitably divert attention from biblical revelation, the only true source of the church's knowledge of the Trinity. From a Barthian perspective, the problem with Chung's speech was not how far it departed from Western precedent, but how closely it followed it!

Still, many have raised a skeptical eyebrow at Barth's objections, and not without reason. As Lamin Sanneh has observed, the impulse to cleave to biblical revelation alone has in practice often meant protecting the hegemony of one local expression of the gospel at the expense of others. In the ninth century, Frankish priests opposed efforts to evangelize the Slavic peoples in their native languages, on the grounds that Pilate had used only Hebrew, Greek, and Latin to compose the inscription placed on the cross of Christ.[18] A similar cultural chauvinism sometimes accompanied the translation of the Bible into the languages of Africa, Asia, and the Pacific. One translation prepared for eastern New Guinea in 1947 employed English loanwords wherever the translator despaired of finding a corresponding indigenous term, such as "ox," "ass," "sheep," "goat"—and "God." Even Karl Barth's denunciation of the *vestigia trinitatis* (images of the Trinity in the created order) did not extend as far as his own use of "Revealer, Revelation, Revealedness," a ternary with roots in, among other things, German idealism's theory of the absolute Subject.

In the end, it seems that the furor sparked by Chung's lecture highlights not so much a new set of questions, but rather the urgency of a very old set of questions that have never been fully resolved. Can Christians faithfully name the persons of the Trinity only by cleaving resolutely to the language and conceptual categories of Scripture? Or can they legitimately repeat what Scripture says in a different way, in the language and categories of their own culture?

If the latter, are some cultures superior to others for expressing the abiding truth of trinitarian faith? If so, which ones? Fourth-century Alexandria? Twentieth-century Basel? Twenty-first-century Beijing? Or alternatively, does "the name of the Trinity" include its translatability into multiple cultural contexts, enabling people of every age and nation to call upon the persons of the Trinity "in their own language"? But if so, then wherein does the unity of trinitarian faith reside, and what defines the limits of its legitimate diversity?

NAMES FROM THE MOUNTAIN IN GALILEE AND THE EMANCIPATION OF WOMEN

Important as the previous issues are, many believe that the main question besetting the church's inherited trinitarian language stems from another source still: the social emancipation of women. For centuries and indeed for millennia, the superiority of men over women has been an axiom of human social order, including in the cultures that gave rise to Judaism, Christianity, and their respective traditions of sacred Scripture. Only recently, and as the result of long and bitter struggle, has the conviction begun to take hold that women are the full ontological, spiritual, and social equals of men. Extraordinarily, Christians from across a wide range of the theological spectrum now assent to this conviction, so relatively late in arriving, as the only view fully consonant with the heart of the canon's witness to Jesus Christ, in whom "there is neither male nor female" (Gal. 3:28 KJV). The disputed question is whether this conviction conflicts with the pervasiveness of male-gendered language for God in the Christian tradition, and, above all, with the words used by Christ to designate the persons of the Trinity on a mountain in Galilee: "the Father and the Son and the Holy Spirit."

To Matilda Joslyn Gage, a nineteenth-century abolitionist and suffragette, the conflict was obvious: "All the evils that have resulted from dignifying one sex and degrading the other may be traced to this central error: a belief in a trinity of masculine Gods in One, from which the feminine element is wholly eliminated."[19] Many have echoed her judgment since. "Father" and "son" are kinship terms used exclusively of human males. To apply them to the Trinity is inevitably to ascribe a value to maleness that is denied to femaleness. At worst, the terms imply that God is male. At best, they suggest that men provide a more fitting analogue for the life of the Trinity than do women. In either case, the terms shore up the assumptions of patriarchal society and militate against the ontological, spiritual, and social equality of women.

In the minds of many others, however, there is no conflict at all. For the persons of the Trinity are called Father and Son and Spirit by analogy, a form of speech midway between univocity on the one hand and equivocity on the other. That is, the first person of the Trinity is "Father" in a way that is neither wholly similar nor wholly dissimilar to a human father. Applied to God, "Father" denotes an eternal, spiritual relationship of divine origin, not male sexuality. Sexuality belongs exclusively to the created order, and human males can be "fathers" only in a derivative and imperfect sense in comparison with God the Father (cf. Eph. 3:14–15). And if one asks why Christians say "Father" and "Son" rather than "Mother and Child," the answer has nothing to do with a supposed superiority of men to women. It simply reflects the revealed sources of Christian faith, and above all Christ's own practice of addressing God as "Father" in prayer.

Presented thus, the argument between traditionalists and progressives seems hopelessly deadlocked. In fact, however, partisans on both sides frequently share a good bit of common ground in their assessment of the language of Father, Son, and Holy Spirit. Traditionalists generally concede to progressives that as a matter of practice, the disputed language has been misunderstood and abused in ways that are detrimental to women, and that such misuses should be weeded out and eliminated wherever possible. Progressives, in turn, generally concede to traditionalists that as a matter of principle, the language can be interpreted in ways that are compatible with the affirmation of women's equality with men, and that such uses should be fostered and encouraged. Underlying this tacit consensus (which is sometimes deeply masked) is the recognition by both parties of the possibilities and ambiguities that attend all analogical language, including "Father, Son, and Holy Spirit."

But if there is so much common ground, is the conflict just a big misunderstanding? Not at all. Close inspection, however, suggests that the conflict is less about the proper use and misuse of the language of "Father, Son, and Holy Spirit" per se than it is about *the status of this ternary within the total economy of trinitarian names.* Traditionalists, for their part, typically argue that "Father and Son and Holy Spirit" belongs permanently at the very center of this economy, that it is in fact *the* most appropriate way of naming the persons of the Trinity tout court. Progressives, in contrast, maintain that "Father, Son, and Holy Spirit" is one valid way of naming the persons of the Trinity among others, but not the name of the Trinity in an exclusive or most appropriate sense. It is this either-or conviction that gives the debate its extremely polarized character, which one theologian has called "as oppositional as any" today.[20] The genuine common ground that exists between the parties is masked as the two contrary assessments of the place of male kinship terminology in trinitarian discourse become the starting points for more global—and frequently antithetical—readings of Scripture, tradition, and the contemporary scene.

But is there really no alternative to the polarizing either-or? Must the language bequeathed to the church from a mountain in Galilee be *either* the most appropriate way of naming the persons of the Trinity, *or* one among many different equally valid ways? The articulation of an alternative that recognized the element of truth in both positions would certainly not magically settle all the points of dispute between traditionalists and progressives regarding the status of male-gendered language for God. But it might make it possible to more easily discern the genuine common ground shared by all parties.

THE NAME OF THE TRINITY IN A TRINITARIAN LIGHT

The church's new posture toward the Jewish people, the growth of global Christianity, and the emancipation of women are developments to be celebrated, invigorating signs of the Spirit's movement in the world today. At the same time, each raises profound questions about the language that Christians use to designate the persons of the Holy Trinity. Singly and together, the developments invite Christians to take a step back from the ordinary self-evidence of the names they use in order to ponder again their logic and significance.

As we have seen, our case studies raise questions that intersect with the church's economy of trinitarian names at different points, which we have signaled by alluding to three different places of sacred memory: the burning bush, the mountain in Galilee, and the morning of Pentecost. Closer inspection has revealed that in each instance, what comes to light is a distinctive pattern of naming the persons of the Trinity, together with a bit of unresolved theological business.

Our last case study directed our attention to a pattern of naming the persons of the Trinity characterized by the male kinship language of Father and Son, and Spirit. Because of its association with the words of the risen Christ at the end of the Gospel of Matthew, let us call this the *christological* pattern of trinitarian naming. The unresolved business with respect to this pattern concerns its status within the total economy of trinitarian names. Is it the most appropriate way of naming the persons of the Trinity, one among an open-ended variety of equally appropriate ways, or something else again?

Our middle case study directed our attention to a pattern of naming the persons of the Trinity characterized by the extraordinary variety of its linguistic expressions drawn from the breadth of human experience across time and space. Because of its association with the outpouring of the Spirit on the day of Pentecost, let us call this the *pneumatological* pattern of trinitarian naming.

Once again, the unresolved business with respect to this pattern concerns its status within the larger economy of trinitarian names. Does this pattern have a dignity and value inferior to that of the christological pattern, at least when its instances are not attested by Scripture or arise from new and unfamiliar cultural contexts (as judged by older siblings in the faith)? Or should this pattern be ascribed a place in the economy of trinitarian names that is fully equivalent to that of the christological pattern?

Our first case study directed our attention to a pattern of naming the persons of the Trinity that is characterized by the giving, receiving, and glorification of the Tetragrammaton, *the* divine name of biblical faith, and by the practice of alluding to the divine name *obliquely*, in keeping with the norms of Jewish religious practice. Because of its association with God's own self-naming at the burning bush, let us call this the *theological* pattern of naming the persons of the Trinity. The issues raised by this pattern are in a certain sense the most challenging of all, both because it has for so long been present only in the shadows of the church's consciousness, and because it is so intimately connected with the question of the church's relationship to the Jewish people. In another sense, however, the questions raised by this pattern are of the same nature as those noted above. What is the place and significance of this pattern of naming the persons of the Trinity within the total constellation of trinitarian names by which the church orients itself in time? Is the pattern of limited significance only, a kind of historical steppingstone on the way to something better, which can be safely left behind once it has served its purpose? Or is it rather an enduringly important dimension of how Christians in every time and place are given to know the persons of the Holy Trinity?

This summary suggests an interesting result. Because each pattern of naming raises questions that concern its status in the total economy of names, it turns out that an effort to answer any of the questions requires us to try to understand how the three patterns of naming the persons of the Trinity are related to each other. Such an endeavor would not necessarily resolve all of the disputed questions that arise in connection with each pattern. But it could clarify the theological space in which such questions might most fruitfully be pursued.

A PROPOSAL

The central hunch of this book is that Christians name the persons of the Trinity most adequately when they take into account three different patterns of trinitarian naming. To recap, the three patterns are these:

- A *theological* pattern of naming the persons of the Trinity that identifies the three persons in terms of the giving, receiving, and glorification of the divine Name, the unspoken Tetragrammaton. This pattern is characterized by its tight orbit around a single personal proper name, which is alluded to obliquely by means of a number of different surrogates and pious circumlocutions, in keeping with the precedent of Jewish custom and the New Testament.
- A *christological* pattern of naming that identifies the three persons as the Father, the Son, and the Holy Spirit. This pattern is relatively fixed, not in the sense that it always appears in a single linguistic form, but rather in that it revolves chiefly around a limited set of male kinship terms, which occurs with relatively minor variations: "Our Father," "Abba," "Son of God," "spirit of adoption," and so forth.
- A *pneumatological* pattern of naming that identifies the three persons by using an open-ended variety of ternaries, such as "Love, Lover, Beloved," "God, Word, Breathe," and so on. This pattern expresses the mutual relations of persons in a variety of context-sensitive ways that multiply and coexist while always leaving room for more.

Furthermore, I propose that Christians understand these three patterns best when they view them in light of the mystery of the Trinity itself. What I mean by viewing the three patterns "in light of the mystery of the Trinity" will become clearer over the course of this book. For now, it is enough to say that it implies that the three patterns are

- *Distinct.* Each pattern has an integrity of its own, both by virtue of its special affinity with one person of the Trinity and by virtue of a distinctive linguistic texture that differentiates it from the other patterns.
- *Equally important.* Each pattern, though principally associated with one person of the Trinity, illuminates the identity and mutual relations of all the persons of the Trinity, doing so in a way that is indispensable for our understanding of eternal mystery of the Trinity and the saving work of the Trinity in the economy of salvation.
- *Interrelated.* Each pattern is inwardly related to the others, so that a full understanding of any of them ultimately requires an understanding of all of them together.

Conversely, my proposal implies that Christian reflection on how most appropriately to identify the persons of the Trinity is seriously threatened whenever Christians

- fail to recognize the distinct integrity of any one of the three patterns of naming,
- permit one pattern of naming to obscure or eclipse any of the others,
- or fail to recognize the interrelatedness of the three patterns.

I think that this proposal is significant for several reasons. It is consistent with the deepest currents of Christian tradition; it provides a framework of analysis that permits a variety of contemporary voices to be heard and contemporary issues to be fruitfully pursued; and it is robustly supported by the witness of Scripture and, above all, its testimony to Jesus Christ. I will not elaborate on these claims now but simply let whatever truth they have emerge over the course of this volume and its sequel.

There is, however, one point I wish to emphasize at the start. My proposal implies that the key to a trinitarian understanding of the name of the Trinity is a recovery of the abiding significance of the unspoken Tetragrammaton for Christian faith. The theological, christological, and pneumatological patterns of naming the persons of the Trinity are all important and indispensable, as we shall see. Nevertheless, the theological pattern occupies a special place in the economy of trinitarian names because it alone orbits a personal proper name, indeed, *the* personal proper name. Precisely for this reason, the pattern of naming that orbits this name stands in relationship to the other patterns as a kind of *fons divinitatis*, fountain of divinity, as the first person of the Trinity stands in relationship to the second and third persons. From its hidden depths the whole constellation of divine names receives its radiance and design.

Part One

A Threefold Cord

The Name of the Trinity in Christian Tradition

Introduction to Part One

> I do not aim foolishly to introduce new ideas; I want only to analyze and with some orderly detail to expand upon the truths set down by others.
>
> —*Dionysius*, The Divine Names

What is the most appropriate way to name the persons of the Trinity? One way to set about answering this question is to investigate how people have named the persons of the Trinity in the past. Christians often meet new challenges, such as those we surveyed in the last chapter, by reexamining their past, seeking there clues that can provide a purifying critique of the present and a guide to the road ahead.

Part 1 explores how the Christian tradition has named the persons of the Trinity from its origin up to the present day. Obviously, we cannot cover this ground in anything like an adequate way, but instead must rely on a series of snapshots that focus on a few key episodes, figures, and schools. While the resulting picture will be incomplete and oversimplified at many points, it will suffice to show that Christians have seldom been content to name the persons of the Trinity in only one way, but instead have drawn upon as many as three distinct patterns of naming to articulate their faith in the Holy Trinity. A key variable in the story we are about to tell, therefore, is *how Christians have configured the available patterns of trinitarian naming in relationship to each other*. At signal points in its history, the Christian tradition has deployed the patterns in a way that implies their distinction, equality, and interrelatedness. More commonly, however, the Christian tradition has failed to sustain this richly threefold vision, a fact that has brought numerous problems and perplexities in its wake.

2

The Name of the Trinity in Early Christian Creeds

The Emergence of a Threefold Cord

> Behind and beneath all the primitive creeds of the apostolic and sub-apostolic era there stands the primal creed and confession of the Christian church, The Shema:
> "Hear, O Israel: The Lord our God is one Lord."
> —*Jaroslav Pelikan*[1]

How did early Christians name the persons of the Trinity? One way to answer this question is by taking a look at ancient creeds. The brevity of creeds makes them a convenient object of study, and their continued authority makes them relevant for Christians today.

In this chapter we will focus on two early Christian authorities of very different kinds, the *nomina sacra*, a sort of visible creed encoded directly into ancient manuscripts of the Bible, and the Nicene-Constantinopolitan Creed (381 CE), the church's first ecumenical confession of faith. Different as they are, the two creeds tell a common story about the logic of trinitarian faith. Both are rooted in the Shema, the church's "primal creed and confession," and both branch out into different patterns of naming the persons of the Trinity. These patterns are only latently visible in the *nomina sacra*, but they come to explicit and enduringly beautiful expression in the Nicene Creed.

THE *NOMINA SACRA*: A VISIBLE CREED

In the ancient world, biblical scribes gave special treatment to certain divine names when copying the sacred Scriptures, setting them off from other names by the use of special orthography. Despite the fact that this practice appears in virtually all surviving manuscripts of the Bible, few people today have any knowledge of it. Since the advent of printing, Bibles have routinely stripped away the visual cues, and today even scholarly editions of the Bible preserve no trace of them. This is a great loss, not only because the practice is inherently fascinating, but also because it illuminates how early Jews and Christians experienced sacred Scripture. By singling out some divine names, while passing over others, the scribal techniques provided readers with implicit guidance about how to read and understand Scripture. Orthography provided, we might say, a kind of visible creed, encoded directly into the sacred text itself.[2]

The Representation of the Divine Name in Jewish Scriptures: A Visible Shema

One of the chief ways Jews of the first century expressed reverence for God was by according special treatment to God's name, the Tetragrammaton. For example, Jews typically avoided pronouncing the divine name, and instead employed some surrogate in its place, such as "Lord" (Heb. *'adonai*, or Gk. *kyrios*). What is less well known is that Jewish scribes also marked out the Tetragrammaton when copying the Scriptures, by writing it in a special way. Scribes used a wide variety of techniques for this purpose. Some used archaic Hebrew characters in texts that were otherwise written in the square Hebrew letters typical of the day. Others wrote the name using specially dyed ink, or replaced the name with a different symbol altogether, such as four dots or four diagonal lines. Whatever the method, the practice of singling out the Tetragrammaton clearly served a religious purpose. At one level, it expressed reverence for the divine name, and so also for the God who bears it. At another, it reminded readers not to pronounce the name when reading the Scriptures aloud. At still another level, the practice gave visible expression to a basic tenet of Jewish faith. For Jews of the Second Temple period, the most basic and common of all creedal confessions was the saying "Hear, O Israel: The Lord is our God, the Lord alone" (Deut. 6:4). Known as the Shema (Heb. *shema'*, "hear") after its first word, the saying was *the* Jewish daily prayer of the time (cf. *m. Ber.* 1:1–4:1). The scribal practice of representing God's name with special characters reinforced the message of the Shema. It served as a kind of visible version of the confession. By underscoring the uniqueness and oneness of God's name, it underscored the uniqueness and oneness of God.[3]

Significantly for our story, Jewish scribes continued to single out the Tetragrammaton for special treatment *even when copying the Scriptures in Greek translation*. One way they did this was by writing the divine name in Hebrew or Aramaic characters, even though the surrounding text was in Greek. The practice is very ancient. It appears, for example, in the Fuad (or

Fouad) papyri, the oldest surviving Greek text of Deuteronomy that we possess, dating from the first or second century BCE. This Fuad papyrus (no. 266, of which only chaps. 17–33 survive) contains the divine name written in Aramaic. We can approximate the way it would have rendered the Shema by substituting modern English and Hebrew characters for ancient Greek and Aramaic, respectively:

> Hear O Israel יהוה is our God, יהוה alone.

We can easily imagine the powerful didactic message that the visible Tetragrammaton would have conveyed to Greek-speaking Jews. Like its counterpart in Hebrew manuscripts, the practice would have functioned to visibly inculcate in readers a practical piety for God's name, guiding them into a reading of Scripture centered in YHWH's uniqueness. Even if hellenized Jews had little or no knowledge of Hebrew, they would have had no difficulty in recognizing the divine Name and the silent message it conveyed: "Hear, O Israel: The LORD is our God, the LORD alone" (Deut. 6:4).

In recent decades, many ancient Greek fragments of the Hebrew Bible have been found that render the divine name in Hebrew letters, suggesting that the practice was common among scribes both before and after the dawn of the Common Era. This knowledge requires a dramatic change in the way many of us picture how ordinary people of the first century experienced the Bible. In 1934, C. H. Dodd, a prominent biblical scholar of the day, wrote, "By merely eliminating the name of God, the [Septuagint] contributed to the definition of monotheism."[4] Dodd implies that the earliest Greek translations of the Bible introduced the God of biblical faith to the Hellenistic world as a deity with only a descriptive title ("Lord") but no proper name. Although we do not know how the earliest copies of the Septuagint handled the Tetragrammaton (no manuscripts survive from that era), we do know that Dodd's judgment gives a very misleading picture of the evidence known to us today. Far from having "eliminated the name of God," the Greek Bible of the New Testament era accentuated it and held it forth as a visible creed.

The *Nomina Sacra*: "Embryonic Creed of the First Church"

Almost from the beginning of the Jesus movement, church-connected scribes developed their own distinctive counterpart to Jewish scribal practice. They consistently marked off certain words from their surroundings by abbreviating them and drawing a line over the characters that remained. These words have come to be known as the *nomina sacra*, the holy or sacred names. C. H. Roberts has suggested that the *nomina sacra* represent "the embryonic creed of the first church."[5] Though the origins of the practice cannot be dated with certainty, its ubiquity and relative uniformity suggest an extremely early origin indeed, in all likelihood well back into the first century, perhaps even "to a time prior to 70 CE." [6]

The *nomina sacra* differ from their Jewish counterparts in two important ways beyond their distinctive visual appearance (i.e., abbreviated words with a line drawn above them). First, Christian scribes marked out the Tetragrammaton by applying special orthography to the conventional oral *surrogate* for the divine name, "Lord" (*kyrios*), rather than to the divine name itself.[7] We can visualize the difference with reference to Psalm 118:26. In a non-Christian Greek translation of the Bible, the passage would have appeared approximately as follows, once again substituting English characters for Greek:

> Blessed is he who comes in the name of יהוה.

In the Christian text, however, we would find the following:

> Blessed is he who comes in the name of $\overline{\mathrm{LD}}$.[8]

This change is noticeable enough, and we will say more about it in a moment. First, however, let us note the other major innovation, which is even more dramatic. From the very beginning (so far as surviving evidence indicates), Christian scribes accorded special treatment *not only* to the customary surrogate for the divine name (i.e., "Lord," Gk.: *kyrios* = $\overline{\mathrm{K}\Sigma}$), *but also* to three additional words, which were also contracted in similar fashion, with a line placed on top:

Theos (God)	Contracted forms = $\overline{\Theta\Sigma}$, $\overline{\Theta\Upsilon}$, and so on
Iēsous (Jesus)	Contracted forms = $\overline{\mathrm{I}\Sigma}$, $\overline{\mathrm{IH}\Sigma}$, $\overline{\mathrm{I}\Upsilon}$, and so on
Christos (Christ)	Contracted forms = $\overline{\mathrm{X}\Sigma}$, $\overline{\mathrm{X}\Upsilon}$, and so on

These four words, Lord, God, Jesus, and Christ, appear as *nomina sacra* in virtually all extant Christian copies of the Scriptures, Old and New Testament writings alike. The number of words treated as *nomina sacra* grew over time, but these four names formed the consistent core of the practice. As has rightly been pointed out, these earliest four words are not merely *nomina sacra* (sacred names), but rather *nomina divina* (divine names), in view of their central place in Christian worship.[9]

What was the nature of the relationship between the Christian *nomina sacra* and their Jewish counterparts? In the 1980s, George Howard proposed that the Christian practice represented "a clear break" with Jewish antecedents. He conjectured that it originated among non-Jewish scribes "who in their copying the LXX [Septuagint, Greek] text found no traditional reason to preserve the Tetragrammaton." At first glance, Howard's hypothesis seems plausible. After all, the Tetragrammaton makes no appearance in the Christian system, whereas it stands out in sharp relief in many Jewish manuscripts. Howard went on to suggest that "it is possible that some confusion ensued from the abandonment of the Tetragrammaton in the NT," and implies that this in turn may have "played a role in the later trinitarian debates."[10] Specifically, the "removal of the Tetragrammaton . . . created a confusion in the minds of early Gentile Christians about the relationship between the 'Lord God' and the 'Lord Christ,'" which led Christians to adopt a high Christology at variance with the views of first-century Christians.[11]

Howard's thesis, however, has won few adherents. Most scholars have perceived far stronger lines of continuity linking the *nomina sacra* with Jewish practice, seeing in the former a distinctively Christian form of piety *for* the divine name, not "a clear break" with it. Typical is the judgment of Larry Hurtado: "Jewish reverence for the divine name, and particularly the Jewish practice of marking off the divine name reverentially in written forms, probably provides us with the key element in the religious background that early Christians adapted in accordance with their own religious convictions and expressed in the *nomina sacra*."[12] Still, it is not immediately obvious how the more common view could be correct. For the fact remains that the Tetragrammaton does not appear among the *nomina sacra*, having been replaced by the symbol $\overline{\text{KΣ}}$ (surrogate for *Kyrios*, "Lord"). How, one might ask, can one express reverence for something by eliminating it?

In fact, it is not hard to see how the symbol $\overline{\text{KΣ}}$ might indeed signify reverence for the Tetragrammaton. One must simply see that the symbol refers to the divine name in two distinct ways, one layered on top of the other, as it were. First, the name of God is designated indirectly, as in ordinary speech, by its conventional oral surrogate, *kyrios*. Second, *kyrios* is set off visibly from its neighbors by special orthography, so that its reference to the Tetragrammaton not be lost. As Schuyler Brown observes:

> The contraction $\overline{\text{KΣ}}$ fulfills then the same function as the writing of יהוה in gold letters in a Hebrew text or the appearance of an unadorned יהוה in a Greek text: by setting off the *nomen sacrum* from the other words it expresses in a positive way the scribe's reverence for the name of God.[13]

Far from being far-fetched or difficult to imagine, Brown's suggestion mirrors the way Europeans (and now Christians around the globe) have handled the Tetragrammaton in translations of the Old Testament since the dawn of printing. The Tetragrammaton is first replaced with its surrogate "Lord," and "Lord" is then printed in capital letters so that the reference back to the Tetragrammaton not be lost—as LORD.[14]

In sum, like its Jewish counterpart, the Christian *nomen sacrum* $\overline{\text{K}\Sigma}$ visibly represents the uniqueness of the Tetragrammaton, but in a distinctive way. Whereas Jewish scribal practice makes the uniqueness of the divine name visible by the representation of the name itself, the Christian symbol makes it visible through its surrogate, as though the uniqueness of the divine name had impressed itself into the surrogate, like a hot seal in soft wax. Early Christians, we may conjecture, might have preferred this more indirect method, because it approximates the way they experienced the divine name in the context of the *oral* recitation and interpretation of the Scriptures, where *kyrios* was routinely used in place of the divine name. Oral discourse was the original matrix of the Christian movement, and it would not be surprising if the scribal practices that emerged from it would seek to maintain, so far as possible, the semantic possibilities of spoken commentary on Scripture.

This brings us to the other major innovation of the *nomina sacra*, the application of special orthography not only to the ordinary surrogate for the Tetragrammaton, *kyrios*, but also to three additional names: God, Jesus, and Christ. Even if the symbol $\overline{\text{K}\Sigma}$ may express reverence for the divine name, surely the application of the same orthography to these additional names points to "a clear break" with such reverence, as Howard surmised. For the effect of such a practice is to place *all four names on the same level*, so far as their visible appearance is concerned. Surely this is a repudiation of the "visible Shema" encoded in Jewish Scripture, if anything is.

To be sure, this aspect of the *nomina sacra* does indeed represent something momentously new. Still, I argue that even the application of special orthography to "Jesus," "Christ," and "God" is best understood not as a break with reverence for the Tetragrammaton, but as its continuation under the new conditions of Christian faith. Indeed, I think it is highly likely the four original *nomina sacra* were selected precisely *in order to give this continuity visible expression*. To see how this might be the case, consider an early Christian text that alludes to the Shema, 1 Corinthians 8:5–6, which Ferdinand Hahn has called "the oldest confessional text" in the New Testament.[15]

> Indeed, even though there may be so-called gods in heaven or on earth—as in fact there are many gods and many lords—yet for us there is one God, the Father, from whom are all things and for whom we exist, and one Lord, Jesus Christ, through whom are all things and through whom we exist.

This passage is both a confession of Christian faith and an evocation of Judaism's primal confession, "Hear, O Israel: The LORD is our God, the LORD alone." Paul's aim is not to "break" with the Shema, but to express its truth in a new way, by placing the figure of Jesus Christ *inside* the ancient confession, as it were.[16] Paul reshapes the Shema by ascribing to Jesus the common surrogate for the divine name, "Lord," thereby implying that Jesus shares the honor and dignity of the "one God." Now consider how 1 Corinthians 8:5–6 would have appeared to early Christians when written with the original four *nomina sacra* (substituting English characters for Greek):

> Indeed, even though there may be so-called gods in heaven or on earth—as in fact there are many gods and many lords—yet for us there is one $\overline{\mathrm{GD}}$, the Father, from whom are all things and for whom we exist, and one $\overline{\mathrm{LD}}$, $\overline{\mathrm{JS}}$ $\overline{\mathrm{CT}}$, through whom are all things and through whom we exist.

This representation is based upon the text as it actually appears in Codex Sinaiticus.[17] Note that the scribe carefully distinguished between profane and sacred uses of "god" and "lord," and handles only the latter as *nomina sacra*. The effect of the scribal practice is to highlight and emphasize the heart of Paul's confession. Moreover, it does so in a way that would accentuate the parallel with the comparable representations of the Shema in Jewish manuscripts of the Bible. We can visualize the point by placing the two passages side by side, approximating how they might have appeared in ancient manuscripts of the first or second century:

Deuteronomy 6:4 (NIV) Hear, O Israel:	1 Corinthians 8:6 For us there is . . .
יהוה our God, יהוה is one.	one $\overline{\mathrm{GD}}$ . . . and one $\overline{\mathrm{LD}}$, $\overline{\mathrm{JS}}$ $\overline{\mathrm{CT}}$.

In both cases, special orthography reinforces the message of the underlying creed. In the first instance, God's uniqueness is emphasized by writing the divine name in Hebrew. In the second instance, Jesus Christ's participation in God's uniqueness is emphasized by applying eye-catching orthography not only to the "one God," as we might expect, but also to "one Lord, Jesus Christ." The singularity of the divine name has rubbed off, so to speak, on the divine names.

In sum, the original four *nomina sacra* served to visibly set in relief the early church's confession of faith, underscoring the church's conviction that its confession of Jesus Christ as Lord was not a deviation from the Shema or reverence for the divine name, but an act of strictest loyalty to both. The fact that Christian scribes do not write the divine name itself is best understood as an assimilation of textual practice to oral speech, where the divine name is routinely indicated by surrogates, and not as an "abandonment" of the divine name. Although the *nomina sacra* do not make the divine name *directly* visible, they do make it *indirectly* visible, in and through its conventional surrogate and the other three divine names. The *nomina sacra*, we may say, express a theology of the divine name(s), one that honors the divine name in the divine names, and vice versa.

The Growth of the *Nomina Sacra:* The Emergence of Patterns of Trinitarian Naming

Over time, Christian scribes came to treat additional words as *nomina sacra*, a process that represents a gradual maturation of "the embryonic creed of the first church."[18] With each new addition, we may surmise, scribes understood themselves to be acting in the spirit of previous precedent, even as they put what they understood to be the heart of the Christian confession into ever fuller relief. Three words appear as *nomina sacra* almost as early as the original four. They are these:

anthrōpos (human being)	Contracted forms: $\overline{\mathrm{ANO}\Sigma}$ and variations ($\overline{\mathrm{ANOY}}$ etc.)
stauros (cross)	Contracted forms: $\overline{\Sigma\mathrm{T}\Sigma}$ and variations
pneuma (spirit)	Contracted forms: $\overline{\Pi\mathrm{NA}}$ and variations

These words have been selected for obvious christological and trinitarian reasons. The first two emphasize Christ's humanity and death, perhaps in response to gnostic teaching in the early church, which denied both. The third term, "Spirit," makes explicit the trinitarian shape of Christian faith. Paul's confession in 1 Corinthians 8:6 is basically "binitarian" in structure, so treating "Spirit" as a *nomen sacrum* would have made no difference to its appearance on the page. But consider how the addition of this term altered the visual appearance of another Pauline passage, 2 Corinthians 13:13 (again substituting English characters for Greek):

> The grace of the $\overline{\mathrm{LD}}$ $\overline{\mathrm{JS}}$ $\overline{\mathrm{CT}}$, the love of $\overline{\mathrm{GD}}$, and the communion of the Holy $\overline{\mathrm{ST}}$ be with you all.

By according the same orthographic treatment to "Spirit" as to the other two persons, ancient Christian scribes made the passage's trinitarian structure visible, and subtly (or perhaps not so subtly) encouraged a trinitarian reading of Scripture generally.

In time, eight additional words came to be commonly treated as *nomina sacra*. These words reflect a further elaboration of the christological and trinitarian contours already visible in the earliest seven *nomina sacra*. The first five

(Savior, mother, Israel, David, Jerusalem) underscore the context of messianic expectation that surrounds the scriptural portrait of Jesus Christ. The further three (Father, heaven, Son) provide an additional set of terms for naming the first two persons of the Trinity ("heaven" appearing chiefly in conjunction with "Father," as in "Our Father in heaven"). Paul, we recall, calls God "Father" in 1 Corinthians 8:6, and although he does not speak of Jesus Christ as "Son," this way of speaking is obviously a natural extrapolation from the passage. Therefore most of the *nomina sacra* that Christian scribes ultimately settled on to designate God and Christ are already contained or implied in Paul's confession in 1 Corinthians 8:6. The terms fall naturally into two patterns, one that represents the relationship of God and Christ by using terms drawn from the Shema ("Lord" and "God"), and one that interprets their relationship in terms of the kinship language of "Father" and "Son." Since "Spirit" is equally compatible with either of these patterns, we can say that the *nomina sacra* draw attention to two different patterns for naming the persons of the Trinity present in the Scriptures.

Actually, the *nomina sacra* draw attention not only to these two patterns of naming the persons of the Trinity, but also to much more besides. "Savior," which has no obvious linguistic connection with either the Shema or the language of Father and Son, appears in Scripture as a designation for both the first and second persons of the Trinity; it thus hints, we might say, at the possibility of yet other ways of naming the persons of the Trinity. In addition, the words that comprise the two patterns we identified also appear in a great variety of combinations among themselves, like a handful of letters that can be combined into dozens of words. We can gather a sense for the range of these combinations from the table below, which is far from exhaustive.

The persons of the Holy Trinity	Names appearing as *Nomina Sacra*
The first person	Kyrios, God, Father Combination names: Lord God, the Lord your God, God the Father, Father in heaven, God of heaven
The second person	Kyrios, God, Jesus, Christ, Son, Savior Combination names: Son of God, Son of Man
The third person	Spirit Combination names: Spirit of the Lord, Spirit of God, Spirit of the Father, Spirit of his Son, Spirit of Jesus, Spirit of Christ, Spirit of Jesus Christ

An impressive feature of the *nomina sacra* is that the list of terms did not grow ever longer with the passing of time, but eventually become fairly set, as though a kind of equilibrium had been achieved. The final list is substantially longer than the original four, but even by the Byzantine period, when the list is substantially fixed, many of the most conspicuous and interesting divine names are still absent (Word, Emmanuel, Advocate, and others). Scribes were no doubt reluctant to introduce *nomina sacra* in cases where ambiguity or confusion might result. But one also senses that the scribal tradition eventually reached a kind of collective judgment that the existing set of terms was sufficient to mark out, if not "all the constellations of the storie" (George Herbert),[19] then nevertheless enough to guide the church in the basic navigation of the Scriptures.

Yet even as the *nomina sacra* attained a stable and mature *Gestalt* in one dimension, they continued to grow and adapt in another. As Christians translated their Scriptures from Greek into languages such as Latin, Coptic, Slavonic, Armenian, and Gothic, they adapted the practice of writing the *nomina sacra* accordingly. This was easy to do, since all that was required was to write the appropriate word as an abbreviation with a line across the top. Like the gospel itself, and the Scriptures that testified to it, the *nomina sacra* were transportable. Here again, perhaps, we see something of the distinctively Christian character of the practice as a whole. The corresponding Jewish custom of writing the Tetragrammaton in Hebrew points back to the language of sacred origins, as though to emphasize that "Mount Zion [is] the place of the name of the Lord of hosts" (Isa. 18:7). As we have seen, it is scarcely right to understand the *nomina sacra* as a "break" with Jewish reverence for the divine name. Still, the *nomina sacra* express this reverence in a distinctively Christian way, as though in the spirit of the saying, "Out of Zion, the perfection of beauty, God shines forth" (Ps. 50:2). Unwritten in itself, the divine name makes its beauty known by shining forth through the medium of other names, first kindling into life "Lord, God, Jesus, Christ, Spirit," and then the other names, until the glowing terms trace in outline the invisible fire that burns on the far side of the sacred page.

THE NICENE-CONSTANTINOPOLITAN CREED: THREE PATTERNS OF NAMING THE PERSONS OF THE HOLY TRINITY

Different as it is in many ways, the Nicene-Constantinopolitan Creed stands in substantial theological and even literary continuity with the *nomina sacra*.

For our purposes, the most important difference between them is the relative explicitness with which they employ different *patterns* of naming to identify the persons of the Trinity. In the *nomina sacra*, we see different patterns of naming in solution, as it were. In the Nicene Creed, we see them crystallized in enduring and enduringly beautiful form.

The Nicene Creed was adopted by a council of bishops in 325 CE for the purpose of repudiating the teaching of Arius and his followers that Christ was God's first and most noble creature, rather than himself divine. The original Nicene Creed of 325 focused almost exclusively on the relationship between God and Christ: it limited its confession of the Holy Spirit to the single phrase "We believe in the Holy Spirit." In 381, the Nicene Creed was revised and amended at the Council of Constantinople, to defend the Holy Spirit against similar misunderstanding and to solidify the triumph over Arianism. The expanded creed is the affirmation still in use among Christians today and is most correctly called the Nicene-Constantinopolitan Creed.

The bishops who composed the original creed in 325 were intensely aware that they were crafting the first ecumenical or churchwide statement of its kind. To ensure broad acceptance of their work, they drew extensively on the format and wording of regional creeds of undisputed antiquity and authority. In addition, the bishops introduced novel words and expressions not found in earlier creeds or Scripture, most notably the phrases "of one being with the Father" (*homoousios*) and "from the being of the Father." At that time and ever since, theologians have been drawn to these novel terms, like moths to a lantern. Important as they are (and we will address them later), our primary interest is not in them but in the other language that the creed uses to identify God, Christ, and the Spirit.

In keeping with the flow of the creed's historical development, we will first examine how God and Christ are named in the creed of 325, and then turn our attention to the Holy Spirit, who did not receive extensive attention from the church fathers until 381.[20]

Naming God and Christ

Despite its brevity, the original Nicene Creed of 325 is a rich, reiterative statement that names God and Christ in a variety of ways for the purpose of rebutting the Arian teaching that Jesus Christ was not divine. Indeed, a careful reading of the creed readily shows that it uses three different patterns of naming God and Christ, each of which affirms Christ's deity in a different way:

- a pattern characterized by oblique reference to the unspoken Tetragrammaton

- a pattern characterized by the vocabulary of Father and Son
- a pattern characterized by an open-ended multiplicity of names

For convenience sake, we will call these the theological, christological, and pneumatological patterns. Let us take a brief look at each of them in turn.

A Theological Pattern Characterized by Oblique Reference to the Tetragrammaton

Sometimes it is easy to overlook something because it is in plain view. So it is with the Nicene Creed's (325) use of a pattern for naming God and Christ that employs oblique reference to the Tetragrammaton. Though it is possible to read the creed many times without being aware that such a pattern exists, it actually constitutes the creed's root structure. We see this immediately when we set the creed alongside its literary antecedents, Paul's confession in 1 Corinthians 8:6 and, before that, the Shema:

Deut. 6:4 (NIV)	1 Cor. 8:6	The Creed of 381 (325)
Hear, O Israel:	. . . for us there is . . .	We believe in . . .
The Lord our God, the LORD is one.	one God . . . from whom are all things and for whom we exist, and one Lord, Jesus Christ, through whom are all things and through whom we exist.	one God . . . maker of heaven and earth, and of all that is, seen and unseen. We believe in one Lord, Jesus Christ, Through whom all things were made.

As this table shows, the Nicene Creed opens by naming God and Christ in a way that directly parallels Paul's confession in 1 Corinthians 8:6: "one God" and "one Lord, Jesus Christ." If Paul himself had had a chance to read this portion of the Nicene Creed, it is hard to imagine that he would have regarded it as anything but a faithful restatement of his own "binitarian" confession. The literary similarity between the two confessions is simply too great to ignore or deny. Moreover, I doubt that Paul would have disapproved of the anti-Arian use to which his words were put. After all, centuries before the Arian crisis, Paul himself had taken the trouble to frame his confession in 1 Corinthians 8:6 as an echo of the Shema, precisely in order to confess Christ's deity. As we saw in the previous section, Paul distributes the key theonyms of the Shema—"Lord" and "God"—to Christ and to God respectively, in order to express the idea that Christ participates in the dignity of the divine name, and so of the one God. Insofar as the Nicene Creed echoes not only 1 Corinthians 8:6, but also that text's own internal allusions, Paul's christologically modified version of the Shema continues to reverberate in the creed's opening members. The first ecumenical creed begins by naming God and Christ, using a pattern of naming characterized by oblique reference to the Tetragrammaton, and thereby makes the anti-Arian point in a supremely potent—and ancient—way.

Were the bishops who framed the creed aware of the full depths of these literary and theological allusions? That is a question we will address more directly in the next chapter. For the present, we can say that by beginning the Nicene Creed in this way, the bishops were consciously following the precedent of other local creeds already known to them, of undisputed antiquity and authority, including the creed used by Christians in Palestine. By confessing their faith with these words, the bishops intended to affirm what earlier generations of Christians had affirmed, in unbroken line, going back to the apostles themselves.[21]

A Christological Pattern Characterized by the Vocabulary of Father and Son

The Nicene Creed also names God and Christ a second time, using a pattern of naming that finds its center of gravity in the kinship vocabulary of Father and Son. This pattern was also anticipated in Paul's confession in 1 Corinthians 8:6, although the Nicene Creed develops it more extensively by using words and phrases drawn from elsewhere in the Scripture. We can make this dimension of the creed visible as follows:

> We believe in . . . the Father. . . .
> We believe in . . . the only Son of God,
> eternally begotten of the Father, . . .
> begotten, not made,
> of one Being with the Father,
> [who] is seated at the right hand of the Father.

We will take up the phrase "of one Being with the Father" at a later point. For the present, note that even apart from this phrase, the creed exploits the possibilities of "Father" and "Son" language in order to make the anti-Arian point in an extremely powerful way. In particular, the composers of the creed hone in on the term "beget" to elucidate the character of the Father-and-Son relationship. The Son is "*eternally* begotten" of the Father, excluding the idea of an origin in time. Again, the Son is "begotten, not made," to distinguish the Son's relationship to the Father from that of every created thing. Thus the creed gives us a second pattern of naming God and Christ that says exactly what the first pattern said, in a different way, using the language of Father and Son.

A Pneumatological Pattern Characterized by the Open-ended Multiplicity of Names

Although the composers of the creed might conceivably have been satisfied to make the anti-Arian point twice (or even once, for that matter), they chose instead to name God and Christ *in a third way*, using yet another pattern of naming, one characterized by the enlistment of an open-ended multiplicity of names. This pattern can by definition be instantiated in many ways, but it takes the following form in the Nicene Creed:

> God of God, Light of Light, True God of True God

Here Christ is named three times, each time in a way that entails a corresponding naming of God. The anti-Arian point is made by employing the same divine names for both God and Christ, while the work of differentiating the persons is performed by grammatical case, or in English translation, by the preposition "of." This pattern of naming has no direct antecedent in Paul's confession in 1 Corinthians 8:6, although arguably it has a certain affinity with Paul's use of the prepositions "from whom" and "through whom" with reference to God and Christ's role in creation. In any case, this pattern of naming *was* a feature of other, more ancient Christian creeds with which the bishops of Nicaea were familiar. For example, the local creed of Caesarea in Palestine (the home church of Eusebius, a key player at the council who presented his church's creed before the council as evidence of his own orthodoxy) contained the following phrase:

> Word of God, God of God, light from light, life from life

Nothing about this is likely to have struck the bishops of Nicaea as problematic. Nevertheless, they themselves used only the middle two phrases, while dropping the first entirely and replacing the last with "true God of true God." No doubt the bishops had their reasons for both changes, but these are somewhat clearer in the second case. "True God" was a favorite name for God among the Arians, because they interpreted the qualifying adjective as applicable only to God and not to Christ. By coining the phrase "true God from true God," therefore, the composers of the creed rebutted the Arian interpretation and introduced a new name for Christ-in-relation-to God at the same time. In so doing, the authors of the creed also illustrated a noteworthy feature of the third pattern of naming: its high degree of context-sensitivity.[22]

The Council of Constantinople: Reaffirming Three Patterns of Naming God and Christ

When the Council of Constantinople revised and expanded the Nicene Creed in 381, the bishops retained almost verbatim the three patterns of naming God and Christ that we have just reviewed. Their only modification was to delete "God from God" from the original creed, trimming back that line to a more economical (though less sonorous) "Light from Light, true God from true God." The Latin and Armenian versions, however, retained the longer form without controversy, illustrating again the adaptability of this particular pattern of naming. In its final form, then, the Nicene-Constantinopolitan Creed names God and Christ by using three different patterns of naming, each of which makes the same anti-Arian point in a different way.

Naming the Holy Spirit

The Nicene-Constantinopolitan Creed is much more fulsome in its treatment of the Holy Spirit than the original creed of 325, which, as we have noted, merely affirms, "We believe in the Holy Spirit." It might seem, therefore, that we should turn our attention immediately to the creed in its expanded form. To do so, however, would be to miss the opportunity to ask an interesting question. How does the original name "Holy Spirit" relate to the three patterns of naming God and Christ that we have just reviewed? Does it belong to one of these patterns, and if so, which one? Or alternatively, is the name equally at home in the context of all three patterns? The question is not only interesting but arguably important too. For if "Holy Spirit" belonged chiefly to one pattern rather than to another, then it might seem that one of the creed's three patterns of naming is more naturally "trinitarian"—as opposed to being merely "binitarian"—than the others. In short, it might tip the scales toward declaring one of the three patterns "more equal" than the others, at least as they come to expression in the Nicene Creed of 325.

In fact, however, the name "Holy Spirit" is equally at home in all three patterns, although it fits into each in a slightly different way. "Holy Spirit" belongs naturally to the theological pattern of naming, because the phrase emerges directly out of the Jewish practice of avoiding the divine name. "Holy Spirit" is equivalent to the circumlocution "Spirit of holiness," where "holiness" serves as a surrogate for the bearer of the divine name (cf. Rom. 1:4).[23] "Holy Spirit" also fits naturally into the christological pattern, because it appears in regular conjunction with the kinship language of "Father" and "Son" in Christian liturgy and Scripture (cf. Matt. 28:19). Finally, "Holy Spirit" is fully at home in the pneumatological pattern that speaks of God and Christ as "Light of Light," and so forth, because it employs similarly generic terms that—while patient of being interpreted in the context of the theological and christological patterns—do not *require* such interpretation, but are fully intelligible in their own right. In sum, when the bishops in 325 affirmed their faith in the "Holy Spirit," they named the third person of the Trinity in a way that could, with equal justification, be understood as the pneumatological completion of all three patterns they used in the earlier portion of the creed.

Turning to the creed of 381, the bishops adopted additional names for the "Holy Spirit" to underscore the deity of the third person of the Trinity and to protect it from the same kind of misunderstanding that had previously attended the second person. The bishops affirmed:

> We believe in the Holy Spirit:
> the Lord, the Giver of life,
> who proceeds from the Father,
> who with the Father and Son is worshiped and glorified.

The bishops have elucidated the name "Holy Spirit" by means of three main clauses, each of which has an affinity with one of the patterns of naming that had previously been used to identify God and Christ. "Lord" names the Spirit in a way that obviously recalls the first pattern of naming, oriented toward the Tetragrammaton.[24] "The Giver of life" names the Spirit in an "occasional way," one that is no more *required* than, say, "Light from Light," but that is nevertheless supremely *apt* for the purposes of underscoring the Spirit's coequal role in the work of creation, alongside the first and second persons. The final phrase does not introduce a new name at all, but simply invokes the language of Father and Son as a third context for understanding the deity of the Holy Spirit. The end result is a remarkable study in literary and theological symmetry, which preserves the balance of the patterns of naming originally introduced in the creed of 325.

Of One Being—From the Being (*Homoousion—ek tēs ousias*)

We have thus far refrained from saying anything about that portion of the creed that commonly attracts the most attention: its use of the phrases "of one being" (*homoousion*) and "from the being" (*ek tēs ousias*). I have not addressed these phrases before, not because they pose any difficulties for the reading I have presented here, and still less because I regard them as in any way wrongheaded or unimportant, but because the words do not directly name any of the persons of the Trinity, and hence are not directly relevant to the immediate object of this inquiry. What the words *do* signify is a much-contested question and has been debated for a long time. Christians spent much of the fourth century trying to come to a common understanding of the terms, coalescing ultimately around the idea that the terms express what is *common* to the three persons of the Trinity: the divine essence. It is not necessary to trace this history or delve into its complexities here. For the purposes of this chapter, it is enough to make three observations.

First, the phrases belong to a slightly different order of discourse than the rest of the creed, standing somewhat closer to what is sometimes called the "second-order" language of theological disputation and debate, as opposed to the "first-order" language of Scripture and worship. Obviously the distinction between first-order and second-order language cannot be pressed too hard, especially when the latter appears in a creed that is commonly used for liturgical purposes! Still, the distinction has some validity that is appropriate to the present case. The phrases originated from the realm of technical theology and were introduced into the creed for the purposes of achieving a greater degree of conceptual precision than was thought to be attainable by its otherwise largely biblical language.

Second, the bishops introduced the phrases in order to *reinforce* its anti-Arian message, a message that they believed was *already* powerfully conveyed in the rest of the creed. In principle, as Athanasius observed, if all the parties of the day had rightly understood the rest of the creed, it would not have been necessary to introduce the phrases in question at all.

Finally, the phrases are fully compatible with all three patterns of naming the persons of the Trinity, without themselves belonging directly to any one of them. This follows from the fact that the phrases do not actually name the persons of the Trinity, but instead express what is common to the three persons.

The Nicene Creed: A Triply Trinitarian Confession

Let us summarize our results. The Nicene-Constantinopolitan Creed uses three distinct patterns of naming to identify the three persons of the Holy Trinity. So far as the relationship of these three patterns is concerned, we may say that they are

- genuinely different. The three patterns differ both by the vocabulary they employ and by the way they deploy that vocabulary. Only one pattern alludes obliquely to the Tetragrammaton; only one is centered by the set vocabulary of Father, Son, and Spirit; and only one is characterized by the open-ended enlistment of multiple names.

- equally important. All three patterns are essential to the fabric of the creed in its final literary form, and all three make the anti-Arian point with comparable intensity and precision.
- intertwined. The root structure "One God . . . one Lord Jesus Christ" flows directly into the elaboration of them in terms of Father and Son, which in turn is explicated in the language of "Light from Light, true God of true God." A full comprehension of any one of the patterns depends upon a right understanding of the others.

In sum, the Nicene-Constantinopolitan Creed is not content to name the subject of Christian worship in a threefold way. Rather, it does so in a *triply* threefold way. Or in loftier terms, the creed uses three patterns of naming the Trinity in a way that is itself an image of the distinction, equality, and interrelationship of the persons of the Trinity.

"A THREEFOLD CORD IS NOT QUICKLY BROKEN"

Different as they are, the *nomina sacra* and the Nicene Creed tell a common story. Early Christians did not identify the persons of the Trinity in only one way, but neither did they multiply names in a random or haphazard fashion. Their faith pressed them to make explicit a distinct variety of different *patterns* of naming according to a certain implicit logic and progression. At the root of this logic stands a pattern of naming that orbits the unspoken Tetragrammaton, in continuity with the Shema, "the primal creed and confession of the Christian church." The original four *nomina sacra* help us to see the importance of this primal pattern of naming as a kind of "first among equals" and to recognize its continued role in the Nicene Creed's confession of "One God," "One Lord Jesus Christ," and "the Holy Spirit, the Lord." At the same time, the growth of the *nomina sacra* over time hints at the equal importance of other patterns of naming, which also come to explicit and enduring expression in the Nicene Creed. Taken together, the two ancient authorities suggest that early Christians named the persons of the Trinity in a *triply* trinitarian way, as though secretly inspired by the wisdom of the proverb "A threefold cord is not quickly broken" (Eccl. 4:12).

3

The Name of the Trinity in Fourth-Century Theology

A Threefold Cord under Stress

> Indeed, to this very day whenever Moses is read, a veil lies over their minds; but when one turns to the Lord, the veil is removed.
>
> —*Paul, in 2 Corinthians 3:15–16*

A threefold cord is not quickly broken, but it is easily stressed if one of its braids is worn, frayed, or severed. Though the analogy is far from perfect, it gives some idea of how the three patterns of naming the persons of the Trinity identified in the previous chapter fared during the fourth century and beyond. One pattern did not pull or bear weight as it should, and partly as a result, the other two were stretched into new positions by the strain of compensation.

THE FADING OF THE DIVINE NAME

Despite the Nicene Creed's triply trinitarian structure, one of its three patterns of naming may have ceased to be sufficiently known and meaningful to be widely recognized, even by those who composed the creed itself. As we noted in the last chapter, "We believe in one God . . . and in one Lord, Jesus Christ" were words already in use when the bishops gathered in Nicaea in 325, by one local creed at least (that of Christians in Caesarea, Palestine), and perhaps by a whole family of such creeds.[1] When the church fathers set out to write a new creed for the universal church, they accepted these words as a suitable framework on which to build. Though they undoubtedly held the words in highest esteem, they did not necessarily still hear in them an oblique reference to the Tetragrammaton. To the degree that they did not, they would no longer have been able to recognize in them an instance of what we have called a *theological* pattern of naming the persons of the Trinity, a pattern that identifies God and Christ by way of oblique reference to the divine name.

Why might Christians of the fourth century have failed to recognize the integrity of this pattern of naming? "The primary reason is quite simple: the move of Christianity from Jewish to Gentile soil led to a widespread ignorance of the Tetragrammaton as the unique and unspoken personal name of God."[2] By the fourth century, few Christian leaders had much understanding of the divine name, the unwritten traditions prescribing its use, and the often subtle ways New Testament writers evoked it indirectly. Indeed, by the fourth century few Christian leaders had much sympathy for any aspect of contemporary Judaism and Jewish practice. The centuries-old rivalry between Jew and Christian had long since hardened into stony mutual repudiation, at least among intellectual elites on both sides.

For evidence of the church's growing estrangement from Judaism and Jewish practice, we need look no farther than the Council of Nicaea itself. One of the controversies resolved at the council was how to calculate the date of Easter. In some parts of the church, it was customary to celebrate Easter on the first Sunday after Passover, a practice that made the dating of Easter dependent on the Jewish calendar. What is more, it required, as a practical matter, a willingness on the part of Christians to consult the Jewish community as to when Passover fell in any given year (a notoriously complex calculation). Other parts of the church used computations that were independent of the Jewish calendar. In the event, the council resolved the issue in favor of disentangling the dating of Easter from the Jewish feast. We catch a flavor of the arguments advanced in support of the victorious position from Emperor Constantine's reflections on the topic, as recorded by Eusebius of Caesarea:

> It was decreed unworthy to observe that most sacred festival in accordance with the practice of the Jews; having sullied their own hands with a heinous crime, such bloodstained men are as one might expect mentally blind. It is possible, now that their nation has been rejected, by a truer system . . . to extend the performing of this observance into future periods also. Let there be nothing in common between you and the detestable mob of Jews! . . . We have received from the Saviour another way. . . . Let us with one accord take up this course, right honourable brothers, and so tear ourselves away from that disgusting complicity . . . [and] not by any resemblance appear to participate in the practices of thoroughly evil persons.[3]

Of course, the Easter controversy does not tell us whether Christians were still sensitive to oblique allusions to the divine name, in the text of the Nicene Creed or elsewhere. But it does suggest that Christians were in no mood to acknowledge themselves in debt to Jewish piety and custom for the practice of their own faith.

The historical record suggests that knowledge of the divine name and understanding of conventions surrounding its use waned steadily during the patristic period, at least among Gentile Christians. This does not mean that Gentile Christians had no knowledge of such conventions at all. Clement of Alexandria, Origen, Eusebius of Caesarea, and Jerome all refer to the Tetragrammaton, and the last three indicate good understanding of customs surrounding its use. Origen and Jerome report that Jews do not pronounce the Tetragrammaton but use the surrogate "Lord" in its place, and Eusebius refers to it as the "unpronounced Tetragrammaton" (*Tetragrammaton anekphōnēton*), a technical term probably drawn from Hellenistic Judaism. These men were the foremost scholars of their day and probably had at least some personal interaction with learned Jews, so it is not surprising that they would have some knowledge of matters important to Jewish faith. Yet even they cannot be said to make the Tetragrammaton the subject of sustained reflection; instead, on a few occasions they refer to it in a chiefly incidental or passing way. If their incidental remarks may be taken to represent the high-water mark of knowledge of the Tetragrammaton among Christians, then it is reasonable to surmise that the general level of knowledge was much below this among less-learned Christians. As we observed, most theologians did not have much firsthand experience of Judaism or knowledge of Hebrew, and hence would have little occasion to gain reliable knowledge about the divine name. And what little information they did possess was apt to be poorly understood, as indeed it is on this point among most Christians today. (Jerome remarks that some Christians, upon encountering the Tetragrammaton in a Greek Bible, mistook the Hebrew characters [י ה ו ה] for Greek letters [Π Ι Π Ι] and pronounced the divine name "Pipi."[4])

In addition to want of knowledge, however, another impediment actively obstructed Christians' ability to recognize a pattern of trinitarian naming oriented toward the Tetragrammaton. Over the first few centuries of the Common Era, Christians increasingly came to share a belief common among educated pagans that the deity could in principle have no name. This was different from the contemporary Jewish view that God's name was not to be pronounced (cf. the phrase *Tetragrammaton anekphōnēton*). Rather, the pagans maintained that God was, in the language of middle Platonism, strictly "unnamable and ineffable" (*akatonomaston te kai arrēton*). God, being beyond comprehension, was also beyond being named, for we can only name that which we comprehend. The doctrine of God's essential namelessness was a pillar of enlightened pagan theism, with a pedigree going back as far as Plato himself (*Parmenides* 137b–144e). It provided sophisticated pagans with a way to affirm the divine principle of the world independently of the myths and practices of this or that local cult. In this respect, too, belief in divine anonymity differed from Jewish beliefs touching on the Tetragrammaton; as we recognized in chapter 2, these beliefs served to emphasize the uniqueness of the biblical deity and the distinctiveness of Jewish worship.[5]

The doctrine of divine anonymity entered the sphere of biblically oriented thought with Philo of Alexandria, the prolific Jewish writer whose allegorical interpretation of Scripture and Platonizing cosmology was prized by Christians (though largely ignored by Jews). Philo himself may well have known of the Tetragrammaton and the written and oral conventions surrounding its use, although the evidence is frustratingly mixed.[6] In any case, what seems clear is that mainstream Christian theology incorporated the belief without much attendant knowledge of or reverence for the divine name. In the early first century, Justin Martyr declared that anyone who thought God could be named was stark mad (*1 Apol.* 61), an opinion echoed by many others after him. By the fourth century, many Christian theologians regarded God's namelessness as virtually self-evident, inherent in the very idea of God. Still, the doctrine did not move to theological center stage until the latter fourth century, when the three Cappadocians (Gregory of Nyssa, Basil the Great, and Gregory Nazianzus) championed it in their battle against the intellectually resurgent Arianism of their day.

In *Christianity and Classical Culture*, Jaroslav Pelikan paints a vivid picture of the role of divine anonymity in the thought of the Cappadocians. On the one hand, it was "the most fundamental of the presuppositions of natural theology" which they brought from classical culture to their biblical exegesis, an assumption so basic that it "underlay and permeated all the other themes of the Cappadocian system."[7] On the other hand, it was a dogmatic principle they consciously wielded to combat the resurgent Arianism of the late fourth century. The Neo-Arians boldly (and in the Cappadocians' view, bizarrely) maintained that God could actually be named with strict propriety. God's name, they held, was Unbegotten (*agennētos*). From this, they argued, one could deduce that the Son was not divine, since the Son was, by universal consent, begotten. Although the Cappadocians might in principle have countered this argument in a number of ways (e.g., by agreeing that there is a divine name, but denying that *agennētos* is it), they did so in fact by affirming God's namelessness. In the words of Gregory of Nyssa,

> We, . . . following the suggestions of Holy Scripture, have learned that His nature cannot be named and is ineffable. We say that every name, whether invented by human custom or handed down by the Scriptures, is indicative of our conceptions of the divine nature, but does not signify what that nature is in itself.[8]

The Cappadocians' strategic appeal to the motif of God's namelessness elevated the doctrine from a background truth to an axiom of fundamental importance for the articulation of Nicene orthodoxy.

Later in this chapter, I will defend the idea that the motif of God's namelessness has an important place in a Christian account of the name of the Trinity, thanks above all to its inner connection with what I have called a *pneumatological* pattern of naming, characterized by the open-ended multiplicity of names. For the present, however, I want to emphasize the negative role that the motif played: it blocked exegetical engagement with the Scripture's testimony to the divine name. The point is an obvious one. If Christian theologians know beforehand that God can have no name, then obviously the Scripture cannot attest to one, even if it at times it *seems* to do just that. Pelikan draws attention to this dynamic in the case of the Cappadocians. Their Bible, he observes, contained "nearly a thousand references, one hundred or so in the Book of Psalms alone, to the term 'name' (the Greek '*onoma*' and cognates), as well as several thousand references to the term 'Lord [*kyrios*],' whether as a rendering of the Tetragrammaton or in its own right as a divine name in the Septuagint, then also in the New Testament for Jesus Christ as Lord." Yet for the Cappadocians, "each exegetical encounter with the very term 'name,' for example in the first petition of the Lord's Prayer, became an occasion for repeating [the] warnings" that the divine essence was unnameable and ineffable. Even biblical texts that "certainly appeared to be a revelation of . . . a divine name if anything was" became "at the hands of the Cappadocians proof texts" for the namelessness of God.[9]

In the Old Testament, the prime example of a revelation of the divine name that, for the Cappadocians, is not really one at all is the theophany at the burning bush. According to Gregory of Nyssa, when Moses asks to know God's name, God's answer is a rebuff, a declaration not of who or even what God is but merely "that God is."[10] For the Cappadocians, God's reply to Moses reaches its climax with the words "I am the one who is" (Exod. 3:14 LXX). In contrast, the continuation of God's reply in the following is scarcely an afterthought ("Tell the sons of Israel, the Lord, the God of our fathers, . . . sent me to you" [3:15]). Without the ability to recognize *kyrios* (or more exactly, $\overline{\text{Κ}\Sigma}$) as a surrogate for the Tetragrammaton, the exegete finds little of interest in Exodus 3:15, whereas 3:14 grabs attention like a flare in the night sky. According to Gregory of Nazianzus, "I am the one who is" is the most "strictly appropriate" name of God, because it indicates "a nature whose Being is absolute" and not "bound up with something else." In contrast, "Lord" and "God" are "relative names," for they describe God in terms of God's relation to the world.[11] Still, the Cappadocians emphasize, "I am the one who is" is not a definition of the divine essence, for this is incomprehensible. It is the self-announcement of "the Being without a name" ("*to on akatonomaston*").[12]

In the New Testament, the declaration that God has given Christ "the name that is above every name" (Phil. 2:9) occasions similar observations. According to Gregory of Nyssa, this passage does not mean that Christ actually received a name from God. "The name above all names" refers not to a name, no matter how exalted, but rather gestures toward the confession "The one who verily 'is' is above all names."[13] Its purpose is to portray Christ as "transcending all the power of names to express."[14]

A final illustration of the power of God's assumed namelessness to overwhelm perception of the divine name is especially fascinating. It concerns the practice of writing the divine name with special orthography, which we discussed in the last chapter. In one of his orations against the Neo-Arians, Gregory Nazianzus cites the scribal practice as evidence of the namelessness of God:

> The divinity is not designated by name. And this not only the arguments [above] demonstrate but also the wise and ancient Hebrews used special characters to venerate the divine and did not allow that the name of anything inferior to God should be written with the same letters as that of "God," on the ground that the divine should not have even this in common with our things.[15]

In 1899, a puzzled commentator remarked about this passage, "While it is well known that Jews never pronounced the name, there seems to be no ground for saying that it was written in a peculiar script."[16] Today we know that such grounds do exist, thanks to the discovery of ancient manuscripts unavailable a century ago. Gregory, it seems, was referring to copies of the Hebrew Bible that rendered the divine name with special characters, perhaps in this case paleo-Hebrew script. Though Gregory approves of the practice, he seems to have misunderstood it as well. Gregory apparently thinks that scribes write the word "God" with special characters to signify God's difference from creatures. So convinced is Gregory that God has no name that he interprets even its special visual representation as further evidence of the same. The Cappadocians cannot see the divine name even when it is before their eyes. Their "most fundamental" of presuppositions has veiled it from view.[17]

To be clear, my point is not that the Cappadocians were simply wrong to affirm the ineffability and namelessness of God, nor that this idea is without importance for an understanding of the name of the Trinity. The contrary is true, as will become clear shortly. My aim, rather, has been to suggest that whatever its merits, the doctrine had the unfortunate effect of *obstructing* a clear perception of the unspoken personal name of God, the Tetragrammaton. While the doctrine of God's namelessness has an important role to play in a well-ordered account of the name of the Holy Trinity, this is not it.

THREE PATTERNS OF NAMING RECONFIGURED

My central claim in the last section was negative. By the fourth century, Christians often did not recognize one of the three patterns of naming the persons of the Trinity encoded in the Scriptures and the Nicene Creed: the one characterized by oblique reference to the unspoken Tetragrammaton. They did not, partly due to unfamiliarity with the Tetragrammaton and Jewish conventions surrounding it, and partly because of an active predisposition to believe that God could in principle have no name. Now I want to turn to the positive side of the issue. Granted that fourth-century theologians had trouble in seeing one pattern of naming the Trinity, how did they make sense of what they could see? We will answer this question by taking each of the three patterns of naming in turn, starting with the one we have just been considering.

The Theological Pattern of Naming

Even as Christians lost the capacity to recognize a pattern of naming characterized by oblique reference to the Tetragrammaton, they did not cease to interpret the pattern altogether. Rather, they lost the ability to *differentiate* it as a distinct pattern in its own right, much as a partially color-blind person "sees" all blues as further shades of green. In this case, the "green" into which the theological pattern faded was the pneumatological pattern of naming, characterized by the open-ended multiplicity of names. So, for example, Christians continued to interpret the words "One God . . . and one Lord," even without knowledge of the Tetragrammaton. Now, however, they understand the words according to their surface semantic meaning only. In effect, "God" and "Lord" became words of the same general *class* as, for example, "Almighty," "King," "Shepherd," and so on. The theological pattern of naming did not cease to exist, but it lost its distinctive character. It continued to inform Christian theology, but in a significantly compromised and "anonymous" way.

We can illustrate these countervailing tendencies with reference to the Shema: "Hear, O Israel: the Lord our God, the Lord is one" (Deut. 6:4 NIV). There is no doubt that Christians of the fourth century regarded the Shema as a cardinal point of reference, indeed, that it was for them nothing less than "the bulwark of the Nicene dogma of the Trinity."[18] On the other hand, however, fading awareness of the divine name effected how this confession was understood. So long as Christians preserve knowledge of the divine name, they instinctively recognize that the Shema is an irreversible sentence. Its singular subject (LORD) and multiple predicates (our God, one) are not interchangeable. It is the bearer of the divine name who is the subject of the confession, who alone can receive the predicates of deity, uniqueness, and oneness, not vice versa. For those without knowledge of the divine name, however, the Shema can be reversed without essential loss of meaning. The Shema's singular subject and multiple predicates become interchangeable. "The LORD our God, the LORD is one" is equivalent to "God our Lord is one God," or for that matter, "God is one."[19] Indeed, we must go a step farther. Apart from an awareness of the divine name, the Shema does not merely become a *reversible* sentence. Under pressure from the doctrine of God's anonymous polyonymy, the nominal subject of the Shema (i.e., "LORD," understood merely as a title rather than as a surrogate for the divine name) must positively give way and assume the position of just another predicate alongside others, to be weighed and assessed in terms of its relative strengths and weaknesses. For the motif of God's transcendent namelessness comes with its own logic of singular subject and multiple predicates, according to which it is the essentially anonymous God who receives every divine predicate even as he transcends them all, including the predicates "One," "God"—and "Lord."

The Pneumatological Pattern of Naming

Turning to the pneumatological pattern of naming, characterized by the open-ended multiplicity of names, its fortunes were nearly the opposite of those of the theological pattern. Far from fading into invisibility, it acquired a new, sharply delineated profile, as theologians increasingly used the pattern to speak about the one divine essence common to the three persons of the Trinity, rather than of the three persons of the Trinity as such. In the second century, Tertullian had used the pneumatological pattern when he spoke of God, Christ, and the Spirit by using the triads Root-Tree-Fruit, Sun-Ray-Apex, and Fountain-River-Stream.[20] Clement of Alexandria did the same when he coined the triad "the One who makes the Sun to Rise," "Sun of Righteousness," and "Dew of Truth."[21] The Cappadocians, too, insisted that the Trinity is rightly spoken of with many names. For them, however, the point of such naming is not so much to identify the three persons as to express what they are or have *in common* by virtue of their shared deity, such as "Good," "Great," "One," "God," and so on. This development is important, and we will have occasion to explore it in greater detail in the next chapter.

Another way in which the pneumatological pattern fared more happily than the theological pattern concerns its relationship to the presupposition of divine ineffability. A moment ago we saw how this presupposition tended to block engagement with the *theo*logical pattern of naming. Now I suggest that the same presupposition interacted with the *pneumato*logical pattern in virtually the opposite way. It served as an intellectual catalyst that spurred Christian theologians to search out and describe the deep logic of God's many names. Why should the same presupposition relate so much more fruitfully with the one pattern rather than the other? There are, I think, two main reasons for this.

A first reason concerns the logic of divine ineffability in the cultural setting of late pagan antiquity. According to the sophisticated monotheism of the day, God's namelessness and polyonymy are but two sides of a single truth. The divine principle of the world may be addressed in many ways precisely because it transcends speech and understanding. In the words of the pagan Maximus of Tyre, "We rely on names for the nameless."[22] To the degree that Christian theologians shared this common belief, which "permeate[d] Greek religious theory," they would have expected the Bible to testify to God's ineffability, to be sure, but also and equally to God's many names.[23] In short, the same preconception that ruled out a search for the *divine name* spurred on a search for the *divine names*.

This is not to say that Christians accepted the pagan theory of God's anonymous polyonymy uncritically.[24] On the contrary, they steadfastly rejected it in one of its most popular forms, according to which "what was really being worshipped under various names and historically sanctioned forms of [pagan] cult was the one ineffable principle of all things."[25] The second-century pagan Celsus expressed this view when he declared that "it makes no difference whether one calls the supreme God by the name used among the Greeks, or by that, for example, used among the Indians or by that among the Egyptians." Origen, the child of a martyr, demurred, observing that Christians "strive to the point of death to avoid calling God Zeus or naming him in any other language."[26] As Origen undoubtedly knew, the God attested by Scriptures had explicitly prohibited such invocations: "Do not invoke the names of other gods; do not let them be heard on your lips" (Exod. 23:13). But if Christians opposed the dialectic of divine ineffability and polyonymy *in this form*, they were more receptive to it when freed from entanglement with the sacred names, rites, and myths of pagan cult. We encounter this "demythologized" form of the doctrine in the Neoplatonist Plotinus, for example, who affirmed the ineffability and unknowability of the supreme principle, even as he elaborated its inconceivable splendor under a variety of names and symbolic titles, such as Creator, Father, King, Beauty, Good, and above all, One. Christians with no sympathy for the syncretism of Celsus might still find much to admire in the philosophically purified meditations of the great Neoplatonists. Indeed, Christians were so sympathetic to the latter that a hymn composed, probably by the Neoplatonist Proclus, could circulate for centuries under the name of Gregory Nazianzus. The hymn reads in part, "You alone are unutterable, though all that is spoken is from you. You alone are unknowable, though all that is thought is from you."[27]

The other reason the cultural motif of divine ineffability interacted fruitfully with Christian theology concerns the nature of the biblical witness. Quite simply, the motif is supremely well suited to illuminate—if not the biblical witness to God *in toto*—then nevertheless an indispensable dimension thereof. To appreciate the sense in which this is so, we can turn again to the Shema. Even if the thesis of ineffable polyonymy is not well suited for elucidating the *subject* of the confession, the situation is different with respect to the *predicate*. The Shema itself characterizes the bearer of the divine name in more than one way, as both "our God" and "one." Elsewhere the Scriptures fill out the sentence "The LORD is . . . ," using a great many other terms, such as Good, a Mighty Warrior, Rock, King, God, my Shepherd, a Stronghold, Powerful, Upright, Pure, and so on. Here, then, we encounter the Bible's own native version of divine polyonymy, in the plethora of divine names that stand in apposition to the divine name. These names elucidate the divine name without competing with it or taking its place, even when in some instances they appear independently in their own right ("God Almighty"). At the same time, the Scriptures also testify that the Lord cannot be likened to anyone or anything, that he is incomparable and without peer (Exod. 15:11; Pss. 35:10; 71:19; 113:5; Isa. 44:7). We therefore understand that no single predicate, nor all of them together, definitively complete the sentence "The LORD is . . ." in such a way as to circumscribe or define the uniqueness of the LORD. In this sense, the bearer of the divine name is also beyond every name, shrouded in "thick darkness" (Exod. 20:21). In sum, the hermeneutical value of the motif of anonymous polyonymy depends on whether it is conceived as a theory of the *subject* or the *predicate* of the Shema. Applied to the subject, it tends to obscure the character of the divine name. But applied to the predicate, it tends to *catalyze* an understanding of the divine *names*. That is, it lends depth and profundity to the understanding of the LORD's deity. It underscores the LORD's inexhaustible glory and the ontological difference between Creator and creation.

Therefore, we have no reason to regret the fact that Christian theologians brought the Hellenistic doctrine of ineffable polyonymy to their engagement with Scripture. On the contrary, here we can celebrate a happy and fruitful encounter between classical culture and Christian theology. Rather, the unfortunate point is the one to which we have already alluded: Christians applied the belief in a way that was color-blind to the difference between the divine name and the divine names. Under these circumstances, they were in no position to distinguish between apt and inapt applications of the hermeneutic of God's nameless many-namedness. It became, in effect, a total theory of the Shema, subject and predicate alike.

The Christological Pattern of Naming

Turning finally to the christological pattern of naming characterized by the vocabulary of Father, Son, and Holy Spirit, our story can be brief. This pattern's fortunes were in good measure a function of those of the other two, being closely intertwined with theirs. Christian theologians needed a way to name the persons of the Trinity. By the late fourth century, however, neither the theological nor the pneumatological patterns were readily available for this purpose. The theological pattern was not available because it had flowed indistinguishably into the pneumatological. And the pneumatological pattern was not available because it was understood as the privileged way of speaking of the one divine essence common to the three persons, rather than of the three persons as such. What was needed was a sturdy, unambiguous way of designating the three persons, and here the vocabulary of Father, Son, and Holy Spirit answered the need admirably. The pattern was all the more ready to assume this role because of the central place it had occupied in the controversies with Arianism. Yet however understandable, the outcome reflects a palpable shift from the Nicene Creed, where the vocabulary of kinship provides but one of three patterns of naming the persons of the Trinity. For the Cappadocians, in contrast, the christological pattern has become something like *the* paradigmatic way of naming the persons of the Trinity, and the standard by which all other names for the Trinity are to be measured.

GREGORY OF NYSSA ON "THE NAME OF THE FATHER AND THE SON AND THE HOLY SPIRIT"

In the previous section I gave a highly schematic—and at many points no doubt oversimplified—account of how the three patterns of naming the Trinity encoded in the Nicene Creed fared over the course of the fourth century. A more adequate account would follow up with a detailed investigation of primary sources. While such an account exceeds the scope of this chapter, we will examine one important text that illustrates the major trends identified above. The text is Gregory of Nyssa's exposition of the phrase "in the name of the Father and the Son and the Holy Spirit," found in his anti-Arian writing

Refutation of the Creed of Eunomius.[28] In the passage, Gregory argues against the claim that God, Christ, and the Holy Spirit can be more properly called "Creator," "product," and "product of product."

Near the beginning of the *Refutation*, Gregory writes that the Lord Jesus Christ appeared on earth to deliver to his apostles a true knowledge of God, in order that humans might no longer think about God "according to their own notions," and in order that the teaching concerning God "which is given to us, as it were, 'through a glass darkly'" in the Old Testament might be "fully revealed to us."[29] The true doctrine concerning God, Gregory maintains, is summed up by Christ himself in his command to baptize "in the name of the Father and of the Son and of the Holy Spirit" (Matt. 28:19). This saying refers both to the diversity of divine persons, indicated by "Father, Son, and Spirit," and to the unity of divine essence, indicated by the singular word "name." "In regard to essence He is one, wherefore the Lord ordained that we should look to one Name: but in regard to the attributes indicative of the Persons, our belief in Him is distinguished into belief in the Father, the Son, and the Holy Ghost."[30] Following the structure of the verse, Gregory divides his exposition into two parts, first addressing "the Father and the Son and the Holy Spirit," and then the phrase "in the name." Speaking of the former, Gregory writes:

> We say that it is a terrible and soul-destroying thing to misinterpret these Divine utterances and to devise in their stead assertions to subvert them,—assertions pretending to correct God the Word, Who appointed that we should maintain these statements as part of our faith. For each of these titles understood in its natural sense becomes for Christians a rule of truth and a law of piety. For while there are many other names by which Deity is indicated in the Historical Books, in the Prophets and in the Law, our Master Christ passes by all these and commits to us these titles as better able to bring us to the faith about the Self-Existent, declaring that it suffices us to cling to the title, "Father, Son, and Holy Ghost," in order to attain to the apprehension of Him Who is absolutely Existent, Who is one and yet not one.[31]

According to Gregory, Christ himself has singled out "Father, Son, and Holy Spirit" from the "many other names" for Deity in the Scriptures, as "better able" to bring us to faith, and sufficient for "the apprehension of Him who is absolutely existent." These appellations, Gregory goes on to explain, teach "not a difference of nature, but only the special attributes that mark the *hypostases*." By them "we know that neither is the Father the Son, nor the Son the Father, nor the Holy Spirit either the Father or the Son, and recognize each by the distinctive mark of His Personal *hypostasis*." Above all, the words permit us to contemplate each person "by Himself" and yet "not divided from that with which He is connected."[32] For Gregory, the vocabulary of Father, Son, and Holy Spirit represents the primary and privileged way of designating the persons of the Trinity. Elsewhere in his writings, Gregory acknowledges that there are other scriptural names indicative of the personal *hypostases*, such as (in the case of the Son) "Right hand," "Only-begotten," and "Word."[33] Yet even so, Gregory still affirms the special significance of the baptismal triad, declaring that "the mystery of godliness is ratified by the confession of the Divine Names [*tōn theōn onomatōn*]—the Names of the Father, the Son, and the Holy Ghost."[34]

Next Gregory turns his attention to the words "baptizing them into the name." Following the singular form of the word "name," Gregory interprets the phrase as a reference to the one divine essence:

> What then means that unnameable name [*to akatonomaston onoma*] concerning which the Lord said, "Baptizing them into the name," and did not add the actual significant term which "the name" indicates? We have concerning it this notion, that all things that exist in the creation are defined by means of their several names. . . . The uncreated Nature alone, which we acknowledge in the Father, and in the Son, and in the Holy Spirit, surpasses all significance of names.[35]

Gregory affirms the ineffability of the divine nature on account of the ontological difference between Creator and creature. We can define created things by the words we use, for "the mention of the name impresses upon the hearer the form of the creature." But we cannot speak of the divine nature in this way, for it "surpasses all significance of names." When Christ spoke of "the name," therefore, he did not refer to any single name at all, but rather gave authority to speak of the uncreated nature by means of a multiplicity of names:

> For this cause the Word, when He spoke of "the name" in delivering the Faith, did not add what it is,—for how could a name be found for that which is above every name?—but gave authority that whatever name our intelligence by pious effort be enabled to discover to indicate the transcendent Nature, that name should be applied alike to Father, Son, and Holy Ghost, whether it be "the Good" or "the Incorruptible," whatever name each may think proper to be employed to indicate the undefiled Nature of Godhead.[36]

This is a Christian version of the dialectic of God's ineffable polyonymy, applied to the Godhead common to the persons of the Trinity. Gregory gives great latitude to the Christian imagination in finding names for the Godhead, in contrast to his insistence on the baptismal names "Father," "Son," and "Holy Spirit." Apparently even the bounds of Scripture may be crossed, so long as the search for appropriate names is guided by "pious effort."

Gregory goes on to say that names predicated of the divine essence may also be said of the persons of the Trinity, thereby enabling another legitimate kind of divine polyonymy. So, for example, one may call the Father "Highest, Almighty, King of kings, and Lord of lords, and in a word all terms of highest significance."[37] Such names, however, do not speak to what differentiates the persons, but rather to what each person is in common with the others, for "all these things the Christian eye discerns alike in the Father, the Son, and the Holy Ghost."[38] A specific application of the last principle appears elsewhere in Gregory's writings in his account of the voice who spoke to Moses from the burning bush. Gregory believes that it was the Son who spoke, because the Scripture initially identifies the speaker as an "angel" (Exod. 3:2), thereby signaling the Son's distinction from Father. But when the Son goes on to declare "I am" (Exod. 3:14), he teaches that he is coessential with the Father. By these words, Christ does not satisfy Moses' request for a *name*, but rather teaches that he has "no name that could possibly give a knowledge of His essence." For this reason, Gregory maintains, Paul in Philippians 2:9 describes the name of the Son as "above every name," "not as though it were some one name preferred above all others, though still comparable with them, but rather in the sense that He Who verily *is* above every name."[39]

If we compare the Nicene Creed's threefold naming of the Trinity with Gregory of Nyssa's reflections on "the name of the Father and the Son and the Holy Spirit," we may be reminded again of a threefold cord under stress. For Gregory, one of the creed's patterns of naming the persons of the Trinity has ceased to pull or bear weight as it should, namely, the pattern centered in oblique reference to the Tetragrammaton. Meanwhile, the other two patterns have assumed new positions. One pattern, characterized by the vocabulary of Father, Son, and Spirit, has become the privileged way of naming the three persons. The other pattern, characterized by ineffable polyonymy, has become the privileged way of speaking of the one divine essence. The cord is in no danger of breaking. But estrangement from the Tetragrammaton and Jewish modes of referencing has stretched it hard.

4

The Dionysian Tradition and the Transformation of Gentile Wisdom

The Eclipse and Rediscovery of the Tetragrammaton

> It was from the Gentiles that I had come to you. . . . And far off, I heard your voice saying, "I am the God who IS."
>
> —*Augustine of Hippo*[1]

In this chapter and the next, we will explore two great schools of thought on the name of the Trinity, which we will dub the Dionysian and Reformation traditions. Both traditions build upon the legacy of the fourth century, but they do so in different ways. To put the matter simply and somewhat misleadingly, the Dionysian school approaches the common tradition from a more pneumatological or Spirit-centered direction, while the Reformation school does so from a more christological or Christ-centered direction. In terms of our metaphor of the threefold cord, each school grasps the common tradition by a different strand. What neither tradition does, however, is restore the theological pattern of naming, centered in the unspoken Tetragrammaton, to its rightful place in the total economy of names.

Our discussion of the Dionysian tradition focuses on Dionysius himself, Augustine of Hippo, and Thomas Aquinas. The story we tell about these towering figures concerns in about equal measure what they have in common and what distinguishes them. What they share is an approach to naming the persons of the Trinity that picks up where we left off at the end of the previous chapter. All three figures accept the Creed of 381 as a settled statement of orthodoxy, as well as the distinction between the ineffable divine essence and the three persons, Father, Son, and Holy Spirit. Without unduly emphasizing the point, we can also say that they tend to think of the divine essence—or rather the effects thereof—as that face of divine mystery that is turned toward the world generally and is most accessible to the wisdom of the Gentiles. They therefore set themselves the task of purifying and transforming such wisdom, so that Christians and others might think rightly of the divine essence and approach the mystery of the three persons by the right path. As for awareness of the unspoken Tetragrammaton, it is all but wholly absent from their thought.

Turning to what distinguishes Dionysius, Augustine, and Thomas, our story relates an ever-richer *reclaiming* of the three patterns of naming the persons of the Trinity that we identified in chapter 2. Dionysius himself focused on one pattern of naming to identify the persons of the Trinity: the christological pattern of Father, Son, and Holy Spirit. Augustine accords this pattern a central place in his writings, too, but he is, if anything, even more interested in exploring the possibilities of the pneumatological pattern of naming the persons, characterized by an open-ended variety of names. Thomas, for his part, gives a secure place to both of the patterns recognized by Augustine. In addition, he gestures, however imperceptibly, toward the existence of yet another pattern, with the surprising result that the Tetragrammaton is not wholly absent from the Dionysian tradition, after all.

DIONYSIUS: THE DIVINE NAMES AND ONE PATTERN OF TRINITARIAN NAMING

> Then there are the names expressing distinctions, the transcendent name and proper activity of the Father, of the Son, of the Spirit.
>
> —*Dionysius*, The Divine Names[2]

The book of Acts tells us that while in Athens, Paul used the language of the Greek poets to preach of "the God who made the world and everything in it" (Acts 17:24), before turning to tidings of the resurrection. This approach, we are told, wooed a handful of newcomers to Christian faith, including one Dionysius the Areopagite (17:34). Centuries later, an anonymous author wrote a number of works under Dionysius's name, including *The Divine Names* (*De divinis nominibus*), the most influential work of its kind ever written. Little is known of the author's identity, apart from what appears from the writings themselves: he was a devout Christian, and he was steeped in the philosophical idiom of late antiquity. In his commitment to biblical authority, respect for Hellenistic wisdom, and reverent orientation toward "the God who made the world," Dionysius the Areopagite—or Pseudo-Dionysius, as he has come to be known—is exemplary of what we have chosen to call a *Dionysian* approach to a Christian theology of divine and trinitarian naming.

Naming the One God: the Nameless God of Many Names

Near the beginning of *The Divine Names*, Dionysius declares: "It is and it is as no other being is. Cause of all existence, and therefore itself transcending existence, it alone could give an authoritative account of what it really is" (1.1 [p. 50]).

These words encapsulate much of Dionysius's own theology and that of the Dionysian family as a whole. Dionysius's theology is first and last a celebration of God's uniqueness as this comes to light *from a certain vantage point*, that of God as creator of the cosmos. Viewed from this perspective, God is knowable as One who is "cause of all existence" and who "transcends existence," or again, as "brimming causality and supreme transcendence" (12.4 [p. 127]). From this double-sided insight into the divine, Dionysius's whole theology of divine naming hangs. Since God is the cause of everything, "The songs of praise and the names for it are fittingly derived from the sum total of creation" (1.7 [p. 56]). But since God "transcends all things in a manner beyond being" (1.5 [p. 54]), none of our naming is adequate to God. Dionysius gathers up both insights in an affirmation that sums up his understanding of the Bible's testimony to the divine names: "Realizing all this, the theologians [the authors of Sacred Scripture] praise it by every name—and as the Nameless One" (1.6 [pp. 54–55]).

In Dionysius's words, we recognize again the motif of God's nameless polyonymy, which already played an important role in the theology of the Cappadocians. For Dionysius, this motif is closely linked to the believer's journey of sanctification and divinization, through an ever more apt use of the names of God. The journey of sanctification entails a series of ascending steps, which move from affirmation, to negation, to the negation of negation, and finally to silence. Ascent from one level to the next is no mere mental achievement, but a matter of spiritual cleansing, illumination, and transformation. At each stage of the journey, Dionysius offers insights concerning the names of God that have remained determinative for the Christian tradition.

The most accessible and ultimately least adequate form of naming is that of affirmation (*kataphatic*, or affirmative naming). Because God is the Creator of all things, all things bear some resemblance to God and thereby make it possible to know and to name God in certain ways. In Platonic fashion, Dionysius distinguishes between two kinds of affirmative names, those that refer to sensible objects, emotions, and actions (Sun, Fire, Wind, Dew, Rock); and those that refer to the intelligible structure of the world (Beauty, Love, Being). The latter are more appropriate to God than the former, and of the latter, the most appropriate name of all is, perhaps, the Good. An enduring insight of Dionysius is that all such affirmative names describe the whole fullness of divine being rather than some aspect of it: "All the names appropriate to God are praised regarding the whole, entire, full, and complete divinity rather than any part of it. . . . Only through perversity would anyone, reared on holy scripture, deny that the attributes of God refer in all their truth and meaning to the complete Deity. . . . I will take it that whatever divine name is explicated it refers to the entire Deity" (2.1 [p. 60]). Since God is not composed of different elements, like created beings, different divine names do not identify different attributes of God, but each describes the one simple being of God from the vantage point of a distinct created effect or cause.[3]

Yet indispensable as they are as a starting point, affirmative names for God must ultimately be left behind in accordance with the insight of holy writ: "Scripture itself asserts that God is dissimilar and that he is not to be compared with anything, that he is different from everything and, stranger yet, that there is none at all like him" (9.7 [p. 118]).

Even our highest affirmative names ("Good," "Life," "Beauty") tell us how God acts upon our finite spirits, not what God essentially is (cf. 2.7 [p. 63]). Hence every affirmative name must be negated (*apophasis*). Throughout *The Divine Names* and his other works, Dionysius delights in composing "veritable litanies and hymns of negation": the divine nature is invisible, infinite, unsearchable, inscrutable, and incomprehensible; there is no perception of it, no image, opinion, name, or expression for it, no contact with it.[4] The celebration of negation drives home the insight that created things fall so far short of their Cause that they are infinitely and incomparably subordinate to him.

Yet even simple negation is not the end of the journey, but prepares the way for a still more appropriate form of speech, one that commentators have sometimes called "eminent discourse." Eminent speech refuses to take either affirmation or negation as final, and instead combines both to propel the inquiring mind to new insight.

> When we talk of God as being without mind and without perception, this is to be taken in the sense of what he has in superabundance and not as a defect. Hence we attribute absence of reason to him because he is above reason, we attribute lack of perfection to him because he is above and before perfection, and we posit intangible and invisible darkness of that Light which is unapproachable [1 Tim. 6:16] because it so far exceeds the visible light. (7.2 [p. 107])

Here simple negation is negated, and a new kind of affirmation created. As Deirdre Carabine explains, "The prefix '*hyper*' [above, super, more than, extra, beyond] . . . provides the key to the central dialectic in Dionysian thought: it indicates something positive, but it is an affirmation which can no longer be thought."[5] In the case of God, negation does not mean *privation* (e.g., that

God lacks reason), but rather *more than* what our names denote (e.g., that God is above and beyond reason).

For Dionysius, our final naming of God is no word at all but ecstatic silence. Dionysius evokes the image of Moses' ascending Mount Sinai into a "cloud" that transcends all language and thought, a "cloud of unknowing," in the language of a later writer in the Dionysian tradition. In the climactic passage of *The Mystical Theology*, the Areopagite writes: "The most divine knowledge of God, that which comes through unknowing, is achieved in a union far beyond mind, when mind turns away from all things, even from itself, and when it is made one with the dazzling rays, being then and there enlightened by the inscrutable depth of Wisdom" (7.3 [p. 109]).

In the end, the nameless Cause of all does indeed give "an authoritative account of what it really is" as only it can do (1.1 [p. 50]). But the Deity so revealed is absolutely unknowable, and union with it is knowledge beyond reason and total ignorance at once.

Naming the Persons of the Trinity: the Father and the Son and the Holy Spirit

The greater portion of *The Divine Names* is occupied with rightly naming the ineffable divine essence. Still, at points throughout his work, Dionysius affirms the central doctrines of Christian faith and in particular the orthodox doctrine of the Trinity. As Dionysius understands it, the doctrine of the Trinity is rightly expressed in the language of Father, Son, and Holy Spirit, as evident, for example, in the following passage:

> Then there are the names expressing distinctions, the transcendent name and proper activity of the Father, of the Son, of the Spirit. Here the titles cannot be interchanged, nor are they held in common. . . . As I have said elsewhere, those fully initiated into our theological tradition assert that . . . the differentiations within the Godhead have to do with the benign processions and revelations of God. (2.3–4 [pp. 60–61])

For Dionysius, the church's distinctive teaching regarding the Trinity is inseparable from the vocabulary of "Father, Son, and Holy Spirit." Nevertheless, he seems to have no interest in elaborating the logic of these words, nor does he adduce further triadic namings of the persons of the Trinity, as Augustine will do. Dionysius is content to let this triad stand on its own as a statement of the church's orthodox tradition. His passion lies elsewhere, in sculpting a right understanding of the awesome transcendence of the One God.

Yet precisely at this point, at the juncture of the divine essence and the three persons, a profound ambiguity emerges in Dionysius's thought, one with serious implications from a Christian point of view. John N. Jones has expressed the issue ably:

> Does Dionysius' highest Godhead preserve Trinitarian identity, or are the Trinitarian elements exclusively economic, existing only on the order of divine manifestation? What is the nature of the 'God beyond God'? . . . Dionysius insists on the total hiddenness of the transcendent God who is beyond names, even the scriptural Trinitarian names of Father, Son, and Spirit. Is Dionysius therefore non-Trinitarian or anti-Trinitarian?[6]

Fortunately, we do not need to resolve the questions that Jones raises. The status of the Trinity in Dionysius's thought is an unsettled question even among specialists, as Jones's essay shows. For our purposes, it is enough to recognize that this ambiguity is a deep and seemingly irresolvable feature of Dionysius's work. Taken by itself, Dionysius's method of affirmation and denial pushes us powerfully toward the recognition of God as the First Cause of all, "the Nameless One" of many names. It is not well suited to make sense of the centrality accorded to certain specific names and affirmations—for example, Jesus, Trinity, Father, Son, Holy Spirit—by the scriptural, liturgical, and doctrinal traditions of the church. Even if we believe that Dionysius himself does attach exceptional status to those names, they do not sit easily with the tenor of his work.

The Divine Name in Dionysius's Thought

Regarding Dionysius's thought concerning the Tetragrammaton, however, there is little controversy. By every indication, Dionysius is simply unaware of it. Certainly he is well acquainted with the other great name of the burning bush, "I am the one who is" (Exod. 3:14 LXX), which provides the scriptural basis for his consideration of the divine name, "Being." Dionysius is deeply struck, too, by Moses' ascent up Mount Sinai into clouds of darkness, which for Dionysius foreshadows every faithful person's ascent into a realm beyond knowing and unknowing. Still, the fact remains that Dionysius appears oblivious to the existence of the Tetragrammaton.

Of course, there is nothing surprising about this. As we noticed in the previous chapter, knowledge of the Tetragrammaton was uncommon among Christians in Dionysius's day. Still, we may wonder how Dionysius would have responded to news of the divine name if he had heard of it. Would he have embraced knowledge of the Tetragrammaton joyfully, as a happy guest might embrace his hitherto unrecognized host? Or would he have gone on exactly as before, as though nothing of importance had happened? We will never know. But it does seem to me that this is one way to weigh the question of the "orthodoxy" of Dionysius's thought—and to show why that question is so difficult to answer.[7]

AUGUSTINE: THE DIVINE NAMES AND TWO PATTERNS OF TRINITARIAN NAMING

> So then, as we direct our gaze at the creator by *understanding the things that are made* [Rom. 1:20, Vulg.], we should understand him as a triad, whose traces appear in creation in a way that is fitting.
>
> —*Augustine*[8]

Augustine of Hippo carries our story forward by introducing a *second* pattern of naming the persons of the Trinity, one that moves from traces of the Trinity in creation to the Trinity itself. To rightly understand Augustine on this point, however, we must begin at an earlier point, with his understanding of the difference between names of the one divine essence, and names of the three persons.

The Distinction between Absolute and Relative Names of God

According to Augustine, the names we predicate of God are said either "by way of substance" or "by way of relationship." Substance names concern the one divine essence, which, Augustine maintains, is absolutely simple and immutable, according to the oracle of the burning bush. As Augustine explains,

> Who can more be than he that said to his servant, *I am who I am*, and, *Tell the sons of Israel, He who is sent me to you* [Exod. 3:14–15, Vulg.]? Now other things that we call beings or substances admit of modifications [*accidentia*], by which they are modified and changed to a great or small extent. But God cannot be modified in any way, and therefore the substance or being which is God is alone unchangeable, and therefore it pertains to it most truly and supremely to be, from which comes the name "being." (*Trin.* 5.1.3 [p. 190])

Because God's essence is utterly without accidents or attributes, it follows that for God "it is the same thing to be as to be great." As Augustine explains,

> Because God is not great by participating in greatness, but he is great with his great self because he is his own greatness. The same must be said about goodness and eternity and omnipotence and about

> absolutely all the predications that can be stated of God, because it is all said with reference to himself, and not metaphorically either or in simile but properly. (5.2.11 [p. 196])

Thus far, everything Augustine has said stands in complete agreement with Dionysius, the Cappadocians, and indeed, with the *Arian* metaphysicians of the fourth century. For the Arians too maintained that what is said of God's substance is said absolutely, for God has no accidents. For the Arians, however, this single principle governs *all* of our names for God, for, according to them, "*Whatever* is said or understood about God is said substance-wise, not modification-wise" (italics added). Augustine denies this:

> With God, though, nothing is said modification-wise. . . . And yet not everything that is said of him substance-wise. Some things are said *with reference to something else*, like Father with reference to Son and Son with reference to Father; and this is not said modification-wise, because the one is always Father and the other always Son. (5.1.6 [p. 192])

As Edmund Hill points out, Augustine here makes "a new distinction" among the names we use for God. We do not distinguish between substance words and accident words, but we do between words that say something of God *absolutely*, and words that say something of God *relatively*. This brings us to Augustine's reflections on naming for persons of the Trinity, for this kind of naming depends on language that implies mutual reference and relationship in the one simple being of God.[9]

Father and Son and Holy Spirit

The first set of relative names that Augustine explores is that of Father and Son and Holy Spirit. It is not surprising that Augustine should begin here for he, like Dionysius, regards this language as virtually inherent in the doctrine of the Trinity itself. This is evident from Augustine's summary of the doctrine in book 1 of *The Trinity:*

> The purpose of all the Catholic commentators I have been able to read on the divine books of both testaments, who have written before me on the trinity which God is, has been to teach that according to the scriptures Father and Son and Holy Spirit in the inseparable equality of one substance present a divine unity; and therefore there are not three gods but one God; although indeed the Father has begotten the Son, and therefore he who is the Father is not the Son; and the Son is begotten by the Father, and therefore he who is the Son is not the Father, and the Holy Spirit is neither the Father nor the Son, but only

> the Spirit of the Father and of the Son, himself co-equal to the Father and the Son, and belonging to the threefold unity. (1.1.7 [p. 69])

When analyzed carefully, however, the triad "Father and Son and Holy Spirit" reveals some surprising and even disconcerting features. Strangely, the language is not actually all that "relational," or at least not as uniformly so, as one would expect. "Father" and "Son" are indeed relational and even *reciprocal* terms, for "neither is said with reference to itself but only with reference to the other" (5.1.6 [p. 192]) The difficulty is the Holy Spirit. For one thing, Augustine states, "Holy Spirit" does not seem to name anything that is distinctive to the third person, for "Holy" and "Spirit" apply just as well to the first and second persons, and indeed to the one divine essence as well. Yet even if we take Holy Spirit as a distinguishing name of the third person, we face another, more serious problem. As Augustine candidly admits, "Relationship, to be sure, is not apparent in this particular name" (5.3.12 [p. 197]). One could introduce a relational element into the name by the use of a preposition or the genitive case, as we do when we say that the Holy Spirit is "the Spirit *of* the Father and *of* the Son." But this sort of relationality could equally well be added to many other names as well. As Edmund Hill observes, "Any word, practically, can be regarded as predicating relationship if it is construed with the genitive, the preposition 'of.'" (203). In any case, even "relationally enhanced" Spirit-language still falls short of the *reciprocity* that is evident in the word pair "Father" and "Son." We can say "Father of the Son" and "Son of the Father," but we cannot similarly transpose the phrase "Spirit of the Father" and say "Father of the Spirit," for "then we should take the Holy Spirit to be his son!" (5.3.13 [p. 198]).

Despite the seriousness of these issues, which Augustine seems almost to delight in pointing out, Augustine is not really too concerned on behalf of the triad "Father, Son, and Holy Spirit." Rather, he defends the adequacy of this form of language by means of two observations, both of which have lasting significance for a Christian theology of the name of the Trinity.

First, Augustine argues, not every personal name of the Trinity must exhibit the same kind of reciprocal relationality as is exhibited by the pair "Father" and "Son." "Nor should the reader be worried by our saying that Holy Spirit . . . is said relationship-wise, on the grounds that there does not seem to be a corresponding name to which this one is referred. . . . This happens in many relationships, where we cannot find two corresponding words to be referred to each other (5.3.13 [pp. 197–98]).

We often refer to reciprocal relationships by using language that is not itself fully reciprocal in character. Augustine offers the example of "pledge," which implies a "pledger," although in fact the latter term is uncommon, in Latin as in English. In effect, Augustine suggests, "Holy Spirit" is a name of this sort. We should not, Augustine implies, demand a conformity to an artificially high standard of trinitarian naming, one that would in effect draw the circle of trinitarian names too narrowly and unnecessarily impoverish our understanding of what counts as a trinitarian name. If we did, then not even "Father, Son, and Holy Spirit" could pass muster!

Second, Augustine suggests that it is permissible, and even in a sense imperative, to go beyond the triad "Father, Son, and Holy Spirit" to other scriptural names for the persons of the Trinity. This is true, in the first instance, of the "Holy Spirit," whose relational character is brought to light by the use of other scriptural terms, such as "Gift" (cf. Acts 8:20; John 4:10). The name succeeds where Holy Spirit does not, for it brings out the distinctiveness and the relationality of the third person. "To get a correspondence here we say gift of the giver and giver of the gift" (5.3.13 [p. 198]). Indeed, Augustine suggests that this name provides the clue for understanding the name Holy Spirit, since He is the Gift of the Father and Son together, who are both Holy and Spirit. But it is also true of the other persons as well. Speaking of the Father, Augustine states that "he is also called Origin relationship-wise, and perhaps other things too" (5.3.14 [p. 198]). And speaking of the Son, Augustine says, "He is also called Word and Image relationship-wise" (5.3.14 [p. 198]).

Lover, Beloved, Love (1 John 4:8, 16)

As fascinated as Augustine is by the triad "Father, Son, and Holy Spirit," he is perhaps even more intent on exploring the possibilities of another form of triadic naming, which employs a variety of different common nouns to move from traces of the Trinity in creation, to the Trinity itself, and vice versa. For our purposes, it is enough to focus on only one of these: Lover, beloved, love.

A question that Augustine poses several times over the course of *The Trinity* is of whom the apostle speaks when he declares, "God is love" (1 John 4:8, 16). "So *God is charity.* But the question is whether it is the Father or the Son or the Holy Spirit or the triad [that is here spoken of], because this triad is not three Gods but one God" (15.5.27 [p. 418]).

Augustine acknowledges that it is natural and proper to take "Love" as a "substance name," one that applies to the divine essence, and so also to each person singly (since according to Augustine the persons and the essence are identical). According to this rule, it is equally true to say that the Trinity is Love, the "Father is Love," "Son is Love," and the "Holy Spirit is Love." Understood in this way, the name works just like other "absolute" names such as Wisdom, Almighty, God, and so forth. Thus employed, the name "Love" generates a string of orthodox affirmations, but ones that do not generate a great deal of new insight.

Yet Augustine clearly believes there is more to the story than this. Augustine points out that the Scriptures often contain obscurities in order to stimulate our investigation (15.5.27 [p. 418]). In this case, Augustine argues that a closer examination of the context of the passage indicates that the saying "God is Love" has special reference to the Holy Spirit. "What is meant is that while in that supremely simple nature, substance is not one thing and charity another, but substance is charity and charity is substance, whether in the Father or in the Son or in the Holy Spirit, yet all the same the Holy Spirit is distinctively named charity" (15.5.29 [p. 419]).

But then Augustine goes another important step further. Having established that "Love" names the Holy Spirit, he extrapolates from it *corresponding names for the Father and the Son.* In effect, Augustine uses "Love" as the "key signature" for unfolding a new ternary that names *all three persons of the Trinity.* Augustine expresses the new triad as "Lover and what is loved and love" (15.10 [p. 402]), and again, in slightly different terms, "One loving him who is from him, and one loving him from whom he is, and love itself" (6.7 [p. 210]). In both cases a similar pattern is at work. Augustine applies the word "Love" to one of the three persons, the Holy Spirit. At the same time, he modifies the word in ways that are appropriate to the first and second persons, in order to illuminate the mutual relations among the persons of the Trinity.

Augustine's *trinitarian unfolding of the saying* "God is love" occupies a key place in the structure of the entire work. Indeed, by Augustine's own account, it marks a decisive turning point in his mammoth fifteen-book work, when he turns from *expounding* the orthodox faith in the Trinity, to *understanding it.* As Augustine himself remarks (15.2.10 [p. 398]): "If we try to recall where it was in these books that a trinity first began to appear to our understanding, it will occur to us that it was . . . when we came to charity, which is called God in holy scripture, the glimmerings of a trinity began to appear, namely, lover and what is loved and love" (15.2.10 [p. 398]).

Augustine goes on to explain that because he understood the doctrine of the Trinity so imperfectly, he then turns to the image of the Trinity in the human being, only to return at the conclusion of the book to the statement. Thus the saying "God is Love," taken as a trinitarian statement, shapes the thematic context or *inclusio* within which Augustine's exploration of the creaturely triads takes shape.

Lord

Before taking leave of Augustine, we will briefly recount his treatment of one term, "Lord," which will prove to be significant for the story we are telling. Augustine is well aware of the important place the term occupies in the

Scriptures. Unlike his contemporary Jerome, however, Augustine seems unaware of the fact that it is commonly employed as a surrogate for the unspoken Tetragrammaton, or indeed that such a name exists at all. In the prayer that closes *The Trinity*, Augustine writes:

> O Lord our God, we believe in you, Father and Son and Holy Spirit. Truth would not have said, *Go and baptize the nations in the name of the Father and of the Son and of the Holy Spirit* (Mt 28:19) unless you were a triad. Nor would you have commanded us to be baptized, Lord God, in the name of any who is not Lord God. Nor would it have been said with divine authority, *Hear O Israel, the Lord our God is one God* (Dt 6:4), unless while being a triad you were still one Lord God. (15.6.51 [p. 443])

As these words indicate, Augustine understands "Lord" to designate what the persons are or have in common rather than what distinguishes them, like other generic or appellative names such as God, Truth, Goodness, and so forth. Yet, Augustine supposes, "Lord" also differs from these other absolute names, for it clearly implies a relationship, in this case with created reality. "As there cannot be a slave who has not got a lord, so there cannot be a lord who has not got a slave" (5.4.17 [p. 203]). From this it follows that "He cannot be everlastingly lord, or we would be compelled to say that creation is everlasting, because he would only be everlastingly lord if creation were everlastingly serving him." Rather, "this relationship title too belongs to God from a point of time, since the creation he is lord of is not from everlasting." To illustrate the temporal reference of the term, Augustine adduces "his being the Lord of the people Israel." Here, Augustine declares, the temporal character of the term is indisputable, for "we can point clearly to the moment when it [Israel] began to be" (5.4.17 [p. 203]).

In fact, Augustine's analysis of the term "Lord" completely misses a crucial dimension of its biblical usage. In extrabiblical speech, it is true, "Lord" is a purely relational term, as Augustine supposes. In the Hellenistic world, deities were routinely designated as the "Lord *of*" this or that. In contrast, biblical speech commonly designates God as "Lord" in an absolute fashion, in a way that has no counterpart in extrabiblical speech.[10] This is because the Old and New Testaments regularly employ "Lord" as a surrogate for the divine name, which is itself used in absolute fashion. In fact, the phrase "Lord *of*" (for "YHWH of") is completely unheard of in the Old Testament, and Augustine's phrase "Lord of the people Israel" never appears in the Scriptures.[11] Being unaware of the Tetragrammaton, however, Augustine has simply assimilated the Bible's distinctive way of using the term "Lord" to the conventions of extrabiblical speech. Augustine imagines that the biblical

God is called "Lord" entirely with reference to creation, rather than with reference to God's eternal identity as bearer of the divine name (cf. 5.4.17 [p. 204]).

In the end, then, Augustine may go beyond Dionysius in reclaiming a second pattern of naming the persons of the Trinity. But Augustine no more than Dionysius has any apparent knowledge of the Tetragrammaton.

THOMAS AQUINAS: THE DIVINE NAME(S) AND THREE PATTERNS OF TRINITARIAN NAMING

> There in Hebrew the name is the *Tetragrammaton*, which certainly is said of God alone. From these sayings it is clear that the Son of God is true God.
>
> —*Thomas Aquinas*[12]

Thomas Aquinas gives elegant expression to both the christological and pneumatological patterns of naming the Trinity previously identified by Dionysius and Augustine. Additionally, however, he does two further things that are of great importance for the argument I am making in this book. For one thing, he draws attention, if not to a third pattern of naming the persons of the Trinity, then nevertheless to the necessary point where such a pattern might be conceived, centered in the unspoken Tetragrammaton. For another, Thomas makes an extremely useful contribution to our understanding of "the most appropriate" way of naming divine reality. He suggests that there can be *more than one* "most appropriate" way of naming, according to the perspective from which divine reality is viewed.

Our discussion of Thomas will focus chiefly on his mature work, the *Summa theologiae*, where Thomas discusses the divine names in two principal locations, first in the *Treatise on God*, and again in the *Treatise on the Trinity* (*ST* 1.33–38).[13] Our discussion will examine these in turn, before returning to a surprising aspect of Thomas's discussion of "The Most Appropriate Name of God," where Thomas draws attention to the root of a *third pattern* of divine naming, one centered in the Tetragrammaton.[14]

"The Names of God" (*ST* 1.13) in the *Treatise on God*

In the *Treatise on God*, Thomas considers our naming of God insofar as it pertains to the one divine essence common to the three persons (*ST* 1.13). At the outset Thomas declares that "we speak of things as we know them" (*ST* 1.13, preface). Since in this life we cannot see the essence of God, which is above all that we can understand, we cannot name God in a way that comprehends the divine essence, as we would define a concept. But we can name God truly on the basis of our knowledge of God's effects, that is, from creatures (*ST* 1.13.1). Negative names (immortal, invisible) do not signify God's essence at all, but rather the radical difference between God and creature: God is not mortal, not visible, and so on, because God is not bodily. But positive names, such as Rock and Wisdom, do signify the divine essence, albeit imperfectly, just as the creatures themselves are imperfect expressions of the divine essence, which contains beforehand in itself the fullness of every creaturely perfection (*ST* 1.13.2). Some positive names are said of God metaphorically (e.g., "Rock"), for they include a finite mode of being in their very definition (i.e., material and lifeless). Such names are predicated primarily of creatures and only secondarily of God. But other positive names are said of God properly, for they express some perfection absolutely, abstracted from the creature's finite mode of being (e.g., Being, Good, Living, and so on). Unlike metaphorical names, names of this sort are predicated primarily of God and secondarily of creatures. Yet even these positive names do not apply properly to God in every respect, for their "mode of signification" applies only to creatures (*ST* 1.13.3). For example, we rightly extol God with many different names that are not synonymous with each other, for each signifies the one divine essence under a different aspect, according to the various and manifold ways in which creatures participate in the divine life. Yet God possesses every perfection in a simple and undivided way, after a fashion that no single name drawn from creatures can adequately express (*ST* 1.13.4). It follows, then, that even our most appropriate names for God are analogical in character. They signify God by evoking a real resemblance of the creature to God, but fall short of naming the divine essence as it is in itself (*ST* 1.13.5).

In general, then, Thomas's teaching in the first five articles of Question 13 follows in the broad contours set by Dionysius's theology of the divine names. (Indeed, Thomas refers directly to Dionysius more times than to any other authors—except Augustine and Aristotle!)[15] Like Dionysius, Thomas's discussion is oriented toward God's uniqueness as this becomes manifest through God's relation to the world as first eternal Cause. This broad similarity is sustained throughout the rest of the Question, and indeed, in certain important ways, throughout the *Summa* as a whole.

The *Treatise on the Trinity* or "What Concerns the Distinction of Persons"

Turning to Thomas's *Treatise on the Trinity*, we detect the massive influence of Augustine. But Thomas's account is more than an elegant restatement of

Augustine's views. Augustine begins his analysis of trinitarian names with "Father, Son, and Holy Spirit," and only then proceeds to examine other personal names such as "Word," "Gift," "Love," etc. In contrast, Thomas appeals to such personal names both *in advance* of the names Father, Son, and Holy Spirit, and also *subsequent* to them. In this way, Thomas gives the discussion of the names of the persons of the Trinity a new and intriguing shape.

Thomas begins the *Treatise on the Trinity* with a discussion of the divine processions. Here Thomas consistently eschews the language of Father, Son, and Holy Spirit in favor of a different triad: "God," "Word," and "Love." Thomas regards these latter names as best suited to indicate the spiritual nature of the divine processions, because they are drawn from higher rather than lower creatures, as in the procession of a word from its speaker. Thomas, in other words, does not treat the christological triad as an all-purpose trinitarian vocabulary that is equally suited to every occasion, but adapts his trinitarian vocabulary to the context at hand. Elsewhere in the *Summa*, "God" figures as a name of the divine essence. Here, however, "God" figures as a *relational* name, *a name for the first person*, from which names for the other two persons are "unfolded." The unfolding in question is not that of semantic reciprocity (as in the case of Father and Son), but rather one that appeals to the common human experience of self-knowledge and self-love. By evoking this analogy with the spiritual dimension of human beings, the triad "God, Word, and Love" prepares the way for the language of Father, Son, and Spirit, providing the conditions that enable its right understanding.[16]

Turning to Thomas's discussion of the three persons, we discover that he introduces the relevant sections with questions "On the Person of the Father" (*ST* 1.33), "On the Person of the Son" (1.34), and "On the Person of the Holy Spirit" (1.36). To this extent, Thomas (like others before him) treats the christological triad as in some sense the ordinary or indexical way of referring to the divine persons. When we look more closely, however, we discover once again that Thomas regards these names as best suited to illuminate the mystery of the divine persons *from a certain vantage point*. "Father," for example, is preferable to the (also permissible) "Begetter" or "Genitor" because "Father" expresses "the full existence of the other term in the relation," whereas the former terms suggest "a relation in which neither term is perfected or complete."[17] Still, Thomas maintains that other names may be used with equal propriety to illuminate the fullness of the mystery of the divine persons. Indeed, Thomas devotes a separate question each to the names "Image" (1.35), "Love" (1.37), and "Gift" (1.38). Thomas considers these names partly because they are given to him by prior tradition, having been discussed extensively by Augustine in *The Trinity*. But Thomas's rationale extends deeper than this. As Thomas explains at one point:

> The Son's being born, which is his personal property, is *denoted by the different names applied to him in order to vary the expressions of his perfection.* For he has the name "Son" in order to show that he is of one nature with the Father; "Splendor," to show that he is coeternal; "Image," to show that he is entirely alike; "Word," to show that he is not begotten carnally. *No one name could be devised to bring out all of these.* (*ST* 1.34.2 *ad* 3; emphasis added)

Here Thomas appeals to an insight that previously informed his discussion of the divine essence, applying it now as a rule for speaking about the second person of the Trinity. Extending what Thomas says to the first and third persons as well, we might say that Thomas believes the divine persons are indeed properly distinguished by the names "Father," "Son," and "Holy Spirit," but that each person demands to be named in other ways as well, for the persons and their mutual relations possess a fullness of being and truth that "cannot be expressed by only one name."[18]

A Third Pattern of Divine Naming Centered in the Tetragrammaton

We now turn to an aspect of Thomas's teaching that is far less well known than what we have surveyed so far: his comments on the Tetragrammaton. These are indeed so rare and brief that they are easily overlooked altogether, and often have been, even by specialists. Nevertheless, they are an important part of the story we are telling in this chapter, for they represent the partial *reemergence* of a third pattern of naming the persons of the Trinity, one that had hitherto gone largely unnoticed in the Dionysian tradition.

The Tetragrammaton and the Deity of Christ in the *Summa contra Gentiles*

A first brief reference to the Tetragrammaton appears in the *Summa contra Gentiles*, written many years before the *Summa theologiae*. In a chapter titled "Refutation of the Opinion of Arius on the Son of God" (*SCG* 4.7), Thomas assembles over twenty brief arguments against the great heresiarch, of which the first several concern Christ's name "Son of God." Although Thomas agrees with his implied Arian interlocutor that "the name of divine sonship is suitable to many—for it belongs to all the angels and saints," Thomas argues that Christ is nevertheless not called the Son of God "by reason of creation" (*SCG* 4.7.4). After several arguments to this effect, Thomas abruptly changes course. The seventh argument reads in part: "Furthermore, . . . Jeremiah (23:5–6) says: . . . 'And this is the name that they shall call Him: The Lord our just one.' There in Hebrew the name is the *Tetragrammaton*, which certainly is said of God alone. From these sayings it is clear that the Son of God is true God."

This argument is structured differently from its predecessors. According to Thomas, the Tetragrammaton is "certainly said of God alone," and not of both God and creatures, like "Son of God." If, therefore, Christ is designated by this name (as a messianic reading of the passage from Jeremiah assumes), then it proves without further ado that Christ "is true God." Thomas, we notice, appeals specifically to the Hebrew text in making his argument, indicating that he is aware that the Latin text alone does not suffice to make his point, for in the Vulgate a name appears in place of the Tetragrammaton that *is* said of God and men, namely, "*dominus*" (Lord).

And that's it. Thomas goes on to his next anti-Arian argument and says nothing more about the Tetragrammaton. Readers not already acquainted with the curious name are apt to shrug and move on. In truth, however, Thomas's brief argument contains a profound puzzle, of which Thomas himself was undoubtedly aware. If it is true that "we name God from creatures," as the Dionysian tradition maintains, then the very existence of a name that is "certainly said of God alone" is precluded from the outset! This Tetragrammaton, it seems, is an impossibility! What's going on here? Is Thomas speaking loosely for the sake of passing on a stray item of Christian tradition? Or can he really have meant what he just said?

The Most Appropriate Name(s) of God in the *Summa Theologiae*

Thomas, it seems, did mean what he said. This becomes clear from Thomas's remarks about the Tetragrammaton many years later in the *Summa theologiae.* While also brief and easily overlooked, these remarks offer a penetrating analysis of the Tetragrammaton and show how it differs from other names. They make crystal clear that Thomas appreciated the singular character of this name.[19]

The passage in question appears in Thomas's discussion of "Is 'He Who Is' the Most Appropriate Name of God?" (*ST* 1.13.11; cf. 13.9). Before writing the *Summa theologiae*, Thomas consistently maintained that the most appropriate name of God is "He Who Is" (Lat.: *qui est*), the name that God revealed to Moses at the burning bush, according to Exodus 3:14. In his earlier writings, Thomas put forward several arguments to support this view, all of which he drew from previous writers, and all of which fit comfortably within the framework of the Dionysian tradition. One argument held that "He Who Is" is God's most appropriate name because being or existence is God's most basic gift to creatures. Another held that "He Who Is" describes God's essence more aptly than any other name, because God's very essence is *to be.* At the same time, Thomas consistently held that the name "He Who Is" falls under the critical caveat that applies to all of our efforts to describe God by beginning with creatures. The name "He Who Is" is made up of subject and verb and therefore implies composition, which is inappropriate to God, in whom essence and existence are identical. In the end, then, "He Who Is," like all other names, falls short of expressing the ineffable mystery of God.

In the *Summa theologiae* 1.13.11 (and related remarks in 13.9), Thomas retracts nothing from what he had previously said on behalf of "He Who Is." But now for the first time Thomas introduces a discussion of the Tetragrammaton, which he says is even more appropriate *from a different point of view*. Thomas's discussion turns on a distinction that he introduces between two different ways in which a name can be "most appropriate." A name may *describe* its object more aptly than other names, or it may *refer* to its object more exclusively than other names (*ST* 1.13.8). (In Thomas's own terminology, a name may be appropriate according to its etymology, or according to the object that the name is designed to signify.) Thomas explains that "He Who Is" is the most appropriate name of God from the first point of view, for "He Who Is" *describes* God more aptly than other names. Thomas's reasons are the same as those he had given earlier in his career (*ST* 1.13.11). From the perspective of reference, however, Thomas judges that the name "God" is actually more appropriate than "He Who Is." To be sure, "God" does not *describe* God more aptly than "He Who Is," but it does *refer* to the divine essence with greater precision, that is, in a more exclusive way. For "God" is a "nature" name that we apply precisely in order to designate the divine essence, just as we use the name "human" to designate the nature or essence of a human being. In contrast, "He Who Is" can truthfully be applied to every creature, insofar as every creature exists! In this respect, therefore, the name "God" is more appropriate than "He Who Is."

Yet the name "God" still harbors a limitation that renders it less than fully apt from the second perspective. It belongs to the character of all "nature names" to be applicable to more than one individual (or to be "communicable," in Thomas's language). This remains true even if there is only one individual that bears a given nature, for people may nevertheless *think* that there are others who bear that same nature, as the name itself permits. For example, some people mistakenly think that there are many gods, all sharing in the nature of divinity. In this respect, nature names are less appropriate to what they signify than are personal proper names, which we use to signify one individual only. Such names are incommunicable, both in reality and in thought.

Thomas's discussion points toward an awesome question. Is there a name that refers to God after the fashion of a personal proper name, which is incommunicable both in reality and in thought? Such a name would "signify God not as to His nature but . . . according as He is considered as 'this something.'" In answer, Thomas suggests that "the Tetragrammaton among the Hebrews" (*ST* 1.13.9) may match this description.[20] Like the name "God," the Tetragrammaton signifies the unique reality of God. But it is even more appropriate than "God" because it signifies not God's nature but "the incommunicable and (if one can use the expression) the singular substance itself of God."[21]

Thomas's analysis of the Tetragrammaton in the *Summa* is astonishing, both for what it does and for what it does not do. What it does is recognize a *second* "most appropriate" name of God alongside the exalted "He Who Is." The result is *two* "most appropriate" names of God, each of which is "most appropriate" in a different way. Given the long unrivaled reign of "He Who Is," this development is surprising enough, especially since it comes virtually without prior warning in Thomas's thought. But what Thomas does *not* do is perhaps even more startling. *He does not try to force the Tetragrammaton to fit within the larger Dionysian framework of his thought.* For the Dionysian tradition, no axiom is more ironclad and fundamental than that "we can name God only from creatures" (*ST* 1.13.5). Thomas's analysis of "He Who Is" honors this axiom, but his analysis of the Tetragrammaton does not. As Thomas himself understood as early as the *Summa contra Gentiles*, the Tetragrammaton manifests a different kind of logic. At the time, he did not explain what this logic is, but now in the *Summa* he does. Unlike "He Who Is," the Tetragrammaton does not *describe* God analogically or metaphorically by beginning with creatures. Instead, it merely refers to God after the fashion of a personal proper name. *Precisely for this reason*, Thomas suggests, it is, in its own way, the most appropriate name of all.

Where did Thomas get the knowledge of the Tetragrammaton on which his analysis is based? Armand Maurer suggests that Thomas came to it through his reading of the Jewish theologian Moses Maimonides, whose *Guide to the Perplexed* was translated into Latin from Arabic in 1240, when Thomas was a teenager.[22] Scholars have often recognized the importance of Maimonides for Thomas's understanding of the divine names, but, as Maurer observes, they have usually focused on his role in shaping Thomas's views of the name "He Who Is." Maimonides' influence on Thomas's view of the Tetragrammaton is addressed much less frequently, as indeed is the fact that Thomas had any view on the subject at all.

In the *Guide*, Maimonides treats the Tetragrammaton and "He Who Is" as two different names, following the precedent of Jewish tradition.[23] He devotes two chapters to the Tetragrammaton and one chapter to "He Who Is." Maimonides' discussion of the Tetragrammaton continually stresses the singularity of this name. In keeping with the standard medieval theory of divine names, Maimonides holds that God's names are derived from God's works or actions. This is true, for example, of "He Who Is." *But it is not true of the Tetragrammaton.* The "Tetragrammaton" is the peculiar name of God; it is a "separated" name (*nomen separatum*). Other names for God ("Judge,"

"Just," "Gracious," "Elohim") are derived from creatures and can be used for both God and creatures. Even the divine name Adonai, which means Lord (and which was used in place of the sacred name, the Tetragrammaton) is shared by creatures. But the Tetragrammaton belongs to God alone, for nothing else shares it with him. This makes it unique among all divine names.

Maimonides goes on to explain that the Tetragrammaton is handled differently than other names on account of its singularity. It is written in sacred Scripture but not pronounced when Scriptures are read. In ancient times, the name was pronounced only by the priests in the temple, when giving the daily benediction ("The LORD bless you and keep you . . ."), or by the high priest on the Day of Atonement. Knowledge of this name is passed down among Jews as a "spiritual secret" (*secretum spirituale*). Even so, the etymology of the name is unknown, and its pronunciation is uncertain. What Maimonides is sure of, however, is that the Tetragrammaton signifies God's unique reality in such a way that nothing else is signified by it.

Thomas had been familiar with Maimonides' *Guide* since his student days and indeed had cited it as an authority in his discussion of "He Who Is" in the *Sentences*, his earliest discussion of the names of God. But for some reason, the young Thomas makes no mention of Maimonides' discussion of the Tetragrammaton. In this, he followed the example of his teacher, Albert the Great, who likewise ignored this aspect of the Jewish theologian's teaching. By the time the mature Thomas came to write the *Summa*, however, he appears to have concluded that the *nomen separatum* deserves a place within a Christian doctrine of the names of God.

The significance of Thomas's analysis of the Tetragrammaton in the *Summa* is greater than implied by the single footnote that Étienne Gilson devotes to it in his *Elements of Christian Philosophy*.[24] Thomas's remarks reflect the outcome of what we may imagine must have been a conceptual tug-of-war in his mind between two competing elements of Christian tradition: the logic of the Dionysian tradition on the one hand, and the logic of the anti-Arian argument that Thomas cites in *Summa contra Gentiles* on the other hand. The remarkable thing, as I noted a moment ago, is that the latter wins, despite the former's incomparably larger role in Thomas's thought. Talk about David and Goliath! For the Dionysian tradition, no axiom is more basic than that "we can name God only from creatures" (*ST* 1.13.5). Following Maimonides, however, Thomas maintains that the Tetragrammaton does not obey this axiom, even if it does not exactly cancel it either. Rather, the Tetragrammaton comes alongside this axiom from the outside, as it were, and places it and the whole edifice it supports in a new context. We *learn* about the Tetragrammaton *from* the Hebrews, but the name itself is not *shared* by any creature at all. The Tetragrammaton does not allow us to *comprehend* the divine essence, but it does allow us to refer to the one who bears it with the exclusivity of a personal proper name.

The boldness of Thomas's analysis of the Tetragrammaton is underscored by an astute observation of Armand Maurer. In the course of Maimonides' own discussion of the name, the great rabbi ventures the suggestion that perhaps it means "Necessary Being." One may well imagine that this suggestion would have been attractive to Thomas. Certainly it has proved attractive to many others in the Dionysian tradition, for a simple reason: it eliminates the most striking difference between the Tetragrammaton and other names, namely, its lack of derivation from creatures. In this sense, Maimonides' suggestion represents exactly what a Dionysian theologian might *wish* to be the case. Thomas, however, makes no mention of Maimonides' suggestion. As Maurer remarks, "It must have occurred to him [Thomas] that if this is its meaning it cannot be said to be underived, as Maimonides himself claims. It would have its origin in existence, which, as the Jewish theologian himself says, is the derivation of the divine name "I am who I am."

If Thomas had adopted Maimonides' suggestion, it would have undercut the anti-Arian argument he had advanced in the *Summa contra Gentiles* (Neoplatonic emanations are necessary beings, too). Rather than do that, Thomas lets the Tetragrammaton fall into the stream of Dionysian theology with the full weight of its singularity, and forces the stream to go around it.

In the end, then, Thomas ventures to suggest that there are *two* "most appropriate" names of the one God, each of which is "most appropriate" in a different way. There remains, as before, the exalted "He Who Is." But now there comes alongside it "the name 'Tetragrammaton' among the Hebrews." Unlike "He Who Is," the Tetragrammaton does not purport to *describe* God at all. Instead, it merely refers to God after the fashion of a personal proper name. That is why it is, in its own way, the most appropriate name of God.

Drawing a Balance

Thomas Aquinas occupies a special place in this chapter. In his thought, God's personal proper name, the unspoken Tetragrammaton, emerges from its long eclipse and comes into view in the startling position of one of two "most appropriate" names of the one God! The reemergence of the Tetragrammaton enables Thomas to recognize three different patterns of divine naming. He recognizes the two patterns of trinitarian naming previously identified by Augustine, and in addition he alludes, however briefly, to the Tetragrammaton as a name for the divine essence, and to its christological implications when predicated of Christ. Perhaps the most extraordinary aspect of Thomas's treatment of the Tetragram, however, is the fact that he does not try to make it conform to the logic of the Dionysian tradition, by insisting that it names God "from creatures." Thomas is the greatest of all the representatives of the Dionysian tradition we have examined, because he was able to recognize the tradition's limits—for the sake of a richer orthodoxy.[25]

At the same time, we should not exaggerate the role that the Tetragrammaton plays in Thomas's thought, which is indeed quite negligible. Nor should we exaggerate the extent to which Thomas draws out its christological and trinitarian implications. Thomas gives no indication that he is aware of the New Testament's practice of using oblique reference to the Tetragrammaton to designate the persons of the Trinity, in the fashion of 1 Corinthians 8 and the Nicene Creed. He treats it as a name that appears in the Old Testament, that is associated with the Jewish people (cf. his phrase "the Tetragrammaton among the Hebrews"), and that signifies the divine nature in a way that is uniquely its own. But even this is a remarkable advance beyond Dionysius and Augustine.

THE DIONYSIAN TRADITION: A SPIRIT-CENTERED APPROACH TO A CHRISTIAN THEOLOGY OF THE NAME OF THE TRINITY

In the end, the Dionysian tradition succeeds to a considerable degree in recovering, on behalf of Christian theology, the full panoply of theonymic patterns encoded in the Nicene Creed. Dionysius makes room for the christological pattern, Augustine for both it and the pneumatological pattern, Thomas for both of these, and in addition, he gestures toward a space where one might conceivably discern a third pattern, centered in the unspoken Tetragrammaton.

At the same time, we have seen that the Dionysian tradition views all three patterns from a certain vantage point, one whose character was already signaled long ago, when Paul preached Christ at the Areopagus, using the language of the Greek poets to speak first of "the God who made the world and everything in it" (Acts 17:24). We can call this a *Spirit*-centered approach to a Christian theology of naming the Trinity, not in the sense that it gives special prominence either to the Spirit, or to what we have called the pneumatological pattern of naming the persons of the Trinity. Rather, the Dionysian tradition is Spirit-centered in the sense that the Spirit's outpouring at Pentecost undergirds its confidence that the riches of Hellenistic culture can be won on behalf of Christian faith. The very Spirit-centered character of the Dionysian approach, however, suggests the legitimacy of a different approach, which would be more emphatically oriented toward the centrality of Christ. To such a tradition we now turn.

5

The Reformation Tradition and the Transformation of Jewish Wisdom

The Rediscovery and Eclipse of the Tetragrammaton

> You will never see the name of the Lord more clearly than you do in Christ. There you will see how good, pleasant, faithful, righteous, and true God is, since He did not spare His own Son (Rom. 8:32). . . . This is the real cabala of the name of the Lord, not of the Tetragrammaton, about which the Jews speak in the most superstitious manner.
>
> —*Martin Luther*[1]

In their own eyes, Martin Luther and Karl Barth approach the mystery of the Trinity quite differently than did the figures we examined in the last chapter. These representatives of what we will call the Reformation tradition see themselves as standing with the Paul of 1 Corinthians, who exposed the foolishness of contemporary wisdom by preaching nothing but "Christ crucified." Broadly speaking, Luther and Barth aim to correct the perceived "Hellenistic bias" of the Dionysian tradition by rooting knowledge of the Trinity exclusively in the Bible's witness to Christ. Luther's corrective is remembered by his advocacy of a "theology of the cross" against a "theology of glory," while Barth's is marked by his rejection of natural theology and of the venerable tradition of seeking analogies of the Trinity in creation (more about this last in a moment). Still, as we shall see, the Reformation tradition's reading of the Bible is no less filtered through a hermeneutical lens than was the Dionysian tradition: its lens simply comes from another source. If Dionysius, Augustine, and Thomas leaned heavily on a baptized version of late classical Neoplatonism, Luther and Barth lean just as heavily on a baptized version of the Jewish mystical tradition known as the Kabbalah. The effect of their dependence is paradoxical. On the one hand, it prompts them to give the Tetragrammaton a far larger place in their reflections on the Trinity than it ever attained in the Dionysian tradition. On the other hand, they confine the relevance of the name to the Old Testament, while imagining it to be superseded by a different name in the New. To continue the story of the name of the Trinity in the Reformation tradition, therefore, we must first say a word about the Jewish Kabbalah and its Christian transformation, the Christian Kabbalah.

THE JEWISH KABBALAH AND ITS CHRISTIAN TRANSFORMATION

The Kabbalah (Heb., tradition) is a form of speculative and mystical Jewish theology that is centrally concerned with the divine name, the Tetragrammaton, YHWH. For most of its history, it was regarded not just as compatible with Jewish orthodoxy, but also as a central component of the same. The tradition arose during the thirteenth and fourteenth centuries in Spain and Southern France, although its roots are far older and quite obscure. Simplifying greatly, one can say that the central passion of the Kabbalah is to show how knowledge of the divine name provides the key to all the major problems of Jewish thought: the harmony of God's mercy and righteousness, the origin of creation, the problem of evil, and so on. In particular, Kabbalah purports to solve these problems by illuminating the divine name's inherent dynamics and movement. The *Zohar*, a classic kabbalistic text, recounts how the divine name gives rise by its own nature to the divine names, the *Sephirot*, which emerge from the Tetragrammaton in a downward movement of emanation and descent. The divine name(s) in turn define the inner structure of all things, of biblical revelation to be sure, but also of language and of being itself. In a word, the Kabbalah offers a fascinating mirror image of the mystical theology of Dionysius the Areopagite. Like Dionysius's work, the Kabbalah can be understood as a biblical transposition of pagan Neoplatonism, but one that gives pride of place—not to the *translatable* name of Exodus 3:14, "I am who I am"—but to the *untranslatable* name of 3:15, YHWH.[2]

Christian Europe took little notice of the Kabbalah until the late 1400s, when a circle of Renaissance humanists began to popularize it in a radically modified form. As Gershom Scholem has emphasized, the Christian kabbalists used the Kabbalah to prove Christianity's superiority to Judaism, its salvation-historical forerunner. In the words of Pico della Mirandola (1463–94), the "father" of the Christian Kabbalah, the Jewish mystical tradition reveals "not so much the Mosaic as the Christian religion. There is the mystery of the Trinity, . . . the same things we read daily in Paul and Dionysius, in Jerome and Augustine."[3] The Christian kabbalists also fused Kabbalah with other esoteric traditions, such as Pythagoreanism, Hermetic philosophy, and their own budding conceptions of magic. The last association was particularly fateful. "What was commonplace in Judaism (and was not conceived of as magic) became prominent in the Christian kabbalists' worldview": "belief in the ability of language—especially names, and in particular, divine names—to influence reality."[4] Thanks largely to its Christian transformation, the Kabbalah became known for centuries as an occult science and sister doctrine of alchemy and astrology.

The Christian Kabbalah's distinctive mixture of apologetic and magical interests appears vividly in one of its quintessential theological claims: the wonder-working power of the Tetragrammaton, unexcelled in its day, has been surpassed by the still more powerful name of Jesus. This is the central claim of *De verbo mirifico* [The wonder-working word] by Johannes Reuchlin (1455–1522), the most learned Christian Hebraist of his day and a principal source of Martin Luther's knowledge of the Kabbalah. (Reuchlin was also the father-in-law of Luther's colleague Philipp Melanchthon.) In *De verbo mirifico* (1494), Reuchlin sets out to discover the name that is supreme in the performance of wonders.[5] Reuchlin praises the Tetragrammaton at length, declaring that it is "the most powerful name, worshipped by those above, obeyed by those below, cherished by earthly nature; which, when imbibed by those who worship consistently, . . . is said to bestow wonder-working powers on the human faculty."[6] Still, Reuchlin maintains, there is one name that is even more powerful than it, the name of Jesus. Just as the new covenant fulfills the old while setting aside its outer form as obsolete, so the name "Jesus" surpasses and antiquates the divine name of the Old Testament. "Jesus" is the *Pentagrammaton*, made up of the same letters as the Tetragrammaton, plus the Hebrew letter *shin* (I-H-Sh-W-H)[7], which mystically signifies (among other things) the transition from ineffability to speech. The divine name of the old covenant was unpronounceable, but that of the new pronounceable, as befits the age of the incarnation. "When the Word descended into flesh, then the letters passed into voice."[8]

Two decades later, Reuchlin proposed another interpretation of the Tetragrammaton. In *On the Art of the Kabbalah* (*De arte kabalistica* [1516]), he wrote,

> Rabbi Hakados says that from the Tetragrammaton comes the name of 12 letters: *Av Ben veRuakh haKadosh*, meaning: "Father, Son, and Holy Spirit." And from this is derived the name of 42 letters: *Av Elohim, Ben Elohim, Ruah hakadosh Elohim, Shalosha beehad, ehad besheloshah*, which means: "God the Father, God the Son, God the Holy Spirit, Three in One and One in Three," What heights and what depths in matters understood by faith alone [*sola fide*]![9]

Once again, Reuchlin locates the significance of the Tetragrammaton in its prefigurative character, but now the name to which it secretly points is "the Father and the Son and the Holy Spirit." The interpretation is deeply ambiguous when viewed against the backdrop of previous Christian reflection on the name of the Trinity. On the one hand, it assigns the Tetragrammaton a clear place in the church's understanding of the name of the persons of the Trinity, something the Dionysian tradition had failed to do, even in the work of Thomas Aquinas. On the other, that space is by its very nature a passing and temporary one, a reflex of Christianity's traditional understanding of the church's relationship to the Jewish people. The Tetragrammaton is the quintessential sign of everything about Judaism that Christianity fulfills according to inward intention and sets aside according to outer form, of everything, in a word, that Christianity renders *obsolete*. Accordingly, from the outset Reuchlin's "rediscovery" of the Tetragrammaton points to its final and permanent—eclipse.[10]

MARTIN LUTHER: THE TETRAGRAMMATON AND THE NAME OF THE HOLY TRINITY

Turning to Martin Luther and Karl Barth, our concern is not with tracing lines of historical descent, but with showing more generally that the two theologians think about the name of the Trinity in ways that repeat basic motifs of the Christian Kabbalah. Our discussion of Luther will focus on his "Excursus on the Tetragrammaton" from his *Lectures on the Psalms* of 1519–21. This fascinating text is especially worth looking at because in it Luther addresses all three patterns of trinitarian naming that are the principal subject of this book.[11]

The excursus begins, "What is this name of the Lord [Lat. *nomen domini*] of which there are many in many different languages?" The question is prompted by a phrase from Psalm 5, but like much of Luther's writings, it is also prompted by some pastoral concerns pressing on the reformer's conscience. The Christian Kabbalah had been making inroads into German popular culture in recent years, and Luther was alarmed by its superstitious nature, which he (mistakenly) attributed to its Jewish roots. Following traditional scholastic protocol, Luther responds to his question by first considering what he takes to be a wrong answer, according to which "the name of the Lord" is the Tetragrammaton. "The Hebrews use ten names of God," he begins, "among which is the famous name they call the Tetragrammaton" (333.2–4). Luther then lets loose what is really on his heart.

> The power of this name, they suppose, affords them I don't know how much protection and might. Meanwhile, they invoke the name of their God in vain, because they do not stop impiously denying and blaspheming the name of Christ, while wanting none the less to save their souls through the name of the Lord. (333.4–7)

Worse yet, Luther laments, Christians too are now following the example of the Jews: "Their superstition has spread among Christians, too, so that they speak, carve, display, and wear these four letters everywhere, caring not at all about whether they are pious or impious, like magicians thinking that they get power through signs and letters" (333.7–10). This opening blast makes clear that Luther's "Excursus on the Tetragrammaton" will be a vigorous polemic against the Christian Kabbalah. Remarkably, though, as it unfolds, it also becomes an exercise in the very same. For in reality Luther's attitude toward the movement was quite complex (he and Reuchlin were condemned together, in the same document, by Pope Leo X in 1517). Luther was a fierce opponent of its magical outlook, which made it, in his mind, guilty of the same errors as the Roman hierarchy and Judaism. At the same time, he was profoundly attracted to some of its signature theological claims, as we shall see.

Luther against the Christian Kabbalah

Writing in an anti-kabbalist vein, Luther quashes the idea that the Tetragrammaton possesses any special power or significance for Christians, or even that it is the name to which the psalmist refers in Psalm 5 (these issues have flowed together in Luther's mind in the "Excursus"). Luther argues that if Christians single out one name above others, it is not the Tetragrammaton but the name of the Father and the Son and the Holy Spirit:

> For if the name Tetragrammaton alone has such power, the church acts foolishly because it blesses and baptizes and conducts all its sacraments, not in this name, but in the name of the Father and Son and Holy Spirit. And it would be astonishing if the church of Christ, which has the Spirit of God, had not yet discovered these things, since it knows everything that is of God. (334.5–9)

Here Luther's argument turns on the theologian's rule of thumb *lex orandi lex credendi* (the rule of prayer sets the rule of belief), which holds that liturgical practice sets the standard for what the church believes. Luther takes it to be obvious that the christological pattern of naming—Father, Son, and Holy Spirit—fills up whatever liturgical space might conceivably have been occupied by the Tetragrammaton, so that by this standard the latter name is basically irrelevant for Christian faith. Luther considers the rejoinder that "when the name of the holy trinity is invoked or of God or of the Lord, at the same time the Tetragrammaton is also invoked" (334.10–11). But he angrily rejects this suggestion by appealing to what he takes to be the liturgical rule of *Jewish* practice, which strictly distinguishes between the Tetragrammaton and other names. "Why, then, is the Tetragrammaton kept separate from other names? Why does it not effect in all situations what it effects in isolation? Can it be so sacred, and other names so profane, that it is polluted if brought into contact with them? Or is it so invidious that it begrudges its glorious strength to other names?" (334.12–15).

"Such," Luther snorts, "would be the fictions of the Jews." Lest there be any misunderstanding, however, he reinforces these arguments with a more fundamental one. Christians should understand that the Tetragrammaton possesses no special power in itself because in fact *no name* does. Conversely, every divine name is a name of power when held in faith.

> We, however, as befits Christians, ought to know this, that without the piety of faith all things are only superstition and worthy of damnation, so much so that neither Christ nor God himself is salvific for anyone, unless they are had through faith. Therefore, any name of God, indeed any word of God, is of omnipotent power for the salvation of body and soul, if it be held with the reverence of faith. For it is not the name but faith in the name of the Lord that does all things. Nor is one name more efficacious than another. (333.11–334.5)

Luther's argument parallels his teaching regarding the efficacy of the sacraments, a flashpoint in his conflict with Rome. For Luther, the kabbalists and the papists share a common failure: they neglect the role of faith.

Having disposed of one false view, Luther returns to the original question, or rather, to a rephrasing of it: "What, then, is the name of God [*nomen dei*], which the prophet in this place (Ps. 5:12) teaches must be loved?" (339.8–9). By replacing "name of the Lord" (*nomen domini*) with "name of God" (*nomen dei*), Luther indicates his determination to steer the discussion away from the Tetragrammaton. The key to the solution, Luther explains, is to recognize that the psalmist here uses "name" in a way that is equivalent to reputation, as in the proverb "Better is a good name than many riches" (Prov. 22:1, Vulg.). "Name" refers not to what God is called, but to what is proclaimed about God. God's name is his good reputation, praise, glory, and tribute. From this it appears that God's name is "not one name only" (339.8). It is many names![12] Luther proceeds to unfurl a great list of scriptural names of God: Wise; Immortal; Love; God of Abraham, Isaac, and Jacob; and more. Perhaps aware that his celebration of divine names might recall the theology of Dionysius the Areopagite, Luther goes on to mention the theologian by name. "And what if we should bring in all of Dionysius' *On the Divine Names*? And, again, the same on *Mystical Theology*, until we have left no name for God? If, in fact, he is not to be comprehended in thought, with what name could he be named?" (340.3–6).

Having raised these Dionysian questions, however, Luther immediately dismisses them and remarks, "Let us leave these things for speculation to those who have more time" (340.6). Luther in the "Excursus" does not want to ascend by negation into the realm of silence and unknowing, but to remain at the level of joyful proclamation and to celebrate the cosmic, all-embracing breadth of divine polyonymy. "Since, moreover, God causes all things for all (1 Cor. 12:6), it must follow that the name of all works is due to God alone. He alone, then, is good, wise, just, truthful, compassionate, forbearing, holy, strong, lord, father, judge—in short, he is whatever can be named anywhere or said in praise about anyone" (340.16–340.19).

As it emphatically sounds the theme of God's polyonymy, Luther's theology of the divine names also has an apophatic or negative dimension of its own. Unlike Dionysius's, however, Luther's negative theology is centered in the cross and its power to illuminate and judge human sin. Immediately after declaring that God "is whatever can be named anywhere or said in praise about anyone," Luther goes on:

> From which idea it comes about that, just as no virtue or work is left for us, so also we cannot claim any name for ourselves. . . . When we recognize and admit these things, we act rightly. For then we hate our works and our name, we renounce and cast [them] away. . . . Truly, here too the cross is the sole judge and witness of the truth. [*Verum et hic crux ipsa sola iudex est testisque veritatis*.] (340.20–21; 341.1–2, 15)

Or as Luther puts it still more impressively shortly later, "In those who lose and forget their own name, dwells the holy and terrible name of God" (352.32–353.1).[13]

To sum up: Luther in his antikabbalist mode finds a secure place for two of the three patterns of divine naming that are the subject of this book. He singles out the christological pattern—"Father, Son, and Holy Spirit"—as the privileged way of naming the persons of the Trinity. And he affirms the pneumatological pattern—characterized by the open-ended multiplication of divine names—as a way of magnifying God's glory and omnipotent rule in creation. As for the Tetragrammaton, it plays no more a role in this aspect of Luther's thought than it did in Dionysius's, with this difference: Dionysius was unaware of the divine name, but Luther has banished it.

Luther the Christian Kabbalist: The Tetragrammaton as a Foreshadowing of "the Name of the Father and Son and Holy Spirit"

It may come as a surprise, therefore, to learn that Luther devotes a large part of the "Excursus" to defending the thesis that the Tetragrammaton is a divine name possessed of significance "different and unique beyond others" (334.20). The apparent contradiction resolves itself when one realizes that the Tetragrammaton's significance resides not in special *soteriological* power but in its character as a symbol of the holy Trinity. Even if divine names are all "of omnipotent power for salvation" when held in faith, still they differ from one another in meaning. A special case concerns divine names that differ according to the pattern of type and antitype, shadow and reality, old covenant and new. In this case, one name signifies in hiddenness what another signifies openly. Along these lines, Luther proposes that we understand the relation between the Tetragrammaton and the name of the Father and the Son and the Holy Spirit. "The name Tetragrammaton is a symbol of the name of the holy trinity, and the name of the Father and the Son and the Holy Spirit, now revealed, was then foreshadowed under four letters" (335.1–2). Surprising or not, Luther's proposal is not original. Behind it, we readily discern the influence of Reuchlin and the Christian Kabbalah, shorn of its magical accoutrements.

Luther employs a variety of different arguments to show that the Tetragrammaton prefigures the name of the Father and the Son and the Holy Spirit. In some of these, Luther deliberately imitates the esoteric methods that he takes to be typical of Kabbalah, saying that he is prepared "to trifle or kabbalize" along with the Jews. A sample from one of these gives an idea of their flavor:

> The meaning [of the Tetragrammaton] is this: *Iod* = "origin," *he* = "this," *vaf* = "and," *he* = "this." Let these be put together grammatically and in Latin this sentence will result: "The origin of this and this." And this fits with the name of the holy trinity in all respects, because the Father in his divinity is the origin of this, that is the Son, and this, that is the Holy Spirit. For these pronouns, "this and this," rather obscurely represent the Son and Holy Spirit, as was suitable to that scripture in which the mystery of the holy trinity was not to be revealed but only indicated. (335.5–335.16)

Luther also uses more conventional arguments to show that the divine name prefigures the name of the Trinity. Luther maintains that the Tetragrammaton differs from all other Old Testament names because it is "ineffable." By this, he means that the name has no known etymology or meaning; it is a nonsemantic sign, as Thomas Aquinas had also recognized. Unlike Thomas, however, Luther argues that the nonsemantic character of the name is an indication that the name was appointed by divine counsel to foreshadow a mystery that transcends the Hebrew tongue and the old covenant dispensation: the mystery of the Holy Trinity. As a nonsemantic sign, the name is appropriate to the time of the old covenant, when "the mystery of the trinity had not been revealed, although it was secretly made known" (337.11–12). That is why God could truthfully tell Moses that he had not appeared to the patriarchs by this name (cf. Exod. 6:3), whereas in fact the Tetragrammaton was well known to them. "The power of this name," that is, faith in the Trinity and the knowledge of Christ, had not yet been revealed to them, nor indeed to anyone else in the Old Testament, except secretly and obscurely (338.3–11).

Luther notes that some Christians have proposed that the Tetragrammaton foreshadows not only the name of the Trinity (that is, "the Father, the Son, and the Holy Spirit") but also the name "Jesus," inasmuch as the latter consists of the Tetragrammaton plus the letter *shin*. According to this theory, which as we saw was advanced by Reuchlin, the incarnation of the Word marks the end of the epoch of the ineffable name of four letters, and inaugurates the yet mightier age of the effable *Pentagrammaton*, "Jesus." Luther admits that he wishes the theory were true, but in the end he rejects it for etymological reasons (338.13–339.7).

Still, Luther concurs with the Christian kabbalists on the more basic point, that the Tetragrammaton occupies a transitory place in the economy of salvation. Its nonsemantic character corresponds to the preparatory nature of the old covenant. Now that the new covenant has dawned, the Tetragrammaton has been replaced by the meaning-bearing term "the Father and the Son and the Holy Spirit." Now that its hidden mystery has been revealed, Luther writes, "there is no need for the Tetragrammaton, no more than there is for the whole of Hebrew, for the knowledge of God" (337.2–3). The divine name certainly remains written in Scripture, but now it is liturgically obsolete, like other symbols and practices of the old covenant, such as circumcision and the dietary laws. In the parlance of contemporary theology, Luther regards the Tetragrammaton as *superseded* by the name of the Father and the Son and the Holy Spirit, that is, fulfilled according to its inner meaning and outmoded according to its external form. Luther concludes that if the Jews refuse to recognize this and continue to treat the Tetragrammaton as ineffable, it is because they shrink in horror from the mystery that has now been revealed (334.17–25).

In the end, then, there is not a great deal of difference between Luther the antikabbalist and Luther the kabbalist, so far as his estimate of the Tetragrammaton is concerned. If Luther the antikabbalist excludes the Tetragrammaton from the sphere of Christian reflection altogether, Luther the kabbalist makes room for it only in the past, which Christians remember as something that has been rendered superfluous for the contemporary knowledge of God.

Luther's Treatment of the Tetragrammaton in Translation

We should not end our discussion of Luther without noticing yet another side of his interpretation of the Tetragrammaton, one that presents a far more positive face than the one we have beheld so far. This concerns Luther's rendering of the Tetragrammaton in his translations of the Bible from the original Hebrew and Greek. Beginning with his first translation of portions of the Old Testament in 1523, Luther consistently rendered the Tetragrammaton in German as HERR, printed in large capital type, with the explanation (in the foreword) that the name is applied exclusively "to the real true God," while other names are often ascribed also "to angels and saints."[14] Thus far, our story is fairly well known, not least because other European translations have followed a similar practice down to the present day, including subsequent German editions of *Die Lutherbibel.* Less well known, however, is that Luther later followed the same procedure *in his translations of the New Testament.* In 1539, Luther directed the printer of his now completed translation of the Bible to use capital typescript for HERR in cases where Luther believed *kyrios* in the Greek New Testament served as a surrogate for the Hebrew Tetragrammaton. Luther adopted this practice not only for citations of the Old Testament in the New, but also when he believed the New Testament writers alluded to the Tetragrammaton in free composition, as, for example, in Matthew 1:20 ("an angel of the LORD") and 11:25 ("I praise you, Father and Lord of heaven and earth"). The result is that the *Lutherbibel* of 1539 visibly signals the special status of the Tetragrammaton in both Testaments, from one end of the canon to the other.[15]

Clearly, there is a tension between Luther's handling of the Tetragrammaton in 1539 and his remarks in the "Excursus" of 1519. Luther the translator goes out of his way to draw attention to the New Testament's oblique reference to the Tetragrammaton, but the mere fact of such reference is hard to square with Luther's earlier doctrine. If the Lord Jesus himself continues to honor the divine name in his teaching and preaching, then it scarcely seems to have been rendered superfluous for the knowledge of God. And if the incarnate Word himself declines to pronounce the name, then its "ineffability" must be something more than a passing shadow of the old covenant. Whence the contradiction in Luther's estimate of the status of the Tetragrammaton in the New Testament? Perhaps part of the answer is that Luther was a better translator than he was a theologian, at least on this score. In any case, one thing is certain. The older Luther's more positive treatment of the Tetragrammaton in translation did not arise from a more favorable view of *Jewish* reverence for the divine name, as Luther's later writings make horrifyingly clear.[16]

But if Luther himself could tolerate this tension in his assessment of the Tetragrammaton, his followers, it seems, could not. After Luther's death, subsequent editions of *Die Lutherbibel* deleted the capitalized HERR from the New Testament and retained it only in the Old Testament. In effect, Luther's heirs made typography conform to theology, not vice versa. By overriding Luther's example on this point, Luther's heirs obscured the connection that Luther spied between the New Testament and the Tetragrammaton. They thus cleared the way for a different interpretation of Lord/*kyrios* in the New Testament, according to which it is not a *reverential surrogate* for the Tetragrammaton, but a *conceptual replacement* of it. To learn more about that alternative, we turn now to a discussion of Karl Barth.

KARL BARTH: THE TETRAGRAMMATON AND THE NAME OF THE HOLY TRINITY

> Into the place . . . of the name of Yahweh that in the end really dwells in Jerusalem in a house of stone—there now comes the existence of the man Jesus of Nazareth, "My Lord and my God."
>
> —*Karl Barth*[17]

Karl Barth's doctrine of the Trinity is often credited with sparking the modern revival of trinitarian theology. One aspect of his doctrine has not attracted much attention, however, and that is the degree to which it rests on an account of the *name* of the Trinity that eerily repeats the key claims of the Christian Kabbalah.

Barth's "Discovery" of the Tetragrammaton

Barth did not always assign much importance to the Tetragrammaton, whether in the doctrine of the Trinity or elsewhere in his theology. Like Thomas Aquinas, he seems to have discovered its significance over time, as a comparison of *Die christliche Dogmatik im Entwurf* (1927) and *The Church Dogmatics* (vol. I/1, German, 1932; English, 1936) reveals.

"Lord" in *Die christliche Dogmatik im Entwurf* (1927)

Barth published his first major treatment of the doctrine of the Trinity in a work titled *Die christliche Dogmatik im Entwurf* [Christian dogmatics in outline].[18] Although the projected multivolume work was never completed, its account of the Trinity anticipates many key features of his later work. Barth begins with a section titled "The Root of the Doctrine of the Trinity," where he introduces the thesis that the doctrine of the Trinity grows exclusively out of a single scriptural confession or root: "Jesus is the Christ or the *kyrios*, the *Lord*." This single root, Barth explains, can also be reformulated as "God reveals Himself as the Lord," in order to bring out the threefold character of God's revelation in Christ, in which God appears as Actor ("God . . ."), as Action (". . . reveals Himself . . ."), and as Result (". . . as Lord") (173). It is this implicit threefold structure that, when fully elaborated, ultimately yields the doctrine of the Trinity. The next section of his exposition Barth titles "Vestigia Trinitatis?" taking the name from Augustine's phrase for traces of the Trinity in creation. Here Barth executes "a defensive maneuver" against the "evil and dangerous" misunderstanding that there exists a *second* root of knowledge of the Trinity alongside God's revelation in Christ. This second root, some suppose, consists in analogies, similitudes, and illustrations of the triune life found in creation (183). Barth gathers up a three-page list of such analogies drawn from the history of Christian thought, such as "Lover, Beloved, and Love," "Base Tone, Fourth, and Fifth," "True, Beautiful, Good," "Subjective Spirit, Objective Spirit, and Absolute Spirit," and so on (184–47). He warns that whenever Christians have sought to supplement the true, scriptural root of the doctrine of the Trinity with this second, fictive root, they have inevitably made the real object of their investigation some god other than the God of revelation.

Finally, Barth develops the doctrine of the Trinity itself, beginning with the affirmation "God reveals himself as Lord," and culminating in a set of three chapters titled "God the Father," "God the Son," and "God the Holy Spirit" (232–89). Barth acknowledges that the specific terms "Father" and "Son" are inadequate in themselves and that theologians have employed numerous alternatives, such as source and stream, sun and light, root and plant, and so on. Nevertheless, for teaching purposes the church has ultimately always returned to "Father," "Son," and their attendant vocabulary (such as "begetting"), while setting the rest aside. The reason is that this language expresses the relationship of the first and second persons in the "comparatively clearest" way, emphasizing their "immediate continuity" in a way that distinguishes them from every merely creaturely relation (262).

In *Die christliche Dogmatik*, then, Barth identifies three patterns of identifying the persons of the Trinity, one of which he repudiates (the open-ended pattern of *vestigia trinitatis*), and two of which he incorporates into his own exposition: the language of "God reveals himself as Lord" on the one hand, and the language of "Father, Son, and Holy Spirit" on the other. We have just seen why Barth thought the language of Father and Son especially apt. But what precisely did Barth understand by the term "Lord"?

In an important discussion of the term, Barth reports that biblical scholars of the day were divided as to the meaning of "Lord" in the New Testament. Some maintained that *kyrios* should be understood "primarily as a translation [*sic*] of the Old Testament name of God Jahweh," while others held that it was "the fervent trumping of everything which the world of Hellenistic religion worshiped in the way of gods, half gods, heroes, Caesars, demons, lords, and lordships." Barth concludes that both views really come to the same thing. He explains: "In either case, it ['Lord'] means a reality that one conceives personalistically, before which one bows in awe, thanksgiving, love, trust, petition, obedience. . . . One bows before the Lord, because the quintessence of superiority, power, and dignity is present in Him" (233). "Lord," according to the Barth of *Die christliche Dogmatik*, derives its meaning from the divine-human encounter, where God is experienced as utterly personal, powerful, and superior. So long as this is clear, it does not matter whether "Lord" is understood with reference to "the Old Testament name of God" or to Hellenistic religion, for in either case the fundamental experience of God is the same.

When *Die christliche Dogmatik im Entwurf* appeared in print, it met a barrage of withering criticism. A particularly juicy target was Barth's doctrine of the Trinity. What was "God reveals himself as Lord," his critics demanded, other than Barth's own *vestigium trinitatis*, an analogy of the Trinity that Barth had drawn from the world of religious epistemology and foisted onto the Bible? Couldn't the same threefold sentence be derived from a host of starting points besides "Jesus Christ is Lord," even from the sentence, "I show myself"?[19] The critics had hit on a sensitive point. If Barth could not sustain his distinction between the one true root of the doctrine of the Trinity and the *vestigia trinitatis*, then the whole structure of his doctrine collapsed. Barth evidently felt the justice of the criticisms, and he soon abandoned the *Die christliche Dogmatik* as a false start.

The "Revealed Name 'Yahweh-Kyrios'" in *The Church Dogmatics*

Several years later, Barth published a revised version of his doctrine of the Trinity in the first volume of *The Church Dogmatics*.[20] He sticks to the general outline of *Die christliche Dogmatik*, while introducing a key modification near the outset. He adds a long exegetical discussion of "the revealed name *Yahweh-Kyrios*" in the opening section on "The Root of the Doctrine of the Trinity." Barth had not previously mentioned this name in *Die christliche Dogmatik im Entwurf* or anywhere else (it actually was Barth's own recent invention). Now, however, he argues that it is what the sentence "God reveals Himself as Lord" is really all about. Indeed, it is what the whole doctrine of the Trinity is about.

> In our demonstration of the root of the doctrine of the Trinity in Biblical revelation we began with and continually returned to the revealed name *Yahweh-Kyrios*, which embraces both the Old Testament and the New. The doctrine of the Trinity is not and does not seek to be anything but an explanatory confirmation of this name. This name is the name of a single being, of the one and only Willer and Doer whom the Bible calls God. (348)

By tracing everything back to "the revealed name *Yahweh-Kyrios*," Barth means to show that his revised doctrine of the Trinity is faithful transcription of the Bible's testimony to God's self-revelation, rather than a modern version of the *vestigia trinitatis*. The name's second half ("*Kyrios*") is familiar enough, but he clearly no longer believes its relationship to "the Old Testament name of God" is a matter of indifference. Now he signals how he thinks the New Testament title must be understood in a New Testament context by prefixing to it *Yahweh*, the transliterated and vocalized form of the Tetragrammaton which Barth (in keeping with the academic conventions of his day) used routinely throughout his career. Thus the Tetragrammaton is the truly new element in Barth's presentation of the doctrine of the Trinity in *The Church Dogmatics*. It is, one could say, "the root of the root" of his doctrine of the Trinity, Barth's primordial answer to the question, "Who is the God revealed in the gospel?"

Let us take a closer look at Barth's exegetical interpretation of the name *Yahweh-Kyrios*, taking its elements one at a time (and not overlooking the all-important hyphen!).

Yahweh

Generally speaking, Barth aims to show that the Old Testament's witness to the name *Yahweh* is *implicitly* trinitarian. This was a point emphasized by the Christian kabbalists, as we have seen, and Barth's embrace of it places him broadly in their tradition. Unlike Reuchlin and Luther, however, Barth makes this point not by appeals to arcana of the name itself, but to a broad sweep of scriptural witness. By his own admission, Barth does not claim to approach Scripture either "naively," innocent of all preconceptions, or "scientifically," in a spirit of objective detachment. Rather, he approaches the Old Testament with a *theological* guide in hand, in this case the conception of God as Self-Revealing Subject (God reveals himself as Lord). As Barth himself freely concedes, this guide has many "human, all too human" antecedents, in nineteenth-century idealism and counterparts in other religions. But Barth's aim is now to show that this guide can also be understood as a faithful redescription and summary of the Old Testament witness to the name Yahweh.

According to Barth, then, the Old Testament testifies to Yahweh in three distinct ways. "Yahweh" refers "a first time" to the unseen God who is invisibly enthroned over all things, who remains forever hidden even in the act of revelation itself. It also refers again "in another way" to God insofar as he is truly known by this or that person, as revelation reaches its goal in human recognition and acknowledgment. These strands of biblical testimony correspond to the first and last elements of the sentence "God reveals himself as Lord," to God the Actor and God the Result. Barth's main interest, however, is not with these, but with a third strand of testimony, which concerns God's ability to be God "the Object," to reveal "*Himself* as Lord."

Barth explains that without ceasing to be the unseen Yahweh enthroned above, Yahweh is also free to assume a perceptible form, in which he "has objectivity for those to whom He is manifest" (316). The Old Testament designates this objective form in a variety of ways, as God's Word, Spirit, Wisdom, and so on. Of these the most important, though, is the very name "Yahweh" itself. This name is not an external attribute of Yahweh, but the form in which the invisible Yahweh in heaven becomes present and manifest on earth. "The name of *Yahweh* is the form in which *Yahweh* comes to Israel, has dealings with it, is manifest to it" (317). Through the name, God chooses a people, makes it his own, and rules it. Accordingly, Israel builds a temple—not for Yahweh, who dwells in heaven—but for Yahweh's *name.* Israel's knowledge, fear, and love of God are all connected to the unseen Yahweh through this *name.* "To have knowledge of the name of *Yahweh*, and to that degree knowledge of *Yahweh* himself, and to participate in His revelation, is to be a partner in the covenant made by Him" (318).

Barth's discussion of the name "Yahweh" is impressive in itself and of strategic importance for his doctrine of the Trinity. By rooting his doctrine of the Trinity in the Old Testament's witness to God's name and covenant with Israel, Barth means to vindicate its biblical character and defend it from the charge of being simply another *vestigium trinitatis* drawn from the world of religious epistemology.

- (Hyphen)

We come now to the small matter of the hyphen, the most unusual and obscure aspect of the "revealed name" *Yahweh-Kyrios*. The hyphen represents a relationship, but what kind? The question is not trivial, for the answer will largely determine what becomes of Barth's "discovery" of the Tetragrammaton.

On several occasions, Barth refers to *kyrios* in the New Testament as a *translation* of the name Yahweh.[21] But, of course, Barth cannot really mean this. Strictly speaking, the name YHWH can be *transliterated*, but it cannot be *translated*, since it is a proper name and without semantic meaning (nor does Barth ever claim that it has such). If we assume, as Barth did, that *kyrios* in the New Testament is connected *in some fashion* with the Tetragrammaton in the Old, then there are basically only two alternatives. Either *kyrios* is a *surrogate* for the Tetragrammaton, following Jewish custom, in which case the unwritten divine name remains a contemporary point of reference whenever *kyrios* is thus used in the New Testament. Or *kyrios* is a *replacement* of the Tetragrammaton, in which case it takes the place formerly occupied by the proper name, while the divine name itself recedes into the past, as the Christian kabbalists supposed.

Kyrios

In truth, there is little doubt about which of these two views Barth held. Barth understood *kyrios* as a successor and replacement of the Tetragrammaton, not as a surrogate for it. Indeed, Barth gives scant evidence that he is even aware of the latter possibility. In contrast, many factors in Barth's formation would have steered him toward the view he actually held. We have already reported that German printers had long since eliminated Luther's use of the capitalized HERR in the New Testament, ensuring that unless Barth deliberately consulted much older editions of the *Lutherbibel*, he would likely have encountered the symbol only in his reading of the Old Testament. Another factor that might have inclined Barth toward the *replacement* view is the influence (however mediated) of the Christian kabbalists. I have already suggested that Barth's triadic interpretation of the Tetragrammaton places him in a certain broad taxonomic alignment with the Christian kabbalists. Is there any evidence that Barth was influenced by or even embraced the view that the name "Jesus" takes the place of the Tetragrammaton?

Yes, there is. Startlingly, the thesis that Jesus and "the name Jesus" replaces the Tetragramaton appears with eerie exactitude at the heart of Barth's commentary on the name *Yahweh-Kyrios*. The decisive sentence is this: "Into the place, not of the Yahweh on Sinai or in heaven, but certainly of the name of the Lord which finally dwells very really in a house of stone in Jerusalem, there now comes the existence of the man Jesus of Nazareth" (318).

Stripped to its basics, the sentence is an exact restatement of Reuchlin's thesis, with a slight "existentialist" twist: Into the place of the name of Yahweh there now comes "the existence of the man Jesus of Nazareth." Barth modifies Reuchlin's thesis by stating that what takes the place of the divine name is Jesus' "existence," rather than the name "Jesus" itself. But this modification permits Barth to then embrace the latter view too, insofar as Jesus' *existence* is denoted by the name "Jesus." As Barth writes a few sentences later, the name Yahweh is replaced by "the historical figure of this Man on his way from Bethlehem to Golgotha, the 'name' of *Jesus*" (318, emphasis original). Barth goes on to state that God's self-unveiling action in Jesus is "incomparably more direct, unequivocal and palpable" than had been God's action in the name Yahweh. Compared with Jesus, "the name of Yahweh" must be regarded as "weak in comparison," indeed as a mere "shadow" and "prophecy of the fulfillment present here" (318). Jesus embodies "God with us" with greater "concreteness and reality" than the name Yahweh ever did. In him, God's presence takes the form of a "unique, contingent, somatic human existence," whereas in the name Yahweh it was "invisible" and "real only in the sphere of the human conception" (318).

For Barth, then, the Tetragrammaton is no more an enduring feature of the economy of salvation than it had been for Reuchlin or Luther. Like the Christian kabbalists, Barth understands the name as a paradigmatic symbol of the Old Testament, the quintessential sign of everything that points forward to—and is antiquated by—the coming of Jesus the Lord. Near the end of his analysis of the name *Yahweh-Kyrios*, Barth borrows the arch-Hegelian term *Aufhebung* to describe this double movement of fulfillment and supersession:

> As the Word became flesh (*logos syntelōn*, word that brings to completion), bringing fully to light what revelation in the Old Testament had always brought to light only in the form of a pointer, it had also to become *logos syntemnōn* (word that cuts off), the dissolution [*Aufhebung*] of this revelation and of its written testimony, not their contradiction, abolition, or destruction, but dissolution [*Aufhebung*] into itself, just as the early light of dawn disappears in the brightness of the rising sun itself (Rom. 9:28): Christ the *telos* (end). (319)

Even if Barth's use of *Aufhebung* is only a rhetorical flourish, it still hints at a real similarity of views between Barth and Hegel regarding the name of God. For Hegel, the "mere" name of God is indispensable as a starting point for religious experience because it indicates the divine subject's freedom for self-determination in a way that a concept cannot. Ultimately, however, the empty name of God must be fulfilled and overcome (*aufgehoben*) by its conceptual determination, so that the actual content of the divine life can be intelligibly expressed. Similarly, for Barth, the name "Yahweh" signals the uniqueness and freedom of the biblical deity at the *beginning* of salvation history. Yet the name also harbors a semiotic deficiency that must be remedied by the coming of "Jesus the Lord." Like Thomas Aquinas, Barth regards the Tetragrammaton as a "pure" proper name without semantic meaning. But whereas for Thomas this emptiness was the source of the Tetragrammaton's *surplus* over other names, Barth follows the Christian kabbalists in viewing it as a *deficit* tied to the name's place in *the old covenant.* Yahweh, Barth maintains, is not really a name at all, but "the refusal to give a name" (317, 322), in which God's self-*veiling* predominates even in the act of revelation itself. Ultimately, however, God's self-revelation must happen in such a way that the moment of *un*veiling predominates. This transpires in Jesus, "the perfect self-unveiling of God" (319), and comes to expression in the confession of "Jesus Christ as *kyrios*," as "Lord."

We cannot be too surprised, therefore, when we discover that the name *Yahweh-Kyrios* actually vanishes soon after being introduced. It makes its last appearance in *The Church Dogmatics* in the context of a discussion of God's "*deitas* or *divinitas*, the divine *ousia*, *essentia*, *natura*, or *substantia*" (349). There, Barth explains, God's essence "is that which makes *Yahweh-Kyrios*, or wherein *Yahweh-Kyrios* is, the One whom He describes Himself to be by this name, the name of the Lord" (349). With this remark, Barth clarifies his understanding of *what sort of name* the expression *Yahweh-Kyrios* is. It is a *descriptive* name, whose meaning is simply "lord" or "lordship." For that reason, it can be replaced by the word "lord" without essential loss. In this, Barth's understanding of the Tetragrammaton differs markedly from Thomas, who takes it as a pure proper name, which cannot be construed as a *description* without destroying its essential character. Having yielded its secret, the "revealed name *Yahweh-Kyrios*" can be put to rest.[22]

The *Aufhebung* of the Covenant and the End of the History of Israel

What are the implications of the *Aufhebung* of the name Yahweh for the deity's covenant with Israel?[23] Does the fate of the divine name foretell the fate of the covenant? In a word, the answer is yes. The climax of Barth's discussion of the name *Yahweh-Kyrios* is a rhetorically powerful account of the incarnation as a summons directed to the people Israel. The incarnation bids the Israelite to turn away from the old form of God's presence—the name that dwells in the temple—and heed the new form of God's presence, which "literally confronts him with God" (319). But Israel took offense at Jesus, the unambiguous self-unveiling of God, and in the name of God crucified him as a blasphemer. Thus the very people who had "Immanuel daily on their lips and in their hearts, did not want this Immanuel in its unconditionally enacted fulfillment" (319). Barth then continues: "But just because Immanuel had been unconditionally fulfilled in Jesus the crucifixion of Jesus was bound to mean something different from the stoning of even the greatest prophet, namely, *the end of the history of Israel as the special people of revelation*, the destruction of the house of stone as the dwelling of the name of the Lord" (319, with emphasis added).

Why exactly did Israel's disobedience "have to" issue in "the end of the history of Israel as the special people of revelation"? The claim would seem to hang in midair if it were not for the fact that Israel's history mirrors the fate of the name Yahweh, as the next phrase indicates ("the pulling down of the house of stone . . ."). Because at a certain point in salvation history, "Yahweh" ceases to be *the* Divine Name and is *aufgehoben* into a higher form, the history of Israel as the special people of revelation must also come to an end. There is food for thought in the fact that Barth's "discovery" of the name *Yahweh-Kyrios* issues finally in *The Church Dogmatics*' first great polemic *contra Judaios*, at the exegetical foundation center of Barth's trinitarian "root."

Father, Son, and Holy Spirit and the *Vestigia Trinitatis* in *The Church Dogmatics*

Having watched the divine name disappear like "the light of dawn . . . in the brightness of the rising sun," let us take a last look at Barth's treatment of the *vestigia trinitatis* and the triad "Father, Son, and Holy Spirit." These two aspect of Barth's thought remain largely constant in the development from *Die christliche Dogmatik im Entwurf* to *The Church Dogmatics*, but there are some shifts of emphasis.

Vestigia Trinitatis

In *The Church Dogmatics*, Barth repeats his criticism of the *vestigia trinitatis* (or "vestiges of the Trinity"), although in a more circumspect and nuanced way. Barth acknowledges that "the finders of the *vestigia trinitatis* had no wish to postulate a second and different root of the doctrine of the Trinity side by side with revelation" (344). Remarkably, Barth goes so far as to agree with the judgment of the Roman Catholic Franz Diekamp, who stated that "the analogies adduced by the Fathers are in the long run only further expositions and multiplications of the Bible concepts, Father, Son, and Spirit, which are already analogical" (340). Barth also admits that his own doctrine of revelation—with its reliance on the schema "God reveals Himself as Lord"—moves "into extraordinarily close proximity to Augustine's vexatious argument." Barth asks, "Have we discovered the root of the doctrine of the Trinity in revelation and not in the end this quite different root?" and concedes that it is impossible to unambiguously escape the appearance of this being the case (397).

Nevertheless, Barth insists that there is a major difference between his method and that of Augustine and his followers. Barth seeks to *interpret*

Scripture's witness to revelation, and in doing so he grasps at creation incidentally and in passing. The other tradition, in contrast, seeks to *illustrate* revelation by consciously beginning with creation itself. Despite their good intentions, the advocates of the *vestigia trinitatis* thereby opened up a dangerous path, which ultimately leads away from revelation and toward the dangerous doctrine of the "analogy of being" (*analogia entis*), the notion that creation harbors within it a path toward knowledge of God independent of God's self-revelation in Christ (334). This doctrine, Barth famously (or infamously) declares in the preface to the volume, is nothing less than "the invention of Antichrist" (xiii), to be avoided at all costs.

Father, Son, and Holy Spirit

As in *Die christliche Dogmatik im Entwurf*, the Barth of *The Church Dogmatics* continues to treat "Father, Son, and Holy Spirit" as uniquely privileged names for the persons of the Trinity. Yet Barth's arguments in favor of these names are even more modest than before. He acknowledges that these same relations can be expressed by other "conceptual ternaries" with equal adequacy. Barth even advances a couple of his own, speaking of them as "Pure Giver," "Receiver and Giver," "Pure Receiver," as "Speaker, Word, and Meaning." But then he adds, "But let us stay clear of the zone of *vestigia trinitatis* on which we have already trespassed" (364). Without elaborating the point, he suggests that, "Father," "Son," and "Holy Spirit" expresses these relations "most simply" (364). Waxing eloquent in a Dionysian vein, Barth acknowledges that what we understand by "the figure of Father and Son" is shot through with worldliness and imperfection, with creatureliness and sin. The figure expresses "a non-knowing knowledge," not a "knowing non-knowledge" (432). Nevertheless, with Thomas Aquinas, Barth maintains that these names are not "optional and ultimately meaningless symbols" whose nonsymbolic content consists originally in creaturely realities. On the contrary, the Father-Son relationship has its original and proper reality in God (as indeed, all creaturely relationships do, according to Barth). The words express not a creaturely but a divine mystery, indeed, *the* divine mystery.

Drawing a Balance

To a greater degree than the other theologians we have considered thus far, Karl Barth gives explicit and sustained attention to all three patterns of trinitarian naming that are the subject of this book. But Barth clearly does not give a *trinitarian* account of the relationship of these three idioms. On the contrary, Barth assigns preeminence to *one* of them—the pattern of the Father, Son, and Holy Spirit—and subordinates the others to it, in one fashion or another. Already in his early work, Barth rejects the pattern of naming the Trinity that operates through open-ended recourse to creation as a dangerous distraction, which contributes nothing essential to the knowledge of God. And in his later work, Barth treats the trinitarian pattern that is centered in the Tetragrammaton in a way that follows the precedent of Luther and the Christian Kabbalah. As a result, Barth's "discovery" of the Tetragrammaton comes to a familiar conclusion. The name Yahweh, together with the Israel's covenant from which it is inseparable, is a shadow, a prophecy, whose limited truth must end in order that its enduring truth may be *aufgehoben* into the lordship of the triune God.

The "eclipse" of the Tetragrammaton in Karl Barth's doctrine of the Trinity is deeply ironic: Barth turned to the Tetragrammaton to defend himself from critics who charged that his analysis of revelation stemmed from a speculative theory of knowledge ("God reveals himself as Lord") and not from the unique character of the biblical witness. Although this charge may not have been wholly fair to Barth, there does seem to be a kernel of truth to it with regard to the specific case of Barth's interpretation of the Tetragrammaton. Barth came to his close study of the Tetragrammaton with a prior commitment to his analysis of revelation as "God reveals himself as Lord," and this commitment sets the parameters within which his understanding of the Tetragrammaton operates.

Arguably, Barth would have been more successful in fulfilling the intentions that led him to the Tetragrammaton in the first place if he had followed the path indicated by Thomas Aquinas, rather than the path of Luther and the Christian Kabbalah. But Barth was in no mood to learn from Thomas Aquinas on this point: in his view, Thomas's doctrine of God was tainted with the problem of natural theology and the *vestigia trinitatis.*

THE REFORMATION TRADITION AND THE REDISCOVERY AND ECLIPSE OF THE TETRAGRAMMATON

The Reformation tradition we have examined in this chapter aspires to correct the Dionysian tradition's "Hellenistic bias" by centering the practice of divine naming and trinitarian naming exclusively in the Christ event as testified by the Scriptures. Insofar as it knows of any legitimate "approach" to this event, it is to be found in the Old Testament's account of YHWH's covenant with Israel, and not in an antecedent account of "the nameless God of many names."

But the Reformation tradition's reading of the Scripture is no less filtered through a hermeneutical lens than that of the Dionysian tradition. The

Reformation's hermeneutical lens simply stems from another source, the Christian Kabbalah. The contribution of the Christian Kabbalah to the Reformation project is ambiguous. On the one hand, the Christian Kabbalah purports to claim for Christian faith the riches of Jewish wisdom, and in particular the riches of the incomparable name YHWH. On the other hand, the Christian Kabbalah transforms Jewish wisdom by subjugating the name YHWH to the pattern of old covenant and new, rendering the Tetragrammaton the quintessential sign of all that has been fulfilled and now belongs to the past. As a result, the Reformation's discovery of the Tetragrammaton reaches its destination in the name's eclipse.

Despite the Reformation tradition's sense of superiority vis-à-vis the Dionysian tradition in general and Thomas Aquinas in particular, there is a real sense in which it never attains the mark set by Thomas's analysis of the Tetragrammaton. For Thomas, the Tetragrammaton signifies God's eternal being as God, irrespective of the distinction between old covenant and new. Moreover, Thomas does not regard the Tetragrammaton's nonsemantic character as a deficit that must be overcome and transcended by meaning-bearing terms, as both Luther and Barth do. On the contrary, for Thomas, the nonsemantic character of the Tetragrammaton is precisely the feature that differentiates it from other divine names, which "name God from creatures," and enables it to be, in its own way, "the most appropriate name of God."

There is a further irony in the Reformation tradition's interpretation of the Tetragrammaton. By declaring the name YHWH—and Judaism's oblique ways of referring to it—a feature of *the old covenant*, the Reformation tradition blinded itself in advance to the possibility that the *New Testament* testifies to the name by using characteristically *Jewish* modes of reference. The Reformation tradition thus obscured for itself a key way in which the New Testament attests to the character of God's uniqueness—as revealed in Jesus Christ himself.

6

Traditions in Conflict

The Trinitarian Revival and the Inclusive-Language Debate

Our survey of how Christians have named the persons of the Trinity ends with the contemporary trinitarian revival and one of its most contentious features: the so-called inclusive-language debate. I have chosen to focus on this debate because of its intrinsic interest, but even more because it permits us to continue the story of the Dionysian and Reformation traditions that we began in the previous two chapters. If the inclusive-language debate is "as oppositional as any" on the theological scene today, then the reasons for this, I want to suggest, are only partly to be found in dispute about the status of male-gendered language in trinitarian discourse.[1] Although this is an undeniably thorny issue, it is also one about which partisans on both sides typically share a considerable amount of common ground, as I suggested in chapter 1. What makes this common ground difficult to claim and cultivate, however, are deeper theological conflicts that arise from the different ways the Dionysian and Reformation traditions *configure* the various elements of Trinitarian discourse. To revert a final time to our metaphor of the threefold cord, the inclusive-language debate is like a tug-of-war in which the teams grab different strands of a single rope and pull. Nonmetaphorically expressed, the debate tends to split the church's pneumatological and christological interests, while leaving its theological interests insufficiently addressed.

Our study will focus on two landmark contributions to the contemporary trinitarian revival: Robert W. Jenson's *The Triune Identity* and Elizabeth A. Johnson's *She Who Is*. Jenson, a representative of the Reformation tradition, is a champion of the unsubstitutable importance of the christological pattern of naming that comes to expression in the kinship vocabulary of Father, Son, and Holy Spirit. Johnson, a representative of the Dionysian tradition, is a champion of the unsubstitutable importance of the pneumatological pattern of naming that names the three persons by using an open-ended variety of context-specific ternaries that always leaves room for more. Both theologians have written extensively on the doctrine of the Trinity, and my discussion of these two books is not intended as a verdict on their larger body of work. Indeed, both authors have subsequently addressed the question of naming the Trinity in ways that are consistent with the constructive aims of this book. Still, I have chosen to focus on these two important works because together they helpfully illustrate what I believe are deeper problems in the logic of the church's inherited trinitarian discourse.

THE TRIUNE IDENTITY: "FATHER, SON, AND HOLY SPIRIT" IS THE PROPER NAME OF THE TRINITY

In *The Triune Identity: God according to the Gospel*, Robert Jenson advances the thesis that "Father, Son, and Holy Spirit" is the *proper name* of the Trinity.[2] To understand Jenson's claim aright, we must see it in the context of his larger interpretation of the doctrine of the Trinity, which belongs broadly to the Reformation tradition of Luther and Barth.

God-Language, Proper Names, and the Identity of the Triune God

According to Jenson, trinitarian discourse "is Christianity's effort to identify the God who has claimed us" (4). Many Christians are reluctant to accept the idea that it is necessary to differentiate the God they worship from other gods, preferring to believe that "everyone worships the same God anyway." What such people fail to realize is that *every religion*, including Christianity, must be able to identify the "god" or supreme principle it worships. Big religious claims, such as "God redeems," are cognitively vacuous unless one can identify *who* one means by "God" and what God does that counts as redemptive (e.g., "Baal sends rain"). Otherwise the claim "God redeems" is no more informative than the statement, "X restores whatever state X defines as good." Religious traditions typically identify "god" by proper names, identifying descriptions, and stories. A proper name is a name that refers to only one person, while an identifying description is a descriptive phrase that fits just the one item to be identified. Some religious traditions maintain that "god" has *no* proper name or essential identifying description, such as Neoplatonism, the funding philosophy of the Dionysian tradition, which we briefly touched on in chapter 3. But even these traditions, Jenson points out, are as dependent upon identifying God as any other. They simply identify God by means of negative characteristics, so that god is known as "the—very specifically—Unidentifiable one" (xi).

Turning to the stories that religions tell about god or the gods, these serve to make a meaningful story out of time by connecting the present with a remembered past and expected future. Religions can do this in one of two basic ways. A religion can tell a story about "the persistence of the past," or it can tell a story of "the anticipation of the future." In the first kind of story, a god prevails by the "cancellation" of time, while in the latter, by virtue of "the success of time itself" (4). History, Jenson maintains, is chock full of gods who cancel time. But the deity of the future has been "historically exemplified" only once: by "the God of Israel" (4). Simply put, the God of Israel is eternal in a different way than other gods. Whereas other gods seek immunity from time by standing behind or above it altogether, the God of Israel transcends time by being faithful in it, by making and keeping promises of a quite specifically historical kind.

Israel's faith identifies God as "Yahweh, the one who rescued Israel from Egypt." The important thing to recognize about the name "Yahweh" is that it was the *only* proper name of Israel's God. Other ancient peoples piled up proper names for God, in order to blur the original uniqueness of its deity and create the impression of a "grandly vague deity-in-general"(5). "Israel made the opposite move," insisting on "the unambiguous identification of her God over against vague intimations of the numinous" (5). The identifying description "the one who rescued Israel from Egypt" encapsulates Yahweh's character as *the* God who is not on the side of established order or natural necessity, who inaugurates Israel's history as the fulfillment of an antecedent promise, and who anticipates a future of fulfillment that is still yet to come (35–36).

Now, according to Jenson, Israel's identification of God confronts one massive problem: death. Death always returns time to the *status quo ante*, to the way things were before. If Israel, too, should finally fall victim to death, then the enterprise of the promise-keeping God would be over. The Hebrew Scriptures, Jenson maintains, do not fully resolve the question of Yahweh's conflict with death, but they do *end* with it. "Son of man, can these bones live?" (39).

Christian faith springs from the belief that the God of Israel has conquered death. The gospel identifies God as the "one who raised Jesus from the dead." Jenson emphasizes that this new identifying description does not take the place of the earlier one, according to which God is "the one who rescued Israel from Egypt." "It is essential to the God who raised Jesus that he is the same who freed Israel" (8). This is entirely consistent with Jenson's claim that the God of Israel is the *only* instantiation of "[the] deity of the future" (4). The Trinity, according to Jenson's analysis, must *not* be a hitherto "unknown" god, as Marcion maintained, but rather must be a new way of identifying the already-identified God of Israel, based on the fact that this same God has raised Jesus from the dead and sent their Spirit of liberation into the world.

We come at last to Jenson's account of the name of the Trinity. Given Jenson's argument thus far, we would expect him to argue that the gospel introduces a new way of naming God, one that supplements and transforms its understanding of the name "Yahweh," but not one that takes its place. After all, Jenson has insisted that the gospel supplements and transforms Israel's earlier identification of God, but does not replace it. For Christians, God is *both* the God who rescued Israel from Egypt *and* the one who raised Jesus from death. Moreover, Jenson has emphasized that "Yahweh" is God's *only* proper name (8). We can only be surprised, therefore, when Jenson claims that at a certain point in salvation history, "Yahweh" ceases to be the God of Israel's proper name, and "Father, Son, and Holy Spirit" steps into its place (10). The claim itself is well known to us from the tradition of the Christian Kabbalah, which, as we saw, worked its way into the theologies of Luther and Barth. But the claim is so at variance with the thrust of Jenson's argument to this point that we can only wonder how he arrived at it.

The answer, it turns out, is by a chain of historical claims. According to Jenson, ancient Israelites stopped saying the name once the need to identify "the true God over against other claimants ceased to be a daily challenge" (7). By the beginning of the Common Era, the name "Yahweh" was simply no longer available for identifying God. "The habit of instead saying 'Lord' has buried it too deeply under the appellative" (8). The biblical God, however, "must have some proper name" (10), and early Christians needed to identify the God of the gospel. A new proper name for the biblical God was, therefore, a historical and religious necessity.

According to Jenson, the name that actually filled the void is "Father, Son, and Holy Spirit." Jenson acknowledges that the triad "Father, Son, and Holy Spirit" did not "fall from heaven." In principle, some other name could have performed the work that Christians eventually came to require of it. Nevertheless, one can see why the tradition settled on this name. For one thing, the elements of this name are rooted in Jesus' own speech:

> "Father" was Jesus' peculiar address to the particular Transcendence over against whom he lived. Just by this address he qualified himself as "the Son," and in the memory of the primal church his acclamation as "Son" was the beginning of faith. "Spirit" was the term provided by the whole biblical theology for what comes of such a meeting between this God and one to whom he takes a special relation. (12–13)

In addition, "Father, Son, and Holy Spirit" became the church's name for its God because it packs into one phrase the content and logic of this God's identifying descriptions (21). God's new proper name differs from his old one in this respect. According to Jenson (who here echoes the teaching of Thomas Aquinas), "Yahweh" was a "pure" proper name, without descriptive content (5). In contrast, "Father, Son, and Spirit" provides a condensed summary of the gospel that expresses faith's "apprehension" (13), "primal interpretation" (18), or "primal experience" (21) of God.

The Curious Fate of the Tetragrammaton in *The Triune Identity*

Jenson is sometimes portrayed as an extreme opponent of all efforts at feminist linguistic reform, but that is not really a fair account of his position. Jenson acknowledges that patriarchy has distorted the church's trinitarian inheritance, and argues that the trinitarian inheritance should be reformed to remedy this distortion (13; cf. 103–59, esp. 143–44). Furthermore, far from rejecting what we have called a *pneumatological* pattern of naming the persons of the Trinity, he deploys it with gusto! Jenson liberally introduces new ideas and vocabulary into received trinitarian doctrine, such as (to take only a few incidental examples) "Subject, Object, Spirit" (148); "Transcendence, Self-expression, Breath of [the] Future"(140); and others. Still, there is no mistaking Jenson's championing of *one* pattern of trinitarian naming in particular: the kinship vocabulary of Father, Son, and Spirit. According to Jenson, this pattern is indispensably important for the logic of trinitarian discourse, and it is so for a simple but telling reason: it is the proper name of the biblical God, as made known in Christ.

Nevertheless, Jenson's claim that "Father, Son, and Holy Spirit" is the proper name of God has some serious problems. The main problem is not, as some have charged, that "Father, Son, and Holy Spirit" has descriptive meaning. As Jenson points out, proper names often have such meaning. A weightier issue is that biblical translators routinely *translate* rather than *transliterate* the words "Father," "Son," and "Spirit," a practice that makes sense only if the church understands the terms as appellative rather than as proper names. The gravest problem with Jenson's claim, however, arises from difficulties that it creates for his own larger trinitarian interpretation. These difficulties center in his interpretation of the Tetragrammaton. Jenson's main argument that "Father, Son, and Spirit" is a proper name might be expressed in the form of a syllogism:

Major premise: The Tetragrammaton is a personal proper name that identifies the true God of biblical faith.
Minor premise: "Father, Son, and Holy Spirit" takes the place of the Tetragrammaton at a certain point in salvation history.
Conclusion: "Father, Son, and Holy Spirit" is a proper name.

The major premise of this argument is one that representatives of both the Dionysian and Reformation traditions have maintained, as we have seen in the previous two chapters. In contrast, the minor premise is a signature belief of the Reformation tradition, with specific roots in the Christian Kabbalah. Whether Jenson's desired conclusion is a valid deduction from his premises is open to debate. What is clear is that the minor premise entails a host of paradoxes and ironies for Jenson's larger project. How can it be that the promise-keeping God of the future leaves his own proper name stranded in the past? Moreover, if the true God can change his proper name once, then why not again? If the Tetragrammaton can be "buried," then perhaps "Father, Son, and Holy Spirit" could as well. In short, Jenson's embrace of the kabbalistic minor premise undercuts the very point he wants to secure: the indispensability of God's proper name.

Drawing a Balance

In *The Triune Identity*, Robert Jenson recognizes in some fashion all the patterns of naming the Trinity that are the subject of this book. Standing in the wake of the Reformation tradition, however, he configures these in a way that assigns priority to one pattern above the other two: the christological pattern of "Father, Son, and Holy Spirit." To speak in an admittedly metaphorical way, and without prejudice to the orthodoxy of Jenson's theology, we might say that he configures the patterns in a "subordinationist" way, assigning supremacy to one pattern above the other two. This "subordinationist" interpretation creates internal difficulties for Jenson's argument: the attribute he wants to capture on behalf of the christological pattern—the status of being a proper name—can be won only by declaring the theological pattern obsolete. But if the theological pattern of naming can be consigned to the past, why not the christological pattern as well?

SHE WHO IS: THE MYSTERY OF GOD IN FEMINIST THEOLOGICAL DISCOURSE

In *She Who Is: The Mystery of God in Feminist Theological Discourse*, Elizabeth A. Johnson asks, "What is the right way to speak about the triune God?"[3] "One right way," she proposes, "is to speak about the Trinity as a symbol of the mystery of salvation, in the midst of the world's suffering, using female images" (212–13). To understand Johnson's thesis fully, we must see it in light of her larger trinitarian proposal, which belongs broadly to the Dionysian tradition.

God-Language, Metaphors, and the Mystery of the Trinity

Johnson prefaces her trinitarian proposal within an account of the general nature of God-language, much as Jenson did in *The Triune Identity*. But whereas Jenson emphasized the vacuity of the word "god" in itself, Johnson celebrates "God" as a symbol of the inexhaustible mystery that surrounds human life in the cosmos. "The reality of God is mystery beyond all imagining. So transcendent, so immanent is the holy mystery of God that we can never wrap our minds completely around this mystery and exhaust divine reality in words or concepts" (7).

Because God is mystery, human speech about the divine is inherently open-ended, always seeking new language to express the inexpressible. God-talk is open-ended, too, because "words . . . are cultural creatures" and "as cultures shift, so too does the specificity of God-talk" (6). Johnson invokes both considerations to warrant her experiment in naming the Trinity:

> Inherited Christian speech about God has developed within a framework that does not prize the unique and equal humanity of women, and bears the marks of this partiality and dominance. This language is now under fire both for its complicity in human oppression and its capacity to rob divine reality of goodness and profound mystery. (15)

Johnson charges the triad "Father, Son, and Holy Spirit" with complicity in the crisis of Christian God-talk. She acknowledges that this language was not intended to affirm that God is male, yet its overuse has fostered the idea that men are better suited to mediate divine mystery than women. She acknowledges that Jesus' own address to God as *Abba* served to identify God not as "a patriarchal figure . . . but [as] a God of the oppressed" (81). Still, she maintains, "to select this one metaphor and grant it sole rights does not follow the pattern of Jesus' speech," which reflected "variety and plurality" rather than "the exclusive centrality" of this one pattern of speech (81). (This is an important point, and we will return to it in the second half of this book.)

Johnson proposes to "shatter the exclusivity of male metaphor, subvert its dominance, and set free a greater sense of the mystery of God" (45). She enlists insights from both feminist theology and "classical theology" to this end. Each tradition offers a valuable criterion for measuring the adequacy of God-talk: the flourishing of women on the one hand, and the adequacy of speech to the transcendent cause of the world on the other. From the classical tradition (which coincides in practice with the Dionysian tradition described in chapter 4), Johnson draws three insights in particular. A first is divine incomprehensibility: "God dwells in unapproachable light so that no name or image or concept that human beings use to speak of the divine mystery ever arrives at its goal: God is essentially incomprehensible" (117).

Second is the analogical character of religious language, with its threefold motion of affirmation, negation, and eminence:

> All words about the divine begin from the experience of the world, and then are negated insofar as they carry reference to the creaturely mode in which the spare, original, strange perfections of the world exist, ultimately being reaffirmed in a transcending movement of the human spirit toward God as eminent source of all. (117)

A third insight is "the necessity of giving to God many names," a principle that Johnson cites in the words of Thomas Aquinas himself (117). Rightly understood, these three insights reinforce feminist theology's commitment to the flourishing of women. For "insofar as God creates both male and female in the divine image and is the source of the perfections of both, either can equally well be used as metaphor to point to divine mystery" (55). In fact, both are needed for "less inadequate speech about God, in whose image the human race is created" (55).

Naming the Trinity by Using Female Imagery

Johnson advances her own proposal for naming the Trinity as one theologically legitimate and religiously fruitful possibility among others. Assuming that "all three *hypostases* of the Trinity transcend categories of male and female" and that "each hypostasis may be spoken of in female metaphors" (211), Johnson invokes the biblical concept of Sophia, the female personification of divine wisdom, to name the persons of the Trinity as "Spirit-Sophia, "Jesus-Sophia," and "Mother-Sophia," and discusses them in that order (see 124–87). She also discusses the persons in that order, unfolding a trinitarian theology that sets out "from below" (123), from Spirit-Sophia's presence "within the widest possible world of everything that exists" (139). In a summary passage, Johnson writes of the three persons:

> God is God as Spirit-Sophia, the mobile, pure, people-loving Spirit who pervades every wretched corner, wailing at the waste, releasing power that enables fresh starts. . . .
>
> God is God again as Jesus Christ, Sophia's child and prophet, and yes, Sophia herself personally pitching her tent in the flesh of humanity to teach the paths of justice. . . .

> God is God again as unimaginable abyss of livingness, Holy Wisdom unknown and unknowable. She is the matrix of all that exists, mother and fashioner of all things, who herself dwells in light inaccessible. (213–14)

Then Johnson carries her experiment in trinitarian naming to its pinnacle by seeking female imagery for the one triune God. She considers various alternatives, such as "Sophia-God as a Trinity of friendship" (218) and as "Sophia-Trinity" (223). Quickly, however, she steers toward the classical tradition and its crowning name for God, derived from the language of being.

Johnson acknowledges that the tradition of Christian ontology is unattractive and obscure to many, but she argues that, rightly understood, it remains an invaluable resource for emancipatory speech about God. "Far from being a dead-weight abstraction, the notion of God as being signifies ultimate reality as pure aliveness in relation. . . .This symbol of divine being can strengthen and embellish discourse about the mystery of God" (240).

Johnson appeals especially to Thomas Aquinas's discussion of "The Most Appropriate Name of God" in *Summa theologiae* (*ST* 1, q. 13, a.11). Noting that Thomas himself appeals here to "a long and venerable tradition," Johnson summarizes key elements of Thomas's discussion as follows:

> [Thomas] finds the term "being" particularly apt because it refers to no partial aspect of God but rather to the whole in an indeterminate way, as to an infinite ocean. Its excellence is further seen in that it highlights the uniqueness of God, for of no one else can it be said that their essence is to exist. At the climax of this argument he proposes that being can serve even to name God in a particularly apt way. He asks "Is HE WHO IS the most appropriate name for God?" Referring to the burning bush scene interpreted metaphysically, he answers in the affirmative: "Therefore this name HE WHO IS is the most appropriate name for God." (242)

Thomas, Johnson says with approval, fills the name "He Who Is" "with all the transcendent significance that accrues to pure, absolute being in his system" (242).

Still, Thomas's discussion is not beyond reproach. For one thing, the masculine grammatical gender of the pronoun "He" (*qui*) "coheres with the androcentric nature of Aquinas's thought as a whole, expressed most infamously in his assessment of women as deficient males" (242). A different kind of problem arises from the location to which Thomas assigns the discussion of the One God within the *Summa*, where it comes before a discussion of the three persons. Following the criticism of Karl Rahner and others, Johnson observes that this sequence tends to isolate the question of the nature of the divine being "from God's free, historic involvement with the struggle and life of the world" (224). Accordingly, Johnson modifies Thomas at two points. First, she places her account of the One God *after* her discussion of the three persons, in order to express the insight that "what the language of being points to is the world's relation to God as the living God" (240). Second, she glosses the name of Exodus 3:14 in female terms:

> If God is not intrinsically male, if women are truly created in the image of God, if being female is an excellence, if what makes women exist as women in all difference is participation in divine being, then there is cogent reason to name toward Sophia-God, "the one who is," with implicit reference to an antecedent of the grammatically and symbolically feminine gender. SHE WHO IS can be spoken as a robust, appropriate name for God. (242–43)

The name "SHE WHO IS," Johnson urges, brings to bear in a female metaphor "all the power carried in the ontological symbol of absolute, relational liveliness that energizes the world" (243).

The Curious Fate of the Tetragrammaton in *She Who Is*

Clearly, *She Who Is* champions what we have called the pneumatological pattern of naming the Trinity, from a vantage point that belongs broadly to the Dionysian tradition. It celebrates the mystery of God, the need for spiritual and moral conversion, and the unapologetic use of cultural resources drawn from outside the life of the church and its Scriptures. But as an heir of Dionysius, *She Who Is* also inherits a problem that dogs that tradition. We may put the problem this way, paraphrasing a question that John N. Jones first posed to Dionysius himself:

> Does *Johnson's* highest Godhead preserve Trinitarian identity, or are the trinitarian elements exclusively economic, existing only on the order of divine manifestation *and human experience*? What is the nature of the "God beyond God"? . . . *Johnson* insists on the total hiddenness of the transcendent God who is beyond names, even the emancipator names of Spirit-Sophia, Jesus-Sophia, and Mother-Sophia. Is *Johnson* therefore non-Trinitarian or anti-Trinitarian?[4]

She Who Is can indeed be read in a constructivist way, as though its trinitarian character were merely a function of the particular human community it serves, rather than an effort to speak a truth surpassing other truths. However, there are excellent reasons to think that Johnson understands her trinitarian proposal differently. As she herself observes, the church's trinitarian tradition has not been content merely to describe "three experiences [that] come to human beings from one God" (198–99). Rather, it affirms that "three corresponding distinctions may be said to exist within one God" (199). The Christian tradition has insisted on this last point, Johnson explains, because it wishes to affirm that "God is *utterly faithful, and does not self-reveal in any guise other than the one which actually coheres with the essence of divine being*" (199, with emphasis added). By embracing this tradition as her own, Johnson places herself squarely with Augustine and Thomas, who, though broadly Dionysian in orientation, are nevertheless firmly trinitarian in outlook.

Perhaps the strongest indication that Johnson does not wish the biblical God to vanish in a fog of apophatic denial, however, is the role that she assigns to what she calls the "sacred Tetragrammaton YHWH" (242). While references to the Tetragrammaton are relatively few in *She Who Is*, they play a crucial role in the book's argument. A case in point is Johnson's discussion of the biblical concept of Sophia. The biblical writers who introduced this image, Johnson argues, were not freely naming God before a limitless horizon of divine mystery. On the contrary, they already knew God "under the revered, unpronounceable name YHWH" (91), and turned to the image of Sophia in order "to universalize the idea of the Jewish God." Their effort was successful because "the controlling context of meaning" remained "the Jewish monotheistic faith" (92), or as Johnson puts it elsewhere, the "divine *self-naming* in the Hebrew Scriptures" (81, with emphasis added).

Here Johnson describes a logic of divine naming that differs markedly from the dominant Dionysian ethos of *She Who Is*. Whereas according to the latter, God's mystery evokes countless names while remaining beyond them all, the former expresses God's mystery by a singular act of "divine self-naming" that sets human "naming toward God" (242) in context and makes it accountable to itself for its truthfulness. By drawing attention to this "other" logic of divine naming at this sensitive point in her proposal, Johnson seems to signal its importance for her own experiment in trinitarian naming. Like Thomas Aquinas before her, it seems, Johnson intends to make room for *two* "most appropriate" names of God, each of which is most appropriate in a different way. There is, as we have seen, the metaphysically resonant name "*Qui est*," rendered by Johnson as "SHE WHO IS," which luminously outlines God's uniqueness against the darkness of divine incomprehensibility. But there is also the name YHWH, which represents God's uniqueness after the fashion of a divinely gifted personal proper name, while remaining utterly dark and opaque in itself.

The reader's expectation that something like this really is Johnson's view is heightened by the following circumstance. At the beginning of her discussion of the name SHE WHO IS, Johnson takes time to ponder God's name revelation to Moses at the burning bush, and points out that God's answer comes in *two* forms, "I am" (Exod. 3:14), and the Tetragrammaton (3:15). She then appeals to none other than Thomas Aquinas himself for understanding the relationship of the names (241–42)! Surely, the reader may think, Johnson means to adopt Thomas's view as her own. It comes as a surprise, therefore, to discover that this is not the case. After briefly identifying several different interpretations of the two names, Johnson turns at last to the one she wishes to endorse:

> Of all the interpretations of the name given at the burning bush, however, the one with the strongest impact on subsequent theological tradition links the name with the metaphysical notion of being. *YHWH means "I am who I am" or simply "I am" in a sense that identifies divine mystery with being itself.* (emphasis added)

As we saw in chapter 4, this is not how Thomas understood the relationship of the names YHWH and "I am who I am." Rather, it is how we speculated a Dionysian theologian might *wish* Thomas had understood them. Thomas, we recall, distinguished the Tetragrammaton sharply from "I am who I am," following the example of Maimonides. Whereas "I am who I am" is rich in meaning, the Tetragrammaton is a pure proper name, with no semantic meaning at all. Thomas's interpretation of the Tetragrammaton was extremely bold, for it meant deviating from a cardinal belief of the Dionysian tradition, that "we name God from creatures." In contrast to Thomas, however, Johnson interprets the Tetragrammaton as a meaning-bearing name that is *equivalent* to "I am who I am." This eliminates the Tetragrammaton's distinctiveness and permits the Dionysian model of divine naming to hold sway unchecked. When at last Johnson summarizes Thomas's climactic account of "The Most Appropriate Name of God," she does not mention the Tetragrammaton at all. "God whose proper name is HE WHO IS is sheer, unimaginable livingness in whose being the whole created universe participates" (242).

In the end, then, it is hard to sustain our original interpretation of the role of the Tetragrammaton in Johnson's presentation, according to which it served to counterbalance and contextualize the Dionysian dynamic of her thought. Human "naming toward God" subsumes *every* divine name in Johnson's theology, *including* the Tetragrammaton. Coherent as this may be from a purely Dionysian perspective, it reopens a question that Johnson herself had wanted to close: whether and to what extent her account of the highest Godhead "is exclusively economic."

Drawing a Balance

She Who Is, a generous and hospitable book, welcomes names without number to give voice to the unfathomable mystery of the Trinity. Even "Father, Son, and Holy Spirit" is welcome, provided it seeks no special privileges. Still, a paradox inheres in the book's hospitality. The Dionysian spirit that animates it insists that every name be a name of the same kind, a creaturely "naming toward God" that unleashes a spark of insight before vanishing into the darkness of ineffable mystery. This creates an *internal* difficulty for Johnson's proposal, for it leaves the reader in the dark concerning Johnson's understanding of the highest Godhead. Does it preserve trinitarian identity, or are the trinitarian elements exclusively economic, existing only on the order of divine manifestation and human experience? Johnson's invocation of the Tetragrammaton seems intended to settle these doubts by gesturing toward an act of *divine self-naming* at the center of biblical tradition. But in the end even the Tetragrammaton is swept up into the vortex of Dionysian naming and ultimately disappears from view.

TWO SCHOOLS AND THEIR DISCONTENTS

Robert Jenson and Elizabeth Johnson are sometimes thought to represent opposite extremes of the modern trinitarian revival. In fact, however, the two theologians agree on many things, even with respect to the status of the kinship language of Father, Son, and Holy Spirit. Jenson agrees that in practice this language has been distorted by patriarchal abuse in the past, and Johnson agrees that in principle it can be understood in a liberative way. Whence, then, the harsh grinding noise when the two proposals come into proximity?

The answer, one might suggest, is that the two theologians champion different strands of a common tradition. Jenson champions the christological vocabulary of Father, Son, and Spirit, while Johnson champions the pneumatological pattern of context-specific ternaries without number. While this is certainly true, I do not think that it gets at the real nature of the tension between their proposals. After all, theologians are entitled to champion different elements of a common tradition as they see necessary in a given case. The real source of the tension, I think, arises from the conflicting way the two theologians *configure* the three patterns of naming the Trinity, with which both are concerned.

Standing in the Reformation tradition with its subterranean influence of the Christian Kabbalah, Jenson configures the three patterns in a way that mirrors the logic of subordinationism. He assigns supremacy to the "Father,

Son, and Holy Spirit" and subordinates the other two patterns to it: the Tetragrammaton is its salvation-historical forerunner, and the pneumatological pattern is its ecclesial-technical expositor. Johnson, meanwhile, standing in the Dionysian tradition, with its subterranean influence of Neoplatonism, configures the three patterns in a way that mirrors the logic of modalism. For Johnson, the differences between the three patterns are only passing distinctions, for all ultimately express the pneumatological pattern, which celebrates the nameless God of many names. The grinding noise comes from these two incompatible configurations when they try—unsuccessfully—to mesh gears.

Sharp disagreement is a hallmark of living traditions. But sometimes disagreement signals an intractable problem in the common tradition that prevailing schools are unable to solve. The result is destructive conflict *between* schools, and perplexing contradictions *within* them. I think that the failure of the Dionysian and Reformation schools to think about how to name the persons of the Trinity in a way that recognizes the equal place and role of all the available patterns is a problem of this kind. The failure turns legitimate disagreements into intractable conflicts, as we see in the contemporary "inclusive-language debate." And it creates problems of coherence within the schools themselves, as illustrated by the curious fate of the Tetragrammaton in the proposals of Jenson and Johnson.

7

"Well, What IS the Name, Then?"

> "The name of the song is called 'HADDOCKS' EYES.'"
>
> "Oh, that's the name of the song, is it?" Alice said, trying to feel interested.
>
> "No, you don't understand," the Knight said, looking a little vexed. "That's what the name is CALLED. The name really IS 'THE AGED AGED MAN.'"
>
> "Then I ought to have said, 'That's what the SONG is called'?" Alice corrected herself.
>
> "No, you oughtn't: that's quite another thing! The SONG is called 'WAYS AND MEANS': but that's only what it's CALLED, you know!"
>
> "Well, what IS the song, then?" said Alice, who was by this time completely bewildered.
>
> "I was coming to that," the Knight said. "The song really IS 'A-SITTING ON A GATE': and the tune's my own invention."
>
> —*Lewis Carroll*[1]

Readers who have persevered to the end of this long historical survey may identify with poor Alice. What began with a reasonably clear question—"How has the Christian tradition named the persons of the Trinity?"—has ended with eye-crossing complexities. In hopes of retaining (or regaining) the reader's goodwill, I will recount the main lessons of our journey thus far and indicate something of the road ahead, under four headings:

Three Patterns of Naming the Persons of the Holy Trinity . . .
  When Configured in Non-Trinitarian Ways . . .
    Generate Problems . . .
      That Might Prove Resolvable If Configured in a Trinitarian Way.

THREE PATTERNS OF NAMING THE PERSONS OF THE HOLY TRINITY . . .

Down through the centuries, the Christian tradition has named the persons of the Holy Trinity in more than one way. No less an authority than the Nicene Creed uses three patterns of naming to identify the three persons, both in themselves and in relationship to one another:

- A pattern characterized by the oblique reference to the Tetragrammaton
- A pattern characterized by the vocabulary of Father, Son, and Holy Spirit
- A pattern characterized by the open-ended multiplicity of names

For convenience's sake, I have referred to these three patterns as the theological, christological, and pneumatological patterns respectively. In the Nicene Creed, the three patterns are clearly distinct, intimately interrelated, and equally important. In this sense, the creed configures the patterns in a *trinitarian* way, which mirrors the distinction, equality, and mutual relation of the three persons of the Holy Trinity.

WHEN CONFIGURED IN NON-TRINITARIAN WAYS . . .

For the most part, however, the Christian tradition has not followed the example of the Nicene Creed, for a simple reason. It lost the capacity to recognize the New Testament's witness to a pattern of trinitarian naming centered in oblique reference to the Tetragrammaton (the theological pattern). Without this capacity, Christian theologians have tended to configure the patterns of naming in ways that deviate, in one fashion or another, from the distinction, equality, and interrelatedness expressed by the creed.

The fourth century was a time of major developments in this regard. Already by the dawn of the century, Christians seem to have largely lost the ability to recognize the theological pattern of naming at all. Evidence of the pattern surrounded Christians on all sides—in their Scripture, creeds, and liturgy—but they could not see it due to fading awareness of the Tetragrammaton. In effect, Christians became color-blind to the difference between the theological and pneumatological patterns, so that the former seemed to vanish even as the latter became nearly ubiquitous. Meanwhile, Christians understood the christological and pneumatological patterns in new ways as well. By the end of the fourth century, Christian orthodoxy had achieved a hard-fought consensus regarding the doctrine of the Trinity, expressed in the newly clarified distinction between the three persons and the one divine essence of the Holy Trinity. An important achievement in its own right, the distinction drew in its wake how Christians understood the relationship of the christological and pneumatological patterns. The former became *the* way par excellence of identifying the three persons of the Holy Trinity (Father, Son, and Holy Spirit), while the latter became chiefly a way of naming the one divine essence (in the culturally refracted form of the dialectic of divine polyonymy and anonymity).

Over time, schools of Christian thought reclaimed for the theological and pneumatological patterns something of what they had lost with respect to the work of naming the three persons of the Holy Trinity. Augustine of Hippo reclaimed the tradition of exploring the divine persons via an open-ended variety of names, and Thomas Aquinas reclaimed the Tetragrammaton as a way of naming the one divine essence. The Reformation tradition went still further in this last respect, by recognizing in the Tetragrammaton a distinctive way of identifying the persons of the Trinity, in themselves and in relationship to one another.

Yet in the final analysis, neither the Dionysian nor the Reformation tradition succeeded in configuring the three patterns of naming on analogy with the Nicene Creed, which gives each of the three patterns equal prominence and weight. Thomas's account of the Tetragrammaton pertains only to the divine essence and not to the three persons as such. And even so, it occupies a vanishingly small place in his thought, wholly out of proportion to the attention he gives to the pneumatological and christological patterns. In contrast, the Reformation tradition accords a much more robust place to the theological pattern and recognizes it as a way of naming the persons of the Trinity. Still, even the Reformation confines the theological pattern's relevance to the Old Testament and maintains that it has been superseded in the New. Thus neither school fully follows the precedent of the Nicene Creed. Neither treats the patterns as distinct, interrelated, and equally important ways of naming the persons of the Trinity in the context of the economy of salvation in its New Testament form.

GENERATE PROBLEMS . . .

The gap between the way the Nicene Creed configures the three patterns, and the way subsequent traditions do, contributes to the emergence of a variety of problems, difficulties, and puzzles. Arguably, the chief of these is the simple fact that the Nicene Creed's precedent on such a sensitive issue is not followed by traditions that regard it as the standard of orthodoxy!

But other problems arise as well, both between and within traditions. Failure to weight the patterns equally creates the conditions for intractable conflict between different schools of thought. This, in large measure, has been the story of the Dionysian and Reformation schools. The schools concur on the centrality of the christological pattern, but they disagree on how it should be "approached" and safeguarded. For the Dionysian tradition, the correct approach is via the pneumatological pattern, and specifically by way of philosophically disciplined reflection on the one divine essence. For the Reformation tradition, the grand highway is scripturally disciplined reflection on the uniqueness of the biblical God as expressed in the divine name, the Tetragrammaton. The result is deep-going conflict between the schools, not so much because the schools adopt different approaches (that is what schools do), but because the schools do not understand their approaches as leading ultimately to the equal importance of all three patterns. Karl Barth's full-throated rejection of the Augustinian tradition of *vestigia trinitatis* reflects this failure from one side, as does the general inability of the Dionysian tradition to make room for the Tetragrammaton on the other. Similarly, the intractability of the modern inclusive-language debate stems in part from the zero-sum nature of the underlying conflict between the Dionysian and Reformation traditions.

Anomalies also crop up that are internal to the traditions themselves and to individual thinkers within them. In the case of Pseudo-Dionysius, the imperative of apophatic negation threatens to erase the Godhead's trinitarian features, or confine them from the outset to a culturally provincial conception of deity (a danger that looms over the whole Dionysian tradition). Again, in the case of Thomas, we encounter the oddity that the most inviolable rule of divine naming—that we "name God from creatures"—is sublimely ignored by one of the two "most appropriate" names of God, the Tetragrammaton. On the Reformation side, the vaunted imperative of naming God exclusively from "revelation" continuously obscures the fact that it has pleased God to make "revelation" unintelligible apart from the church's reliance on intellectual resources that belong to the wider culture. In Barth, this blind spot takes a particularly ironic form. In the name of combating the Thomistic error of natural theology, Barth assigns unique importance to the name *Yahweh-Kyrios* as the guarantor of scriptural integrity of his naming of God as Revealer, Revelation, and Revealedness. In point of fact, however, it is a neologism that resolves ultimately into the concept "lordship," leaving the Tetragrammaton in a place far beneath that assigned to it by—Thomas Aquinas!

We could draw attention to more such oddities, but this suffices to suggest a path forward. By restoring to its rightful place the theological pattern of naming the persons of the Trinity, centered in oblique reference to the Tetragrammaton, we can open the door once again to a balanced interpretation of the three patterns of naming the persons of the Trinity, one that accords each of them a secure place in the whole economy of divine names.

THAT MIGHT PROVE RESOLVABLE IF CONFIGURED IN A TRINITARIAN WAY

In part 2 of this book, therefore, I want to explore the possibility that each of the three available patterns represents a "most appropriate" way of naming the persons of the Holy Trinity, each time from the perspective of one of the persons of the Trinity. Accordingly, the three patterns are to be understood "in a trinitarian way," as distinct, interrelated, and equally important. Such an approach is not only consistent with the defining beliefs of the Christian tradition, as expressed by the Nicene Creed, but also has the potential to give these beliefs fresh and powerful expression. Furthermore, it may help resolve formerly intractable problems that arise when the patterns are configured in non-trinitarian ways.

Part Two

Distinguishing the Voices

The Name of the Trinity in the Scriptures of the Old and New Testaments

Introduction to Part Two

Oh that I knew how all thy lights combine,
  And the configurations of their glorie!
Seeing not onely how each verse doth shine,
  But all the constellations of the storie.

—*George Herbert*[1]

What is the most appropriate way of naming the persons of the Holy Trinity? In part 2, we will seek to answer this question by listening again to the primal sources of the Christian tradition, the Scriptures of the Old and New Testaments. The answer most in keeping with this witness, I will propose, is that there are three most appropriate ways, each of which is most appropriate by virtue of its special affinity with one person of the Trinity in particular.

This part of our investigation into the doctrine of the Trinity will be an exercise in the theological interpretation of Scripture, or better, perhaps, in biblical dogmatics. By whatever name, it straddles the line between systematic theology and scriptural interpretation. It is more occupied with scriptural exegesis than is much contemporary systematic theology, and more avowedly theological than much biblical exegesis. Although this combination of interests has become more common in recent years, a word about my specific assumptions is in order.[2]

A first assumption I make is that it is possible to arrive at a deepened understanding of the Scriptures by reading them in light of the church's doctrinal traditions. This is what might be called the catholic moment in my approach to biblical interpretation. While my goal is to describe the Scripture's testimony as fully and faithfully as possible, I make no claim to reading the Scripture from a neutral or disinterested vantage point. On the contrary, I avowedly bring to my reading of the Bible certain elements of Christian tradition (to be discussed later in this volume, at the appropriate time) to serve as a guide. I do not do so reluctantly, fearful that my reliance on church doctrine will distort my vision, but gratefully, trusting that it will guide me to see things that I might otherwise miss.

A second assumption that informs my approach is that it is possible to arrive at a deepened understanding of Christian teaching by interpreting it in light of the Scriptures. This is what might be called the evangelical moment in my approach. By returning to the Scriptures, the primal sources of Christian tradition, I believe that it is possible to purify, deepen, and renew inherited doctrinal insights. In the particular case at hand, the aspect of church teaching that I am trying to understand better is how Christians most appropriately name the persons of the Trinity. My assumption, simply put, is that by listening again to the witness of the Old and New Testaments, I can deepen and enrich existing accounts of how Christians most appropriately identify the persons of the Holy Trinity.

My two working assumptions do indeed imply a circularity of method. Still, I think that it is a benign circularity that parallels the church's experience with Scripture over time. The church has *always* come to the Scriptures with hermeneutical presuppositions that have been shaped, in part, by its own *previous* encounters with Scripture (the catholic moment). Each new encounter with Scripture, in turn, has had the capacity to purify, deepen, and extend existing insights (the evangelical moment). One expression of this virtuous circle, which also provides inspiration for this study, is the *nomina sacra*, the ancient system of orthography discussed in chapter 2. From the start (or very close to it), Christians read Scripture "glossed" by the original four *nomina sacra*—$\overline{\mathrm{K\Sigma}}$, $\overline{\Theta\Sigma}$, $\overline{\mathrm{I H \Sigma}}$, and $\overline{\mathrm{X\Sigma}}$ (Lord, God, Jesus, and Christ)—which guided the reading of the Bible by emphasizing terms drawn from the Shema and the name "Jesus Christ." But the Bible, thus interpreted, acted back upon the *nomina sacra* in turn, prompting scribes to add new names to the original list, such as Father, Son, Spirit, and others.

A final word concerns the limits of my investigation. In part 2, my focus will be the question of how to name the persons of the Trinity *as revealed in the economy of salvation*. In this volume I will *not* try to draw consequences for how Christians most appropriately name the immanent or eternal Trinity.[3] Readers should recognize that this implies a significant limitation to the scope of the present volume. The thesis that there are three "most appropriate" ways of naming the persons of the Trinity can be fully sustained only by addressing *both* the Trinity's self-revelation in the economy of salvation *and* its implications for our understanding of the eternal Trinity. Because the present volume is focused only on the first of these, its conclusions must be regarded as a kind of "preliminary report," pending further examination and testing in volume 2 of this work, *The Divine Name(s) and the Holy Trinity: Voices in Counterpoint.*

Why limit the scope of our investigation in this volume in this way? The reason is this: The economy of salvation is the source of everything Christians dare to affirm about the eternal Trinity. Hence, it makes sense to first describe the Trinity's self-naming in the economy of salvation as fully and carefully as possible, before proceeding cautiously to draw conclusions about the eternal Trinity. By limiting ourselves in the present volume to the question of the Trinity's self-naming in the economy, we protect ourselves from a premature appeal to the immanent Trinity, which might distort our ultimate conclusions by truncating what we learn by attending patiently to the witness of the Scriptures.

8

Declaring the Name of Lord in the Old Testament I

Divine Uniqueness, Presence, and Blessing in the Book of Exodus

The Bible never explicitly asks or answers the question "What is the most appropriate way of naming the persons of the Trinity?" What it does do, however, is testify to God's *name declaration* and to its important place in the economy of salvation. Indeed, if the scriptural witness to the economy of salvation has something like a spine or backbone, it is apt to be found very near God's *name declaration*, a theme that runs through the Scriptures from Genesis to Revelation like (to change metaphors) a mighty mountain chain. In this chapter and the three that follow, my aim is to trace the contours of God's name declaration as these emerge over the course of the Christian canon, with the aim of showing how they ultimately yield what we may justifiably call three most appropriate ways of naming the persons of the Holy Trinity.

THE UNITY-IN-DIFFERENCE OF THE OLD AND NEW TESTAMENTS

My approach to Scripture, as I stated, makes no claim to being neutral or disinterested. I avowedly bring to my reading of Scripture certain elements of Christian tradition to serve as a guide, trusting that they will help me to see things that I might otherwise miss. A first doctrinal constellation on which I will lean concerns the relationship of the Old and New Testaments. While differences of emphasis and nuance abound, the Christian tradition has nevertheless concurred on two cardinal points:

- The Old and New Testaments comprise a single coherent witness to the Holy Trinity and to the Trinity's gracious works in the economy of salvation.
- The mystery of the Trinity is anticipated by the Old Testament's witness to the "one God," yet first openly revealed in the context of the New Testament's witness to the Spirit-empowered sending of Jesus Christ and the Christ-centered outpouring of the Holy Spirit.

If both of these affirmations are true, as I take them to be, then we can draw a couple of inferences for our present topic with a high degree of confidence.

- We can expect the Old Testament's witness to God's name declaration to introduce certain themes that are recognizably sustained throughout the rest of the canon. If it did not, then the first point above would not obtain, and the canon's unity would fall to the ground.
- We can also expect the New Testament's witness to God's name declaration to evince a perfectly harmonized blend of *consistency* and *novelty* vis-à-vis that of the Old Testament. For, again, if it did not, the second point would not obtain, and the distinctiveness of the New Testament's witness falls to the ground.[1]

Again, I think these assumptions stand very near the center of the church's consensus regarding the unity-in-difference of the Old Testament and New Testament. Together they guide our interpretation of the Scripture's witness to God's name declaration by alerting us to dangers on either side, like opposing shoals of a narrow harbor. They alert us to the danger of undervaluing the *consistency* of the canon's witness on the one side, an error that leads in the extreme case to Marcionism; and they alert us to the danger of undervaluing the *novelty* of the New Testament's witness on the other, an error that minimizes the decisiveness of the incarnation and the outpouring of the Holy Spirit for a Christian understanding of God. A test of any interpretation of God's name declaration in the Christian canon—including this one—is whether it safely sails past these two shoals.

In this chapter and the next, then, our aim is to trace the contours of the Old Testament's witness to God's name declaration, putting special emphasis on those contours that extend into the New Testament and enliven its witness as well. The specific focus of this chapter is the book of Exodus.

GOD'S NAME DECLARATION IN PRIMORDIAL FORM: EXODUS 20:24

Our first text is a single verse from Exodus 20. To this point in the story, God's actions have constituted one mighty display of God's incomparable uniqueness, one great demonstration that "I am the Lord" (Exod. 6:6, 8, 29; 12:12; 15:26; etc.). As moments internal to this display, as it were, God has acted graciously toward Israel, by coming to rescue it from Egypt, and by blessing the people with the gift of the law, encapsulated in the Ten Commandments. Just so, by coming to Abraham's descendants and blessing them, God has fulfilled the promise he made at the beginning: "You shall know that I am the Lord" (Exod. 6:7).

But now an implicit question hangs in the air: What next? What can possibly happen now that this promise has been fulfilled, that is not either an anticlimax on the one hand or a non sequitur on the other? God himself provides the answer in Exodus 20:24, a verse that follows immediately after the giving of the Ten Commandments:

> In every place where I cause my name to be remembered
> I will come to you
> and bless you. (Exod. 20:24b)

These words gather together everything God has done heretofore—demonstrate his uniqueness, enact his presence, bestow his blessing—and reinstates them as a promise that qualifies Israel's history, and the world's, for all time to come. *God will cause his name to be remembered, and wherever this happens, there he will come again and bless again.* By proving faithful to this promise, God's future way with Israel and the world will exhibit both consistency and novelty vis-à-vis who he has already shown himself to be and what he has already done in the past.

Brief as it is, Exodus 20:24 enunciates several themes of great importance not only to the book of Exodus but also to the church's whole canon:

1. The first of these is the incomparable uniqueness of God. To say that God is unique is to say more than that he is one in a numerical sense. It is to say that God is *this* one, who can be likened to no other. In Exodus 20:24 this theme is sounded by the pronoun "I," by the string of active verbs, and above all by the phrase "my name." Just as God is unique and without comparison, so too his name (Heb. *shem*), which in this context refers *both* to God's personal proper name, the Tetragrammaton, *and also* to the cloud of association that clings to it, that is, to God's reputation, honor, and glory. Between God's I, his name (*shem*), and the name's own dense cloud of connotation, there is a harmony that belongs to God's very being as God. God's business in the world is to make this harmony known, to announce it, repeat it, develop it, vindicate it, and glorify it without end. Nothing the Bible says about God's name declaration in the Old or New Testaments can be understood apart from this first and most basic theme.[2]

2. A second theme announced in Exodus 20:24 concerns the intimate relation that exists between God's uniqueness on the one hand and his "coming"

and "blessing" on the other. All of the benefits that God has to bestow are comprehended in God's uniqueness, but they are applied by God's presence and blessing. To put it another way, if God is zealous on behalf of his name and its glory, then he expresses this zeal quite specifically by these two activities above all. Coming and blessing are, as it were, the preferred ways God elaborates, vindicates, and magnifies the harmony first announced by his name.

3. A final theme important to our passage is the relationship of God's self-naming to the human naming of God. The latter is important to our verse: "To remember God's name" means quite specifically to use it in worship, in invocation, petition, thanksgiving, and praise. The point to notice, however, is that God retains the initiative in determining how this will happen. God "causes" the people to remember his name, in the place of his own choosing, following rules that he has set down beforehand. God's rules are simple and salutary: they prohibit the worship of other gods and require altars made only of earth or uncut stone (Exod. 24:24–25). Even so, it is clear: God's use of the divine name enables its proper human use and provides a standard and criterion for such use.

THE NAME THEOPHANIES OF THE BOOK OF EXODUS

The subtle nexus of patterns primordially expressed in Exodus 20:24 reappears over the rest of the book of Exodus countless times, with many variations of detail and emphasis. At bottom, everything the Old Testament tells us about God's name declaration—no, everything the Christian canon tells us—is an elaboration of the patterns encoded in this verse. The purpose of the rest of this chapter is to make good on this claim with specific reference to the three great name theophanies of the book of Exodus: Exodus 3; 6; and 32–34. Exodus 6 is the simplest of the three, and so we begin with it.[3]

God's Name Declaration in Exodus 6

As the scene opens, God tells a bitterly discouraged Moses that he will indeed deliver the Israelites from Pharaoh, despite the negligible progress made so far. As though to drive home this word of comfort, God speaks the following words:

> "I am the Lord. [3]I appeared to Abraham, Isaac, and Jacob as God Almighty, but by my name 'The Lord' I did not make myself known to them. [4]I also established my covenant with them, to give them the land of Canaan, the land in which they resided as aliens. [5]I have also

> heard the groaning of the Israelites whom the Egyptians are holding as slaves, and I have remembered my covenant. [6]Say therefore to the Israelites, 'I am the Lord, and I will free you from the burdens of the Egyptians and deliver you from slavery to them. I will redeem you with an outstretched arm and with mighty acts of judgment. [7]I will take you as my people, and I will be your God. You shall know that I am the Lord your God, who has freed you from the burdens of the Egyptians. [8]I will bring you into the land that I swore to give to Abraham, Isaac, and Jacob; I will give it to you for a possession. I am the Lord.'" (Exod. 6:2b–8)

According to Walther Zimmerli, the basic picture here is that of "an unnamed someone" who "steps out of that unknown state by revealing his personal name, by making it recognizable."[4] Despite the enduring value of Zimmerli's classic study, he exaggerates slightly at this point. God was not previously *unknown* before his appearance to Moses, since he "appeared" formerly to the patriarchs as "God Almighty" (v. 3). The point is that God did not then "make myself known to them" *by the divine name* (lit., "but my name YHWH I did not *announce* to them").[5] This gap in the patriarch's knowledge is crucial. For despite it, God is still making good on his promises to them. The implication is clear. If God can be counted on to honor a pledge contracted as "God Almighty," *then how much more*, we are to understand, can he be counted on to perform what he now promises to do on the strength of the divine *name*, the Tetragrammaton.

For indeed, it is the Tetragrammaton that is the center of the passage. "I am the Lord" anchors the divine speech at beginning and end, like the fixed poles of a vibrating string, and it appears again near the speech's exact middle, the point of a sounding string's greatest amplitude. The "fundamental" tone of the speech, we may safely say, is the affirmation of God's uniqueness, of God's who-ness, of God's incomparable identity and the sovereign mystery, especially as all this is contained in God's *name*. In 6:3 God emphasizes the peerless status of the Tetragrammaton, both by designating it alone as "my *name*" (*shem*)—a practice followed elsewhere in the canon with almost perfect consistency—and also by a significant shift of verbs. Previously God "appeared" (*wa'era'*) to the patriarchs as God Almighty (*El Shaddai*) but did not "announce to them [*lo' noda'ti lahem*] my name YHWH." God thereby signals that the announcement of God's name marks a new and decisive step in his dealings with Israel and with the world.[6]

With this, our attention shifts to the passage's "overtones," the promises God makes to Moses. There are two sets of promises, whose contents correspond to the pattern of Exodus 20:24b, "I will come to you and bless you." In 6:6b, we find the promises of God's coming. God vows to demonstrate God's saving nearness with "mighty acts of judgment," that is, dramatic, onetime events that accomplish their purpose and then recede into the past. God will "free you from the burdens of the Egyptians," "deliver you from slavery," and "redeem you with an outstretched arm." In verse 7, we discover the promises of God's blessing. Here the emphasis falls on God's creation of lasting, life-giving relationships that flourish into the future. "I will take you as my people, and I will be your God"; "I will bring you into the land"; "I will give it to you for a possession."

Among God's promised blessings, we find this especially important vow: "You shall know that I am the Lord your God" (6:7). Here God's basic self-declaration appears in an augmented form, looking forward to the end result that is to be accomplished by the fulfillment of all God's promises. When God has performed all that he has said, God's name declaration will reach its goal in the creation's knowledge of God's uniqueness. Israel will arrive again at the beginning—"I am the Lord" (6:8)–and know it for the first time (6:7). Significantly, the verse identifies God in a way that elaborates the Tetragrammaton with the theonym "God," a cousin of which also appeared in the cognomen "God Almighty" (El Shaddai). By this we may understand that saving history reaches its goal in a knowledge of God that is anchored in the divine name even as it is amplified and expounded by other divine names.

God's Name Declaration in Exodus 3:1–18

Whereas Exodus 6 *begins* with God's self-naming, Exodus 3 *builds* toward it with consummate literary artistry. In the story of the burning bush, we find what may rightly be called the Bible's only description of the *revelation* of his name, for it is the only passage that clearly purports to relate the original disclosure of his name, if not generally, then at least to Moses. In a sense, every other account of God's name declaration is but a repetition and explication of this inexhaustible event.

After calling to Moses from the bush, and warning him to remove his sandals, God speaks words that resonate with God's uniqueness, presence, and blessing:

God's uniqueness:	I am the God of your father, the God of Abraham, the God of Isaac, and the God of Jacob. (v. 6)
God's presence:	I have observed the misery of my people who are in Egypt; I have heard their cry on account of their taskmasters. Indeed, I know their sufferings, and I have come down to deliver them from the Egyptians, (vv. 7–8a)

God's blessing:	and to bring them up out of that land to a good and broad land, a land flowing with milk and honey, to the country of the Canaanites, the Hittites, the Amorites, the Perizzites, the Hivites, and the Jebusites. (v. 8b)

God's initial self-introduction makes no reference to the Tetragrammaton and instead provides what we might call an identifying description that connects God with the patriarchs of old. The divine uniqueness is visible, but as though at a great and hazy distance. The vagueness of God's initial self-introduction creates an uneasy sense of narrative tension that lurks beneath the surface of the story and drives it forward.

Sensing, perhaps, that God's commission rests on the insecure foundation of God's fuzzy self-introduction, Moses deflects it by questioning the adequacy of his own person. He echoes back God's words in the key of deferral and self-abnegation:

Uniqueness:	Who am I
Presence:	that I should go to Pharaoh,
Blessing:	and bring the Israelites out of Egypt? (v. 11)

God responds with words of reassurance:

God's presence:	I will be with you;
God's uniqueness:	and this shall be the sign for you that it is I who sent you:
God's blessing:	when you have brought the people out of Egypt, you shall worship God on this mountain. (v. 12)

Notice the abrupt reversal of the familiar order of uniqueness and presence. Now the affirmation of presence comes first, as though to shore up Moses' confidence at its weakest point. Meanwhile, however, the character of God's uniqueness has become, if anything, murkier than ever. God promises to give Moses a sign that it is really "I who sent you." But since God offers to give this sign only after such a time as all doubt must be resolved, one way or the other, it is not clear what good it does Moses now. Nor, indeed, is it clear what purpose such a sign could serve in any case. After all, Moses can scarcely doubt that it is "I who sent you." The question that oppresses him, rather, is "Who is this 'I,' anyway?"

And so Moses asks the natural question:

> If I come to the Israelites and say to them, "The God of your ancestors has sent me to you," and they ask me, "What is his name?" what shall I say to them? (v. 13)

God's answer, we must observe at the outset, is threefold. He replies, and replies again, and replies again. Christians have a long and strangely tenacious history of overlooking this fact or otherwise obscuring it, a point we have already had occasion to notice. For the record, then, God's three replies to Moses' question are as follows:

> I am who I am [*'ehyeh asher 'ehyeh*] (v. 14a)
> I am [*'ehyeh*] (v. 14b)
> YHWH [*yhwh*] (v. 15)

Furthermore, we must insist without further ado, of these replies, it is the last that offers the climactic and decisive answer to Moses' question. This conclusion has been foreshadowed from the beginning of the passage by the requirements of literary composition, which demand that the story's building suspense be resolved by the *last* of three replies. But the conclusion becomes simply inescapable when one takes the time to examine God's three replies in their larger literary context. We therefore quote Exodus 3:14–18:

> 14God said to Moses, "I am who I am." He said further, "Thus you
> shall say to the Israelites, 'I am has sent me to you.'" 15God also said
> to Moses, "Thus you shall say to the Israelites, 'The LORD, the God of your ancestors, the God of Abraham, the God of Isaac, and the God of Jacob, has sent me to you':
> This is my name forever,
> and this my title for all generations.
> 16Go and assemble the elders of Israel, and say to them,
>
> 'The LORD, the God of your ancestors, the God of Abraham, of Isaac, and of Jacob, has appeared to me, saying: I have given heed
> to you and to what has been done to you in Egypt. 17I declare that
> I will bring you up out of the misery of Egypt, to the land of the Canaanites, the Hittites, the Amorites, the Perizzites, the Hivites, and the Jebusites, a land flowing with milk and honey.'
>
> 18They will listen to your voice; and you and the elders of Israel shall go to the king of Egypt and say to him, 'The LORD, the God of the Hebrews, has met with us; let us now go a three days' journey into the wilderness, so that we may sacrifice to the LORD our God.'"[7]

Upon careful examination, this passage clearly indicates that God does indeed satisfy Moses' request for God's name, and that he does so by means of the last of his three replies, and by means of it alone. God's other replies are never really even in serious contention. For one thing, God amplifies only the Tetragrammaton with the words, "This is my name forever" (v. 15). For another, God connects only the Tetragrammaton with the original self-designation, "the God of Abraham, of Isaac, and of Jacob," thus explicitly resolving the narrative tension that has been building from the beginning of the passage (v. 16). Finally, God assumes only of the Tetragrammaton that it will be accepted and indeed used by the elders of Israel, which was, of course, the point of Moses' question in the first place (v. 18).

For the purposes of this chapter, however, there is an even more telling way in which this passage signals the climactic significance of the Tetragrammaton. Of God's three replies, only it appears in conjunction with the characteristic motifs of God's self-declaration: divine presence and blessing. Indeed, it does so twice. The first time is in the words that God instructs Moses to speak to the elders:

> God's uniqueness: The LORD, the God of your ancestors, the God of Abraham, of Isaac, and of Jacob,
> God's presence: has appeared to me, saying: I have given heed to you and to what has been done to you in Egypt. [17]I declare that I will bring you up out of the misery of Egypt,
> God's blessing: to the land of the Canaanites, the Hittites, the Amorites, the Perizzites, the Hivites, and the Jebusites, a land flowing with milk and honey. (vv. 16–17)

The second time is in the words that God foretells the elders will speak to Pharaoh.

> God's uniqueness: The LORD, the God of the Hebrews,
> God's presence: has met with us;
> God's blessing: let us now go a three days' journey into the wilderness, so that we may sacrifice to the LORD our God. (v. 18)

These verses seldom receive even a small fraction of the attention that is poured on verses 14–15. Nevertheless, they are supremely important. In these verses, God revisits the wonderful promises he originally made to Moses and repeats them, now backing them up with the full faith and credit of his name, the Tetragrammaton. God declares his name, not once, not twice, but thrice (vv. 16a, 18a, 18b), and thereby sweeps away the haze of ambiguity that formerly surrounded God's uniqueness. What is more, God presents his promises of presence and blessing in a new, more brilliant light. According to verse 18, the elders of Israel will profess before Pharaoh that *they themselves* have met with the LORD, and they will proclaim that God is "the LORD *our God.*"

In sum, Exodus 3:1–18 has been carefully composed to emphasize the singular status of the Tetragrammaton as the linguistic token par excellence of

God's uniqueness, and therefore the guarantor par excellence of God's promised presence and blessing.[8]

Exodus 3:14: "I am who I am" and "I am"

But if so, how should we understand God's first two replies to Moses, "I am who I am" and "I am"? Bernard Joseph Ratzinger, writing before he became Pope Benedict XVI, points us in the right direction: "God gave a name to himself in front of Moses and clarified it in the formula: 'I am who I am.'" "I am who I am" and "I AM" are not themselves the divine name but clarifications of it. Even if the Christian tradition has sometimes allowed these commentaries to overshadow the text on which they comment, still their towering significance is beyond dispute.[9]

A striking feature of God's first reply, "I am who I am," is that it is a complete sentence, a complete thought in its own right. It differs in this way from God's other replies, both of which are parts of the larger sentence: "Thus you shall say to the Israelites, X . . . has sent me to you" (3:14b). The sheer self-sufficiency of "I am who I am" contributes much to its mystery. Lacking every external contextual clue, one cannot initially tell how the reply bears on Moses' question. Is it an answer? A rebuff? The prelude to an answer yet to come? To someone who enters the story from Moses' perspective, God's first reply might be any of these, or something else yet again.

What is crystal clear is that "I am who I am" is a tautology.[10] With these words, God declares who he is by referring God to—God! And that, I believe, is the key point. When God first introduced himself at the beginning of the story, God expressed who he is in a relative way: "I am the God of your father, the God of Abraham, the God of Isaac, and the God of Jacob" (3:6). Now, prompted by Moses' question, God expresses who he is absolutely: "I am who I am." Whether or not this is God's *name* is not yet clear. What is clear is that God has expressed his uniqueness in a way that is dependent on nothing else besides God. Viewed in this light, the question of translating the phrase proves to be less important than is sometimes supposed. Any translation that preserves the saying's tautologous character conveys the crucial point, whether it be "I am who I am," or "I will be who I will be," or "I will be there as the One I will be there."

Narrowly considered, God's second reply, "I am," is just a shortened version of the first. Coming on the heels of "I am who I am," it reverberates with something of the original's serenely self-contained character. Viewed in its larger literary context, however, God's second reply sets out afresh. For "I am" is no longer nestled inside a tautology, but the subject of a sentence (a synthetic sentence, in Kant's terminology) that *is* responsive to Moses' question:

Thus you shall say to the Israelites, "*I am* has sent me to you." (3:14b)

These words shimmer with unexpected humor, like a wink after a long, inscrutable gaze. God's first reply, it now appears, was not a rebuff after all, or at least not a total one. Rather, it provides the necessary prologue that will enable Moses to understand God's *second* reply. Hidden within the serene self-sufficiency of "I am who I am" was a genuine answer to Moses' question, an answer that now openly appears in God's readiness to come to the aid of Moses and Israel. We might paraphrase the deep logic of God's first two answers this way: I am "I am who I am"; *therefore* I can be "I am who I am" *for you.*

We have barely scratched the surface of this endlessly fascinating verse. But however tempting it is to tarry, we must not box off Exodus 3:14 from what comes next. Although we cannot regard 3:14 as God's *climactic* reply to Moses' request for a name (for reasons explained above), we should nevertheless recognize that it bears upon the interpretation of 3:15 in a very important way. Prior to God's further reply in 3:15, it is not yet clear (at least from Moses' point of view) that "I am who I am" and "I am" are *wordplays* that anticipate a reply yet to come: the Tetragrammaton. In light of 3:15, however, it becomes clear that God's initial replies are *puns* that anticipate and elucidate God's third and final answer to Moses: the Tetragrammaton. This truth is inevitably lost in translation, but it is important nevertheless. "I am who I am" and "I am" are *not* self-enclosed after all, at least not in this respect. *They are God's own playful commentaries on God's name, the Tetragram.* Taken by themselves, "I am who I am" and "I am" might equally well be the self-enunciation of any deity. Seen in light of Exodus 3:15, however, they are the uniquely apt self-description of the God whose name is YHWH.

Exodus 3:14 and 3:15 Together

God's replies to Moses' question express God's uniqueness, each in a different way. "I am who I am" and "I am" express God's uniqueness by virtue of what they *mean*, albeit with subtle differences of color. The Tetragrammaton, in contrast to both, expresses God's uniqueness merely by what it *is*.[11] These two main ways of expressing God's uniqueness illuminate and protect each other. The Christian tradition has not always recognized this. On one side, it has sometimes become so enthralled by the radiance of Exodus 3:14 that it has failed to register 3:15 altogether. On the other, it has sometimes sought to reclaim the importance of 3:15 by repudiating the tradition of theological reflection on 3:14. Both extremes are unfortunate. In truth, both "I am" and the Tetragrammaton are "most appropriate" names of God, albeit in fundamentally different ways, as Thomas Aquinas recognized long ago. "I am who I am" illuminates and protects our understanding of the Tetragrammaton by driving home the insight that God's uniqueness is beyond every finite category, even (or perhaps especially) the category of named gods of the ancient Middle East. *Deus non est in genere*![12] Yet the Tetragrammaton also illuminates and protects our understanding of "I am who I am" by referring even this august description to the living God who bears the divine name.

Nevertheless, if there is no relationship of superiority and inferiority between these two kinds of names, there is a relationship of priority and logical sequence. The Tetragrammaton precedes "I am who I am," not in a literary or temporal sense, but in a logical sense, by virtue of its status as a personal proper name that fixes the referent of biblical discourse and of every other discourse that aspires to move in the orbit of the God attested by Scripture. The Tetragrammaton, we might say, leans on "I am who I am" for its elucidation in the language of "Being." But language about Being becomes discourse about the one true God only insofar as it willingly yields to the priority of the Tetragrammaton. Whenever Christian theology overlooks or withholds or denies this priority, it threatens its own integrity from within. For if the names of Exodus 3:14 were to disappear, the rest of the canon's witness to the living God would remain, however much our understanding of it might be impoverished. But if the divine name of Exodus 3:15 were to disappear, the canon itself would cease to exist as sacred Scripture.

God's Name Declaration in Exodus 32–34

The last name theophany recounted in the book of Exodus occurs immediately after Israel's primordial sin: the worship of the golden calf. The story uses God's name declaration to explore how God responds to Israel's catastrophic failure to be what it was called into being to be: the people where God "causes God's name to be remembered" (cf. Exod. 20:24). The story illustrates how the proper name YHWH, though void of any conventional semantic meaning, acquires specific connotation over the course of God's history with Israel, though void of conventional semantic meaning of its own.

The Profanation of God's Name and the Possibility of Supersessionism

Forgetfulness of God and God's name is the starting point of the story. Wearied by Moses' delay in coming down from the mountain, the people complain, "As for this Moses, *the man who brought us up* out of the land of Egypt, we do not know what has become of him" (32:1). Failing to remember who really led them to freedom, the people proceed to orchestrate a theophany in caricature.

Uniqueness:	The people gathered around Aaron, and said to him, "Come, make gods for us, who shall go before us." (32:1b)
Presence:	So all the people took off the gold rings from their ears, and brought them to Aaron. He took the gold from them, formed it in a mold, and cast an image of a calf. (32:3–4b)
Blessing:	They rose early the next day, and offered burnt offerings and brought sacrifices of well-being; and the people sat down to eat and drink, and rose up to revel. (32:6)

Here the notes of uniqueness, presence, and blessing appear transposed into the farcical key of idolatry. The Scriptures emphasize the gravity of the crisis as starkly as possible. God first responds by contemplating something like an anti-Exodus. Previously, God had prefaced the promises of deliverance with some variation on the words, "I have observed the misery of my people" (3:7, 16). Now God begins by saying, "I have seen this people, how stiff-necked they are" (32:9b). God then declares:

God's uniqueness:	Now let me alone,
God's presence:	so that my wrath may burn hot against them and I may consume them;
God's blessing:	and of you I will make a great nation. (Exod. 32:10)

God vows to destroy Israel, descended from the patriarchs, and promises to establish a new people in its place, descended from Moses. These are dire words. But they are also exceptionally interesting when heard in light of the traditional Christian teaching of supersessionism. Supersessionism maintains that God ultimately deals with Israel very much along these lines. In the fullness of time, God does transfer the status of election from Israel to the church, the spiritual family of Christ. Early on, Christians noticed the similarity between the two accounts. In *The Epistle of Barnabas* (ca. 100–135), the author explicitly appeals to the story of the golden calf, in what is perhaps the first explicit formulation of Christian supersessionism. He warns, "Watch yourselves now and do not become like some people by piling up your sins, saying that covenant is both theirs [i.e., 'the Jews'] and ours [i.e., 'the Christians']. For it is ours." He continues:

> They permanently lost it, in this way, when Moses had just received it. . . . For the Lord says this: "Moses, Moses, go down quickly, because your people, whom you led from the land of Egypt, have broken the law." Moses understood and cast the two tablets from his hands. And

> their covenant was smashed—that the covenant of his beloved, Jesus, might be sealed in our hearts.[13]

Barnabas locates the point when God breaks covenant with Israel in the sin of the golden calf. Other Christian writers located the point elsewhere, such as the crucifixion of the Messiah, or Israel's subsequent failure to heed the preaching of the gospel. Still others, such as Augustine and Aquinas, located the reason for Israel's obsolescence at a still deeper level, in God's original design for a "fulfillment" of Israel's history that would render all the visible markers of its corporate life "dead and deadly."[14] Despite these differences, they all agree with Barnabas, that God has in fact made another people to be God's people in Israel's place.

In defense of the teaching of supersessionism, it proposes nothing that God has not already contemplated, in even more severe form, in the terrible words, "Now let me alone, so that my wrath may burn hot against them and I may consume them; and of you I will make a great nation" (Exod. 32:10).

The Reaffirmation of God's Name and the Vindication of the Covenant

It is all the more important, then, to recognize that the story of the golden calf raises the possibility of supersessionism *only to emphatically reject it.* At the critical moment, "the Lord changed his mind about the disaster that he planned to bring on his people" (Exod. 32:14). Significantly, Moses himself—the intended cornerstone of God's new people—intercedes for Israel. "Moses implored the Lord his God, and said, 'O Lord, why does your wrath burn hot against your people, whom you brought out of the land of Egypt with great power and with a mighty hand?'" (v. 11). Moses does not deny the gravity of Israel's sin, but appeals instead to God's oath, sworn "by your own self," to multiply Abraham's descendants (v. 13). Moses warns that God's reputation will suffer if he destroys Israel, for the nations will conclude that he took Israel from Egypt with evil intent. At heart, Moses intercedes for Israel by invoking *God's name.* Moses reminds God not only of the name itself ("O Lord!"), but also of the dense cloud of association, connotation, and overtone that surrounds it, not because the name itself *means* anything, but because God has put it at the head of his dealings with Israel and the world.

In response to Moses' appeal, God relents, but only in part. God punishes many of the wrongdoers, but more terrible still, he declares that he will no longer accompany the people on their pilgrimage. "Go up to a land flowing with milk and honey; but I will not go up among you, or I would consume you on the way, for you are a stiff-necked people" (33:3). With these words, the story begins to focus in a fascinating way on the theme of God's *presence* in the midst of a manifestly sinful people. Apparently Moses has convinced God that self-consistency requires that he *bless* the people, by giving them the land to dwell in, as promised. But God is not prepared to "go up among you," that is, to be present among his sinful people. Still, Moses does not give way. With awesome tenacity, Moses insists on the inseparability of God's presence and blessing. What is possession of the land without God's accompanying? At last God signals acquiescence: "My presence will go with you, and I will give you rest" (v. 14). Not content with victory, Moses continues to harp on the point, declaring, "If your presence will not go, do not carry us up from here. For how shall it be known that I have found favor in your sight, I and your people, unless you go with us?" (33:15–16). Again, and for a final time, God declares, "I will do the very thing that you have asked" (v. 17).

This is the backdrop of the third and final name theophany in the book of Exodus, the only one that takes place on the top of Mount Sinai, the primordial site of God's holy presence. Emboldened, perhaps, by God's comforting words, Moses asks to see the divine glory. God assents, declaring:

> I will make all my goodness pass before you, and will proclaim before you the name, "The Lord"; and I will be gracious to whom I will be gracious, and will show mercy on whom I will show mercy. (33:19)

The next morning, events unfold as God had said. God puts Moses in the cleft of a rock and covers him with his hand, so that Moses will not be undone by the sight of God's presence.

> [5]The Lord descended in the cloud and stood with him there, and proclaimed the name, "The Lord." [6]The Lord passed before him, and proclaimed,
> "The Lord, the Lord,
> a God merciful and gracious, slow to anger,
> and abounding in steadfast love and faithfulness,
> [7]keeping steadfast love for the thousandth generation,
> forgiving iniquity and transgression and sin,
> yet by no means clearing the guilty,
> but visiting the iniquity of the parents
> upon the children and the children's children,
> to the third and the fourth generation." (34:5–7)

This last great name declaration of the book of Exodus is a nonidentical repetition of the previous two (Exod. 3 and 6). Once again, God is so zealous for the divine name that he declares it repeatedly, and makes it known precisely in its repetition. At the same time, God's name declaration in Exodus 34 exhibits some distinctive features. Previously, the note of God's *uniqueness* predominated, and God's presence and blessing sounded as overtones within it. Now the overtone of God's presence swells in volume to an unprecedented degree, to the point where Moses must take cover in the cleft of a rock. In advance of the event, God promises that he will make the divine goodness "pass before you" and "will proclaim" the divine name "before you," and in the event itself God is said to have "descended," and "stood with him there," and "passed before him," and so forth (30:17–23; 34:5). Indeed, it is tempting to say that the "fundamental" note of God's name declaration in this instance is that of God's presence, and God's uniqueness and blessing are heard as overtones within it.

Special importance attaches to the sayings "I will be gracious to whom I will be gracious, and will show mercy on whom I will show mercy" (33:19), and its much longer counterpart that begins with the words, "a God merciful and gracious . . ." (34:6). There can be little doubt that these divine self-characterizations are best understood as further *paraphrases* of the divine name. The first is a tautology, recalling God's first reply to Moses at the burning bush, and the second comes at the climax of a series of repetitions of the divine name. Like "I am who I am," these paraphrases comment on the divine name, but unlike it, they draw out the bare affirmation of God's uniqueness into a portrait of God's abiding character. The import of these paraphrases is that God's faithfulness toward sinful Israel is not the adventitious result of God's passing fancy, nor even the happy result of Moses' bold intercession. Rather, it is the sovereign expression of God's being as God. Prior to this point, one might have supposed that God's name was implicated in what became of Israel only insofar as God's oath and reputation were at stake. Certainly God's oath and reputation cling closely to his name, but nevertheless only because God has freely created a world wherein to "cause my name to be remembered" (20:24). But now, in light of God's words to Moses at the cleft in the rock, we see that God's name is implicated more deeply yet. In God's mercy and faithfulness toward Israel, what comes to light is nothing more or less than the eternal radiance of God's name, YHWH, which being paraphrased is "I am who I am," which being paraphrased is "a God merciful and gracious, slow to anger, and abounding in steadfast love and faithfulness" (34:6; cf. Num. 14:18; Neh. 9:17; Pss. 86:15; 103:8; 145:8; Jonah 4:2; Nah. 1:3).

Whether the teaching of supersessionism is a legitimate expression of the gospel or a disastrous distortion of it—that is a problem that cannot be resolved on the basis of reading a single text, even one as suggestive as Exodus 32–34. Nevertheless, our examination of this passage suggests that at the deepest level the problem touches on the Christian understanding of the name of God. Even though—or rather, precisely because—the Tetragrammaton is a name without conventional semantic meaning, its connotation derives wholly from the One who declares it eternally and who also declares it temporally in the context of covenant with Israel. At the very outset of this history, God briefly entertained the possibility of abandoning Israel on account of its wickedness, only to reject this possibility as incompatible with God's name. This strongly suggests that wherever Christian theology retains a lively sense of the Tetragrammaton as the mark of God's uniqueness, doctrines of supersessionism can indeed be formulated, but they can never settle down into a fixed and well-justified feature of Christian thought. Wherever Christian theology loses such a sense, however, whether because it has ceased to remember the name, or because it thinks the name itself is obsolete, or because it believes itself bound to proclaim some other name as the primary mark of God's uniqueness—then the question of supersessionism remains not only alive but also positively dangerous in the highest degree.

9

Declaring the Name of Lord in the Old Testament II

Divine Uniqueness, Presence, and Blessing Elsewhere in the Old Testament

Although we cannot survey God's name declaration in the rest of the Old Testament in a single chapter, it is important to show that the patterns found in the book of Exodus—characterized above all by the subtle interplay of God's uniqueness, presence, and blessing—are repeated elsewhere in the Old Testament when God's self-naming is thematic.

One way we can explore this point is by focusing chiefly on the saying, "I am the Lord" and its variants. The declaration appears for the first time in Genesis 15:7, and recurs frequently thereafter in the most varied settings in the Old Testament. Like a musical motif that returns often throughout a complex score, the saying gives unity and thematic coherence to the canon's diverse witnesses.[1] It tunes the otherwise often discordant elements of Scripture to the primordial melody of God's uniqueness and sets them in movement toward the inexhaustible goal of the knowledge of God: "You shall know that I am the Lord!" At the same time, the saying in its many canonical settings makes clear that "the primordial melody of God's uniqueness" has a recognizable cadence and progression of its own, constituted by the mutual coinherence of divine uniqueness, presence, and blessing.

Even with respect to the one saying "I am the Lord," our review must be highly selective. For the sake of variety, we begin with its connection to the theme of divine blessing.

GOD'S NAME DECLARATION AND GOD'S BLESSING

The important thematic connection between God's name declaration and God's blessing has not always received the attention it deserves. One reason for this may be that the Scriptures express this connection in a variety of ways rather than by one or two fixed expressions. Consider the following examples (with added emphasis):

God's uniqueness:	I am the Lord
God's presence:	who brought you from Ur of the Chaldeans,
God's blessing:	*to give you this land to possess.* (Gen. 15:7)

God's uniqueness:	I am the Lord your God
God's presence:	who brought you out of the land of Egypt,
God's blessing:	*to be their slaves no more; I have broken the bars of your yoke and made you walk erect.* (Lev. 26:13)

God's uniqueness:	I am the Lord your God,
God's presence:	who brought you up out of the land of Egypt.
God's blessing:	*Open your mouth wide and I will fill it.* (Ps. 81:10)

Notice the diversity of the third element in contrast to the relative stability of the first two. If one assumes (perhaps unconsciously) that fixity of form is a prerequisite of theological weightiness, one might even overlook the third element entirely. A better interpretation, I would argue, is that the third member is just as important as the others but places the emphasis at a different point. The first element emphasizes God's uniqueness as such, as concentrated specifically in God's name; the second stresses God's presence as remembered in a completed event of the past; the third element places the emphasis upon God's blessing in the here and now, as the renewal of God's life-giving benefits. Viewed in this light, variation in the third element is not a deficiency but the sign of its special "charism," which is to refract the wealth of God's name into a spectrum of endless color, hue, and intensity.

God's blessing is comprehensive, even when viewed in its endless variety. It does not communicate a part of God to a part of life (for God has no "parts"), but conveys everything that God is to the whole of life. This is expressed paradigmatically in the following example:

Uniqueness:	I am the Lord your God,
Presence:	who brought you out of the land of Egypt,
Blessing:	*to be your God.* (Num. 15:41; cf. Lev. 11:45)

All the benefits that God has to confer upon God's people are comprehended in the words "your God." It is not accidental that the Tetragrammaton appears in the first member of the triad, where the point is God's uniqueness as such, but not in the third, which concerns God's uniqueness as blessing, the conferral and reception of God's uniqueness in the mode of gift. The Tetragrammaton cannot be modified by pronouns and prepositions (the Bible never speaks of "your YHWH" or "our YHWH" or "YHWH of Israel"), but the divine names that derive from common nouns (*El*, *Adonai*, *Elohim*, etc.) can be modified in this way. Precisely this grammatical feature enables the latter names to express God's deity with a nuance and context-specificity that is unavailable to the divine name. From here the path is short to a host of other "divine names" that appear in the context of the affirmation "the LORD is . . . ," such as "my banner" (Exod. 17:15); "their inheritance" (Deut. 18:2); "peace" (Judg. 6:24); "a God of knowledge" (1 Sam. 2:3); "my rock," "my fortress," "my deliverer" (2 Sam. 22:2); "king" (1 Chr. 16:31); "your strength" (Neh. 8:10); "a stronghold for the oppressed" (Pss. 9:9); "righteous" (11:7); "their refuge" (14:6); "my chosen portion and my cup" (16:5); "my shepherd" (23:1); "my light," "my salvation" (27:1); and so on.

The comprehensive nature of God's blessing is also expressed by the gift of the law, which is addressed to the whole of Israel's life. We see this with paradigmatic clarity in the Ten Commandments:

God's uniqueness:	[2]I am the LORD your God,
God's presence:	who brought you out of the land of Egypt, out of the house of slavery;
God's blessing:	[3]you shall have no other gods before me. [4]You shall not . . . [5]You shall not . . . [7]You shall not . . . [8]Remember . . . [12]Honor . . . [13]You shall not . . . [14]You shall not . . . [15]You shall not . . . [16]You shall not . . . [17]You shall not . . . (Exod. 20:2–17; cf. Deut. 5:6–21)

The entire list of commandments (which stands representatively for the Torah as a whole) is simply a single elaboration of God's blessing as it adapts itself to the contours of Israel's life. That God's blessing appears now in the *imperative* rather than *indicative* mode is indeed an important key change in the melody of God's blessing, but not a departure from the melody as such. As the prevenient gift of God's life-giving power, God's blessing always has something of the character of an imperative about it ("Be fruitful and multiply!"). By means of the Torah, God blesses in a way that both enables and demands Israel's response in every sphere of life. It is no coincidence that the saying "I am the LORD/your God" is especially common in the great book of the law, Leviticus, where it appears *over fifty times* in contexts both grand and humble.[2]

We can hardly end this section without citing a passage that expresses the connection between God's name declaration and God's blessing with singular force and profundity, although it departs from the rhetorical pattern we have considered thus far ("I am the LORD . . .). I am thinking of the Aaronic blessing:

> [22]The LORD spoke to Moses, saying: [23]Speak to Aaron and his sons, saying, Thus you shall bless the Israelites: You shall say to them,
>
> [24]The LORD bless you and keep you;
> [25]the LORD make his face to shine upon you, and be gracious to you;
> [26]the LORD lift up his countenance upon you, and give you peace.
>
> [27]So they shall put my name on the Israelites, and I will bless them. (Num. 6:22–27)

The threefold repetition of God's name anchors the blessing in the affirmation of God's uniqueness even as each line pours it out like so many streams of luxurious perfumed oil. God's blessing is also God's keeping, which is also God's shining face, which is also God's grace, which is also God's countenance lifted up, which is also God's peace. And all of these together brim over with the riches of "my name."

GOD'S NAME DECLARATION AND GOD'S PRESENCE

As we have seen, the Old Testament often portrays God's name declaration in conjunction with some account of God's coming to be present with God's people. The paradigmatic instance is the almost reflexive association of the phrase "I am the LORD" with "who brought you out of the land of Egypt." But the Bible links God's name declaration and God's presence in many other ways as well. We think, for example, of the great name theophanies of the book of Exodus (see chap. 8), which in a supremely concentrated way portray God's advent and presence at the burning bush and on Mount Sinai. Or we notice (to take a less familiar example) how God's name makes God's angel the concrete representative of God's person and authority in the following passage: "Be attentive to him and listen to his voice; do not rebel against him, for he will not pardon your transgression; *for my name is in him*" (Exod. 23:21, emphasis added). In all these examples, God's presence is distinguished by its discrete, delineated form.

A particularly vivid example appears in the biblical traditions that speak of God's being present where God causes God's name to *dwell* (Deut. 26:2; cf. 12:11; 14:23; 1 Kgs. 8:43; Ps. 74:7; etc.). The reference is to the divinely sanctioned sites of worship, and ultimately to the temple at Jerusalem. In these witnesses, we recognize something like an intensification of the earlier promise: "In every place where I cause my name to be remembered, I will come to you . . ." (Exod. 20:24b–25). As God's history with Israel takes settled form in the land of promise, God causes God's name to dwell at a fixed location, which becomes the locus of God's reliable presence. The whole land is full of God's blessings, but God's presence is concentrated at a particular locale. The interrelationship of God's blessing and promise is beautifully illustrated in the following passage:

> [23]In the presence of the LORD your God, in the place that he will choose as a dwelling for his name, you shall eat the tithe of your grain, your wine, and your oil, as well as the firstlings of your herd and flock, so that you may learn to fear the LORD your God always. [24]But if, when the LORD your God has blessed you, the distance is so great that you are unable to transport it, because the place where the LORD your God will choose to set his name is too far away from you, [25]then you may turn it into money. With the money secure in hand, go to the place that the LORD your God will choose; [26]spend the money for whatever you wish—oxen, sheep, wine, strong drink, or whatever you desire. And you shall eat there in the presence of the LORD your God, you and your household rejoicing together. (Deut. 14:23–26)

Notice the plurality and mobility and even fungibility of God's blessings in contrast with the singularity and stability of God's presence, even as the one God is the source of both.

Despite what is sometimes said, the Bible never depicts God's name as an instrument that humans can use to manipulate God's presence, as though God were a cosmic Rumpelstiltskin whose power depends on anonymity, or a domestic servant who must come when called. God always retains the initiative, according to the paradigmatic promise, "In every place where *I cause* my name to be remembered . . ." (Exod. 20:24b). Nevertheless, the Bible certainly portrays God's name as a site of grave danger, where humans repeatedly fall victim to the *illusion* of divine control. The temple traditions themselves testify to this. According to 2 Samuel 7, God rejected King David's plan to build a temple in Jerusalem as a foolish impertinence.

> [5]Go and tell my servant David: Thus says the LORD: Are you the one to build me a house to live in? [6]I have not lived in a house since the day I brought up the people of Israel from Egypt to this day, but I have been moving about in a tent and a tabernacle. (2 Sam. 7:5–6)

God goes on to declare that a "house for my name" (13a) shall indeed be erected, but not by David. The builder shall be David's *son*, of whom God makes the following resonant promise:

> I will establish the throne of his kingdom forever. [14]I will be a father to him, and he shall be a son to me. When he commits iniquity, I will punish him with a rod such as mortals use, with blows inflicted by human beings. [15]But I will not take my steadfast love from him, as I took it from Saul, whom I put away from before you. (2 Sam. 7:13b–15)

Here two traditions come together, one that describes the temple as the dwelling place of God's name, and one that describes God's relationship to Israel and Israel's king by using the vocabulary of father and son. In a later chapter we will have occasion to look more closely at this passage, which serves as midwife for the birth of messianic hope in both the Old Testament and the New. For now, the point I want to emphasize is that the two traditions work together to make a common point. God's presence is beyond human manipulation, and precisely therefore it is utterly reliable.

In the final analysis, the reliability of God's presence is not a function of the temple per se, but of the name that he has caused to dwell in it. Just as God once freely chose the temple, so he remains free to abandon it. This is God's warning through the prophet Jeremiah, on account of Israel's sins:

> [12]Go now to my place that was in Shiloh, where I made my name dwell at first, and see what I did to it for the wickedness of my people Israel. [13]And now, because you have done all these things, says the LORD, . . . [14]I will do to the house that is called by my name . . . what I did to Shiloh. (Jer. 7:12–14)

Still, not even the destruction of the temple signals the permanent rejection of God's people. The work of the exodus may be undone, Jerusalem razed, the temple destroyed, and the people driven into exile. Yet God will come to his people again:

	[7]Therefore, the days are surely coming, says the LORD, when it shall no longer be said,
Uniqueness:	"As the LORD lives
Presence:	who brought the people of Israel up out of the land of Egypt,"
	[8]but
Uniqueness:	"As the LORD lives
Presence:	who brought out and led the offspring of the house of Israel out of the land of the north and out of all the lands where he had driven them."
Blessing:	Then they shall live in their own land. (Jer. 23:7–8)

The sure sign of God's presence thus is not the temple itself, but the name for which it was built. For that reason, Israel can trust that its life in God's presence is as enduring as the heavens.

> [35]Thus says the LORD,
> who gives the sun for light by day
>   and the fixed order of the moon and the stars for light by night,
> who stirs up the sea so that its waves roar—the LORD of hosts is his name:

[36]If this fixed order were ever to cease from my presence, says the Lord, then also the offspring of Israel would cease to be a nation before me forever. (Jer. 31:35–36)

GOD'S NAME DECLARATION AND GOD'S UNIQUENESS

A striking feature of the association between God's name and God's uniqueness in the Bible is that it does not seem to weaken with time. It is just as prominent in the latest strata of tradition as it is in the earliest. From a philosophical perspective, this is surprising, perhaps even offensive. One might expect the felt need to mark out a god by name would be strongest at the early stages of a religion's development, when it is still necessary to distinguish its own patron deity from others. The rise of "monotheism" would, however, seemingly render the very concept of "God's name" more and more superfluous, as God's uniqueness came to be included in the concept of "deity" as such.[3] Generally speaking, this is the course that pagan monotheism took, as evidenced by its conviction of the "namelessness" of God.[4] But, as Christopher Seitz has observed, it is not the course that the Old Testament witness takes. Rather, the later strata of biblical tradition (such as Malachi, Zephaniah, and Second and Third Isaiah) continue to articulate God's uniqueness *precisely* by means of the divine name, even as the tradition becomes increasingly "monotheistic." Indeed, if these witnesses trend in a common direction, it is toward the hope that Israel will be joined by the nations in recognizing together that "the Lord is God."[5]

The oracles of Second Isaiah, for example, are filled with references to God's name, in which we easily recognize the familiar motifs of God's uniqueness, presence, and blessing. God's blessing comes to the fore in many passages, such as this one:

[3]For I will pour water on the thirsty land, and streams on the dry ground;
I will pour my spirit upon your descendants, and my blessing on your offspring.
[4]They shall spring up like a green tamarisk, like willows by flowing streams.
[5]This one will say, "I am the Lord's," another will be called by the name of Jacob,
yet another will write on the hand, "The Lord's," and adopt the name of Israel.

(Isa. 44:3–5; cf. 41:17–20; 43:25; 44:3; 49:8–21; 51:3, 8, 11; 54:10, 13; 55:12; 56:7; 62:3–5; 65:17)

And God's presence comes to the fore in other passages, such as this:

> 7How beautiful upon the mountains are the feet of the messenger who announces peace,
> who brings good news, who announces salvation, who says to Zion, "Your God reigns."
> 8Listen! Your sentinels lift up their voices, together they sing for joy;
> for in plain sight they see the return of the LORD to Zion.
> 9Break forth together into singing, you ruins of Jerusalem;
> for the LORD has comforted his people, he has redeemed Jerusalem.
> 10The LORD has bared his holy arm before the eyes of all the nations;
> and all the ends of the earth shall see the salvation of our God.
>
> (Isa. 52:7–10; cf. 41:10; 41:13; 42:13; 45:3; 52:10; 54:10; 57:15; 59:19–20; 64:1–2)

Without doubt, however, the note that predominates is that of God's uniqueness, which God sounds directly through the declaration of God's name:

> I am the LORD, that is my name;
> my glory I give to no other, nor my praise to idols.
>
> (Isa. 42:8)

> Thus says the LORD, the King of Israel, and his Redeemer, the LORD of hosts:
> I am the first and I am the last; besides me there is no god.
>
> (Isa. 44:6)

> I am the LORD, and there is no other; besides me there is no god.
>
> (Isa. 45:5a)

The comprehensive theme of Second Isaiah is God's new exodus. It shall be greater than the first because God's salvation of Israel will also be a light to the nations, so that "my salvation may reach to the end of the earth" (49:6). Beholding what God does for Israel, the nations will turn to the LORD, and be saved. And so the petition will be fulfilled that was made at the dedication of the temple in Jerusalem, that "all the peoples of the earth may know your name" (1 Kgs. 8:43; cf. Isa. 64:2; Jer. 16:21; Pss. 100:4; 145:21).

> 22Turn to me and be saved, all the ends of the earth!
> For I am God, and there is no other.
> 23By myself I have sworn, from my mouth has gone forth in righteousness a word that shall not return:
> "To me every knee shall bow, every tongue shall swear."
>
> (Isa. 45:22–23)

REPRISE: PSALM 113 AND THE BLESSING OF GOD'S NAME

In this chapter, we have attempted to trace the contours of the Old Testament's witness to God's name declaration as this appears outside the book of Exodus. By way of conclusion, I wish to trace these outlines one last time, as they appear in Psalm 113.[6] This psalm differs from most of the texts we have considered thus far because the voice that speaks in it is the human voice of the psalmist rather than the voice of God. In the psalmist's voice, we hear the familiar notes of God's name declaration echoed back in thanksgiving and praise.

Psalm 113 opens with a threefold call to praise the name of the LORD:

> 1Praise the LORD!
> Praise, O servants of the LORD; praise the name of the LORD.
> 2Blessed be the name of the LORD from this time on and forevermore.
> 3From the rising of the sun to its setting the name of the LORD is to be praised.

Echoing the threefold summons to praise, the psalmist sets forth three reasons why praise is due, beginning with God's uniqueness:

> 4The LORD is high above all nations, and his glory above the heavens.
> 5Who is like the LORD our God, who is seated on high,
> 6who looks far down on the heavens and the earth?

With the shortest possible strokes, the psalmist portrays God's uniqueness as encompassing both his *incomparable identity* and his *uncircumscribable mystery*. The psalmist emphasizes God's identity through the continued repetition of his name, and God's mystery by the simple images that evoke the "infinite qualitative distinction" between this God and everything else.

But if God is indeed so utterly unique, so beyond every category and comparison, then how does it come about that God's name is known and praised at all? The psalmist answers this implied question by further explicating God's uniqueness, now in terms of his redeeming presence:

> 7He raises the poor from the dust, and lifts the needy from the ash heap,
> 8to make them sit with princes, with the princes of his people.

With plunging suddenness, the infinitely exalted God comes alongside the poor and needy and raises them up to royal rank. This image encapsulates the whole story of Israel's exodus from Egypt, and behind it, perhaps, the story of creation, when God raised the first parents out of the dust and made them to be in the image of God (Gen. 1–2). Still the psalmist is not finished and expresses God's uniqueness one last time, as it takes shape in God's blessing:

> [9]He gives the barren woman a home,
> making her the joyous mother of children.
> Praise the LORD![7]

The closing image of Psalm 113 depicts God's blessing not as harmless domesticity, but as the comprehensive transformation of life from sterility to fruitfulness. In the barren woman become joyous mother, we recognize the story of Israel's origins from Sarah, and before that, the story of the human family, in Eve's fruitfulness, east of Eden. In every instance, God's blessing is both gift and charge. It bestows life, home, and progeny, but it also yokes them to life before God. In the woman's never-ending rounds of chores and satisfactions, we see in microcosm how *fine-grained* and *all-consuming* is God's blessing.

Psalm 113 provides a fitting counterpart to the verse with which we opened this chapter, "In every place where I cause my name to be remembered, I will come to you and bless you" (Exod. 20:24b). Together the two passages epitomize the Old Testament's testimony to God's name declaration and its characteristic notes of divine uniqueness, presence, and blessing. But the verses do something more as well. They provide an account of how God "tunes" or proportions human speech to speak fittingly of God. God accomplishes this by proclaiming his name and causing it to be remembered. As this happens, human beings are transformed by the divine blessing, caught up into the divine presence, and given to know the uniqueness of God. Between God's self-naming and our naming of God, there is neither univocity, nor equivocity, but analogy, an analogy of the blessing of God's name.

GOD'S NAME DECLARATION IN THE OLD TESTAMENT: THE INTRODUCTION OF ENDURING THEMES

We have come to the end of our survey of God's name declaration in the Old Testament. Let us encapsulate some of the main themes we have found.

The Uniqueness of the One God

The Old Testament is not an optional, minor, or dispensable part of the Christian canon's witness to God's name declaration in the economy of salvation. On the contrary, it introduces certain themes whose contours support the Christian canon as a whole, like a spine or backbone. Of these none is more basic than the testimony that God is one (Deut. 6:4; Mark 12:29). "One" in the context of the Old Testament, however, means much more than numerical oneness. It means qualitative oneness, in the sense of *this* one and no other. "I am the Lord your God, who brought you out of the land of Egypt, out of the house of slavery; you shall have no other gods before me" (Exod. 20:2–3). The Old Testament is the indispensable starting point for understanding the Christian canon's testimony to God's name declaration because it is the primary school in which we learn to recognize the qualitative uniqueness of God.

God's Self-naming and Our Naming of God

Another theme introduced in the Old Testament and sustained throughout the rest of the canon concerns the relationship between God's self-naming and our naming of God. To put the matter as simply as possible, the Old Testament depicts both, but according to a certain order, whereby God's self-naming enables the human naming of God and provides the norm for such naming. That is the premise of the third commandment (Exod. 20:7; Deut. 5:11). To use God's name in vain, by swearing a false oath, for example, is to use it in a way that contravenes God's own use of the divine name, which is unfailingly truthful.

None of this is to deny that the Old Testament's portrait of God's self-naming and our naming of God is rich and multidimensional. By its own account, *all* Scripture testifies at some level to the human "naming of God," inasmuch as humans are the authors of Scripture, *including* its variegated records of God's self-naming. Again, we can say that *all* Scripture is an expression of *God's* self-naming, or at least of God's speaking, insofar as God's word and Spirit enable humans to produce and interpret Scripture (cf. Jer. 1:2; Ezek. 1:3; cf. Matt. 22:43; 2 Tim. 3:16). Still, even after we have taken this rich multidimensionality into account, we are left with a picture that gives priority to God. To speak in an admittedly anthropomorphic way, the canon wants to be understood according to the logic of Exodus 20:24: "You need make for me only an altar of earth and sacrifice on it your burnt offerings and your offerings of well-being, your sheep and your oxen; in every place where I cause my name to be remembered I will come to you and bless you." Though composed of only dirt and stone (20:25), it is *the* written record where God is pleased to cause his name to be remembered.

God's Self-naming as the Manifestation of Divine Uniqueness, the Enactment of Divine Presence, and the Bestowal of Divine Blessing

Another theme introduced in the Old Testament and sustained in the New concerns what God typically accomplishes by declaring his name. Speaking again as simply as possible, God typically accomplishes three things: God manifests his uniqueness, enacts his presence, and bestows his blessing. Of these, the first is primary, and the others are its inward elaborations. This is not to deny that the Old Testament portrays God as using his name in a host of different ways not explicitly mentioned in this short summary, such as when foretelling the future (Isa. 42:8–9; 44:6–7; etc.), delivering the weak (Ps. 35:10), magnifying God's creatures (Job 40:6–41:34), pronouncing judgment (Ezek. 20), and so on. Still, it is to claim that this wider circle of witnesses finds its center of gravity in the uses of the divine name central to the story of the exodus—the display of uniqueness, the enactment of presence, the bestowal of blessing—as though these three were somehow melodic phrases internal to the divine name itself.

The Divine Name and the Divine Names

A final theme introduced in the Old Testament and sustained throughout the rest of the canon concerns the actual nomenclature that God uses when declaring his name. Speaking once again as succinctly as possible, the Tetragrammaton is indispensable to this nomenclature, but so too are other divine names.

The Tetragrammaton enjoys a certain priority to other divine names not because of anything that it may mean (for it is not clear that it means anything at all) but simply because of what it does: point. As a personal proper name, and indeed, as God's *only* personal proper name, the Tetragrammaton is the linguistic token of God's uniqueness par excellence. When God introduces who God is with the words, "I am . . . ," the word that immediately follows is most often the Tetragrammaton. When God speaks of "my name," as in Exodus 20:24, the term that God intends is the Tetragrammaton. Empty in itself, the name's "sense" is the cloud of association and disassociation revealed over the course of salvation history, a cloud that, though visible in part, infinitely exceeds what can be known or said about its bearer.

And yet, as important as the Tetragrammaton is, other names are *equally important* in their own way in the economy of God's name declaration in the Old Testament. When God affirms his uniqueness with the words "I am the Lord," he frequently elaborates the affirmation with some further self-designation, as in the opening of the Decalogue, "I am the Lord *your God.*"

Though the Scriptures do not dub these predicative nouns God's *name* (*shem*), they are not therefore any less integral to the scriptural portrait of God. They exegete the divine name, bringing the sheer darkness of its infinite depths to light. In large stretches of biblical narrative and poetry, God is known only by these other terms, and the Tetragrammaton vanishes from sight.

In sum, the Old Testament portrays God's uniqueness by using different *kinds* of terms that cannot easily be brought under a single classification. Although we could speak of God's proper name on the one hand and of God's titles, cognomens, and epithets on the other, it seems better to speak simply of the divine name and the divine names.

10

Declaring the Name of the Trinity in the New Testament I

The Differentiation of Divine Voices

. . . God said . . .

(Luke 12:20)

. . . Jesus said . . .

(Matthew 4:7)

. . . the Spirit said . . .

(Acts 8:29)

The New Testament's portrait of the Trinity's name declaration in the economy of salvation is a perfect harmony of consistency and novelty vis-à-vis the Old Testament. It portrays God declaring—not a new name (truly a misapprehension of the first order)—but the old name in a new, cosmos-restoring way, by the sending of Christ Jesus and the outpouring of Holy Spirit. We have seen that in the Old Testament, God speaks with a single incomparable voice, marked by the great pronoun "I . . ." and by the great divine name ". . . the LORD." Turning to the New Testament, we continue to hear this ancient voice of old, sounded by the One to whom Jesus prays, "Hallowed be your name!" (Matt. 6:9). Yet now we hear this voice speak in a radically new way, and as though for the first time. For now it speaks by directing us to listen to Christ and to the Spirit, in whose voices we recognize again the *one* voice, each time modulated in a different way. To put the matter in musical terms, it is as though the infinitely rich voice of the "one God" were revealed by the sending of Jesus Christ and the outpouring of the Holy Spirit to be in truth the simultaneous interplay of a three-note chord.[1]

Our goal in this chapter and the next is to trace the acoustic contours of the new, trinitarian space wherein we hear again God's old, old voice and name. The special concern of this chapter is not yet with the form of words that God, Christ, and the Spirit use to express the bonds that unite them—not yet "the name of the Trinity." That will be the theme of the next chapter. For now, we will direct our attention to a point that lies just "behind" this form of words, to the persons of the Trinity themselves, and to the characteristic voices with which they speak. Our aim, in brief, is to learn to *distinguish the voices* of the persons of the Trinity, to recognize their characteristic timbres, textures, and frequencies.[2]

To assist us in this endeavor, we will seek guidance from another constellation of church teaching, what is known as the doctrine of appropriation.[3] This doctrine maintains, in part, that the persons of the Trinity always work together in the economy of salvation, even as each person does so in a characteristic way that reflects its distinctive place in the divine life. So, one may say, the first person originates every divine work, the second accomplishes it, and the third perfects it and brings it to completion. Applied to our current theme, the teaching implies that the persons of the Trinity work together to declare the name of the Trinity, even as each person does so in a distinctive and characteristic way. Specifically, I propose that a special affinity exists between each person of the Trinity and one of the characteristic moments of God's name declaration. The first person declares the divine name in a way that has a special affinity with the manifestation of divine uniqueness, the second with the enactment of divine presence, and the third with the bestowal of divine blessing. It is this affinity, I suggest, that gives each person's "voice" its characteristic tone and timbre, of uniqueness, of presence, and of blessing respectively.

To explore these claims in the rest of this chapter, we will focus on a single passage of Scripture that appears in both parts of the Christian canon, "Blessed is the one who comes in the name of the Lord!" (Ps. 118:26).

BLESSED IS THE ONE WHO COMES IN THE NAME OF THE LORD!

Our saying encompasses all of the characteristic elements of God's name declaration that we have come to know from the Old Testament: uniqueness, presence, and blessing. At the same time, it sets these before us in a distinctive dramatic form that involves three actors: a throng of people who welcome a victorious king, the king himself, and God, in whose name the king comes. Each actor is chiefly associated with a different moment in the familiar economy of God's name declaration. The victorious king is chiefly associated with the moment of presence: he is "the one who comes." The crowds are chiefly associated with the moment of blessing, for they declare the king "blessed!" even as they bask in the blessings he brings. Finally, God is chiefly associated with the moment of uniqueness, for it is in God's name that the king comes, and the people rejoice.

To repeat, this saying appears in both the Old Testament and the New, where its wording is virtually identical in both contexts. Nevertheless, the saying's import for the "acoustic shape" of the divine life is dramatically different in each case, as we shall see.

Psalm 118:26 in Its Old Testament Context

In the Old Testament the saying "Blessed is the one who comes in the name of the Lord" appears only once, near the conclusion of Psalm 118. The psalm is a royal hymn of thanksgiving, originally composed to commemorate deliverance from national danger. Most of the psalm unfolds responsively, as the king narrates God's victory in battle, and the people reply with shouts of praise. The psalm is dominated by these two alternating human voices, and God's own voice is rarely heard.

At one point, however, God's voice enters the psalm, albeit indirectly, by way of the king's report. At the head of his recital, as a kind of summary of all that follows, the king declares:

> Out of my distress I called on the Lord;
> the Lord answered me and set me in a broad place.
> (Ps. 118:5)

The words "the Lord answered me" depict the advent of God's voice into the psalm for the first and only time. Brief as it is, the phrase is the psalm's theological and dramatic heart. It marks the occasion of sacred memory that gives rise to the whole psalm and ultimately leads to the celebration in the temple. In content, what verse 5 records is God's fulfillment, at a given time and place, of the primordial promise he made on Mount Horeb: "In every place where I cause my name to be remembered, I will come to you and bless you" (Exod. 20:24). We can visualize the correspondence of promise and fulfillment as follows:

	God's uniqueness	God's presence	God's blessing
God's promise (Exod. 20:24)	In every place where I cause my name to be remembered	I will come to you	and bless you.
God's promise fulfilled in the person of the king (Psalm 118:5)	Out of my distress I called on the LORD;	the LORD answered me	and set me in a broad place.

Everything God promised according to Exodus 20:24 is fulfilled in Psalm 118:5, viewed now from the perspective of the human partner to God's covenant. The king is himself the "place," so to speak, where God has caused his name to be remembered, where God came, and where God blessed. Seen in light of Exodus 20:24, even the king's cry of distress and invocation of God is the result of God's prior initiative.

The psalm continues antiphonally as ruler and people ascribe the king's victory on the battlefield not to themselves but to the LORD. Three times the sovereign recounts how he prevailed against overwhelming odds by fighting "in the name of the LORD":

> All nations surrounded me;
> in the name of the LORD I cut them off!
> They surrounded me, surrounded me on every side;
> in the name of the LORD I cut them off!
> They surrounded me like bees; they blazed like a fire of thorns;
> in the name of the LORD I cut them off!
> (vv. 10–12)

Three times the assembly shouts in return:

> The right hand of the LORD does valiantly;
> the right hand of the LORD is exalted;
> the right hand of the LORD does valiantly.
> (vv. 15–16)

At last the king declares, "Open to me the gates of righteousness, that I may enter through them and give thanks to the LORD" (v. 19). The people respond by once again attributing the astonishing triumph to God, "The stone that the builders rejected has become the chief cornerstone. This is the LORD's doing; it is marvelous in our eyes" (vv. 22–23). At last the people welcome the king with the climactic cry:

> Blessed is the one who comes in the name of the LORD.
> (v. 26)

With these words, the focus of the psalm turns and rests on the figure of the king. And yet the king is important not for his own sake but because God's uniqueness, presence, and blessing become visible in him. He represents not his own name but the name of the LORD. He can "come" because God first came to him. He is called "blessed" because God first blessed him. Victorious, on the far side of danger, he is a living icon of the living God.

Viewed in its Old Testament context, "Blessed is the one who comes in the name of the LORD" summarizes a drama played out among three voices. But of these, one—and only one—is divine, the incomparable voice of the LORD, who answered the king's cry for help on the field of battle. God's voice, recorded in 118:5, resonates with its characteristic timbre of divine uniqueness, together with its inalienable overtones of presence and blessing. These overtones set the two creaturely voices ringing, as it were, causing them to vibrate sympathetically according to their own distinctive pitch and tenor. Still, the reverberations are only that. They are not divine voices in their own right.

Psalm 118:26 in Its New Testament Context

Turning to our saying in its New Testament setting, we immediately recognize a basic continuity of dramatic structure, involving a crowd, an approaching king, and the One in whose name the king comes. At the same time, we also recognize a number of novel features. In the Old Testament the royal figure is unnamed; in the New Testament it is Jesus of Nazareth. In the Old Testament, the "name of the LORD" is indicated directly in the original Hebrew text; in the New Testament it appears indirectly, by the use of a pious surrogate in its place (*kyrios*, or, more precisely, $\overline{\text{K}\Sigma}$). In the Old Testament, the saying appears once, in a single psalm of medium length; in the New Testament, it appears multiple times in a much larger and more complex literary context, that of the four Gospels (Matt. 21:1–16; Mark 11:1–10; Luke 19:28–40; John 12:12–19). Finally, in the Old Testament, the saying comes *after* the king's climactic struggle; in the New Testament, it comes *before* the climactic struggle.

All these differences are important. In what follows, however, we will focus on yet another difference. In the New Testament setting of Psalm 118:26, we hear, as before, the voice of the LORD, who hears and answers the petitions of the king (cf. Gospel of John, below). But now we also hear this one divine voice *twice repeated*, first in the voice of the king, and then again in the inspired voices of the crowds, each time in a different way. The nonidentical repetition of the *one* divine voice, and the resulting simultaneity of divine voices—this is *the* radically new thing in the New Testament setting of Psalm 118:26. It is the opening up of a threefold acoustic space within which we hear the distinct voices of the persons of the Holy Trinity.

At the same time, this new thing stands in perfect continuity with the Old Testament. For each of the three divine voices simply enunciates from a different location in the drama and with greater purity and distinctness one of the familiar tones that has characterized God's name declaration from the very beginning. The first person has a special affinity with the manifestation of divine uniqueness, the second with the enactment of divine presence, and the third with the bestowal of divine blessing. It is this affinity between person and acoustic location in the economy of God's name declaration that gives each person's voice its characteristic tone and timbre. Let us now look at each of these, beginning with the Holy Spirit.

THE THIRD PERSON'S DISTINCTIVE VOICE AND ROLE: BESTOWING DIVINE BLESSING

The Holy Spirit speaks in a voice that has a special affinity with the bestowal of divine blessing. The Spirit speaks *indirectly*, through the inspired voices of those blessed by God. Consider Luke's account of the crowds who greet Jesus as he draws near to Jerusalem.

> [37]As he was now approaching the path down from the Mount of Olives, the whole multitude of the disciples began to praise God joyfully with a loud voice [Gk. *phonē megalē*] for all the deeds of power that they had seen, [38] saying,
>
> "Blessed is the king who comes in the name of the Lord!
> Peace in heaven, and glory in the highest heaven!"
>
> (19:37–38)

The cry of the multitude is unmistakably human: loud, spontaneous, jubilant. This stands in strict continuity with this saying as it appears in its Old Testament context. Indeed, if anything, we might say that the Gospels portray the crowds as all too human, at least when viewed from the vantage point of later events. Before long, we know, the throng will dissolve, and even Jesus' closest disciples will abandon him. Certainly the text gives no explicit indication that the crowd's acclamation of Jesus is divinely inspired.

Still, there is more to the scene than this. At the outset of the Gospel, the third evangelist portrays those who welcome Jesus with cries of benediction as inspired by the Holy Spirit. He does this persistently, as though enunciating a theme of great importance. Elizabeth, upon hearing Mary's voice, "was filled with the Holy Spirit and exclaimed with a loud cry, 'Blessed are you among women, and blessed is the fruit of your womb'" (1:41–42). Zechariah, initially struck dumb because of doubt, was later "filled with the Holy Spirit" and declared, "Blessed be the Lord God of Israel, for he has looked favorably on his people and redeemed them. He has raised up a mighty savior for us in the house of his servant David" (1:67–69). Similarly, Simeon, guided into the temple by the Holy Spirit, praised God and "blessed" Mary and Joseph upon seeing the infant Jesus (2:25–35). By the time the Gospel gets to Anna, there is no mention of the Holy Spirit, but there does not need to be. The pattern has been established beyond all mistaking, and we scarcely doubt that when the ancient widow "began to praise God and to speak about the child to all who were looking for the redemption of Jerusalem" (2:38), she too was speaking at the prompting of the Spirit.

Seen against this backdrop, the crowd's acclamation of Jesus on the outskirts of Jerusalem marks the resumption of a familiar pattern, that of the Spirit-inspired benediction of Jesus of Nazareth as the coming King and Savior. After a long period of suspension, the pattern of Spirit-enabled blessing resumes as the promised king enters the royal city at last. The divinely initiated character of the event is confirmed by what comes next.

> 39Some of the Pharisees in the crowd said to him, "Teacher, order your disciples to stop." 40He answered, "I tell you, if these were silent, the stones would shout out." (Luke 19:39–40)

The Pharisees think that the crowds speak by their own power and authority, or at Jesus' private behest. But that is not the case. The crowds shout as they do because the Spirit enables them so to speak. If they were silent, the benediction would still ring out: the Holy Spirit would simply awaken other instruments to the task. True, the text does not mention the Holy Spirit's agency, but, then, as in the case of aged Anna, there is no need to. How else can stones shout, apart from the inspiration of the Spirit?

The voice of the Holy Spirit is distinctly audible in the New Testament setting of Psalm 118:26, together with its distinctive vocal register of blessing given and received. The Holy Spirit magnifies "all the deeds of power" (Luke 19:37) that proceed from God, speaking through a multiplicity of cries and shouts and voices. It is free to speak not only through humans, but also through rocks, even as it is permanently tied to neither. It speaks by enabling others to speak, freeing them to bless the one whom God has blessed, and to receive his blessings in turn, of which the Spirit itself is the crown and glory (cf. Luke 3:16; Acts 2).

THE SECOND PERSON'S DISTINCTIVE VOICE AND ROLE: ENACTING DIVINE PRESENCE

Jesus Christ, the Word made flesh, speaks in a voice that has special affinity with the enactment of divine presence. We sense the characteristic timbre of Jesus' person and voice in Mark's account of Jesus' entry into the royal city.

> [1]When they were approaching Jerusalem, at Bethphage and Bethany, near the Mount of Olives, he sent two of his disciples [2]and said to them, "Go into the village ahead of you, and immediately as you enter it, you will find tied there a colt that has never been ridden; untie it and bring it. [3]If anyone says to you, 'Why are you doing this?' just say this, 'The Lord needs it and will send it back here immediately.'" [4]They went away and found a colt tied near a door, outside in the street. As they were untying it, [5]some of the bystanders said to them, "What are you doing, untying the colt?" [6]They told them what Jesus had said; and they allowed them to take it. (Mark 11:1–6)

The scene opens with Jesus and the disciples coming toward the city together. But immediately Jesus' special relation to the events that are about to unfold distinguishes him from the rest. As the coming one, Jesus does not merely foresee and foretell what is to happen, although he does that (he knows where the donkey is tied, that the disciples will be challenged, and so on). More fundamentally, Jesus orchestrates the circumstances of his entry, causing events to unfold as they do, beginning with the word "Go!" Jesus' voice is that of a human being, but it is also qualitatively different than that of others, for everything surrounding his entry into Jerusalem unfolds according to his own purpose and intent.

Jesus' "qualitative difference" from others is underscored by his self-designation as "the Lord" (11:3). Lord (*kyrios*) is the surrogate for the Tetragrammaton that the crowds will use when citing Psalm 118:26, in which context it refers unambiguously not to Jesus but to the one in whose name he comes, the Lord, the first person of the Trinity. And yet by applying this same word to himself, Jesus hints that the divine name also in some sense belongs to him. In this way Jesus, to use Richard Bauckham's phrase, signals his inclusion in the identity or uniqueness of God, the one to whom he prays and in whose name he comes.

At the same time, the careful reader detects a subtle grammatical distinction between the two uses of the term "Lord." When the crowds praise God with the words of Psalm 118:26, "Lord" appears without a preceding article, in conformity with its biblical usage as a surrogate for the proper name YHWH.[4] The special nuance can be simulated in English by similarly dropping the article, thus: "Blessed is the one who comes in the name of Lord." As in Greek, the ear detects the hidden presence of a proper name, to which "Lord" is made to conform. (The important nuance is sadly lost by conventional translations, which introduce the unwarranted article "the" in keeping with standard English usage.) In contrast, Jesus designates himself as "*the* Lord" (v. 3), with the article, a usage consistent with (although not necessarily limited to) a titular or honorific understanding of the term, such as "Master" or "Sir." The subtle grammatical distinction preserves the insight that Jesus, though included in the uniqueness of the one God, is not identical with the one to whom he prays, nor does he relate to the divine name in precisely the same way.

The double aspect of Jesus' relation to the first person—encompassing unity and difference—is further emphasized by two details that allude to the book of Zechariah. We are told that Jesus approached Jerusalem from near the Mount of Olives. According to Zechariah, this is the very spot from which the LORD will come to Jerusalem to vanquish his enemies and establish his reign over all the earth.

> [3]Then the LORD will go forth and fight. . . . [4]On that day his feet shall stand on the Mount of Olives, which lies before Jerusalem on the east. . . . [5]Then the LORD my God will come, and all the holy ones with him. (Zech. 14:3–5)

By alluding to this passage, the evangelist signals that the LORD's own coming transpires in Jesus' entry into Jerusalem. To understand how this is so, however, we must notice another allusion to the book of Zechariah, which concerns the advent of another figure, Israel's human king.

> Rejoice greatly, O daughter Zion! Shout aloud, O daughter Jerusalem! Lo, your king comes to you; triumphant and victorious is he, humble and riding on a donkey, on a colt, the foal of a donkey. (9:9)

Jesus' entry into Jerusalem fulfills this prophecy as well, as explicitly claimed in the Gospel of Matthew (21:4–5). Taken together, the two allusions require us to understand the affinity between Jesus and the enactment of divine presence in a rich and nuanced—let us say it—in a *trinitarian* way. The first citation from Zechariah makes clear that what transpires in Jesus' entry is the LORD's own coming! And yet, mysteriously, the LORD accomplishes his advent in the person of another. Jesus, therefore, is neither himself simply identical with the LORD, nor merely a human icon of the LORD's having come, as in Psalm 118. He is the *advent* of the LORD, personified. It is this that gives Jesus' voice its special resonance in the economy of God's name declaration.

THE FIRST PERSON'S DISTINCTIVE VOICE AND ROLE: MANIFESTING DIVINE UNIQUENESS

The first person speaks in a voice that has a special affinity with the saving display of divine uniqueness. The voice of the first person resonates throughout the whole pericope of Jesus' entry into Jerusalem, for everything unfolds "in the name of LORD." Yet just as God's voice entered Psalm 118 with particular vividness at one particular point (v. 5), so also it enters in the New Testament context. All four Gospels locate this point immediately after Jesus' arrival in Jerusalem, although the Synoptics and John portray it in different ways.

In the Synoptics, Jesus goes to the temple immediately upon entering Jerusalem, signaling a shift in focus to the first person, the one in whose name Jesus comes. According to Matthew and Luke, Jesus casts out the money changers, exhibiting zeal on God's behalf. As a warrant for his action, Jesus cites Isaiah 56:7, "My house shall be called a house of prayer" (Matt. 21:13; Luke 19:46; Mark 11:17). With these words, the voice of the first person of the Trinity enters the tableau for the first time, albeit indirectly, by way of Jesus' citation of Scripture. In the corresponding chapter of Isaiah, God declares that "soon my salvation will come, and my deliverance be revealed" (56:1). Envisioned is the saving enlargement of God's covenant to all who "love the name of the LORD" (56:6), when "my house shall be called a house of prayer for all peoples" (56:7). Jesus' cleansing of the temple—and by implication everything he is, says, and does—stands in service of this saving glorification of God's name, when "the glory of the LORD shall be revealed, and all people shall see it together, for the mouth of the LORD has spoken" (40:5).

In John, the voice of first person enters the tableau even more directly. John relates that upon his arrival, Jesus is informed of "some Greeks" who would like to see him, suggesting that Jesus himself is the place where the nations gather, rather than the temple, which John does not mention (cf. John 12:20–26). Immediately thereafter, Jesus alludes obliquely to his imminent death, and then lifts up a prayer that contains only a single petition: "Glorify your name" (John 12:28). The petition encapsulates everything that the gospel drama is about, from the viewpoint of the first person: the glorification of God's name, the saving manifestation and vindication of God's uniqueness on earth. What follows is one of the most stunning verses in the New Testament:

> Then a voice came from heaven, "I have glorified it, and I will glorify it again." (12:28)

The mediating veils of indirect discourse and scriptural citation fall away as we hear the voice of the first person speaking directly. This voice is unmistakably the source of everything that is divine in the voices of Christ and the Spirit, and yet it speaks with a characteristic timbre and emphasis of its own. *The first person's voice is characterized by zeal for the glory of his own name.* Zeal for the glory of the divine name, the unspoken Tetragrammaton, is the past and the future, the beginning and the end of everything that the first person does: "I have glorified it, and I will glorify it again." At the same time, when we hear the first person's voice in concert with those of the second and third, we understand that the glorification of *this* name transpires in perfect fidelity to the ancient promise: "I will come to you and I will bless you" (Exod. 20:24).

CONCLUSION

> The naming of God, in the originary expressions of faith, is not simple but multiple. It is not a single tone, but polyphonic.
>
> —*Paul Ricoeur*[5]

Our aim in this chapter has been to learn to *distinguish the voices* of the persons of the Trinity. We have seen that what gives each person's voice its characteristic timbre is a certain affinity that exists between each person and a particular role and location in the undivided work of declaring the divine name. This result is in keeping with the doctrine of appropriation, which leads us to expect that every action common to the three persons belongs to each of them in a different way. The result is also in perfect harmony with the witness of the Old Testament. For each voice simply enunciates with greater purity and distinctness one of the familiar tones that has characterized God's name declaration from the very beginning.

To put the matter in musical terms, what in the Old Testament we hear as the "overtones" of divine presence and blessing concealed in the uniqueness of the one divine voice, in the New Testament we hear as distinct voices in their own right. The infinitely rich voice of the "one God" is revealed by the sending of Jesus Christ and the outpouring of the Holy Spirit to be in truth the simultaneous interplay of a three-note chord. Each note occupies a different point in trinitarian space and sounds the richness of the divine life at a particular range and frequency, now of divine blessing, now of divine presence, and now of divine uniqueness, the sourceless source of all the music of the divine life.

11

Declaring the Name of the Trinity in the New Testament II

Three Voices in Triple Repetition

Our sketch of the Trinity's name declaration as attested by the New Testament is almost done. We must connect what we have found, so far, with the main question of this book: "What is the most appropriate way of naming the persons of the Trinity?" To advance our investigation a further step, we will take up another aspect of the doctrine of appropriation. Ever mindful that the Trinity works in undivided unity, this aspect maintains that "every attribute and action common to three persons of the Trinity belongs *primarily* to one of them."[1] So, for example, Christians commonly ascribe creation primarily to the first person, redemption to the second, and consummation to the third, even though they know that all three persons work together to create, redeem, and consummate. As Bruce Marshall reminds us, "the primacy here in question is that of likeness (*similitudo* as the medievals put it) rather than of causality or existential dependence."[2] To employ a (very imperfect) musical analogy, we might speak of three voices who always sing together while taking turns carrying the melody, according to a certain real affinity between voice and melodic phrase, so that at any given point only one voice is in the fore while the others support it.

These considerations set the stage for an interesting question. Granted that the persons of the Trinity work together to declare the name of the Trinity, *to which person does this work primarily belong?* Or to put the question in terms of our musical analogy, which person takes the lead in sounding the form of words that best illuminates the mutual relations of God, Christ, and the Spirit?

- Does the first person take the lead? If so, then we would expect the name of the Trinity to resound in a way that has a special affinity with the first person, whose voice, as we saw in the last chapter, resonates with the mystery of *divine uniqueness* at the source of the divine life.
- Or does the second person take the lead? In that case, we would expect the name of the Trinity to be declared in a way that has a special affinity with the second person, whose voice resonates with the mystery of *divine presence* at the heart of the divine life.
- Or does the third person take the lead? Then we would expect the name of the Trinity to have a special affinity with the third person, whose voice resonates with the mystery of *divine blessing* that surrounds and glorifies the divine life.

There is, of course, yet another possibility. It could be that the persons of the Trinity work together in each of these ways, so that the work of declaring the name of the Trinity belongs principally to each of them in turn. Each "sounding" of the name of the Trinity would be the work of the three persons together, but each would have a special affinity with the voice of one person of the Trinity in particular. In that case, the characteristic form of the Trinity's name declaration would be a kind of threefold repetition. Each repetition would be a perfect harmonic unity of uniqueness, presence, and blessing, insofar as each was the undivided work of the three voices together. At the same time, each repetition would be different from the others, insofar as each would especially sound one of these three notes in turn, according to the special timbre and register of its leading voice.

I believe that it is this last answer that is most in keeping with the breadth of the New Testament's witness. Furthermore, I propose, each repetition of the Trinity has a special affinity with one of the three patterns of naming that we identified in the first portion of this book.

- The repetition that belongs primarily to the first person has a special affinity with the pattern of trinitarian naming characterized by oblique reference to the Tetragrammaton.
- The repetition that belongs primarily to the second person has a special affinity with the pattern of naming characterized by the vocabulary of Father, Son, and Holy Spirit.
- The repetition that belongs primarily to the third person has a special affinity with open-ended enlistment of ordinary forms of speech.

Let us test the validity of these claims against the testimony of Scripture. Afterward we will venture a preliminary answer to the main question of this book, "What is the most appropriate way of naming the persons of the Trinity?"

THE FIRST PERSON TAKES THE LEAD: THE MYSTERY OF THE TRINITY AS THE MANIFESTATION OF DIVINE UNIQUENESS

One way the Trinity reveals the divine life in the economy of salvation gives special prominence to the first person, whose voice sounds the mystery of divine uniqueness at the source of the divine life. This repetition of the name of the Trinity has a special affinity with the pattern of trinitarian naming that tightly orbits the Tetragrammaton, the personal proper name of the first person. We can illustrate this pattern by taking a look at the opening verses of the book of Revelation.[3]

Revelation 1:1–8

The book of Revelation signals the cardinal importance of the first person of the Trinity in its first verse:

> The revelation of Jesus Christ, which *God gave him* to show his servants what must soon take place; he made it known by sending his angel to his servant John. (1:1, with emphasis added)

Everything flows from the primordial initiative of God, even "the revelation of Jesus Christ." But *who is "God"? Who is the ultimate source of the saving revelation of Jesus Christ?* That is the question that Revelation immediately sets about to answer. The climactic response appears in verse 8:

> "I am the Alpha and the Omega," says the Lord God, who is and who was and who is to come, the Almighty.

What we have here is in fact a *triple* answer to the question "Who is God?" introduced by God's own self-identification. All three answers consist in an oblique reference to the Tetragrammaton, signaling its supreme importance as a sign of the uniqueness of "God," the ultimate source of the revelation of Jesus Christ. In addition, the last two answers pair the unspoken Tetragrammaton with other divine names, in a manner consistent with the usage of the Old Testament.

The easiest of the three answers to decipher is the middle one, "Lord God." "Lord" should be understood as a surrogate for the Tetragrammaton, as signaled by its lack of an article ("says Lord God" would be a more accurate translation in 1:8). "God," of course, is an appellative name that commonly follows after the Tetragrammaton in the Old Testament and especially in the Septuagint (Greek).

A more striking allusion to the divine name is the first one, "I am the Alpha and Omega." This answer is unique because it is spoken directly by God, in God's own voice. The phrase "Alpha and Omega" has a double significance. Taken according to its surface meaning, it affirms God's sovereignty over history, God's precedence to every past and subsequence to every future (cf. Isa. 44:6). In addition, however, the phrase likely contains a veiled reference to the Tetragrammaton, which was sometimes transliterated into Greek as ΙΑΩ (*iota*, *alpha*, *omega*).[4] The implication is that God's sovereignty over history is rooted not merely in what God does—in God's power, say—but in who God is, the bearer of the divine name.

The last answer to the question "Who is 'God'?" pairs an allusion to the Tetragrammaton with the epithet "Almighty," evoking the Old Testament name *LORD Sabaoth*. Superficially, the phrase "He [Gk.] who is and who was and who is to come" resembles a familiar trope of Hellenistic religion, the *Dreizeitenformel* (Ger., lit., three-times formula), by which pagan deities regularly proclaimed their unchanging self-sameness in past, present, and future. An example is the following:

> Zeus was, Zeus is, Zeus shall be. O mighty Zeus![5]

John, however, twists the motif to signify the Deity attested by Scripture. The phrase begins not with the *past* tense, as one might expect, but with the *present*, citing God's first reply to Moses at the burning bush ("He Who Is," Exod. 3:14 LXX). The two remaining elements of the name then correspond to past and future, creating an exact parallel with God's *first* self-naming: "I am [the present] the Alpha [the past] and the Omega [the future]." The most extraordinary part of the threefold name is its final element. In place of the expected "who will be," which would have rounded off the phrase by employing the verb "to be" a third time, we find "*who is coming*." Not only is this the "wrong" verb; it also is the "wrong" tense! (Translations often sadly obscure this by writing "is to come" [KJV, NIV, RSV, NRSV] rather than "who is coming" [YLT].) But the unexpected substitution is in keeping with the deeper significance of the phrase as an interpretive paraphrase of the unspoken Tetragrammaton. The bearer of *that* name, we are given to understand, is the "God" whose very identity it is "to come." As Sean McDonough puts it, "John does not simply talk about God's coming as an incidental attribute. *It is rather a part of his name, his identity.* The coming of God to his creation is not simply a future possibility for John, it is an inevitable consequence of God's being who he is."[6]

Taken as a whole, verse 8 represents not three different answers to the question "Who is God, the ultimate source of the revelation of Jesus Christ?"

but one answer expressed in three different ways. At the heart of this one answer stands the Tetragrammaton, a name that is obliquely signaled in a variety of ways but never directly spoken or written. A more emphatic delineation of the unique identity of the first person of the Trinity is difficult to conceive. At the same time, its full significance becomes apparent only when we examine how the opening verses of Revelation identify—not only the *first* person of the Trinity—but the *second* and *third* as well.

Revelation 1:1–8 and the Third and Second Persons of the Trinity

Revelation 1:1 and 1:8 are theocentric bookends that bracket a fully trinitarian portrait of the divine life. We see this unmistakably in the book's opening salutation:

> Grace to you and peace from *he* who is and who was and who is to come, and from the seven spirits who are before his throne, [5]and from Jesus Christ, the faithful witness, the firstborn of the dead, and the ruler of the kings of the earth. (1:4–5, with "he" [Gk.] instead of "him" [NRSV])

The greeting is unusual among early Christian letters for its explicitly trinitarian structure. Though we have already discussed the phrase "he who is and who was and who is to come" (1:8), its appearance here, for the first time in the letter, requires a further comment. The phrase appears in place of the customary reference to "God the Father," not because John has anything against the latter term (he uses it in v. 6), but because his aim is to signify at the outset *who* this "Father" is. An extraordinary feature of the phrase is that it ("he who . . .") appears in the *nominative* case in Greek, even though the syntax of the salutation makes this a grammatical "error" of the most egregious kind. But there is no error: John purposefully introduces a grammatical solecism in order to imply that the phrase is "a single indeclinable noun," like a Hebrew proper name.[7] The deviant grammar is yet one more indication that John intends the phrase to allude to a name that does not explicitly appear on the surface of the text itself: the unspoken Tetragrammaton.

Naming the Third Person: The Seven Spirits Who Are before His Throne

Unlike the salutations of most letters in the New Testament, John the Seer's includes an explicit reference to the Holy Spirit. Admittedly, John has chosen "an unusual way of designating the Holy Spirit,"[8] to the point where some have suggested that "the seven spirits who are before his throne" (v. 4) is really a reference to seven angels, and not to the divine Spirit at all. Once again, however, John has simply pushed language into unusual shape, this time in order to illuminate the Spirit's relationship to the first person *as bearer of the unspoken name.*

John's unusual phrase alludes to a vision from Zechariah, in which the prophet beholds a lampstand on which are seven lamps, an allusion to the sacred menorah that stood in the temple before the throne of YHWH. An angel explains that the seven lamps are "the eyes of the Lord, which range through the whole earth" (Zech. 4:10b). By means of the phrase "the seven spirits," John suggests that the Holy Spirit is equivalent to "the eyes of the Lord" referred to in Zechariah. The identification of "the seven spirits" with the "eyes of the Lord" becomes more explicit a little later in the letter. In Revelation 5:6, we read:

> Then I saw between the throne and the four living creatures and among the elders a Lamb standing as if it had been slaughtered, having seven horns and seven eyes, which are the seven spirits of God sent out into all the earth.

Here "seven eyes" are explicitly identified with "the seven spirits of God," making it difficult to suppose that John intends anything other than the Holy Spirit. Yet, arrestingly, the seven spirits/eyes are said to belong to a slaughtered Lamb, a clear reference to Jesus Christ. To whom, then, do the spirits/eyes belong, to God or to Christ? John seems to indicate both. Like other New Testament writers, John understands the first person of the Trinity to be the ultimate source of the Spirit, even as Jesus Christ is its proximate source as the Spirit is poured out on the earth in the end times (cf. Acts 2:33; John 20:22). John's language is equivalent to the teaching that "the Holy Spirit proceeds from the Father through the Son." John, however, expresses this in a way that emphasizes the first person's identity as bearer of the divine name.[9]

Naming the Second Person: the Faithful Witness—Look! He Is Coming with the Clouds

The opening salutation identifies Jesus Christ as "the faithful witness, the firstborn of the dead, and the ruler of the kings of the earth" (Rev. 1:5). The implication seems to be that Jesus Christ's relation to "He who is and who was and who is to come" encompasses both unity (as indicated by the parallel triadic structure) and difference (as indicated by the distinctive content of Jesus' titles). The precise nature of these, however, is not initially clear. In particular, the names applied to Jesus in verse 5 do not seem to settle the question of whether Jesus is to be viewed as an exalted creature or as divine—or to put it another way, as external or internal to the eternal life of "He who is and who was and who is to come."

All ambiguity is removed over the course of the rest of the book, however, beginning with the very next verses:

> [5]To him who loves us and freed us from our sins by his blood, [6]and made us to be a kingdom, priests serving his God and Father, to him be glory and dominion forever and ever. Amen.
>
> 7 Look! He is coming with the clouds;
>   every eye will see him,
> even those who pierced him;
>   and on his account all the tribes of the earth will wail.
>
> So it is to be. Amen. (1:5b–7)

That Jesus is internal to the life of God is made clear in the first instance by the flow of worship indicated here. Jesus Christ, we are told, has made priests who serve "his God and Father." Yet the doxology in which this affirmation appears is directed to Jesus Christ "forever and ever." In the last days, it appears, priests serve God by rendering praise to Jesus Christ! Yet a still more striking indication of Christ's inclusion in the deity of God comes in the following words, "Look, he [Jesus] *is coming* with the clouds, and every eye will see him!" The key verb ("to come") is the same one that formed the climax of God's name in verse 4b. The verb has scarcely ceased to reverberate before it tolls afresh, this time predicated of Jesus Christ! The repetition is a theological tour de force. Jesus' coming, we are given to understand, is no incidental or contingent event. It is internal to God's own coming to creation, nay, more, to God's own identity as "he who is and who was and who is coming." Jesus Christ is, quite literally, the one who comes "in the name of the Lord." John does not thereby designate Jesus as a second God, "but includes him in the eternal being of the one God of Israel who is the only source and goal of all things."[10]

THE SECOND PERSON TAKES THE LEAD: THE MYSTERY OF THE TRINITY AS THE ENACTMENT OF DIVINE PRESENCE

Another way the Trinity reveals the divine life in the economy of salvation gives special prominence to the second person, whose personal distinction it is to sound the mystery of divine presence at the heart of the divine life. This repetition of the name of the Trinity has a special affinity with the vocabulary of Father, Son, and Spirit. We can illustrate this pattern by taking a look at the closing verses of the Gospel of Matthew.[11]

Matthew 28:16–20

The passage reads as follows:

> [16]Now the eleven disciples went to Galilee, to the mountain to which Jesus had directed them. [17]When they saw him, they worshiped him; but some doubted. [18]And Jesus came and said to them, "All authority in heaven and on earth has been given to me. [19]Go therefore and make disciples of all nations, baptizing them in the name of the Father and of the Son and of the Holy Spirit, [20]and teaching them to obey everything that I have commanded you. And remember, I am with you always, to the end of the age. (Matt. 28:16–20)

The climax of the Gospel of Matthew is a christophany, a manifestation of the victorious presence of Christ to the disciples. The christophany has been prefigured by events earlier in the Gospel, as at the time of his birth, his baptism in the Jordan, and his glorification on the Mount of Transfiguration. Yet compared with these earlier intimations of divine presence in Christ, this christophany is unique in a striking way. Previously the epiphanies of Christ had always been accompanied by some audible or visible sign of the first and third persons of the Trinity, such as the voice from heaven or the descending dove. Now at the conclusion of the Gospel, however, the first and third persons of the Trinity are completely invisible and inaudible. Christ alone is seen and heard. Christ's divine presence fills the mountaintop as fully and exclusively as did the presence of the Lord on Mt. Sinai, reaching out to the margins of the narrative so that room scarcely remains for the disciples themselves.

Yet in its very Christ-centeredness, Matthew 28:16–20 is also thoroughly and utterly trinitarian in conception. The first and third persons are indeed invisible and inaudible in *themselves*, but they become indirectly visible and audible *in Christ*. The first person is indirectly visible in Christ's very aliveness, in his having-being-raised-from-the-dead. And the Spirit is indirectly audible in Christ's promise of abiding presence to the end of the age (unlike Luke and John, Matthew, we recall, has no independent account of the gift of the Spirit to the followers of Jesus). The passage is every bit as trinitarian, therefore, as Revelation 1:4–8, but its trinitarianism is of a different sort, centered in the victorious presence of the second person rather than the uniqueness of the first.

The passage's "trinitarianism of the second person" is elaborately conveyed by the compositional structure of Christ's speech. The speech consists of an intricate set of nesting triads that consistently point toward the first and third persons, even as they repeatedly center in Jesus Christ, "the Son." At the largest compositional level, Jesus' speech is structured around the triad of announcement, command, and promise:

Announcement (v. 18b)	Command (vv. 19–20a)	Promise (v. 20b)
All authority has been given . . .	Go therefore . . .	And remember . . .

Christ is the explicit subject of all three elements of the triad; the personal pronouns "I" or "me" appear in all three segments. Even so, the first and final elements of the triad point indirectly to the first and third persons of the Trinity respectively.

In the announcement (18b), Jesus declares that "all authority in heaven and on earth *has been given* to me." The logical but unstated subject of the verb is the first person, the one who possesses "all authority" and thus is able to grant it to Christ. (The verb is best understood as an instance of the so-called divine passive, discussed at greater length in chap. 12.) Our passage presupposes, then, that the first person has not only raised Jesus from the dead, but also exalted him and invested him with divine authority (cf. Phil. 2:5–11). In this sense, Christ is transparent to the first person, who, though unseen and unheard, becomes indirectly visible in him.

In the promise (v. 20b), Jesus declares "Lo, I am with you always (lit., 'I with you am,' *egō meth' hymōn eimi*) to the end of the age." Again, the emphasis falls upon Christ himself, and yet in such a way that Jesus becomes transparent to the person and presence of the Holy Spirit. As noted, the Gospel of Matthew lacks a distinct account of the bestowal of the Holy Spirit to the community of disciples. What Luke portrays as Pentecost, and John as Jesus' bestowing of the Spirit by breathing on the disciples (20:22), Matthew in effect folds into the promise of the risen Christ, "I am with you always." The reference to the Holy Spirit is concretely indicated by a verbal echo between Christ's words in Matthew 28:20 and the words spoken by the angel of the Lord at the time of Jesus' birth, "The child conceived in her is from the Holy Spirit" (1:20b), which fulfill the prophetic word, "Look, the virgin shall conceive and bear a son, and they shall name him Emmanuel," which means, "God is with us" (1:23, Gk. *meth' hēmōn ho theos*; cf. 18:20).

When we turn to the command, the middle element of Christ's speech, we make an interesting discovery. Of the three main parts of Jesus' speech, only it consists of a further set of three parts!

Announcement	**Command**			Promise
	Go therefore and make disciples of all nations,	baptizing them in the name of . . . ,	and teaching them to obey everything . . .	

Again, Christ's person and commanding authority is evident in all three elements, but once again, there is a subtle affinity between the three subelements and the persons of the Trinity. In Jesus' command to "make disciples *of all nations*," we hear in the background the note of God's universal sovereignty over creation, just as in the command to "teach them to obey," we hear the note of the Spirit's role in the edification and sanctification of Jesus' followers.

Turning to the central element of this triad, we discover that it too opens into a more complex structure: "Baptizing them in the name of the Father and of the Son and of the Holy Spirit."

Go therefore . . . ,	**baptizing them in the name**[12]			and teaching them . . .
	of the Father	and of the Son	and of the Holy Spirit,	

The series of nesting triads comes to a conclusion at last in the saying "the Father and the Son and the Holy Spirit." Like the sun finally rising above the horizon at dawn, the verse makes explicit the trinitarian nature of the passage that has been subtly signaled from the beginning; indeed, it makes explicit the trinitarian nature of the whole *Gospel*, which has also been prefigured since the opening chapters. The saying's trinitarian orientation is obvious, not merely in its threefold vocabulary, but also in its grammatical parallelism, which places all three terms on the same level. At the same time, we should not fail to see that the saying "the Father and the Son and the Holy Spirit" has a distinctive center and concern of its own. Consistent with the composition of the passage as a whole, its central concern becomes visible in *its* middle element, "*the Son*," the one whose presence dominates the pericope from top to bottom and side to side. The theme of presence is further emphasized by the association of the triadic formula with baptism, the rite whereby new disciples are initiated into the bonds of the fellowship of Christ. In sum, Matthew 28 does not deploy the language of "Father, Son, and Spirit" as a generic or all-purpose trinitarian vocabulary, but quite specifically in a way that finds its center of gravity in the second person and the mystery of victorious divine presence enacted in him.

THE THIRD PERSON TAKES THE LEAD: THE MYSTERY OF THE TRINITY AS THE BESTOWAL OF DIVINE BLESSING

Still another way the Trinity reveals the divine life in the economy of salvation gives special prominence to the third person, whose voice resonates especially with the mystery of divine blessing that surrounds and glorifies the divine life. This repetition has a special affinity with that pattern of trinitarian naming characterized by an open-ended variety of language drawn from many sources and contexts. We can illustrate this pattern by taking a look at the story of Pentecost as recounted in Acts 2. Pentecost, we remember, was originally an agricultural festival celebrated to give thanks for the blessings of God (cf. Exod. 23:16; Deut. 16:10; Num. 28:26). By dating the outpouring of the Spirit to the day of Pentecost, Luke signals continuity with God's blessings in the past, but also the surpassing greatness of God's blessings in the present, which are all comprehended in the *one* blessing of the gift of the Holy Spirit.[13]

Acts 2

Luke's account begins in this way:

> [1]When the day of Pentecost had come, they were all together in one place. [2]And suddenly from heaven there came a sound like the rush of a violent wind, and it filled the entire house where they were sitting. [3]Divided tongues, as of fire, appeared among them, and a tongue rested on each of them. [4]All of them were filled with the Holy Spirit and began to speak in other languages, as the Spirit gave them ability. (Acts 2:1–4)

The voice of the Holy Spirit has a distinctive tenor that distinguishes it from that of the first and second persons. The advent of the Spirit is signaled at first by signs and wonders of untamed natural power, by primordial wind and fire. Quickly, though, it modulates out of this cosmic register and comes to rest, not over one or two of the most outstanding disciples, but over the whole assembly, enabling everyone to speak ordinary languages in an extraordinary way. Plain men and women talk in everyday tongues—but not their own! Rugged day-to-day languages from around the world are put to use—but by speakers of one homely dialect from backwater Galilee. In this blessed event of the ordinary transformed, we recognize the distinctive tenor of the Spirit's voice.

Still, the wonders of Pentecost are just beginning. We have heard *how* the Spirit empowers the disciples to speak, but not *what* they say. Significantly, this report first comes to us from the perspective of those who *hear* them:

> [5]Now there were devout Jews from every nation under heaven living in Jerusalem. [6]And at this sound the crowd gathered and was bewildered, because each one heard them speaking in the native language of each. [7]Amazed and astonished, they asked, "Are not all these who are speaking Galileans? [8]And how is it that we hear, each of us, in our own native language? . . . [11]In our own languages we hear them speaking about God's deeds of power." (2:5–8, 11)

The key sentence is "in our own languages we hear them speaking about God's deeds of power." The first half of the sentence ("in our own languages") is important because it shows that the miracle of Pentecost is as much about the capacity of the nations to *hear* the message of the Galileans, as it is about the backwater countryfolk themselves. But the second half of the sentence is even more important for our purposes, because it reports the contents of their message for the first time: "We hear them speaking about *God's deeds of power*" (*ta megaleia tou theou*). Unremarkable though it may seem, the phrase "God's deeds of power" provides a hermeneutical key for understanding how the gospel was proclaimed and heard on the morning of Pentecost. The assembled crowds, we must remember, were all Jews (v. 5), like the Galileans themselves. Nevertheless, the term used to designate the Deity is not a surrogate for the Tetragrammaton (e.g., "Lord"), as one might expect, but simply "God" (*theos*), the most universal, ordinary, and "translatable" of all divine names. The phrase "deeds of power" is similarly broad in scope. The root word comes from the adjective *megaleios*, meaning magnificent, excellent, splendid, wonderful, marvelous. Used in the plural and saying something about God, it may refer either to the greatness of God himself or the greatness of God's deeds, or both. While most translations single out God's deeds ("the mighty works of God" [RSV]; "the wonderful works of God" [KJV]), the old Thayer lexicon happily draws out both dimensions of the phrase by translating it as "the glorious perfections of God and his marvelous doings."[14]

Thus the abundance of preachers and hearers, of sermons and languages, is now multiplied exponentially by the superabundance of their common theme: "the glorious perfections of God and his marvelous doings." Limitations of narrative method prohibit Luke from recounting what each person hears in detail, and we must simply let our mind's ear imagine the plenitude of divine names and praises that filled the air, in languages "from every nation under heaven" (1:5). Still, Luke does recount *one* sermon in greater depth, and we can look to it for further lessons about naming the Trinity in a pneumatological key.

Peter's Sermon

Peter's speech on the morning of Pentecost contains no striking names for the persons of the Trinity after the fashion of Augustine's Lover, Beloved, and Love. It would be surprising if it did, given the context of the sermon, and the Gospels' portrait of Peter. Still, it does reveal the sprouts from which this type of naming grows. The sermon is quite long, so I will quote only as much as is helpful for the present discussion.

> [14]But Peter, standing with the eleven, raised his voice and addressed them, "Men of Judea and all who live in Jerusalem, let this be known to you, and listen to what I say. . . . [16]This is what was spoken through the prophet Joel:
>
> [17]'In the last days it will be, God declares,
> that I will pour out my Spirit upon all flesh,
> and your sons and your daughters shall prophesy,
> and your young men shall see visions,
> and your old men shall dream dreams. . . .
> [21]Then everyone who calls on the name of the Lord shall
> be saved.' (NRSV)
>
> [22]"Men of Israel, hear these words: Jesus of Nazareth, a man attested to you by God with mighty works and wonders and signs which God did through him in your midst, as you yourselves know—[23]this Jesus, delivered up according to the definite plan and foreknowledge of God, you crucified and killed by the hands of lawless men. . . . [32]This Jesus God raised up, and of that all of us are witnesses. [33]Being therefore exalted at the right hand of God, and having received from the Father the promise of the Holy Spirit, he has poured out this which you see and hear. . . ." (RSV)

Throughout his sermon, Peter names the persons of the Trinity differently according to the different "strata" of his speech, depending on whether he is (1) citing Scripture, (2) quoting the words of Jesus, or (3) speaking freely in his own words. In the first stratum, the quotation of Scripture, Peter identifies the first and the second persons by using an oblique reference to the Tetragrammaton, "Lord" (cf. 2:20–21, 25, 34), as illustrated above by the citation from the prophet Joel, "Everyone who calls on the name of the Lord shall be saved."[15] In a second stratum of discourse, Peter recites Jesus Christ's own words. This stratum is quite thin, consisting entirely in the one affirmation that Jesus "received from the Father the promise of the Holy Spirit" (33), a reference to Jesus' words at the beginning of *Acts*, when he spoke of the Holy Spirit as "the promise of the Father" (1:4). These two strata of Peter's discourse are not happenstance assemblages of words from here and there, but correspond exactly to the two patterns of trinitarian naming we have previously examined in this chapter, one in which the dominant voice is the scripturally attested voice of the "Lord," and one in which the dominant voice is that of Jesus himself.

This brings us to the "surface" stratum of Peter's sermon, the apostle's own free discourse, where he speaks spontaneously to the crowds in relative independence of the authoritative words of Scripture or of Christ. The crucial thing to note is that here Peter speaks of God, Christ, and the Spirit *in a way that is keyed to the experience and language of his audience.* Peter consistently speaks of the first person as "God," picking up the crowd's own report of what they had heard the apostles proclaim "in our own native language." ("God" does not appear in the citations of Scripture, nor in the recollected words of Christ, except where Peter himself inserts it.) Analogously, he speaks of Jesus as "a man *attested to you* by God with mighty works and wonders and signs which God did through him *in your midst, as you yourselves know*" (v. 22 RSV). He invites the crowd to recollect and confirm what they themselves know to be true about Jesus, including his death by their own complicity, because they saw it and heard it with their own eyes and ears. Peter emphatically declares, "*This* Jesus," whom "*you yourselves* know," is he whom "God raised up" (vv. 22, 32).

Finally, Peter speaks of the Holy Spirit too in terms of his audience's firsthand experience. The key sentence is this:

> Being therefore exalted at the right hand of God, and having received from the Father the promise of the Holy Spirit, he has poured out *this that you both see and hear.* (v. 33)

In context, "this that you both see and hear" is virtually a synonym for "Holy Spirit," a way of saying the same thing that exploits the immediate context at hand. The phrase names the Spirit in terms of what the assembly has experienced for itself: the hurly-burly in the streets, the strange eloquence of peasants, and the wonder of hearing of God's splendors recounted in one's own native tongue. Peter's impromptu naming of the Spirit removes the fog of ambiguity that surrounded these events (they are not the effect of new wine!) and reveals them to be tokens of the superlative blessing of God.

At the end of the sermon, the convicted audience asks, "Brothers, what should we do?" Peter tells them to be baptized in the name of Jesus, and then they too "will receive the gift of the Holy Spirit." (Augustine cites this passage as evidence that one of the names of the Holy Spirit is "Gift"; *Trin.* 15.35.) Peter then explains:

> For the promise is for you, for your children, and for all who are far away, everyone whom the Lord our God calls to him. (2:39)

Peter's sermon ends with something like a reprise of all three "strata" of his discourse. "Promise" echoes Christ's distinctive way of referring to the Holy Spirit, while "Lord" echoes the language of Scripture. Still, the emphasis seems to fall on the last theonym, "*our God*," giving the last word, in a sense, back to the congregation of people "from every nation under heaven" (v. 5), and to the way in which they experienced and heard the miracle of Pentecost.

Threefold Naming: God, the *Megaleia* of God in Christ, and "this which you see and hear"

Peter's speech is virtually a compendium of all the patterns of naming the Trinity that we have investigated in this chapter. In it, we hear echoes of the patterns of trinitarian naming that we saw more fully developed in Revelation 1 and Matthew 28. At the same time, we have recognized in Peter's sermon a *third* way of naming the persons of the Trinity in which the distinctive voice and rhetoric of the Holy Spirit come to the fore. In the particular case at hand, this pattern comes to expression by naming the first person as "God"; the second person as the one singled out by "deeds of power, wonders, and signs"; and the third person as "this that you both see and hear." To be sure, this language is quite ordinary and heavily imbued with the particular context in which it first arose. Still, the humility of the language and its context-specificity is part of the point, for it is characteristic of the Holy Spirit to rest on the ordinary wherever it may be, bless it, and transform it into praise of "the glorious perfections of God and his marvelous doings" (Thayer).

THREE MOST APPROPRIATE WAYS OF NAMING THE PERSONS OF THE TRINITY

The texts we have examined in this chapter suggest that the persons of the Trinity work together to reveal their common life together, even as they do so in three different ways, each of which has a special affinity with one of the persons of the Trinity and one of the patterns of naming that we identified in part 1 of this book. Which of these three is the most appropriate way of naming the persons of the Trinity? The answer, I believe, is "All of them!"

The idea that there can be more than one "most appropriate" name is not new: it goes back to Thomas Aquinas's analysis of the names of the burning bush in *Summa theologiae* (1a.13). What makes it possible for a name to be "most appropriate" in a given instance is its special aptness to a particular context or frame of reference. In the case of the three patterns of naming we have investigated in this book, that context is the life of the Trinity itself and the varied ways in which God, Christ, and the Spirit make themselves known in the economy of salvation.

- The pattern of naming that employs oblique reference to the Tetragrammaton is *a* most appropriate way of naming the persons of the Trinity by virtue of its affinity with the first person of the Trinity and the mystery of divine uniqueness that is the source of the divine life.
- The pattern of naming that employs the vocabulary of Father, Son, and Spirit is *a* most appropriate way of naming the persons of the Trinity by virtue of its affinity with the second person of the Trinity and the mystery of divine presence at the heart of the divine life.
- The pattern of naming that employs an open-ended variety drawn from common experience is *a* most appropriate way of naming the persons of the Trinity by virtue of its affinity with the third person of the Trinity and the mystery of divine blessing that radiates from the divine life.

Therefore we recognize three most appropriate ways of naming the persons of the Trinity, each of which is most appropriate in a different way, because of its affinity with a different person of the Trinity as revealed in the economy of salvation.

Interlude

The Name of Jesus Christ and the Name of the Trinity

> A beautiful breathing instrument of music the Lord made man, after His own image. And He Himself also, surely, who is the supramundane Wisdom, the celestial Word, is the all-harmonious, melodious, holy instrument of God.
>
> —*Clement of Alexandria*[1]

We now have an answer to our question, "What is the most appropriate way of naming the persons of the Trinity?" Still, the answer is tentative, because it rests so far on a slender survey of the New Testament. Beginning with the next chapter, therefore, we will test whether it holds up against a more fine-grained examination of the biblical witness. Our second journey through the Scriptures, however, will proceed by a new route. Rather than move from the Old Testament to the New, tracing the contours of God's name declaration, we will focus this time on the Gospels' portraits of Jesus Christ, the Word made flesh, attending especially to the characteristic ways in which he speaks about himself, the Spirit, and the One to whom he prays.

Why adopt this new procedure at this point? One reason is to address a concern some may have about the argument so far. The objection would go like this: "I see what you mean about there being three different patterns of naming the persons of the Holy Trinity. Still, I do not see how you can say that they are all equally important. The mystery of the Trinity is revealed in and through the person of Christ, through his relationships to the One to whom he prays and the Spirit in whom he lives. Therefore, it seems that what you call the *christological* repetition of the name of the Trinity must be the most important of the three—the one that comes to expression in the vocabulary of Father, Son, and Holy Spirit." "Furthermore," my interlocutor might continue, "you have argued that there is a connection between the three patterns of naming the Trinity and the voices of God, Christ, and the Spirit. But Christ speaks vastly more often than either God or the Spirit in the New Testament. So again, it seems, the christological repetition must be more important than the other two, in keeping with the greater prominence of Christ's voice over the voices of the other two persons of the Trinity."

I have sympathy for the concern that prompts this objection. A major test for any doctrine of the Trinity is its capacity to bring the central figure of Christian faith into focus, or to put it another way, to illuminate the divine depths opened up by the person who bears the name "Jesus." If it could be shown that one pattern of naming were more or less important in this regard, then that would count heavily against my proposal. However, I do not think this is what we find. When we attend carefully to the Gospels' portraits of Christ Jesus, we discover that *all three repetitions of the name of the Trinity meet and intersect in him.* In the wonderful phrase of Clement of Alexandria, Christ Jesus is the "all-harmonious, melodious, holy instrument of God." Through him, all the music of the triune life is made known, whether in a christological, theological, or pneumatological key.

Upon reflection, we realize that this is just what the doctrine of appropriation would lead us to expect. Like the other persons of the Trinity, Jesus Christ participates in every work of the Trinity in the economy of salvation. If, therefore, the persons of the Trinity really do proclaim who they are together in three different ways, then we should expect to find this reflected in Jesus Christ and in his own characteristic ways of speaking.

In the final chapters of this book, therefore, we will trace the Gospels' portraits of Jesus Christ three times, concentrating each time on a different dimension of his characteristic speech about himself, the Spirit, and the one to whom he prays. Each dimension, as we shall see, corresponds to one of the three "most appropriate" ways of naming the Trinity that we have already identified. And each serves to bring Jesus Christ himself into focus in a different but equally indispensable way.

12

Hallowed Be Your Name!

Jesus the Manifestation of Divine Uniqueness and the Name of the Trinity in a Theological Key

In every place where *I cause my name to be remembered*
I will come to you and bless you.

—*Exodus 20:24b*

"Wherever Jesus appears, the Trinity is understood."[1] These words of Julian of Norwich express a profound truth. Those seeking knowledge of the Trinity do well to look at Jesus, for wherever he is, there the Trinity is too. One way that we may contemplate Jesus is specifically with reference to his characteristic ways of speaking about himself, the Spirit, and the One to whom he prays, as these are portrayed by the Gospels in their final canonical form.

In the twentieth century many who have embarked on this path have been deeply impressed by Jesus' custom of opening prayer with the address "Father!" This, they note, casts light not only on the One to whom he prays, but also on Jesus himself—the Beloved Son!—and on the Holy Spirit, the bond of mutual love between them. Just so, they have maintained, the Trinity is understood wherever Jesus appears, through this telling feature of his speech.

Others approaching the figure of Jesus from a different angle have been equally impressed by his custom of proclaiming God's coming reign in parables and signs of power. This too, they say, casts light on the One to whom Jesus prays, whose unfathomable mystery is revealed by Christ as "the Parable of God" and applied by the Spirit, who gathers up the wounded words of ordinary life and transforms them into hymns to the everlasting Trinity. Just so, they argue, the mystery of the Trinity becomes visible through this decisive feature of Jesus' speech.

In the following two chapters I will argue that both of these ways of discerning the mystery of the Trinity in Jesus' characteristic patterns of speech are indispensably important. One brings to focus the mystery of divine presence enacted in him, the other the mystery of divine blessing bestowed in him. At the same time, I maintain that neither alone, nor even both together, are sufficient to sound the depths of the ways the Trinity is made known in Jesus. Crucial as they are, they leave another dimension of this mystery underexposed: the manifestation of divine *uniqueness* in him. To bring into focus this dimension, which—to change images—is the sourceless source of the divine mystery in its fullness, we must carefully attend to yet another characteristic feature of Jesus' speech: his practice of showing reverence for the Tetragrammaton by avoiding its direct use.[2]

THE DIVINE NAME AND PERIPHRASTIC SPEECH IN THE GOSPELS' PORTRAIT OF JESUS

> Whoever has the word of Jesus for a true possession can also hear his silence.
>
> —*Ignatius of Antioch*[3]

An example of how Jesus shows reverence for the divine name by avoiding its direct use is found in Mark's account of his trial before the high priest.

> Again the high priest asked him, "Are you the Messiah, the Son of the Blessed One?" Jesus said, "I am; and
> 'you will see the Son of Man seated at the right hand of the Power,'
> and 'coming with the clouds of heaven.'" (Mark 14:61–62)

Here both Jesus and the high priest use circumlocutions in place of the divine name. "The Blessed One" and "the Power" are not freestanding designations that stand independently in their own right, like "God," but stand-in names used in place of the divine name. Jesus and the high priest use different circumlocutions, but they have no difficulty in understanding each other. Each perceives the other to be making a veiled reference to the one God who is distinguished from every other reality in heaven and on earth by the bearing of the unspoken divine name.

From a historical point of view, it is not surprising that the Gospels should portray Jesus as avoiding the direct use of the divine name. By the first century, such avoidance was normative across the variety of Second Temple Judaisms, an axiomatic feature of what later rabbinic tradition would refer to as "oral Torah" or "oral law."[4] It would be startling if Jesus did not honor the practice. The more important question is whether Jesus assigned any importance to it, or whether he regarded it, as many Christians subsequently would, as something essentially perishable destined to become "dead and deadly," along with the rest of Jewish ceremonial law.

The Avoidance of Oaths and the Dominical "Amen"

We can get an initial answer to these questions by looking at Jesus' teaching regarding oaths. By Jesus' day, the idea had arisen in some circles that oaths became less binding in proportion to how indirectly they invoked God's name and person: the less direct the invocation, the less binding the oath. This interpretation in effect treats the practice of referring to God circumlocutiously as a buffer that conveniently distances the speaker from the holiness of God, like the insulation of an electric wire. The thicker the insulation, the less the majesty of God and God's name is implicated. Jesus angrily rejects this view.

> Woe to you, blind guides, who say, "Whoever swears by the sanctuary is bound by nothing, but whoever swears by the gold of the sanctuary is bound by the oath." You blind fools! For which is greater, the gold or the sanctuary that has made the gold sacred? And you say, "Whoever swears by the altar is bound by nothing, but whoever swears by the gift that is on the altar is bound by the oath." How blind you are! For which is greater, the gift or the altar that makes the gift sacred? So whoever swears by the altar, swears by it and by everything on it; and whoever swears by the sanctuary, swears by it and by the one who dwells in it; and whoever swears by heaven, swears by the throne of God and by the one who is seated upon it. (Matt. 23:16–22)

The target of Jesus' condemnation in this passage is not the custom of using "buffers" in place of God's name. Quite the contrary: as Gustaf Dalman observed about this passage over a century ago, "Even he appears to approve the non-pronunciation of the name of God."[5] Jesus' scorn is directed rather at the premise that such circumlocutions serve to *replace* the divine name rather than to *refer* to it. "Swearing by heaven is looked upon by Jesus as equivalent to swearing by God" because "*a real name of God was being intentionally avoided.*"[6] The higher righteousness to which Jesus calls his disciples elsewhere in Matthew is not the explicit use of God's name, as might be the case if he regarded the practice of name avoidance as essentially perishable, but adherence to a yet more rigorous form of it: the eschewing of oaths altogether (5:34).

Dalman suggests that Jesus' teaching on oaths is connected to another highly distinctive feature of his customary speech: his habit of underscoring his teaching with the word "Amen."[7] "As Jesus, in forbidding the oath, had in view the guarding against a misuse of the divine name, so here, too, one may speak of a conscious avoidance of the name of God." Lacking recourse to the use of oaths, "He had to seek for some other mode of emphasis, and found it in the solemner 'Amen.'"[8] Again, Jesus' zeal for the divine name comes to expression not in a tendency toward pronouncing it, but in a heightened desire to signal its unique status—by avoiding its direct use.

Jesus' teaching on oaths suggests that zeal for the holiness of the divine name was more than a superficial feature of Jesus' piety and teaching, or at least this is what his teaching on oaths suggests. Still, most of the Christian tradition has not generally regarded this particular teaching as an especially central aspect of his person and work, for understandable reasons. Do we still find similar evidence of Jesus' passion for the divine name when we turn to what the tradition has found central? Indeed, we do. For evidence of this we turn to the Lord's Prayer.

Hallowed Be Your Name! The Avoidance of God's Name as a Sign of the Uniqueness of God

The first petition of the Lord's Prayer is a plea for the hallowing or sanctification of God's name (Matt. 6:9). To hallow or sanctify the name of God is to vindicate its holiness, to remove from it every besmirching obscurity, and to make it shine forth with the radiance of a single truth only: "I am the Lord!" By placing this petition at the head of the prayer, Jesus indicates that every good thing that his disciples may hope from God flows from this source.

But doesn't the phrase "your name" refer in this context quite generally to God's reputation and honor? Certainly it does! The cloud of connotation that surrounds God's name must be made radiant if the petition is to be fulfilled. But the phrase *also* refers quite particularly to the Tetragrammaton, the linguistic token at the center of the cloud of connotation, announced to Moses at the burning bush. Jesus leaves the Tetragrammaton unspoken not because God's reputation has somehow miraculously broken free from its orbit, but because he alludes to it indirectly, by means of the phrase "your name," which in context is itself a circumlocutious way of gesturing unambiguously toward one name above every other.[9]

Jesus' indirect mode of reference to the divine name is not an incidental feature of the first petition but a decisive clue to its meaning. It enables us to understand the significance of Jesus' use of the passive voice: "Hallowed *be* your name!" From a purely grammatical point of view, the passive voice always creates potential ambiguity since the logical subject of the verb is left unspecified. In the case of the first petition, the ambiguity is evident in the variety of proposals that have been made regarding *who* is supposed to hallow

God's name, such as the church, creation, and so on. Once Jesus' customary practice of name avoidance is taken into account, however, the ambiguity disappears. Jesus is actually calling upon *God* to sanctify his own name, albeit in a way that intentionally avoids explicit reference to God, by means of what biblical scholars sometimes call "the divine passive."[10] The first petition must therefore be understood as *an appeal to God's own zeal on behalf of his name*, as attested throughout the Old Testament and especially in passages such as this from the prophet Ezekiel:

> [22]Thus says the Lord God: It is not for your sake, O house of Israel, that I am about to act, but for the sake of my holy name, which you have profaned among the nations to which you came. [23]I will sanctify my great name, which has been profaned among the nations, and which you have profaned among them; and the nations shall know that I am the Lord, says the Lord God, when through you I display my holiness before their eyes. (Ezek. 36:22–23)

The sanctification of the divine name by anyone besides God does not even come into question, because all others (i.e., Israel and the nations) are the agents of its profanation in the first place. The only one who can sanctify the divine name is its bearer, the Lord, by purifying the cloud of connotation that surrounds it, burning off everything common between it and the false language of humans and making it shine forth with the radiance that comes only from within. What this will mean in practice is the redemption of Israel and the enlightenment of the nations. Wretched, sinful, and dispersed though it is, Israel will be redeemed because it is the place where God has chosen to "cause his name to be remembered" (cf. Exod. 20:24) on earth, and the nations will behold it, so that they too may know that "I am the Lord." Still, God will not act for the sake of Israel or the nations. He will act out of truthfulness to himself, in fidelity to who he is as bearer of *this* name.

The first petition of the Lord's Prayer is a human counterpart to Ezekiel 36, spoken now in a context of final eschatological expectation. It asks God to fulfill what is promised there with irrevocable fullness and completeness, to vindicate on earth the harmony that exists in heaven between the Lord, his name, and the name's corona of glorious connotation. Precisely in this context of eschatological expectation, we can discern the special significance of Jesus' practice of avoiding the pronunciation of the divine name. The practice of name avoidance points away from the one who offers the petition for the hallowing of God's name to the one who alone can fulfill it. It expresses final impatience with every human use of God's name and eschatological longing for its vindication by God. It acknowledges our inability to say God's name in a way that corresponds to the eternal uniqueness of its bearer. It renders a verdict on human God-talk and bids our vacuous and self-serving invocations to cease. It represents an unsaying and a nonsaying, an apophaticism—not of the divine *names*, but of the divine *name*. It divests itself of the divine name, in hopeful longing that God will cause it to be remembered throughout heaven and earth, as only God can do.

Unlike the apophaticism of Dionysius (which is well and good in its place), the apophaticism of the first petition is inseparable from *the last* of God's three replies to Moses at the burning bush, the nameless name of Exodus 3:15, and from the Jewish practice of nonsaying that points to it. Knowingly or not, those who pray this prayer do not refrain from voicing the divine name because it has become obsolete, together with all the distinctive marks of Jewish religious life (as Otto Weber and others have maintained),[11] but rather because they conform to the pattern of Jewish oral law, following the example of Jesus himself. Whenever Christians pray this prayer as Jesus taught them, they render up silent witness to this unspoken name. What is more, they demonstrate, in the most concrete way imaginable, that the Incarnation and outpouring of the Holy Spirit has not rendered obsolete all forms of Jewish cultic practice, not even among Christ's own disciples in the present day.

JESUS' NAME AVOIDANCE AS THE STARTING POINT OF A PATTERN OF TRINITARIAN IDENTIFICATION

Reverence for the divine name, expressed by its nonpronunciation, is the very wellspring of Jesus' speech, a token of his longing for the eschatological vindication of God's name. It is the silent source from which all his audible speech flows, his address to God as "Father," his teaching about the kingdom in parables, and so on. It is also a form of speech that spills over with christological and trinitarian implications that saturate the New Testament from top to bottom. Even as Jesus points away from himself toward the Bearer of the divine name, he opens up a space where the name can be hallowed and made manifest—in Jesus himself.

The Synoptic Witness: The Trinitarian Implications of Jesus' Use of the Divine Passive

One way this becomes evident in the Synoptic Gospels is in Jesus' use of the divine passive, a mode of expression so typical of him that a full listing of instances would amount to a virtual recapitulation of his public teaching.

The Divine Passive and the One to Whom Jesus Prays

By its very nature, the divine passive points away from Jesus and his listeners to the One to whom Jesus prays. A great majority of instances (italicized below) are in the future tense:[12]

> Blessed are those who mourn, for they *will be comforted.* (Matt. 5:4)
>
> Blessed are the merciful, for they *will receive* mercy. (v. 7)
>
> Blessed are the peacemakers, for they *will be called children of God.* (v. 9)
>
> Do not judge, so that you may *not be judged.* (7:1)
>
> The heirs of the kingdom *will be thrown* into the outer darkness. (8:12)
>
> But the one who endures to the end *will be saved.* (24:13)
>
> Do not judge, and you will not *be judged*; do not condemn, and you will not *be condemned.* Forgive, and you will *be forgiven.* (Luke 6:37)
>
> On that night there will be two in one bed; one *will be taken* and the other left. (17:34)
>
> All who exalt themselves *will be humbled*, but all who humble themselves *will be exalted.* (18:14)

The logical subject of these and similar verses is God, the bearer of the divine name. What the ensemble depicts is the future revolutionary outworking of the name's eschatological vindication, the retuning of the universe into harmony with God. When this will happen is not stated, but it will bring reversals of a revolutionary kind.

The Divine Passive, Jesus, and the Spirit

The rigorously theocentric and eschatological character of the divine passive is the necessary starting point for understanding its christological and pneumatological implications. The divine future they anticipate is even now coming to light—in Jesus himself and in the gift of the Spirit! Consider the story of the paralytic let down through a hole in the roof made by his friends.

> When Jesus saw their faith, he said to the paralytic, "Son, your sins *are forgiven.*" (Mark 2:5)

Now the divine passive truly does introduce an ambiguity, one of a christologically pregnant kind. On the one hand, the divine passive points to God as the agent of forgiveness, as in the verses above. On the other, it appears as part of Jesus' own present-tense, declarative word of pardon. The result is a volatility of reference: *Who* forgives the paralytic's sins? God or Jesus? The volatility prompts some to take offense.

> Now some of the scribes were sitting there, questioning in their hearts, "Why does this man speak in this way? It is blasphemy! Who can forgive sins but God alone?" (vv. 6–7)

Jesus responds by placing his own action in light of the agency of God: "The Son of Man has authority on earth to forgive sins" (v. 10), the implication being that God has given Jesus such authority. Thus the "agent" signaled by the divine passive is neither God alone, nor Jesus alone, but God-working-in-Jesus to inaugurate the vindication of his name on earth. This is the typical form of words that Jesus employs in performing deeds of power. He does not say, "I clean you!" "I will save her," but "*Be made clean!*" (Matt. 8:3), "She *will be saved*" (Luke 8:50), and so on. In these and similar passages, the divine passive, a mode of theocentric speech par excellence, overflows with christological connotation as Jesus becomes the site where God's name-vindication becomes visible in the world.

The christological significance of the divine passive is raised to a still higher power in sayings that pertain to Jesus' originating purpose and ultimate destiny, such as these:

> I must proclaim the good news of the kingdom of God to the other cities also; for I *was sent* for this purpose. (Luke 4:43)
>
> But after I *am raised up*, I will go ahead of you to Galilee. (Matt. 26:32)
>
> Jesus came and said to them, "All authority in heaven and on earth *has been given* to me." (28:18)

Here the divine passive relates God's agency to Jesus' whole person and life span, and not just to individual acts of power. As before, the passive verbs point silently away from Jesus to the bearer of the divine name as the ultimate agent at work in him. But now the event they announce is Jesus himself in the fullness of his being, from origin to ultimate destiny. The result is a sophisticated and powerful message concerning the relationship of God and Christ, and first and second persons of the Trinity. Jesus is distinct from the one whose name he honors, even as the bearer of that name becomes indirectly visible in him.

Jesus also uses the divine passive in contexts where the Holy Spirit is thematic. In such cases the Spirit is simply identified with neither Jesus nor God but is a third alongside them, as in the following verse from John:

> Jesus answered, "Very truly, I tell you, no one can enter the kingdom of God without being born of water and Spirit." (3:5)

The divine passive "being born" points back to God as the ultimate agent of new birth, while the distinctive role of the Spirit is signaled by the preposition "of" (Gk.: *ex*: "out of").

Another interesting example comes from Matthew:

> When they hand you over, do not worry about how you are to speak or what you are to say; for what you are to say *will be given to you* at that time; for it is not you who speak, but the Spirit of your Father speaking through you. (10:19–20)

The phrases "will be given to you" and "the Spirit of your Father speaking through you" describe the same thing from different points of view. The first silently points to the bearer of the divine name as the source of what the disciples will say, while the second explicitly foregrounds the agency of the Spirit who comes from the "Father." The equivalence implies that the bearer of the divine name works by the Spirit, for he surely is one and the same with the Father.

Humble as it is as a mode of theological expression, the divine passive conveys a message whose full import is trinitarian in depth. The countless divine passives that circumscribe Jesus' ministry are silent clues pointing to the fulfillment—*in* him and *by* the Spirit—of the great divine passive at the heart of the Lord's Prayer: "Hallowed be your name!"

The Johannine Witness: The Giving, Receiving, and Glorification of the Divine Name

The Gospel of John repeats in a more elaborate and explicit form the picture of trinitarian relations expressed by the divine passive in the Synoptics. Once again, the heart of the matter is Jesus' reverence for the divine name.

Jesus Christ and the Divine Name: "Your Name That You Have Given Me"

The Fourth Gospel portrays Jesus as referring several times to the divine name, as when he declares, "I have come in my Father's name" (5:43) and "The works that I do in my Father's name testify to me" (10:25). These sayings concisely summarize the christological import of Jesus' use of the divine passive in the Synoptic Gospels: Jesus is the one who "comes" and "works" in the divine name and precisely so manifests its glorification on earth. The sayings do not employ the technical vocabulary of later dogmatic reflection, but they nevertheless express a Christology of the highest order, by portraying Jesus as the visible expression of God's name on earth. Still, it is true that Jesus' references to God's name in these passages leave the precise nature of the mutual relation between himself and God underexposed.

In John 17, however, we encounter a dense constellation of four references to God's name that illuminates the mutual relations of God and Christ in an extraordinary way. The verses appear at the beginning, middle, and end of Jesus' prayer in the Garden of Gethsemane.

> I have made your name known to those whom you gave me from the world. (17:6a)
>
> Holy Father, protect them in your name that you have given me, so that they may be one, as we are one. (17:11b)
>
> While I was with them, I protected them in your name that you have given me. (17:12a)
>
> I made your name known to them, and I will make it known, so that the love with which you have loved me may be in them, and I in them. (17:26)

In the first and last verses, Jesus speaks of the divine name in a way that overlaps materially with John 5:43 and 10:25: Jesus is the one who reveals/manifests/makes known the name of the One to whom he prays. In 17:11–12, however, Jesus expresses a still more intimate relationship to the divine name by the extraordinary phrase "your name that you have given me." As before, Jesus identifies the one to whom he prays as the primordial bearer of the divine name, for the name in question is "*your* name." Yet now Jesus reveals himself to be a bearer of the divine name, too, because it has been given to him.

I judge the references to the divine name at the heart of the high-priestly prayer to be the high point of John's trinitarian theology of the divine name and among the most profoundly illuminating affirmations in the entire New Testament. They express a pattern of mutual relations between God and Jesus that is fully consistent with the picture presented by means of the language of "God" and "Word," and "Father" and "Son" elsewhere in the Gospel, but they do so in a distinctive way, centered in the giving and receiving of the divine name. If this evangelist can testify that "from his fullness we have all received, grace upon grace" (1:16), then this is not only because Jesus is the Word of God made flesh, and the only begotten Son of the Father, but also because he is the receiver of the unspoken divine name, the one who bears it to make it known.[13]

Jesus Christ and the Divine Name: "I am"

The giving and receiving of the divine name expressed in John 17 is best understood in relationship to Jesus' "I am" sayings, another distinctive feature of the Fourth Gospel.[14] Seven times over the course of the narrative, Jesus declares "I am" in an absolute fashion, without any elucidating predicate. The seven absolute "I am" sayings are these:

> Jesus said to her, "I am, the one who is speaking to you." (4:25–26 mg., Gk.)
>
> He said to them, "I am; do not be afraid." (6:20 mg., Gk.)
>
> "You will die in your sins unless you believe that I am." (8:24 mg., Gk.)
>
> Jesus said, "When you have lifted up the Son of Man, then you will realize that I am." (8:28 mg., Gk.)
>
> Jesus said to them, "Very truly, I tell you, before Abraham was, I am." (8:58)
>
> "I tell you this now, before it occurs, so that when it does occur, you may believe that I am." (13:19)

On the seventh and climactic occasion, "I am" appears three times in quick succession.

> [4]Then Jesus, knowing all that was to happen to him, came forward and asked them, "Whom are you looking for?" [5]They answered, "Jesus of Nazareth." Jesus replied, "I am." Judas, who betrayed him, was standing with them. [6]When Jesus said to them, "I am," they stepped back and fell to the ground. [7]Again he asked them, "Whom are you looking for?" And they said, "Jesus of Nazareth." [8]Jesus answered, "I told you that I am." (18:4–8 mg., Gk.)[15]

As Larry Hurtado observes, the naked declaration "I am" is "as strange sounding and mysterious in Greek as it is in literal translation."[16] While the words relate meaningfully to their immediate context, they are syntactically odd and virtually without parallel in nonbiblical religious texts. The deep truth to which they point is further signaled by their sevenfold repetition (a sign of divinity, fullness, and perfection) and by the response they evoke: in one case Jesus' audience prepares to stone him (8:59; the punishment prescribed for blaspheming "the Name" in Lev. 24:16), and in another case the arresting party falls to the ground at his feet (John 18:6).

To understand this feature of the Fourth Gospel, we must see it against the background of biblical passages that link the phrase "I am" with the Tetragrammaton.[17] Far from being limited to Exodus 3:14–15, such passages are quite common in the Septuagint, thanks to God's ubiquitous declaration "I am the Lord!" (*egō eimi kyrios*), and are especially characteristic of Ezekiel and Isaiah 40–55, where the saying evokes the Lord's incomparable uniqueness and proven character as Creator, Redeemer, and Consummator of all things. Significantly, Isaiah several times reports God's self-declaration "I am the Lord" in the abbreviated form "I am!" (LXX: 41:4; 46:4; etc.). In such cases, the short form is materially identical with the longer one: "I am" = "I am the Lord." On three occasions, the Septuagint renders God's self-declaration with the extraordinary phrase, "I am I am"! (LXX: *egō eimi egō eimi*; Heb. *anoki anoki hu*). So, for example, Isaiah 43:25 reads:

> I, I am He [Gk. *egō eimi egō eimi*, lit., "I am I am"]
> who blots out your transgressions for my own sake,
> and I will not remember your sins.

In this and similar passages, the author of Second Isaiah creates a virtual synonymy between the phrase "I am" and God's personal proper name, which is implied rather than explicitly stated. Though Second Isaiah wrote before the practice of avoiding God's name became customary, the synonymy he created has obvious relevance for understanding the Gospel of John, written during the Second Temple period, when the custom was universally normative among Jews. Distinct from God's personal name yet closely linked to it, the words "I am" permit one to evoke God's name while leaving the name itself unspoken.[18]

Viewed against the backdrop of Isaiah 40–55, the profound significance of Jesus' sevenfold declaration "I am!" becomes clear. Jesus thereby enacts his identity as the one who has been given the divine name in order to make it known (cf. John 17), even as he does so in a way that continues to honor the custom of avoiding the direct use of the Tetragrammaton itself. This conclusion is supported by the many material parallels between Jesus' "I am" sayings and those of God in Second Isaiah. Jesus declares, "Before Abraham was, I am" (John 8:58), just as God uses the phrase to express God's eternity (Isa. 44:6; 48:12); Jesus uses the phrase when foretelling his passion (cf. John 13:19), just as God uses it to emphasize the power to foresee and bring about future salvation (Isa. 43:9–10). This last seems to be implied, too, by the climactic repetition of "I am" in John 18. When the Roman soldiers and temple police come to arrest Jesus, he confronts them with a question, "Whom are you looking for?" to which they answer, "Jesus of Nazareth." (vv. 4–5). Jesus' reply sets in motion the events that lead to Jesus' passion and the salvation it brings. The narrator records the reply in threefold form:

> "I am." "I am." "I told you that I am." (vv. 5, 6, 8)

Jesus' free acknowledgment of who he is appears simultaneously as a threefold declaration of the divine name, toward whose saving revelation all Scripture points and all creation pines.

Upon hearing Jesus' reply, the armed squad sent to arrest him drops to the ground (v. 6). At a surface level, it is just barely possible to imagine that they are so startled by Jesus' candor as to fall. As elsewhere in John, however, the event contains a deeper significance. In the background we detect a reference to Isaiah 45:18–24:

> Turn to me and be saved, people from the end of the earth.
> I am God, and there is no other.
> By myself I swear . . . that to me every knee shall bow. (Isa. 45:22–24 LXX)

Falling to the ground, the temple police and Roman soldiers represent Israel and the nations bending the knee before God's self-declaration in Christ. Quibblers may object that a few armed men on a nighttime raid are not yet the "every knee" of which Isaiah speaks. But they are its symbolic representation and inauguration. In the words of Richard Bauckham, the scene is "the Evangelist's way of indicating that Jesus' passion, which in Gethsemane he undertakes irrevocably in its totality, is both the achievement of salvation and the revelation of God's glory to all, such that the unique identity of the one God is demonstrated and wins the recognition of all."[19]

The Holy Spirit and the Divine Name

Although the Holy Spirit is seldom explicitly thematized in the Johannine passages we have just considered, the Spirit's presence and power are implied in the wider context of what transpires when Jesus makes known "your name that you have given me" (17:11–12). The challenge of describing this more precisely is bound up with the complex relationship of Christology and pneumatology in the Fourth Gospel. Still, it is suggestive that Jesus' first "I am" statement (to the Samaritan woman at the well; 4:26) is immediately preceded by the saying that "those who worship him [God] must worship in spirit and in truth" (4:24). Regardless of how one interprets "spirit" in this immediate context (whether as a reference to created or uncreated Spirit), the Holy Spirit's role in enabling people to recognize Truth is a conspicuous theme of John's Gospel. Jesus instructs the disciples on this point in John 16.

> [13]When the Spirit of truth comes, he will guide you into all the truth; for he will not speak on his own, but will speak whatever he hears, and he will declare to you the things that are to come. [14]He will glorify me, because he will take what is mine and declare it to you. [15]All that

> the Father has is mine. For this reason I said that he will take what is mine and declare it to you. (16:13–15)

This passage opens up a pneumatological perspective that complements our understanding of Jesus' references to God's name in John 17. Just as it is Christ's work to make known "your name which you have given me," so it is the Spirit's work to "take what is mine and declare it to you." Understood in its fullest scope, the manifestation of the divine name is a trinitarian event, one that involves its giving, receiving, and acknowledgment, so that those who worship God may do so "in spirit and in truth."[20]

Psalm 118:26 as Dominical Speech

The final instance of Jesus' speech that we will examine is his citation of Psalm 118:26, "Blessed is the one who comes in the name of the LORD!" as recorded by Matthew and Luke. In a previous chapter we explored the implications of this verse as it appears on the lips of the jubilant crowds who welcome Jesus' entry into Jerusalem. Now we turn our attention to its soteriological implications as it appears on Jesus' own lips.

Jesus is portrayed as using a conventional surrogate (*kyrios*) in place of the divine name (YHWH) when citing Psalm 118:26, in keeping with his practice elsewhere (Matt. 4:7; Mark 12:29; etc.). That an allusion to the divine name is genuinely intended in these instances is underscored by the fact that "Lord" (*kyrios*) appears in the original Greek without a preceding article, an omission that signals its use as a surrogate for a proper name.[21] What gives this particular dominical citation of Scripture its special poignancy is its appearance in the context of his lament for Jerusalem, "the city that kills the prophets and stones those who are sent to it!" (Matt. 23:37–39; Luke 13:34–35; cf. Matt. 21:9; Luke 19:38). Implicit in this context is the tension that arises when the holiness of God's name encounters the sinfulness of Israel, a tension we also saw in Ezekiel 36.

Luke incorporates the pericope into his account of Jesus' Galilean ministry, just after a body of teaching material that concludes with the saying "Some are last who will be first, and some are first who will be last" (Luke 13:30). "At that very hour," we are told, some Pharisees warn Jesus that Herod wants to kill him (v. 31). Jesus sends back the message that he will carry on as before to the very end, which will in any case occur in Jerusalem (outside Herod's jurisdiction), "for it is impossible for a prophet to be killed outside of Jerusalem" (v. 33). The reference to Jerusalem prompts Jesus to declare what is on his heart, which is not fear of Herod or of death, but agony on behalf of the royal city and her offspring, the people Israel:

> Jerusalem, Jerusalem, the city that kills the prophets and stones those who are sent to it! How often have I desired to gather your children together as a hen gathers her brood under her wings, and you were not willing! [35]See, your house is left to you. (vv. 34–35)

Jerusalem and her children are "first" in Jesus' desire (cf. 2:32), but they will be "last" because of their refusal to receive him. They will get what they have chosen (your house), but it will be empty and desolate. Jesus' verdict is reluctant, but nevertheless final and irrevocable, or so it seems. All that remains is to pronounce sentence, which Jesus proceeds to do:

> I tell you, you will not see me until the time comes when . . .

The reader expects what follows to consummate somehow the word of condemnation. What in fact follows, however, is another reversal:

> . . . you say, "Blessed is the one who comes in the name of the Lord." (Luke 13:35)

Jesus' sentence on Jerusalem, it seems, is not ultimate destruction after all. Rather, it is instead a season of deprivation ("You will not see me"), followed at last by its tardy but joyous recognition of Jesus as royal envoy and bearer of salvation from the Lord. Surprising though it may be in context, this outcome is consistent with the way God vindicates his name in the course of salvation history, as in Ezekiel 36:22–24. God acts to redeem Israel, not on account of its righteousness, for it has none, but for God's own name's sake.

Others, however, interpret Jesus' words as though spoken ironically: Israel will acknowledge Jesus' coming, but only after it is "too late."[22] Indeed, such a reading rightly detects a strata of judgment that is genuinely present in Luke's text. When Jesus enters the holy city on the eve of Passover, the words of Psalm 118:26 are jubilantly exclaimed not by its inhabitants generally, but rather by "the whole multitude of the disciples" (Luke 19:37–38). All the rest, it seems, have indeed missed their chance. This impression is immediately confirmed by Jesus' ominous words that follow after his entry into the royal city. Addressing Jerusalem, he laments, "Your enemies . . . will crush . . . you and your children . . . because you did not recognize the time of your visitation from God" (19:43–44).

Nevertheless, a reading of Luke 13:34–35 that stops here sees but half the picture. The same disciples who spread their cloaks before Jesus on Sunday have abandoned him by Friday, thus aligning themselves with "the city that kills the prophets" and those who have missed the visitation of God. Still, God did not pronounce "too late!" on them. On the contrary, God gathered the scattered company of disciples and made them the firstfruits of a renewed

Israel. The Gospel ends with a picture of the disciples "continually in the temple blessing God" (Luke 24:53), making it the center of God's restored people. Acts begins by citing the expectation of Christ's coming again to "restore the kingdom to Israel" (1:6), an event that looks beyond even the present season of the Spirit to that time (known only to the Father) when Jesus "will come in the same way as you saw him go into heaven" (1:11). In view of all this, it seems quite possible to understand Luke 13:35 according to its plain sense. It looks forward in hopeful anticipation to a time when corporate and official Israel will join the disciples in acclaiming Jesus as "the one who comes in the name of the Lord."

Matthew's account of Jesus' prophetic citation of Psalm 118:26 is virtually identical to Luke's, with the important exception that he places it *after* Jesus' royal entry into Jerusalem, on the very eve of his arrest and execution (Matt. 23:37–39a). The effect is to emphasize the verse's character as prophecy concerning some future event not narrated by the Gospel itself. Jesus, it seems, looks beyond his own impending death to his future Parousia and to the consummation of God's reign on earth. At that time, Jesus foretells, those who presently reject him will hail him with the very words of messianic acclamation that greeted his humble entry into Jerusalem. Or will it then be too late? Will the glorious Son of Man ultimately spurn those who greet him with these words? If this were so, then Jesus' words here would be little more than a cruel jeer. It is better to take Jesus' words in a way that parallels their canonical function in Luke, where they point to a future time when those who currently reject Jesus will repent and acknowledge him. Understood in this way, the saying maintains the link that exists between *the glory of God's name* and *the salvation of God's people, Israel*, a link that it is the very purpose of Jesus' existence to forge irrevocably: "He will save the people from their sins" (Matt. 1:21).[23]

THE NAME ABOVE EVERY NAME: THEOCENTRIC TRINITARIANISM IN PHILIPPIANS 2

The pattern of Jesus' speech that we have traced in this chapter appears elsewhere in the New Testament canon as well. In the remaining paragraphs of this chapter, we will focus on a single passage, Philippians 2:5–11.[24] Although the passage is among the oldest in the New Testament, it exhibits an understanding of the "economy" of the divine name that corresponds closely to what we have already encountered, not least in the Gospel of John. The passage reads:

[5]Let the same mind be in you that was in Christ Jesus,

[6]who, though he was in the form of God,
did not regard equality with God as something to be exploited,
[7]but emptied himself, taking the form of a slave, being born
in human likeness.
And being found in human form,
[8]he humbled himself and became obedient to the point of death—
even death on a cross.
[9]Therefore God also highly exalted him
and gave him the name that is above every name,
[10]so that at the name of Jesus every knee should bend,
in heaven and on earth and under the earth,
[11]and every tongue should confess that Jesus Christ is Lord,
to the glory of God the Father.

The story told here unfolds in three movements that correspond to the three persons of the Trinity. In the first, the primary agent is "Christ Jesus," who freely yields his divine estate in costly obedience toward God, leading to his death on the cross (vv. 5–8). Christ's stark downward trajectory recalls the mysterious figure of the Servant in Second Isaiah (53:7, 12); it also recalls God's own condescension as described, for example, by Psalm 113, which portrays God as looking "far down on the heavens and the earth" in one verse and raising up "the needy from the ash heap" in the next (cf. vv. 6–7). Viewed against the backdrop of passages such as Psalm 113, Christ's readiness to humble himself for the sake of the needy is an imitation of the pattern already previously delineated by the bearer of the divine name, and already recognized to be worthy of universal adoration (cf. Ps. 113:1–3).

The main character of the story's second movement is God, who exalts Jesus and bestows on him "the name that is above every name" (Phil. 2:9). Surely Richard Bauckham is correct when he declares that it is "inconceivable that any Jewish writer could use this phrase for a name other than God's own unique name."[25] God honors Jesus' self-donation with God's own: the gift of the divine name. This need not mean that God divests himself of the name, anymore than that Christ Jesus' *kenōsis* necessarily implies the loss of divine status. As George MacDonald rightly wrote, "A name is one of those things one can give away and keep all the same."[26] Rather, God manifests his own identity as bearer of the divine name *by giving it to another*, in a manner wholly consistent with Jesus' saying "Your name that you have given me" (John 17:11).

The giving and receiving of the divine name inaugurates the story's third movement, when the whole living cosmos acclaims "Jesus" as the receiver of the name to the glory of the one who gives it, "God the Father." The acclamation transpires in the confession "Jesus Christ is Lord!" (Phil. 2:11). Once again the passage makes its point by using a surrogate in place of the divine name, in this case the conventional Greek reverential substitute "Lord" (*kyrios*). Even in this vision of cosmic and eschatological fulfillment, creation magnifies God's name while avoiding its direct use, thus pointing away from itself and back toward the One who hallows it. Although the passage does not expressly speak of the Holy Spirit, it seems reasonable to think that the Spirit's agency is at least implied by creation's praise. Elsewhere Paul expressly says, "No one can say 'Jesus is Lord' except by the Holy Spirit" (1 Cor. 12:3). If it is permissible to read the present passage in light of this remark, then we may infer that here too creation's acclamation of Jesus is a work accomplished by the Holy Spirit.

Paul's letter to the Philippians, then, portrays God, Christ, and the Spirit relating to the divine name in a trinitarian way: the first person gives the divine name, the second person receives it, and the third person (by implication) glorifies it, by awakening its universal acclamation and praise. At the same time, there is an important sense in which their threefold action accomplishes a single thing—the display of God's saving uniqueness in Christ—for the sake of a single ultimate goal: the glorification of God.

THE THEOLOGICAL PATTERN: THE MOST APPROPRIATE WAY OF NAMING THE PERSONS OF THE TRINITY?

Our survey in this chapter shows that one way the New Testament portrays the mutual relations of God, Christ, and the Spirit is by means of oblique reference to God's personal proper name, the unspoken Tetragrammaton. Taken together, this body of witness comprises what I earlier called a *theological* pattern of naming the persons of the Trinity.[27] We encountered this pattern once before, in our exploration of Revelation 1:1–8 in chapter 11. In that case, we arrived at the pattern by tracing the contours of the Trinity's own self-declaration, as these emerge over the course of the canon's witness from Old Testament to New Testament. In this chapter we have arrived at the same pattern by an altogether different route, by beginning with Jesus Christ's own characteristic patterns of speech. The fact that both of these routes have brought us to the same destination powerfully supports the conclusion that the pattern we have identified is a significant element of the New Testament witness. It retains an identifiable integrity across differences of genre, literary idiom, and theological outlook.

Should we therefore conclude that the theological pattern of naming is *the* most appropriate way of naming the persons of the Trinity? There certainly seem to be some good reasons for thinking so.

1. Above all, the theological pattern of naming orbits a name of unsurpassed importance to the Christian canon, the Tetragrammaton. The Tetragrammaton is referenced over six thousand times in the Old Testament and alluded to obliquely another two thousand times or more in the New. This density of use and allusion vastly outstrips that enjoyed by any other divine name, and makes the Tetragrammaton the single most characteristic literary feature of the Christian canon, bar none. The only other name of comparable prominence for Christians is "Jesus," whose meaning ("YHWH is salvation") also points to the Tetragrammaton! Clearly, a pattern of naming that identifies the persons of the Trinity in terms of the giving, receiving, and glorification of this name (cf. Phil. 2:5–11; John 17) is of supreme moment for Christian faith.

2. The theological pattern of naming the persons of the Trinity is of unsurpassed importance, too, because of the particular *kind* of name that it orbits. The significance of the Tetragrammaton resides not in what it means (for it has no certain meaning), but in what it is: a personal proper name. As a proper name, it refers to the subject of Christian worship in a way that is logically prior to other names and descriptions. It directs our words and our silences toward their proper goal by pointing to the one to whom alone all worship is properly directed.

3. Although lacking conventional semantic meaning, the Tetragrammaton is surrounded by a corona of connotation that reflects the one who bears it as he is attested by sacred Scripture. At the heart of this corona is the event of God's self-naming, an event that is utterly personal, gracious, and free. The Tetragrammaton thereby safeguards the truth that the name of God is not a human attainment but a divine gift, to be received ever anew wherever God causes his name to be remembered. Precisely so, the pattern of naming centered in the giving, receiving, and glorification of the divinely gifted Tetragrammaton has foundational importance for Christian faith.

4. Finally, the theological pattern of naming is crucially important by virtue of the fact that it employs surrogates in place of the divine name, in continuity with Jewish custom and following the example of Jesus Christ himself. Far from being a husk of ancient piety that can be set aside without loss, the practice connects us with Jesus' own zeal for the hallowing of God's name. It expresses impatience with every merely human use of God's name and eschatological longing for its perfect vindication by God, an event that the New Testament portrays as already accomplished in Christ by the power of the Spirit, and as yet to happen.

These are weighty considerations. Still, I do not think that they demonstrate that the theological pattern is *the* most important way of naming the persons of the Trinity. Rather, they show that the theological pattern is *a* most appropriate way of naming the persons of the Trinity, by virtue of its special affinity with the first person of the Trinity. The first person of the Trinity is the source and the mystery of divine uniqueness at the source of the divine life. The special value of this pattern is its power to illuminate the mystery of the Trinity from this vantage point in particular.

13

Our Father in Heaven!

Jesus the Enactment of Divine Presence and the Name of the Trinity in a Christological Key

> In every place where I cause my name to be remembered,
> *I will come to you* and bless you.
>
> —*Exodus 20:24*

In this chapter we will explore another path by which it is possible to arrive at a way of naming the persons of the Trinity. Once again we begin with Jesus' characteristic patterns of speech as illustrated by the Lord's Prayer. In Luke's account we read,

> [1]He was praying in a certain place, and after he had finished, one of his disciples said to him, "Lord, teach us to pray, as John taught his disciples." [2]He said to them, "When you pray, say: Father . . ." (Luke 11:1–2; Matt. 6:9)

The word "Father" has a special place in the Lord's Prayer. It is the only element of the prayer that is not a petition. "Father" does not ask God to meet some need or protect against some danger. Indeed, it does not ask God to do anything at all. Rather, it simply addresses God, by means of a human kinship term that implies an already existing familial relationship between God and the one who speaks. As a form of address, "Father" implies that God is already well-disposed toward the one who prays and will hear and answer every petition accordingly. The term finds its divine counterpart in God's words to Jesus when he was baptized in the river Jordan by John. In Mark, we read:

> And just as he was coming up out of the water, he saw the heavens torn apart and the Spirit descending like a dove on him. [11]And a voice came from heaven, "You are my Son, the Beloved; with you I am well pleased." (Mark 1:10–11; cf. Luke 3:21–22; Matt. 3:17; cf. John 1:32–34; 2 Pet. 1:17)

The voice from heaven speaks directly to Jesus; everyone else listens in (cf. Luke 3:21–22). With the words, "You are my Son, the Beloved; with you I am well pleased," God does not command or question, promise or threaten. God simply announces the disposition of love and satisfaction with which God bends toward Jesus, a disposition reflected in the kinship term that God uses of him: "my Son." The descending Spirit is the gift that proceeds from the wellspring of paternal love and envelops Jesus like a womb. All four Gospels place an account of this sort near the beginning of their compositions, thereby providing an interpretive guide for the evangelical drama that follows. "Father, Son, and Spirit" is not a chance grab bag of unrelated terms, but a privileged set of mutually interpreting designations that leads to the heart of the gospel. Through them, God, Christ, and Spirit make themselves known to us in terms of the relationships of origin, mutual presence, and availability that characterize their eternal life together, relationships that, by the Father's sending of the Son and Spirit, they open up to the world as well.

A WARNING SIGN

The figure I have just sketched is a well-known motif of Christian theology, one that has appeared countless times with many variations of detail and emphasis over the last century or more.[1] Before elaborating it further, however, we do well to take note of a warning sign. The danger arises not from the picture itself, which (whatever the deficiencies of my own presentation) portrays something real and important. Rather, the hazard arises from the temptation to emphasize this dimension at the expense of others that are neglected, cropped off, or made to play the role of negative foil.[2]

Wittingly or not, many theologians have done just this. They have celebrated the trinitarian implications of Jesus' address to God as "Father" in a partial and one-sided way that underplays or denies the importance of other features of Jesus' speech, such as his use of parables and his reverence for the divine name, the unspoken Tetragrammaton. While we might profitably examine either or both of these points, we will concentrate on the latter.

> Whereas in Judaism awe of the Holy One led to fear of the very name of God, both cult and fear, both accumulation and concealment of names, are now overcome by the one word "father." . . . The name of God is no longer a mystery enveloped in silence as in the Synagogue.[3]
>
> The kingdom of *Elohim*, the kingdom of the heavens, must have, as it were, two levels. As the kingdom of *Abba*, it belongs to the One who

> is beyond *Yahweh-Elohim*, whom the Jewish hearers of Jesus did not know because he was yet unrevealed in their life. Into this kingdom no one can enter except the Son, who comes from it without having left it.[4]

> As a matter of course, Jewish prayer avoided naming YHWH. . . . Respect for God's transcendence nurtured a climate of fear that forbade all familiarity. Jesus on the contrary, wants the Father to be called by his name in prayer.[5]

> When we turn to the Scriptures of the New Testament, we find a radical deepening of the Old Testament doctrine of God, for "Father" is now revealed to be more than an epithet—it is the personal name of God in which the form and content of his self-revelation as Father through Jesus Christ his Son are inseparable. "Father" is now the name of God that we are to hallow, as our Lord Jesus taught us: "Our Father who art in heaven, hallowed be your name."[6]

> The name "Father" is the one best calculated to manifest the novelty of the God of Jesus, as compared not only with the God of the Greeks but [also] with the God of the Jews. . . . Compared with the God of Israel the God of Jesus represents a revolution in so far as God is the God of grace before being the God of the law.[7]

> Everything that Christ taught, everything that makes the NT new, and better than the Old, everything that is distinctively Christian as opposed to merely Jewish, is summed up in the knowledge of the Fatherhood of God. "Father" is the Christian name of God.[8]

The problem with these views is not merely that they reinforce Christian stereotypes of Judaism as harboring a distant and fearsome conception of God, although that is true and bad enough. The problem furthermore is that they distort the New Testament's portrait of Jesus himself, by suppressing the reverence for God's unspoken name that informs his speech. Nor is this the only aspect of the New Testament witness that this same perspective tends to hide. The same authors who emphasize "the Father's" superiority to the Tetragrammaton often also emphasize its superiority to Jesus' language for God as employed in parables, suggesting that "Father" is a "proper name" for God, whereas other terms Jesus employs are merely "metaphors" or "similes." (We will have more to say on this last point in the next chapter.)

In view of the preceding, it is scarcely surprising that some theologians have swung to the other end of the spectrum by challenging the significance of the language of Father, Son, and Spirit altogether. Yet however understandable, this response commits a similar error of one-sidedness and one-dimensionality. The better course, I maintain, is to recognize that this pattern of language tells the truth, but it does not tell the whole truth. Or rather, it *does* tell the whole truth, but—and this is the key point—it does so from a particular vantage point, one that emphasizes the mystery of divine presence in the life of God and the economy of salvation. As important as this perspective is, it must be held in balance with—rather than played off against—other equally important dimensions of mystery, the manifestation of divine uniqueness, and the bestowal of divine blessing.

THE OLD TESTAMENT ROOT OF THE CHRISTOLOGICAL REPETITION

To assess the christological pattern of naming the persons of the Trinity rightly, we must spend at least a moment in exploring its roots in the Old Testament, even if we cannot do these justice. As many have recognized, the New Testament's language of Father and Son draws on the Old Testament's depiction of God's relation to the people Israel generally and to the Davidic king in particular. What has not always received the emphasis it deserves is the simple fact that the Old Testament portrait of God as Father *complements* rather than *competes with* its portrait of God as bearer of the divine name. Indeed, as Jon Levenson shows in his wonderful study of the patriarchal narratives, *The Death and Resurrection of the Beloved Son*, what gives the ordinary kinship relations portrayed in the Bible their incomparable shape is the way they are thwarted and fostered, bent and remade by the matchless force of YHWH's paternal love for the firstborn or chosen son.[9]

The story of the binding of Isaac is paradigmatic. YHWH's claim on the favored child is more basic than even that of the human parents; that claim asserts itself in the command that Abraham sacrifice his son and so lose him forever. Although the sacrifice is averted, Abraham truly yields his paternal claim to God. "The natural father hands over the son born outside the course of nature to the divine father whose due he is."[10] God responds by restoring the child, now God's own, to Abraham, and what is far more, by promising to make from him a people that will endure forever before God.

> By myself I have sworn, says the Lord: Because you have done this, and have not withheld your son, your only son, [17]I will indeed bless you, and I will make your offspring as numerous as the stars of heaven and as the sand that is on the seashore. (Gen. 22:16–17)

The natural stream of human kinship runs from fertility to barrenness, life to death, wholeness to loss (cf. Gen. 1–3). In contrast, the mark of YHWH's paternity is loss and recovery, death and resurrection, as the ordinary bonds of human kinship are dissolved and remade in the fire of YHWH's love for the firstborn child.

As the biblical story unfolds, the story of YHWH's paternity repeatedly focuses on two themes. One is the demonstration that the bond between YHWH and the beloved son is stronger than every countervailing force. The other is the manifestation of just who the beloved son is. Both sources of narrative tension are in play in this paradigmatic verse from Exodus.

> Then you shall say to Pharaoh, "Thus says the LORD: Israel is my firstborn son. I said to you: 'Let my son go that he may worship me.'" (Exod. 4:22–23)

The enslavement of the Israelites is intolerable not just (or even primarily) because it inflicts suffering, but because it separates YHWH and the beloved child. YHWH's demand for release reveals paternal love, but just as much the identity of the beloved child: "*Israel* is my firstborn son!" As the story moves to its conclusion, YHWH's zeal for the divine name ("You shall know that I am the LORD!") works itself out as the mighty demonstration of a fatherly love able to restore the endangered son to his rightful place in God's presence.

The unconditional force of YHWH's paternal love is also thematic in biblical traditions concerning the divine sonship of the Davidic king. An example is 2 Samuel 7, a passage of great importance to many New Testament writers. As the scene opens, David, with royal magnanimity, announces his intention to build "a house" or temple for the LORD (v. 2). The LORD, however, spurns David's plan as an impertinence. God scarcely needs David to dictate how he will dwell among the people. Why, David owes his very kingship to God's singling him out as a child and to God's ceaseless companionship since then (vv. 5–9). Nevertheless, God will not so much reject David's plans as turn them on their head. God will allow David's *son* to build a temple for him. Moreover, God will use the same offspring to build a house (i.e., a royal dynasty) for David. The following passage, more than any other, ignites the flame of messianic expectation in the biblical tradition:

> 13He shall build a house for my name, and I will establish the throne of his kingdom forever. 14I will be a father to him, and he shall be a son to me. When he commits iniquity, I will punish him with a rod such as mortals use, with blows inflicted by human beings. 15But I will not take my steadfast love from him, as I took it from Saul, whom I put away from before you. (vv. 13–15)

The extraordinary thing about these verses is not only their unconditional nature, but also how, in the figure of the future king, they mingle two distinct discourses of divine presence, one connected with the dwelling of YHWH's name on earth, and the other with YHWH's paternal love for the chosen child. Henceforth YHWH's zeal for the divine name will have its earthly counterpart in the humiliation and exaltation not only of the people Israel, but also, as a kind of epitome and instrument in service of the same, of David's royal offspring. Subsequently other passages elaborate this complex of themes with reference to God's Spirit, such as the following:

> [1]A shoot shall come out from the stump of Jesse, and a branch shall grow out of his roots. [2]The spirit of the LORD shall rest on him, the spirit of wisdom and understanding, the spirit of counsel and might, the spirit of knowledge and the fear of the LORD. (Isa. 11:1–2; cf. Isa. 7:14–17; 9:6–7)

Obviously the passages we have considered scarcely exhaust the biblical sources of the New Testament's language of Father/Son/Spirit; a fuller account would need to consider many other sources, including wisdom traditions and apocalyptic writings. Still, we have seen enough to establish the simple but important point with which we began this section: the Old Testament portrait of God as Father *complements* rather than *competes with* its portrait of God as bearer of the divine name.

THE CHRISTOLOGICAL REPETITION IN THE NEW TESTAMENT

Turning to the New Testament, we expect to discover the language of Father, Son, and Spirit attested in a way that manifests both consistency and novelty in relation to its Old Testament antecedents. Indeed, this is just what we do find. Both trajectories appear in the following passage, which appears in all the Synoptic Gospels:

> [42]"What do you think of the Messiah? Whose son is he?" They said to him, "The son of David." [43]He said to them, "How is it then that David by the Spirit calls him Lord, saying, [44]'Lord said to my Lord, "Sit at my right hand, until I put your enemies under your feet"'? If David thus calls him Lord, how can he be his son?" (Matt. 22:42–45 NRSV alt. via Gk.; cf. Mark 12:35–37; Luke 20:41–44)

As in the Old Testament passages considered above, God's identity is here expounded by means of two distinguishable motifs: God is bearer of the divine name (where "Lord" is not preceded by "the" or "my" in vv. 43, 44, Gk.), and God is Father of the beloved Son, the Messiah. Note that the two motifs *complement* rather than *compete with* each other. The motif of divine fatherhood in no way replaces that of God's name, as we should expect if it were true, as Gottlob Schrenk claimed, that the name of God is no longer "enveloped in silence as in the Synagogue," having been "overcome by the one word 'father.'"[11] On the contrary, God's fatherhood and the unspoken Tetragrammaton peacefully coexist in this passage, the former *expounding* the latter in the direction of God's powerful protective care for the beloved. ("My right hand" here implies a place not only of authority but also of proximity and safety; cf. Ps. 139:10: "Your right hand shall hold me fast.") Schrenk notwithstanding, we discover strict *continuity* between the Old and New Testaments along this line of analysis, not discontinuity.

Were Schrenk and others therefore wholly wrong to think that the New Testament's use of father language exhibits profound novelty over against the Old Testament? Not at all. But the novelty lies at a different point. This ancient bit of messianic exegesis so emphasizes *God's* fatherhood that the Messiah's *Davidic* sonship is wholly eclipsed. David's relation to the Messiah is not that of father to son, but of servant to master. The extraordinary implications of this eclipse are spelled out in another New Testament message:

> [1]Long ago God spoke to our ancestors in many and various ways by
> the prophets, [2]but in these last days he has spoken to us by a Son,
> whom he appointed heir of all things, through whom he also created
> the worlds. [3]He is the reflection of God's glory and the exact imprint
> of God's very being, and he sustains all things by his powerful word.
> When he had made purification for sins, he sat down at the right hand
> of the Majesty on high, [4]having become as much superior to angels as
> the name he has inherited is more excellent than theirs. [5]For to which
> of the angels did God ever say, "You are my Son; today I have begotten you"? Or again, "I will be his Father, and he will be my Son"? (Heb. 1:1–5)

This passage uses the designation "Son" to articulate a trinitarian/christological vision of the highest order. Very compactly expressed, we may say that here "Son" represents a transference of identity—not from a human family to God's family—but from *God's side* to humanity. God's Son is not merely one in a continuing series, not even the highest, but a qualitatively new event in the history of salvation. The Son is with God in the beginning and the end, prior even to creation itself. And yet, for all of the grandeur of this vision, it remains in continuity with the Old Testament's reverence for the divine name. "The Majesty on high" is a buffer phrase used in place of the divine name, indicating that even here reverence for the divine name remains an integral dimension of the theological vision represented.[12]

In the remainder of this chapter, we will fill out our portrait of the language of Father, Son, and Spirit in the New Testament. Having emphasized the lines of continuity that connect this witness with the Old Testament generally and with reverence for the divine name in particular, we permit this point to retreat somewhat into the background (without forgetting it entirely), in order to concentrate on the novel element in the use of this language: its capacity to articulate Jesus Christ as the advent and enactment of God's victorious presence in the world.

FEATURES COMMON TO THE FOUR GOSPELS

The language of Father, Son, and Spirit appears, explicitly and by implication, in all four Gospels, albeit in significantly varying degrees. For example, Mark, the earliest of the Gospels, employs it rather sparingly, albeit at key junctures in his narrative, while John, the most recent Gospel, employs it much more abundantly. Some have concluded from this that the language proliferates in proportion to how "high" an author's Christology is.[13] John uses it so much because he has a "higher" Christology and a more robust trinitarian vision than Mark. This view assumes that the language of Father, Son, and Spirit serves as a kind of all-purpose theological vocabulary that writers draw upon at will to emphasize the deity of Christ, the preexistence of the second person, and so on. (It also assumes that John's Christology and trinitarian vision are higher than Mark's, which I do not believe, but set that aside for the present.)

Marianne Meye Thompson has provided a helpful corrective to this view of divine kinship language in her study *The Promise of the Father: Jesus and God in the New Testament*.[14] Thompson focuses on biblical imagery for God as Father, but her observations are relevant for understanding the language of Son and Spirit as well. Thompson argues that throughout the New Testament, Father language is consistently used in connection with *a limited number of theological motifs*. When readers notice an increase in the frequency of divine kinship language from one book to another, say by comparing Mark and John, this does not bear witness to an indiscriminate proliferation of Father imagery for God, but rather to a "disciplined appropriation of the terminology" in keeping with a limited set of themes, such as God's giving or granting the kingdom to his children, the language of prayer, and the relationship of Jesus to God.[15]

The soundness of Thompson's general thesis can be illustrated by looking at one motif she mentions, "the language of prayer." At issue here is Jesus' practice of opening prayer with the address "Father!" Mark, which records the fewest instances of "Father" among the Gospels, also quotes only one prayer of Jesus, in the Garden of Gethsemane:

> He said, "Abba, Father, for you all things are possible; remove this cup from me; yet, not what I want, but what you want." (Mark 14:36)

In contrast, the other Gospels report Jesus' prayers in greater abundance. In addition to the prayer in the garden (Matt. 26:39, 42; Luke 22:42; cf. John 12:27–28), they record Jesus' praying to God in thanksgiving and praise (Matt. 11:25 / Luke 10:21; John 11:41), in intercession for his followers (John 17), in intercession for his enemies (Luke 23:34), in death (Luke 23:46), and on other occasions besides. Strikingly, in all of these prayers the word "Father" plays *exactly the same role*: Jesus uses it as a term of address, whether at the opening of the prayer or in the context of the prayer itself. In short, the difference between Mark and the other Gospels is not that Mark uses Father in a different or less theologically resonant way, *but that he reports fewer of Jesus' prayers*. The more frequent attestation of "Father" in Matthew, Luke, and John simply reinforces a motif already visible in Mark: it is characteristic of Jesus' address to God. Jesus addresses God not as though to establish a relationship that does not yet exist, but in a way that assumes a preexisting relationship of kinship, mutual relatedness, and tender care.

Another feature common to the Gospels, irrespective of how frequently they use "Father" for God, is extraordinary care in portraying *who* uses the term. The word is used almost exclusively by Jesus alone. This is true not only when the "Father" appears without modifier ("Father!"), but also when qualified by various personal pronouns ("my Father," "your Father," "our Father," etc.). Mark is exemplary in this regard. While he records relatively few instances of the term, they all appear on Jesus' lips. The second evangelist even refrains from using the word in constructing his own narrative frame! (In contrast, Mark shows no such restraint with regard to "Son of God," freely using it in the introduction to the Gospel [1:1] and placing it on the lips of others [3:11]). Matthew and Luke show the same reserve in the use of "Father," a fact that is all the more striking given the greater frequency with which they report the term. This feature of the Synoptic Gospels is not the result of chance. It is a subtle but powerful way the Synoptic writers underscore Jesus' identity as the "Beloved," the one through whom God's paternal zeal enters at last triumphantly on the scene.[16]

Interestingly, it is in John that we find a few (instructive) deviations from the general rule. While in the overwhelming majority of cases it is Jesus who speaks of "the Father," the term is occasionally used by others, but in an uncomprehending way (cf. 8:19, 14:8). Additionally, the evangelist himself uses the term on a few occasions, most notably in the Gospel's prologue:

> No one has ever seen God. It is God the only Son, who is close to the Father's heart, who has made him known. (1:18)

This rare editorial use of the term "Father" clarifies the evangelist's own understanding of the term. Jesus' (almost) exclusive use of the term signifies his own status as "God the only Son," whose primordial privilege it is to be "close to the Father's heart" (lit., "bosom/breast"). Because Jesus comes from this place of incomparable proximity to God, he is able to address God as "Father" and re-present his Father's presence in the world, thereby making it possible for others also to become "children of God" (1:12–13; cf. 3:5; 20:21–23).

The Gospels also employ the designation "Son" or "Son of God" in certain common ways irrespective of how frequently the term appears. An example concerns the narrative of Jesus' baptism that each writer places near the beginning of his Gospel. While these accounts differ in many points of detail, they also show important similarities. Every Gospel writer cites words from Isaiah 40:3 near the beginning of the baptism pericope: "'Prepare the way of the Lord, make his paths straight'" (Matt. 3:3; Mark 1:3; Luke 3:4; John 1:23). Similarly, every Gospel writer concludes the account with the affirmation that Jesus is the (Spirit-anointed) Son of God. (The Synoptic writers depict this affirmation as God's own, while John places it in the mouth of John the Baptist.) Other differences notwithstanding, this common framing of the beginning of Jesus' public ministry is highly significant. It signals a common conviction among the evangelists that the victorious coming of the Lord to his people prophesied by Isaiah and by John the Baptist is accomplished in the person of God's beloved Son, Jesus. To call Jesus "Son of God" is to say that he brings God's saving presence into the world. At the same time, such language portrays the saving mystery of divine presence as a trinitarian event that occurs through the mutual presence of Father and Son in the power of the Holy Spirit.

While we could profitably explore Thompson's thesis at greater length, we have seen enough to lend support to her thesis that the language of Father (and by implication of Son and Spirit as well) is not an all-purpose trinitarian vocabulary that the Gospel writers use in an indiscriminate way, regardless of narrative context. Rather, as Thompson maintains, it is a context-sensitive vocabulary that is particularly apt for expressing a limited range of motifs, including the language of prayer and Jesus' relation to God. At the same time, we can venture to elaborate on Thompson's thesis by making it more precise. Even with respect to Jesus' "relation to God," the language of Father, Son, and Spirit is not an all-purpose vocabulary, equally apposite for illuminating this relation from every point of view. As Thomas Aquinas recognized, who the Son is in relation to God is so superabundantly rich that it can and must be thematized in more than one way (*ST* 1.34.2 *ad* 3). Just as the language of the giving and receiving of the divine name is especially apposite for articulating Jesus' relation to God from the perspective of God's uniqueness, as we saw in the last chapter, so also the language of Father, Son, and Spirit is particularly apposite for illuminating it from a different point of view: that of the mystery of mutual presence, availability, and solicitous care at the heart of the divine life.

FEATURES DISTINCTIVE TO THE GOSPELS

The language of divine kinship appears in the Gospels not only in the common ways sketched above, but also in ways that are unique to the different compositions and reflect marked differences of literary style and theological concern. Yet even in their distinctiveness, these instances too share a family resemblance with each other and with the common features already recognized.

Matthew: Jesus, the Son of God, Emmanuel

Matthew's Gospel begins with an account of the "genealogy [or birth] of Jesus the Messiah, the son of David, son of Abraham" (1:1), making the relation of father and son thematic to Jesus' story from the outset. Curiously, however, the lengthy genealogy that follows does not establish what the superscript leads us to expect. The line of patrilineal descent ends not with Jesus himself but with Joseph, who is characterized as the "husband of Mary, of whom Jesus was born, who is called the Messiah" (1:16). In its surprising twist, the passage recalls an earlier genealogy, that of Abraham, which also concludes with an unexpected shift from male to female: "Now Sarai was barren; she had no child" (Gen. 11:30). And like that genealogy at the beginning of Israel history, this one sets the stage for an account of how the chosen or beloved son is destined from before birth to be God's own. The child whom Mary bears is "from the Holy Spirit" (Matt. 1:20), conceived while she is still a virgin. Like Isaac, though in a still more radical way, he owes his existence to the creative initiative of God. Jesus' divine sonship is silently signaled by the divine passive, "of whom Jesus was born" (1:16). But it is explicitly affirmed a few verses later in the wake of the holy family's flight from Herod: "Out of Egypt I have called my son" (2:15). Jesus' birth gathers up all the various elements of Israel's identity as beloved child—God's initiative in the birth of the patriarchs, Israel's deliverance from Egypt, the Messiah as son of David and Son of God—while giving resounding emphasis to the last of these: Son of God.

The evangelist's understanding of the awesome significance of Jesus' divine sonship is immediately spelled out after the angel foretells the child's birth.

> All this took place to fulfill what had been spoken by the Lord through the prophet: "Look, the virgin shall conceive and bear a son, and they shall name him Emmanuel," which means, "God is with us." (Matt. 1:22–23)

The name "Emmanuel" expresses *in nuce* Jesus' significance as the "son" foretold by the prophet. He is "God is with us," the personal embodiment of God's saving presence with his people. This is how Jesus' divine sonship surpasses every previous instance of sonship in Israel's history, while gathering them up in itself. His sonship is not the outcome of a transference of paternity from human father to God, as was Isaac's, consummated on a mountain in Moriah. It is the source and abiding mystery of his whole existence. From first to last, he is the filial expression of God's paternal love, God's enacted presence on earth.

The link between divine sonship and divine presence so emphatically made at the outset of the first Gospel is reaffirmed at key points thereafter. In Matthew's account of the transfiguration, the disciples initially retain their composure upon seeing Jesus' radiance; they are not terrified or sleepy, as in Mark and Luke. Yet this abruptly changes when the divine voice declares Jesus to be God's Son:

> Suddenly a bright cloud overshadowed them, and from the cloud a voice said, "This is my Son, the Beloved; with him I am well pleased; listen to him!" [6]When the disciples heard this, they fell to the ground and were overcome by fear. [7]But Jesus *came and touched them*, saying, "Get up and do not be afraid." (17:5b–7; with emphasis)

That Jesus "came and touched" the disciples is striking. Elsewhere in the Gospel, others often come to Jesus, but he is seldom said to come to them (cf. 5:1; 8:2, 5; 9:14, 28; 14:15; 15:1; 17:19; 18:1; 26:17; etc.). But here it is Jesus who comes to the frightened disciples, as though to explicate the words of the voice from heaven: "This is my Son." Similarly, the story that begins by recounting how Jesus "*came walking toward them* [i.e., the storm-tossed disciples] on the sea" ends with the acclamation "Truly you are the Son of God" (14:33). Both stories represent the significance of Jesus' divine sonship in spatial and tactile terms, as Jesus' own overcoming of the distance that separates him from the fearful and endangered. As "the Son, the Beloved," Jesus is the one in whom the divine presence draws near to comfort and to save.[17]

Luke: "The Disappearance of the Father"

The Third Gospel also explores Jesus' identity as beloved Son of the Father, using motifs of presence and absence, proximity and distance, separation and reunion, being lost and being found. An example is the story of the boy Jesus in the temple, which vividly recounts Jesus' separation from his human parents, who have lost track of him and must search anxiously for him in the crowds. Meanwhile the child is calmly and joyfully present in the temple, unperturbed by the commotion. The climactic words, "Did you not know that I must be in my Father's house?" (Luke 2:49) are the first spoken by Jesus in the Gospel. They signal Jesus' identity as the beloved Son, but just as much, they hint at an abiding proximity that exists between Jesus and his divine parent that transcends the vicissitudes of human kinship relations.

Another example is the story of the Prodigal Son. Remarkably, this one parable, which so obviously concerns the themes of presence and absence, separation and reunion, life and death, contains more than twice as many references to "father" as all of Jesus' other parables together (12 out of a total of 17). Although the parable does not explicitly identify God as Father, or Jesus as Son, its portrait of the human father illuminates the deep significance of Jesus' hospitality toward sinners. Jesus tells the parable because "all the tax collectors and sinners were *coming near* to listen to him," prompting the Pharisees and scribes to grumble, "This fellow *welcomes* sinners and eats with them" (Luke 15:1–2). The parable prods us to see the welcome that Jesus offers sinners as an efficacious sign of the heavenly Father's love for the lost children of Israel, powerfully applied through fellowship with Jesus.

A final example concerns the remarkable phenomenon that Robert L. Mowery has called "The Disappearance of the Father" in Luke–Acts.[18] Mowery points out that while the Gospel of Luke contains sixteen or seventeen references to God as Father, Acts contains only three, all of them in Acts 1–2. Thus the final twenty-six chapters of Acts contain no references to God as Father at all! What accounts for this very one-sided distribution? One author has proposed that the answer is to be found in "the apparently minimal use of 'Father' in the communities described in the Book of Acts."[19] While a historiographical explanation of this sort cannot be ruled out, it seems unlikely in light of other evidence we possess about the language of early Christian communities (cf. Gal. 4:6; Rom. 8:15, 29; 1 Peter 1:2; etc.). A more likely explanation, I think, is to be found in the literary design of Luke–Acts. As we noted above, the third evangelist takes pains in the Gospel to portray Jesus as the *only* person who speaks the word "Father," thereby emphasizing Jesus' special status as *the* Son. The evangelist continues to follow this rule in composing Acts, deviating from it only once, in Peter's sermon on the morning of Pentecost. And even in this one case (which is the final reference to God as Father in Luke–Acts), Peter is actually quoting Jesus' own words concerning the gift of the Holy Spirit (Acts 2:33; cf. 1:4). The reason that Father disappears from Luke–Acts as a designation for God, therefore, is to be sought in the mystery of Jesus' ascension into heaven, which marks the end of Jesus' directly reported speech in the composition (though see 9:4). For Luke, the ascension does not mean the *end* of the mystery of Jesus' presence as such, but it does mean its relocation to a heavenly realm not directly accessible to human experience. Even in its absence, the language of God as Father signals the mystery of divine presence in Jesus of Nazareth, now hidden until its glorious revelation again in the end of days (cf. Acts 1:11).

John: "I am in the Father and the Father is in me" (John 14:10)

The affinity between the language of divine kinship (Father, beloved Son, and Spirit) and divine presence is an especially pronounced feature of the Fourth Gospel. From the abundance of material we will consider a single illustration, John 14:8–21. The passage begins with Philip's request of Jesus: "Lord, show us the Father, and we will be satisfied" (v. 8).

In one sense Philip's appeal is understandable, since Jesus has spoken often and mysteriously of the Father since the beginning of John (120 times in the Gospel as a whole, nearly twice as frequently as the other Gospels combined). Perhaps Philip hopes that Jesus will clarify what he has said by pointing to the heavens and declaring a vision after the style of Ezekiel or Daniel. Still, Philip's words betray a basic misunderstanding—not so much of who "the Father" is—but of who *Jesus* is.

> Jesus said to him, "Have I been with you all this time, Philip, and you still do not know me? Whoever has seen me has seen the Father. How can you say, 'Show us the Father'?" (14:9)

Instead of pointing to the heavens, Jesus redirects Philip's attention to Jesus himself and to his being-there with Philip over the long haul ("I have been with you all this time!"). Philip must still learn and appropriate a truth that the evangelist declared at the beginning of the Gospel: "No one has ever seen God. It is God the only Son, who is close to the Father's heart, who has made him known" (1:18). To know the unseeable Father is to know Jesus himself as he sojourns among the slow of heart and mind. Jesus' reply continues:

> [10]"Do you not believe that I am in the Father and the Father is in me? The words that I say to you I do not speak on my own; but the Father who dwells in me does his works. [11]Believe me that I am in the Father and the Father is in me; but if you do not, then believe me because of the works themselves." (14:10–11)

Here Jesus goes beyond the initial request to impart a deeper lesson. It is possible to know the Father because of the works that he performs in Jesus.

But it is possible to know the Father in a still deeper way. This deeper knowledge rests on the truth that "I am in the Father and the Father is in me" and "the Father dwells in me." With these words, Jesus illuminates his own identity by referring to the mystery of mutual love, presence, and availability that characterizes the relationship of Father and Son. So complete is the closeness and proximity of Father and Son that each is *with* and even *in* the other. This is a depth dimension of good news that Jesus brings into the world: "God's being is one of communion."[20]

At the conclusion of his reply to Philip, Jesus connects the previous themes to the gift of the Spirit:

> "I will ask the Father, and he will give you another Advocate, *to be with you forever*. [17]This is the Spirit of truth, whom the world cannot receive, because it neither sees him nor knows him. You know him, because *he abides with you*, and *he will be in you*. [18]*I will not leave you orphaned; I am coming to you*. [19]In a little while the world will no longer see me, but *you will see me*; because I live, you also will live. [20]On that day you will know that *I am in my Father*, and *you in me*, and *I in you*." (14:16–20, with emphasis added)

I have italicized all the phrases that emphasize closeness, proximity, and presence to underscore how prominent they are in this passage. Jesus' imminent departure will not leave the disciples orphaned, without a Father in the world. The Holy Spirit will come and abide "with" and "in" the disciples "forever." These words extend the bonds of mutual presence that have hitherto characterized the relationship of Father, Son, and disciples in a new, pneumatological direction. Jesus' departure, when seen from another perspective, is his arrival again in the Holy Spirit: "I am coming to you." In the final analysis, then, the knowledge of the Father that Jesus reveals is trinitarian in scope. It is being adopted into the "with" and "in" that characterizes the life of Father, Son, and Spirit together. To speak of the Trinity as Father, Son, and Spirit is to say that this "with" and "in" is stronger than every experience of rupture, loss, death, and separation. It is to say, "Because I live, you also will live."[21]

THE CHRISTOLOGICAL REPETITION ELSEWHERE IN THE NEW TESTAMENT

We encounter the language of Father, Son, and Spirit not only in connection with Jesus' own speech in the Gospels. We also encounter it elsewhere in the New Testament, where it expresses the invincible bonds of mutual presence that characterize the life of the Trinity and the Trinity's action in the world.

In the interests of space, we will focus on a single passage, the eighth chapter of Paul's letter to the church in Rome.

In Romans 8, Paul sets forth a vision of the new creation that God has planted in the moribund world through Christ and the Spirit. The pattern of trinitarian divine agency that has informed the letter from its beginning moves into bold relief, as in the following remarkable declaration:

> If the Spirit of him who raised Jesus from the dead dwells in you, he who raised Christ from the dead will give life to your mortal bodies also through his Spirit that dwells in you. (v. 11)

As Robert W. Jenson has observed, this verse expresses the logic of trinitarian discourse with utmost conceptual compression: "The Spirit is *of* him *who* raised *Jesus*." From the prepositional structure of this phrase, Paul develops "a rhetoric and argument which sweeps justification and the work of Christ and prayer and eschatology and ethics and predestination into one coherent understanding."[22] All this is correct. What is especially important for our purposes, however, is that Paul elects to use a particular trinitarian vocabulary to flesh out the logic so compactly signaled in 8:11—the kinship vocabulary of Father, Son, and Spirit. The key passage is this:

> 14For all who are led by the Spirit of God are children of God. 15For you did not receive a spirit of slavery to fall back into fear, but you have received a spirit of adoption. When we cry, "Abba! Father!" 16it is that very Spirit bearing witness with our spirit that we are children of God, 17and if children, then heirs, heirs of God and joint heirs with Christ—if, in fact, we suffer with him so that we may also be glorified with him. (vv. 14–17)

Paul, as we have seen, has more than one trinitarian vocabulary at his disposal, more than one way of expressing the mutual relations that constitute the shared life of God, Christ, and the Spirit. He can speak, for example, of the giving, receiving, and glorification of the divine name, as he does in Philippians 2. That pattern informs other portions of Romans, especially chapters 9–11, and even peeks through at points in chapter 8 (cf. v. 39). Still, in Romans 8 Paul chooses to deploy the language of divine kinship in a particularly prominent way. In the passage above, he invokes the motif to interpret his readers' experience of Spirit possession and prayer as signs of gracious incorporation into the fellowship of God and Christ, Father and Son. He elaborates it further by speaking of Christ as "the firstborn within a large family" (v. 29), of creation's longing for the revelation and freedom of "the children of God" (vv. 19, 21), and so on.

Notice, then, that Paul's trinitarian argument, couched in the language of Father, Son, and Spirit, sweeps toward a climactic hymn of praise that celebrates—not so much the manifestation of God's uniqueness, as in Philippians 2—as *the unvanquishable bond of mutual presence* that unites the redeemed with God through Christ:

> If God is for us, who is against us? [32]He who did not withhold his own Son, but gave him up for all of us, will he not with him also give us everything else? . . . [35]Who will separate us from the love of Christ? Will hardship, or distress, or persecution, or famine, or nakedness, or peril, or sword? . . . [37] No, in all these things we are more than conquerors through him who loved us. [38]For I am convinced that neither death, nor life, nor angels, nor rulers, nor things present, nor things to come, nor powers, [39]nor height, nor depth, nor anything else in all creation, will be able to separate us from the love of God in Christ Jesus our Lord. (Rom. 8:31b–32, 35, 37–39)

According to this passage, God the Father does that which he spared father Abraham from doing. He surrenders his own beloved Son to the alien realm of death, thereby revealing his heart to be moved by an inconceivably tender mercy for those at risk of eternal separation from God. But the love uniting Father and Son is unconquerable, and therefore the Son's submission to death is the annihilation of death and its minions, and every creature gathered within its folds is already victorious over every threat. Nothing—no, nothing—can separate them from the Spirit of love that unites Father and Son.

THE CHRISTOLOGICAL PATTERN: THE MOST APPROPRIATE WAY OF NAMING THE PERSONS OF THE TRINITY?

Once again we have found it possible to arrive at a way of naming the persons of the Trinity by beginning with Jesus' own characteristic patterns of speech, as portrayed by the Gospels in their final canonical shape. In this case the language that we have explored is centered in the vocabulary of Father, Son, and Spirit. We have seen that this pattern is patient of multiple forms of expression; it takes different shapes across different authors and genres. At the same time, we have seen that it maintains a recognizable integrity across authors and genres. Should we therefore conclude that *this* pattern represents the most appropriate way of naming the persons of the Trinity?

Again, there seem to be some good reasons to suppose that it does.

1. The language of Father, Son, and Holy Spirit has one great distinguishing feature that differentiates it from the other patterns of trinitarian naming we have examined in this book. It provides a way of designating the persons of the Trinity that is relatively simple, fixed, unambiguous, and pronounceable. This differentiates it from the theological pattern we examined in the previous chapter, which has a fixed center but not a fixed form of expression since it employs a variety of pious circumlocutions. In contrast, the christological repetition gathers together many forms of Jesus' speech—my Father, our Father, Son of Man, Son of God, Spirit of the Father, and so forth—and stabilizes them in a single, coordinated phrase.

All of this suits the christological pattern of naming for use in liturgical contexts where clarity and brevity of expression are desirable. It also provides a kind of shorthand that is convenient for many pedagogical purposes where it is desirable to identify the persons of the Trinity in a simple, clear, and unambiguous way.

2. The language of Father, Son, and Spirit finds its primary home in the context of mutual address spoken within the context of already existing relations. Two of the three elements of the name—Father and Son—are in the first instance forms of personal address, spoken in the context of a lived relationship of availability and directedness of each to the other. The third, Holy Spirit, receives its specific connotation by virtue of the Spirit's role in originating and sustaining the relations of personal address. In this way the language emphasizes—not merely relationships of origin (the Son comes from the Father), but also relations of mutual presence between Father, Son, and Holy Spirit. The language expresses divine presence as *copresence*, enacted through relationships of mutual orientation, availability, and love.

Here again we seem to encounter an advantage over the other two patterns of naming. Personal names can also be used as terms of address, but they do not ordinarily bring the nature of mutual relations to the surface.

3. The language of Father, Son, and Holy Spirit draws centrally on human kinship language. Kinship language designates a sphere of human experience that is deeply vulnerable to experience of rupture, upset, disappointment, death, and loss. Although the language is not predicated of human experience and of the Trinity in a univocal way, the language does provide a way of saying that the bonds uniting the persons of the Trinity are *stronger* than all of the forces that threaten to annihilate human persons at the level of their basic relatedness to one another.

4. Finally, the language of Father, Son, and Spirit is weighted toward emphasizing the uniqueness and centrality of "the Son," Jesus Christ. Surely the vocabulary is also concerned with the first and third persons respectively, but they appear "transcribed" into an idiom whose keynote is that of divine

presence concentrated in the second person. The uniqueness of the first person remains thematic, but it is now articulated in a key whose special character is not the articulation of uniqueness as such, but rather presence: the first person is the *Father* of the Son. Similarly, the third person, as the bestower of divine blessing, remains thematic but now articulated in the key of presence: the Holy Spirit is the Spirit of the Father in and by whom the Son is begotten, in and by whom the Son has access to the Father, and in and by whom the fellowship of Father and Son is extended to include others, brothers and sisters of Christ and children of God.

Moreover, in its firm linguistic form, the christological repetition mirrors Jesus Christ himself, whose life also exhibits a definite shape and character that is sustained throughout his history from conception to death and resurrection. In him, God's presence also has a certain delimited character. Because of this limited vocabulary, the christological repetition lends itself to expression as liturgical formula, as in the iconic expression "the Father and the Son and the Holy Spirit." If the theological pattern glows like a hidden fire through the billowing clouds of the ever-changing coverings, the christological pattern shines like Jesus' brilliant raiment on the Mount of Transfiguration, bringing the church's fragmentary knowledge of the mystery of Jesus, God, and the Spirit to brilliant, focused expression.

The previous considerations are substantial. Still, I do not think that they warrant the conclusion that the christological pattern represents *the* most appropriate way of naming the persons of the Trinity. Rather, they support the conclusion that it represents *a* most appropriate way, by virtue of a strong affinity, aptness, or congruity between the pattern's distinctive linguistic texture on the one hand, and the mystery of the Trinity as gathered together and focused in the second person on the other hand. The christological pattern is not an all-purpose theological vocabulary that is employed with equal appropriateness in every context, or that is equally well suited to expressing every dimension of the mystery of the Trinity. But neither is it a chance assemblage of unrelated terms without a distinct integrity of its own. Rather, in the christological repetition, the persons of the Trinity declare the mystery of their life together *from a certain perspective: one that accords centrality to the second person of the Trinity and to the victorious divine presence that he brings into the world.*

14

"Your Kingdom Come!"

Jesus the Bestowal of Divine Blessing and the Name of the Trinity in a Pneumatological Key

> In every place where I cause my name to be remembered,
> *I will* come to you and *bless you.*
>
> —*Exodus 20:24*

In the last two chapters we have seen that the Gospels portray Jesus as speaking in plurality of ways of and to the One to whom he prays. He addresses God as "Father" in prayer, but he also shows reverence for his Father's name by avoiding its direct use. We have seen, too, that each of these features of dominical speech "unfolds" into corresponding ways of regarding Jesus himself and the Spirit, so that the Gospels actually present us with not one but at least *two* patterns of naming the persons of the Trinity. Still, even this inventory understates the pluriformity of Jesus' characteristic speech about God. In this chapter, we will explore yet another of its facets: his proclamation of the kingdom of God with signs of power and—of special concern to us—*with parables.* As we shall see, this form of speech, too, unfolds into a corresponding way of speaking about the Trinity, characterized by a limitless ability to unfurl the blessings of the triune life in ever new forms of speech, which multiply and coexist while always leaving room for more.

In our exploration of the kingdom of God in Jesus' proclamation, we will again start with the Lord's Prayer. The first petition, for the hallowing of God's name, is followed by prayer for the quick coming of the kingdom. An interesting feature of the second petition is that it seems to have circulated from very early times in more than one form. Much of the early church knew it by these words:

> Your Holy Spirit come upon us and cleanse us.[1]

Even those who received the prayer in the form best known to us today possessed it, as we do, in two different versions. Luke's is the shorter:

> Your kingdom come! (11:2)

Matthew transmits it in amplified form:

> Your kingdom come. Your will be done, on earth as it is in heaven. (6:10)

Matthew has not added a new petition but reformulated the same one in a new way, perhaps in order to make it more accessible to an audience for whom the original language had become obscure. The first image of God as coming king makes room for another, of God as creator of heaven and earth. The diverse forms of the second petition are deeply instructive as to the meaning of the petition itself. The coming of God's kingdom simply *is* the Holy Spirit's entering fully into a moribund creation to quicken, purify, and perfect it. Moreover, it belongs to the distinctive glory of the Spirit to accomplish this one task in an infinite variety of ways, according to the superabundant wealth of divine blessing it brings and the varied forms of creation itself.

JESUS' TEACHING IN PARABLES AS A PATH TOWARD NAMING THE PERSONS OF THE TRINITY

> [Christ] will be called the Son of unicorns, for . . . the unicorn is irresistible in might and unsubjected to man.
>
> —*Basil the Great, of Caesarea*[2]

What the Spirit comes to do on earth, however, it first does in Jesus. According to his Gospel portraits, Jesus is not merely a herald of the coming kingdom, as though he stood outside it like a footman at the gate. He is himself the Spirit-saturated advent of the kingdom he proclaims. To use the splendid word coined by Origen, Jesus is the *autobasileia*, the kingdom of God in person.[3] He himself, his words and actions, bestow the kingdom and its blessings on others.

One way the kingdom breaks out in Jesus is through his signs of power, which signal the loosening grip of sin, death, and sorrow like the thawing of ice in spring. "If it is by the finger of God that I cast out the demons, then the kingdom of God has come to you!" (Luke 11:20). It belongs to the essence of Jesus' works of power to be many and varied. He expels demons, but he also gives sight to the blind, makes the lame walk, heals the sick, forgives the sinner, feeds the hungry, and raises the dead, all according to the fullness of his power and the needs of those around him. The joy he ignites is inherently pluriform, prompting multitudes "to praise God joyfully with a loud voice for *all the deeds of power* that they had seen" (Luke 19:37).

Another way the kingdom breaks out in Jesus is through the parables he tells, often introduced with some variation of the words: "The kingdom of heaven is like . . ." (Matt. 13:31, 33, 34; etc.). Like Jesus' works of might, the parables of the kingdom are many and varied, but even more so. The sheer number is astonishing.[4] The Synoptics alone record well over 120 instances of parabolic speech, and John records many others of a distinctive kind. The parables are also diverse in genre, encompassing not only parables in the strict sense (e.g., the Prodigal Son), but also similes, similitudes, allegories, metaphors, aphorisms, example stories, and so on. They also touch on numerous facets of the natural and social world, including food production: farming, vineyard keeping, fishing; domestic activities: marketing, cooking, looking for things lost; economic activity: construction, banking, investing; government enterprise: war making; crime: assault and battery, theft, murder; labor relations: landlord-tenant relations, relations among laborers; domestic relations: family tensions, village emergencies, masters and servants, father and sons; the legal system: judges, courts; and so on. Finally, every one of the parables has a potentially limitless variety of applications, according to its own plenitude of meaning, the ever-varying circumstances in which it is heard, the person who hears it, and the nature of the hearer's response.

This last point is important. A crucial feature of Jesus' proclamation of the kingdom is that it requires a response from those who will receive its blessings. Jesus comes on the scene, declaring, "*Repent*, for the kingdom of heaven has come near" (Matt. 4:17), that is, "Renew your minds, turn Godward, change your life!" The need for response is clearly visible in many stories of healing (cf. "*Your faith* has made you well" [Matt. 9:22]), and it is also implied when Jesus declares at the end of a parable, "Let anyone with ears to hear listen!" (Mark 4:9). Jesus' parables open with a familiar scene of the everyday, but as they unfold, ordinary expectations are upset and some new view of reality appears that invites or warns the listener to think again. The parables insinuate themselves into the hearer's imagination and from there exert pressure on the total person to change the hearer's life, to be renewed, to repent. Just in this way, by enlisting the active participation of those who hear his parables of the kingdom, Jesus conveys the kingdom's blessings to others.

One way the parables have blessed the church down through the ages is by nourishing its christological and trinitarian imagination, prompting Christians to think and speak about the mystery of the Trinity in ways they otherwise would be unlikely to do. Although we could illustrate this point with reference to virtually any parable in the Gospels, we choose the one that follows immediately after the Lord's Prayer in Luke's account, the Visitor at Midnight:

> Suppose one of you has a friend, and you go to him at midnight and say to him, "Friend, lend me three loaves of bread; [6]for a friend of mine has arrived, and I have nothing to set before him." [7]And he answers from within, "Do not bother me; the door has already been locked, and my children are with me in bed; I cannot get up and give you anything." [8]I tell you, even though he will not get up and give him anything because he is his friend, at least because of his persistence he will get up and give him whatever he needs. (Luke 11:5–8)

For anyone who wishes to extract a single didactic point from every parable, the story presents few challenges. The parable teaches persistence in prayer, for if even an annoyed neighbor will eventually respond to an unrelenting request, then "how much more will the heavenly Father give the Holy Spirit to those who ask him!" (Luke 11:13). Yet while this interpretation is correct as far as it goes, it scarcely breaks the surface of the parable's tantalizing depths.

Some of the main elements of the story—a father at home with his children, a hungry sojourner from far away, an uncertain and precarious welcome—are the same as those found in the parable of the Prodigal Son (Luke 15:11–32). But the Visitor at Midnight assembles these pieces in a starkly different way, as though the better-loved parable were being seen through Alice's looking glass. The story begins with the arrival of the hungry sojourner, whose legitimate expectation of hospitality is imperiled, first by his host's lack of resources ("I have nothing to set before him!"), and then by village indifference ("Don't bother me!"). The father figure is not the embodiment of unconditional love and merciful welcome, but of lack of sympathy and self-protection. Safe and warm in bed, the father prefers the comfort of himself and his children over the claims of an unknown stranger, even when mediated by a neighbor. The hero of the story is the empty-handed but persistent friend, who risks upsetting his fellow villager for the sake of showing hospitality to the hungry sojourner. If the purpose of the parable were simply to encourage persistence in prayer, to what point are all these details?

And then there is the matter of the "three loaves." The bread of hospitality is the very heart of the story. It is what the tired visitor longs for, what the persistent friend lacks, what the sleepy father has but is reluctant to give. The number "three" fits naturally into the story's realism and yet has a luminous significance that shines beyond the edges of the story world. It recalls Abraham and Sarah's primordial act of hospitality toward the three strangers under the oaks of Mamre. Genesis tells us that Sarah took three seahs of flour and baked them into cakes for the strangers (18:6). We are not told how many cakes Sarah made from this quantity of grain, but later artistic representations of the scene depict three loaves of bread. Theophanes the Greek, teacher of Andrei Rublev, the great Russian iconographer, portrays the three angels sitting at a semicircular altar table, on which sit two loaves, while Sarah approaches from the right foreground, bringing the third. With sound canonical insight, Theophanes draws from the parable of the Visitor at Midnight to supply details missing from the story of Genesis, as though each story were a commentary on the other.[5]

Centuries before Theophanes, theologians such as Jerome and Augustine had already detected in the three loaves an allusion to the Trinity. In a letter to his friend Marsella, Jerome wrote:

> Our riches are to meditate in the law of the Lord day and night (Ps. 1:2), to knock at the closed door (Matt. 7:7), to receive the "three loaves" of the Trinity (Luke 11:5–8), and, when the Lord goes before us, to walk upon the water of the world (Matt. 14:23–25).[6]

The one who knocks persistently on the closed door receives "the 'three loaves' of the Trinity," implying that the Trinity is the one who opens the door to give, and the gift itself. Augustine interprets the passage along similar lines. In one of his sermons, he extols the riches that come to the person who imitates the dogged neighbor:

> But when you have gotten the three loaves, that is, fed on and understood the Trinity, you have that whereby you may both live yourself, and feed others. Now you need not fear the stranger who comes out of his way to you, but by taking him in may make him a citizen of the household: nor need you fear lest you come to the end of it. That Bread will not come to an end, but it will put an end to your indigence.

Augustine's interpretation harmonizes imagination and literary insight, connecting a figural interpretation of the three loaves with the parable's deep concern with hospitality to the stranger. Augustine goes on to draw out of the parable a new way of naming the persons of the Trinity:

> It is Bread, God the Father, and it is Bread, God the Son, and it is Bread, God the Holy Ghost. . . . God who gives to you, gives you nothing better than himself. O you greedy one, what else were you seeking for? Or if you seek for anything else, what will suffice you whom God does not suffice?[7]

Augustine's words illustrate the power of Jesus' parables to generate new and unexpected ways of naming the persons of the Trinity. Augustine's triadic naming was a passing style, prompted by this text for use on one occasion, and perhaps never repeated again. Yet it is not any less profound, memorable, and truthful for that. It is an illustration, however humble, of how Christians have named the persons of the Trinity in a pneumatological key by adapting ordinary language to a new and sacred purpose.

ANOTHER WARNING SIGN

> With what can we compare the rise of metaphor in recent theology, or what parable shall we use to describe it? It is like the kudzu plant, which begins as one sprout among many, but ends up hiding everything under its smothering embrace.[8]

Before continuing our exploration of a Spirit-centered way of naming the persons of the Trinity, it is well to take note of another warning sign. One reason why contemporary debate about naming the Trinity is so polarized is that theologians often grab hold of one dimension of Jesus' characteristic speech and emphasize it to the detriment of other dimensions. We drew attention to that danger in the last chapter, in our discussion of Jesus' address to God as "Father," which some (often more conservative) theologians have played off against his reverence for the divine name and indeed against the Old Testament generally. Something analogous sometimes happens with respect to Jesus' teaching in parables. In this case, however, it is other (often more progressive) theologians who latch onto this one aspect of Jesus' speech and make it the paradigm for understanding everything he says. We can illustrate this point with reference to the remarkable career of the concept "metaphor" in Christian theology of the last fifty years.

Around the middle of the last century, biblical scholars typically defined the term "metaphor" as a simile without "like" or "as." Starting about the mid-1960s, however, scholars began to define the term "metaphor" more broadly, for example, speaking about the unfamiliar (the kingdom of God) in terms of the familiar (a mustard seed).[9] According to this new understanding, *all* of Jesus' parabolic sayings (whether allegories, aphorisms, example stories, and so on) are really metaphors, regardless of literary genre. The expanded definition was especially popular among American scholars seeking new literary approaches to the parables that would free them from the (as they saw it) overly confessional and church-centered categories of a previous generation of German scholars (Word of God, revelation, etc.). In time, younger American theologians made the new parable research the starting point for their work in systematic theology. The result was yet another massive expansion of metaphor's domain. In *Speaking in Parables: A Study in Metaphor and Theology* (1975), theologian Sallie McFague argued that not only are Jesus' parables all metaphors, so too are the *Gospels*, for they too speak of the unfamiliar (God) in terms of the familiar (Jesus). In fact, the whole Bible is metaphorical, for metaphor is "the crucial constitutive of language" (32). "Metaphor is, for human beings, what instinctual groping is for the rest of the universe—the power of getting from here to there" (56). For us, "there is no other way" (62).[10]

McFague's work proved inspirational for a generation of theologians eager to adopt a revisionist posture toward Christian tradition. If Jesus talked about God by using metaphors, and if that's all anyone can do anyway, then it is appropriate for contemporary Christians to devise new metaphors for God in keeping with their insight and experience. "Father, Son, and Holy Spirit" is a worn-out metaphor that has been killed by overuse, and new trinitarian metaphors should be used in its place, such as "Creator, Redeemer, Sustainer," "Mother, Lover, Friend," and so on. Feminist theology's love for the concept of metaphor elicited a strong negative reaction from defenders of tradition, who insisted that "Father, Son, and Holy Spirit" was not a metaphor at all (unlike the Bible's talk about God as Mother, which was), but was rather a datum of revelation, a proper name, or something of the kind. Ever since, the polarized inclusive-language debate has generally fallen out along these two lines, both of which originate in a different aspect of Jesus' characteristic speech.[11]

I have already explained why I find many traditionalists' claims on behalf of the language of "Father, Son, and Spirit" unpersuasive. But what is wrong with progressive claims on behalf of metaphor? Nothing, I think, so long as metaphor is thought to say something that is important and true about the way biblical language works. Rather, problems arise when one supposes that it says *everything* that is important and true. To put it another way, the concept of metaphor becomes problematic for biblical interpretation when it becomes the main organizing concept for a general theory of human understanding.

As theologian Hans Frei pointed out some years ago, the problem with such general theories is that they tend to overwhelm the unique contours of the biblical witness from the outside, like kudzu on a country road.[12] This danger is not unique to contemporary theology. We encountered a version of it in the Cappadocian's presupposition of God's anonymous polyonymy, which blocked their ability to recognize the Bible's testimony to the divine name. Today, an overly generalized theory of theology as metaphor has a similar weakness. Because it knows in advance that all speech about God is metaphorical, it cannot register the important role played in the economy of biblical God-talk by something that is not—the Tetragrammaton. As Thomas Aquinas recognized, the Tetragrammaton does not name God "from below," as metaphors do, but serves rather to fix the ultimate referent of biblical discourse, while leaving other forms of speech (metaphors, narratives, analogical discourse, etc.) free to speak about that referent in the terms most appropriate to them.

It turns out, then, that the danger that comes from an overemphasis on Jesus' parabolic speech is the same as that which comes from an overemphasis on his address to God as Father. Both tend to underplay his reverence for the divine name. To help recover a sense of the Tetragrammaton's importance for the kind of discourse we are examining in this chapter, and for Jesus' own parabolic speech, we will turn once again to the Old Testament.

THE OLD TESTAMENT ROOT OF A SPIRIT-CENTERED WAY OF NAMING THE TRINITY

> The name of the LORD is a strong tower;
> the righteous run into it and are safe.
>
> —*Proverbs 18:10*

Like the pattern of naming we examined in the last chapter, the pneumatological pattern is best understood as a kind of nonidentical *repetition* of God's name and its ineffable cloud of connotation. But whereas the christological pattern repeats the divine name in terms of God's unvanquishable love for the chosen child, the pneumatological pattern repeats it as God's superabundant glory and blessing, conveyed by a limitless variety of terms drawn from many spheres of life. The relationship between the divine name and its explication is visible in the subject-predicate structure of the sentence, "The LORD is . . . my shepherd, my light, my shield," and so on. In such sentences the conjunction of subject and predicate catalyzes a rich semantic transaction. On the one hand, common nouns are nominalized, freed from their contexts of ordinary generic meaning and made to share in the incomparable uniqueness of God's name. On the other, the name itself is explicated by means of what it is not, with its uncircumscribable cloud of connotation gathered within the ambit of a single intelligible word or phrase. Such sayings are metaphors, perhaps, but metaphors of a distinctive kind by virtue of their location in a literary context whose infinite web of allusion spins around a single proper name. The ancient Christian practice of designating the predicative terms used in these and similar sentences as "divine names" was quite astute, insofar as it expressed the terms' assimilation toward a point of infinite uniqueness.[13]

A narrative illustration of the unity-in-difference of God's name and names is the story of Hagar in the wilderness. Oppressed by jealous Sarah and abandoned by spineless Abraham, Hagar flees into the desert in despair. There she unexpectedly meets "an angel of the LORD," who addresses her by name and bids her return home, sweetening the bitter words with a promise: her offspring will be multiplied "so . . . that they cannot be counted for multitude" (Gen. 16:10). The story then relates an extraordinary thing.

> [Hagar] named the LORD who spoke to her, "You are El-roi"; for she said, "Have I really seen God and remained alive after seeing him?" (16:13)

Hagar's bold naming of God fills the foreground of the story, at the very moment we realize—in the background, as it were—that the "angel of the LORD" is really the LORD himself. Whether Hagar knows she is speaking to the LORD is not clear, nor is it important to the story being told. The important thing is that *the reader* realizes that Hagar aptly names the LORD in terms of her own experience of unexpected rescue and blessing. Henceforth "El-roi" *is* one of the names of the LORD, an indispensable repetition of everything he is as viewed from the vantage point of a cruelly mistreated slave. Figuratively speaking (and why not?), we might say that Hagar's promised offspring are the numberless divine names that designate God in and out of the church's canon, beginning with the Old Testament's own Elohim, El, El-Olam, El Shaddai, and so on. These and other names (many drawn originally from other ancient Near Eastern cults) never replace God's personal proper name, but frequently enough they operate independently in its stead, repeating what it says in other terms, even as the divine name itself recedes wholly into the background, as in the opening chapter of Genesis or the Elohistic Psalms. Without El-Roi and countless other divine names, the blessed offspring of Hagar's naming, the Bible could not portray the LORD as the unique God he is.[14]

If Hagar is the earthly mother of the divine names, then her most splendid daughter is surely Lady Wisdom, the feminine personification of divine wisdom, and a figure of great importance in the immediate historical background of the New Testament. For sheer luxuriance of linguistic apparel, she has no equal, as the following passage indicates:

> 22There is in [Wisdom] a spirit that is intelligent, holy, unique, manifold, subtle, mobile, clear, unpolluted, distinct, invulnerable, loving the good, keen, irresistible, 23beneficent, humane, steadfast, sure, free from anxiety, all-powerful, overseeing all, and penetrating through all spirits that are intelligent, pure, and altogether subtle.
> 24For wisdom is more mobile than any motion;
> because of her pureness she pervades and penetrates all things.

> 25For she is a breath of the power of God,
> and a pure emanation of the glory of the Almighty;
> therefore nothing defiled gains entrance into her.
> 26For she is a reflection of eternal light,
> a spotless mirror of the working of God,
> and an image of his goodness.
> 27Although she is but one, she can do all things,
> and while remaining in herself, she renews all things;
> in every generation she passes into holy souls
> and makes them friends of God, and prophets;
> 28for God loves nothing so much as the person who lives with wisdom.
> 29She is more beautiful than the sun,
> and excels every constellation of the stars.
> Compared with the light she is found to be superior,
> 30for it is succeeded by the night,
> but against wisdom evil does not prevail.
>
> (Wisdom 7:22–30)

As Elizabeth A. Johnson points out in *She Who Is*, the writers who introduced the image of Lady Wisdom into biblically oriented discourse were not freely speculating against a limitless horizon of divine mystery, as McFague's general theory of metaphor implies. They were seeking to express YHWH's incomparable uniqueness in a way that would be intelligible and attractive to people of their time, when enthusiasm for Isis, the many-named Egyptian goddess of motherhood and fertility, was sweeping the Greco-Roman world. The biblical writers captured and transformed Isis's extravagant polyonymy by bringing it under "the controlling context of Jewish monotheistic faith." At the same time, they expanded the biblical portrait of God by presenting him "in the garb of the goddess," in a way that would prove to be of great importance to the writers of the New Testament.[15]

A SPIRIT-CENTERED WAY OF NAMING JESUS CHRIST

Turning to the New Testament, we expect to discover the kinds of discourse we have just explored attested in a way that manifests both consistency and novelty vis-à-vis its Old Testament antecedents. And indeed, this is just what we do find. As before, the pleroma of "divine names" is best understood as a kind of nonidentical repetition of the divine name, but now this repetition reveals a christological focus and trinitarian breadth that is quite new. We will explore these claims beginning with the naming of Christ, and toward the end of the chapter we will turn to the naming of the Trinity. Our starting point this time will be the Gospel of John.

Johannine Witness: Jesus' Predicative I am Sayings[16]

The phrase "kingdom of God" seldom appears in the Fourth Gospel, and nowhere do we find the array of stories and pithy sayings that are so integral to the Synoptics' portrait of Jesus. One thing we find instead is a curiously symmetrical constellation of fourteen "I am" statements, spoken by Jesus on various occasions over the course of the Gospel. Half of these we have already considered, the seven "absolute" sayings that (in the Greek) appear simply in the form "I am!" (see chap. 12). The other seven, of special interest to us now, are the so-called predicative I am statements (here with capitalization added):

> I am the Bread of Life. (John 6:35; cf. 41, 48, 51)
> I am the Light of the World. (8:12; cf. 9:5)
> I am the Gate for the Sheep. (10:7, 9)
> I am the Good Shepherd. (10:11, 14)
> I am the Resurrection and the Life. (11:25)
> I am the Way, and the Truth, and the Life. (14:6)
> I am the True Vine. (15:1, 5)

Clearly, the two sets of seven sayings are to be understood in light of each other.[17] The seven absolute sayings have logical priority because they signal Jesus' unique identity as the one who makes known "your name that you have given me" (John 17:11–12). Still, it is the seven predicative sayings that first bring to light the wealth of blessing bestowed wherever God "cause[s] my name to be remembered," as he now accomplishes with eschatological fullness in Jesus Christ. The relationship of the two sets of sayings exactly parallels that between God's absolute self-declaration "I am the LORD!" (Isa. 45:5–6; etc.) and the expanded declaration "I, the LORD, am your Savior and your Redeemer, the Mighty One of Jacob" (Isa. 60:16). The absolute sayings declare the mystery of God's uniqueness manifested in Christ, and the predicative sayings declare the mystery of divine blessing bestowed in him.

The sevenfold repetition of the sayings connotes fullness and perfection in both cases, but each time in a somewhat different sense. The selfsame repetition of the absolute "I am" hints at the perfect revelation of a single unchanging truth, while the ever-varied predicative statements hint at a plenitude of divine richness. It would have been a simple matter for the author of the Fourth Gospel to have included an eighth or ninth or tenth predicative saying, such as "I am the water of life." Yet here any addition would have been a subtraction, because any attainable number would fall short of the fullness implied by the perfect number seven. For this reason, Origen was justified in describing such sayings as "countless."

> Although Jesus was one, he had several aspects; and to those who saw him he did not appear alike to all. That he had many aspects is clear from the saying, "I am the way, and the truth, and the life," and "I am the bread," and "I am the door," and *countless* other sayings.[18]

One certainly is free to call Jesus' predicative "I am" statements metaphors, and there is an important sense in which that is just what they are: similes without "like" or "as." But there is also an important sense in which they are his names, nonidentical repetitions of the one divine name that he has been given to make known. There is *taxis*, or sequential order, between Jesus' divine name and his divine names, but not a relationship of superiority and subordination. To know Jesus as "I am," the disciples must also know him as Bread and eat of him; as Light and walk in him; as Gate and go through him; as Good Shepherd and follow him; as Resurrection and be raised to life in him; as Way and tread him; as Vine and grow from him. He is both the one and the other, just as the one to whom he prays is "I am who I am" (Exod. 3:14), "the Lord" (3:15).

The Synoptic Witness: The Irreducible Element of the Odd

> No estimate of Jesus deserves to be taken seriously which does not do full justice to [the] irreducible element of the odd in the portrait of our Lord.
>
> —*Reginald E. O. White*[19]

Although the Synoptic Gospels have no exact counterpart to Jesus' predicative "I am" sayings, they, no less than John, portray Jesus as the person through whom God's blessings are bestowed. In the Old Testament, God's blessing is often conveyed by a stranger (Gen. 14), a mysterious "angel" (Gen. 16), or a sojourner on the road (Gen. 18), who ultimately proves to be transparent as "the Lord." Similarly, one way Jesus conveys the blessings of the kingdom of God is precisely by virtue of what is enduringly enigmatic, odd, and challenging in him. Consider the following motifs.

Jesus the Parable of God

Just as Jesus' parables contain familiar elements in startling juxtaposition, so too the man himself. He teaches not only in the synagogue but also on the beach. He dines with scrupulous Pharisees, but also with tax collectors and street women. He enters Jerusalem to the acclamation of multitudes, but dies on a Roman gibbet, abandoned by his followers. He is buried in a borrowed tomb, but dines again with his friends three days later. The enigmatic in Jesus is not something that wears off with time, but an inextinguishable dimension of who he is and always will be. No matter how well we think we know him, no matter how aptly we think we name him, he interrupts the flow of our trusts and the ordinary self-evidence of our words and challenges us to repent, to reorder our language and our lives from the bottom up. Just in this way, Jesus comes to us and blesses us again.[20]

The parable-like character of Jesus' existence is accentuated by his self-designation as "the Son of Man." Whatever the original historical or theological connotations of the name (now perhaps unrecoverable), the title considered in its final literary setting is "unique and mysterious." "It is more like one of Jesus' parables or riddles. Jesus can use it freely in public, people can understand that it refers to Jesus, yet no one seems to grasp the deep theological import Jesus gives it."[21] Just so, the title challenges the hearer, resists closure, and keeps the question of Jesus' identity perpetually alive. Consider the following passage:

> He asked them, "But who do you say that I am?" Peter answered him,
> "You are the Messiah." 30And he sternly ordered them not to tell any-
> one about him. 31Then he began to teach them that the Son of Man
> must undergo great suffering, and be rejected by the elders, the chief
> priests, and the scribes, and be killed, and after three days rise again.
> (Mark 8:29–31)

Jesus does not reject Peter's confession, but neither does he allow it to stand unqualified, as though "the Messiah" provided the sufficient and comprehensive answer to the question "Who do you say that I am?" By immediately referring to himself by the opaque title "Son of Man" and alluding to the strange destiny of his rejection and death, Jesus supplements and decenters Peter's confession and renews the question of his own mysterious identity. Even after he has been recognized as the Christ, "the Son of the living God" (Matt. 16:16) he remains—all the more!—the enigmatic Son of Man.

Jesus the Least of These

Jesus unnerves us by the company he keeps, by those with whom—and *in* whom—he chooses to be found. In Matthew 25:31–46, he tells a parable about the judgment of the nations at the end of days. Then "the Son of Man" will come "in his glory" to do justice on the earth, separating people from one another as a shepherd separates the sheep from the goats. He will put those "blessed by my Father" on his right hand, at the same time explaining to them why they are now invited to enter the kingdom. The Son of Man will relate a series of past encounters when he was in need and the blessed showed him kindness and mercy.

> I was hungry and you gave me food, I was thirsty and you gave me something to drink, I was a stranger and you welcomed me, [36]I was naked and you gave me clothing, I was sick and you took care of me, I was in prison and you visited me. (25:35–36)

Strangely, however, the blessed themselves will be unable to remember these encounters, though surely any meeting with the Son of Man, who now sits before them "on the throne of his glory," would be difficult to forget. "When was it," they will ask, when we saw you in need and did you some kindness? Then the Son of Man will answer, splitting the darkness of history with the sword of his mouth: "When you did it to the least of these, you did it to me" (cf. 25:40). And so it will go again for those on his left hand, who also encountered the Son of Man but passed him by. Unnamed to the end, the Son of Man unriddles who he is by declaring his self-identification with human beings in need.

Jesus the Stranger

It is not surprising that Jesus began his public ministry a stranger.[22] What is deeply odd is that he remains one as resurrected Lord. Mary Magdalene mistook him for a gardener; two disciples did not know him on the road to Emmaus; the fishermen did not recognize his figure or voice when he called to them loudly from the shore. The resurrection, it seems, *intensifies* an incognito characteristic that was there from the beginning, when John the Baptist declared, "Among you stands one whom you do not know" (John 1:26). According to Revelation, the triumphant Christ bears a name "that no one knows but himself" (19:12).

And yet the "strangerliness" of Jesus is not a mask he puts on to hide from others. It is how he reveals who he really is, how he becomes transparent to the one who sent him.[23] Few have expressed this insight more movingly than Charles Wesley in his hymn, "Come, O Thou Traveler Unknown."

> Come, O thou Traveler unknown,
> Whom still I hold, but cannot see!
> My company before is gone,
> And I am left alone with Thee;
> With Thee all night I mean to stay,
> And wrestle till the break of day.
>
> I need not tell Thee who I am,
> My misery and sin declare;
> Thyself hast called me by my name,
> Look on Thy hands, and read it there;
> But who, I ask Thee, who art Thou?
> Tell me Thy name, and tell me now.

Wilt Thou not yet to me reveal
Thy new, unutterable Name?
Tell me, I still beseech Thee, tell;
To know it now resolved I am;
Wrestling, I will not let Thee go,
Till I Thy Name, Thy nature know.

'Tis Love! 'tis Love! Thou diedst for me!
I hear Thy whisper in my heart;
The morning breaks, the shadows flee,
Pure, universal love Thou art;
To me, to all, Thy bowels move;
Thy nature and Thy Name is Love.[24]

In this lyric Wesley interprets the identity of Christ by evoking the Genesis account of the mysterious stranger who wrestled with Jacob at night, a story that eerily mingles themes of anonymity, struggle, physical intimacy, and blessing (Gen. 32:22–32). In Genesis, a wounded Jacob pleads to know his opponent's name, but receives no answer. Instead, Jacob receives a blessing in parting that leads him to exclaim "I have seen God face to face!" (v. 30). Similarly, Wesley's lyric, which noticeably lacks any reference to the proper name "Jesus," never wholly lifts the veil of mystery that cloaks the unknown traveler. Rather, as in Genesis, the cloak of anonymity becomes transparent without being removed, when at last the divine blessing is received as a whisper in the heart: the stranger's "new, unutterable Name" is—Love.

A SPIRIT-CENTERED WAY OF NAMING THE PERSONS OF THE TRINITY

The pattern of naming we have examined in this chapter serves not only to illuminate Christ as the bestowal of divine blessing, but also the Trinity revealed in him under the same aspect. In some instances this is already hinted at in Jesus' own speech, as in the following verse:

> [1]I am the true vine, and my Father is the gardener. [2]He cuts off every branch in me that bears no fruit, while every branch that does bear fruit he prunes so that it will be even more fruitful. (John 15:1–2 NIV)

Because the second person is the vine, we may name the first person of the Trinity the gardener, and the third—by implication—the pruning knife! Where we typically find a fuller deployment of the pneumatological pattern, however, is not in Jesus' own direct discourse, but rather elsewhere in the New Testament. One thinks, for example, of the following passages:

> In the beginning was the Word, and the Word was with God, and the Word was God. [2]He was in the beginning with God. [3]All things came into being through him, and without him not one thing came into being. What has come into being [4]in him was life, and the life was the light of all people. [5]The light shines in the darkness, and the darkness did not overcome it. (John 1:1–5)

Or again:

> [15]He is the image of the invisible God, the firstborn of all creation; [16]for in him all things in heaven and on earth were created, things visible and invisible, whether thrones or dominions or rulers or powers—all things have been created through him and for him. [17]He himself is before all things, and in him all things hold together. . . . [19]For in him all the fullness of God was pleased to dwell. (Col. 1:15–17, 19)

Or again:

> He is the reflection of God's glory and the exact imprint of God's very being, and he sustains all things by his powerful word. (Heb. 1:3)

The influence of Jewish wisdom traditions is evident in these passages. In adapting them to their own purposes, early Christians focused rigorously on God's relation to Christ, but they did not squelch the impulse toward rhetorical variation, reiteration, and fullness. The second person is identified as "Word," "Image," "Reflection," "Exact Imprint," "Firstborn of all creation," while the first person is identified or referred to by means of such phrases as "God," "the invisible God," "God's glory," "all the fullness of God," and "God's very being." The fullness of language used to name God and Christ mirrors the fullness of the work wherein their glory is made known: the cosmos as a whole. These passages, it is true, do not speak explicitly of Holy Spirit, but this lack is made up for by the variety of ways the Spirit is attested elsewhere in the New Testament: as dove, wind, rushing sound, tongues of fire, voice from heaven; as "the Spirit of God" (Matt. 3:16), "Spirit of truth" (John 14:17), "Spirit of holiness" (Rom. 1:4 mg.); "Spirit of life" (8:2); "Spirit of the living God" (2 Cor. 3:3), "Spirit of wisdom and of revelation" (Eph. 1:17 NIV), "Spirit of grace" (Heb. 10:29), "Spirit of glory" (1 Pet. 4:14 NIV); as "Advocate" (John 14:16), pledge, seal (2 Cor. 1:22; Eph. 1:13–14), and so on.

Rich as the Scriptures themselves are, it is to the life of the church that we must look for the fullest unfolding of the name of the Trinity in a pneumatological key. Here is an example from the end of the first century that appears in the *Odes of Solomon*, which may have been considered canonical by some portions of the early church.

> 1A cup of milk was offered to me,
> and I drank it in the sweetness of the Lord's kindness.
> 2The Son is the cup,
> and Father is he who was milked;
> and the Holy Spirit is she who milked him;
> 3because his breasts were full,
> and it was undesirable that his milk should be released without purpose.
> (19.1–3)[25]

This is a metaphor, parable, or allegory, but just so it is also a way of naming the persons of the Trinity: "He who was milked," "the Cup," and "She who milked." The image is undeniably bold, but not fundamentally different in kind from the pattern first set forth in the Gospel of John. Who could count all the ternaries that faith has subsequently coined? Here are a few: "God, Word, and Wisdom"; "God, Offspring, Similitude" (Irenaeus); "the One who makes the Sun to Rise, Sun of Righteousness, Dew of Truth" (Clement of Alexandria); "Root, Tree, Fruit"; "Sun, Ray, Apex"; "Fountain, River, Stream" (Tertullian); "Lover, Beloved, Love"; "Unity, Equality, Connection"; "God, Beginning, Goodness and Love" (Augustine); "Archetype, Image, Purifying Sun" (Basil the Great); "Rose, Flower, Fragrance"; "Sun, Ray, Radiance" (John of Damascus); "Power, Wisdom, Goodness" (Peter Abelard); "Our Table, our Food, our Server"; "Light, Wisdom, and Strength" (Catherine of Siena); "Eternal sovereign truth, eternal sovereign wisdom, eternal sovereign love"; "Might, Wisdom, Love"; "Joy, Bliss, Delight"; "Maker, Keeper, Lover"; "Being, Increase, Fulfillment"; "Nature, Mercy, Grace"; "Fatherhood, Motherhood, Lordship" (Julian of Norwich); "A Brightness, a Flashing Forth, a Fire" (Hildegaard of Bingen); "Works, Words, and Will"; "Might, Medium, Servant"; "Fist, Fingers, Palm" (William Langland); "Deep of the Omnipotence, Deep of Uncreated Wisdom, Breathtaking Goodness" (Gertrude of Helfta); "Life, Light, Joy" (William of Auvergne); "Lover, Beloved, Co-Beloved" (Richard of St. Victor); "Unity, Equality, and Union"; "This, It, and the Same"; "the Loving Love, the Lovable Love, and the Love Which Is the Bond of Loving Love and Lovable Love" (Nicholas of Cusa); "Deliverer from the Hand of Death, Distributor of Mercies, Bestower of Immortality"; "Awesome Judge, Healer of Souls, Distributor of Gifts"; "God without Beginning, Liberator, Distributor of Gifts"; "God without Beginning, Healer of Our Souls, Giver of Mercy"; "Righteous Judge, Bridegroom, Tree of Life"; "Refuge, Fountain, Purifier"; "Him Who Is by Nature Good, True Vine, Sun of Life"; "Light That Has No Beginning, Most Pure Light, Enlightener"; "Creator of All, Joy of Creatures, Fragrance of Immortality"; "Love, Love Born from Love, Sent Love"; "Eternally Existing One, Sun of Righteousness, Spirit of Truth"; "Seer, Rock of Faith, Fountain"; "Uncreated, Only Begotten, Heavenly Fire"; "God without

Beginning, Only Begotten, Cup of Immortality"; "Source, Word, Stream"; "Divinity, Divine Fire, Power from on High"; "All-Pure Light, Sun of Righteousness, All-Holy Spirit"; "Uncreated Fire, Word from the Very Beginning, Spirit of God"; "First and Inexpressible Light, Light Pouring Forth from Light, Cosharer in Glory"; "Light, Outpouring from the Light, Source of Good Things" (Liturgical Canons and Hymns of the Armenian Orthodox Church); "My Hope, My Refuge, My Shelter" (Orthodox Prayer Book); "Fountain of Divine Compassion, Savior and Salvation, Spirit of Consecrating Grace"; "the One Who Draws, the One Who Sprinkles, the One Who Seals"; "God, Word, Breath"; "Life, Life Bestowed, Life Imparted"; "Truth That Sends, Truth That Comes, Truth That Is Conferred"; "First, Second, Third"; "the One Who Allures, the One Who Assures, the One Who Bears Witness"; "Almighty, Fountain of Bliss, River of Raptures" (Charles Wesley); "Pure Giver, Receiver and Giver, Pure Receiver"; "Speaker, Word, and Meaning" (Karl Barth); "Primordial Being, Expressive Being, Unitive Being" (John Macquarrie); "*Sat*, *Cit*, and *Ananda*" (Abhishiktananda); "Mother Sophia, Jesus Sophia, Spirit Sophia"; "Unoriginate Love, Love from Love, Mutual Love" (Elizabeth A. Johnson); "Subject, Object, Spirit"; "Transcendence, Self-expression, Breath of the Future" (Robert W. Jenson); "*Dao*, *De*, *Qi*" (Paul S. Chung); "Fountain, Offspring, and Wellspring"; "Womb of Life and Source of Being, Life of Life and Death of Death, Brooding Spirit" (Ruth Duck); "Source, Well-Spring, Living Water" (David S. Cunningham); "Overflowing Font, Living Water, Flowing River (*Book of Common Worship*); "Abba, Servant, Paraclete"; "Our Life, Our Mercy, Our Might"; "Our Rainbow, Our Ark, Our Dove"; "Our Sovereign, Our Water, Our Wine"; "Our Light, Our Treasure, Our Tree" (Gail Ramshaw); "Parent Ancestor, Brother Ancestor, Holy Spirit" (Charles Nyamiti of Tanzania); "Planner, Performer, Enabler" (Thian Nun Piang [Myanmar]); "Sun, Brilliance, Warmth," "Perfume, Sprinkling, Aroma" (Van Kung [Myanmar]); "Mountain Peak, Cool Air, Freshness" (Lam Thien Loc [Vietnam]).[26]

To be sure, it is possible to draw meaningful distinctions among these different ternaries. Some are to be understood chiefly as identifying *vestiges* of the Trinity in creation ("Rose, Flower, Fragrance"), while others are understood chiefly as naming the persons of the Trinity themselves (God, Offspring, Similitude). Among the latter, some illuminate chiefly the inner relations of the Godhead ("Lover, Beloved, Love"), while some emphasize the loving activity of the three in the world ("Awesome Judge, Healer of Souls, Distributor of Gifts"). Some involve nouns that abstract wholly from material reality (Unity, Equality, Union), while others are vividly material (Table, Food, Server). Some are personal in character (Maker, Keeper, Lover), some are not ("Source, Wellspring, Living Water"). Still, it would be wrongheaded to turn these distinctions into separations, as though only some of them were relevant for naming the persons of the Trinity. For the truth is that we find *all of these categories* represented even among those personal names most solemnized by tradition, such as "Father" and "Son" (drawn from material creatures), "Holy Spirit" (employing terms common to all three persons), "Image" (impersonal), "Gift" (named with reference to the order of salvation), and so on. As Karl Barth himself correctly observed, "The analogies [of the Trinity] adduced by the Fathers are in the long run only further expositions and multiplications of the Bible concepts, Father, Son, and Spirit, which are already analogical."[27] Rather than be overanxious to draw the circle of trinitarian naming too narrowly, then, we should let ourselves appreciate the glorious fullness of the name of the Trinity in a pneumatological key.

THE PNEUMATOLOGICAL PATTERN: THE MOST APPROPRIATE WAY OF NAMING THE PERSONS OF THE TRINITY?

For a third time we have arrived at a way of naming the persons of the Trinity by beginning with Jesus' own characteristic patterns of speech. In this case, we began with Jesus' practice of proclaiming the kingdom of God in parables, and ended with a pattern characterized by a seemingly endless ability to unfold the glory of the Trinity in ever-new forms of speech, which multiply and coexist while always leaving room for more. Should we conclude that this pattern is *the* most appropriate way of naming the persons of the Trinity? Again, there are good reasons for thinking that it is.

A great advantage of this pattern of naming is precisely the extraordinary breadth with which it intersects human language and experience in the world. In contrast to the theological pattern, which tightly orbits a single personal proper name, and the christological pattern, which makes uses of a limited selection of human kinship terms—the pneumatological pattern paints with an immeasurably fuller linguistic palette. "Names" in the context of the pneumatological pattern encompass not only the vast sea of common nouns ("Word," "Advocate"), but also nominal phrases ("Giver of Life"), prepositions ("Light of Light"), adjectives ("Almighty"), and other forms of speech besides. Precisely so, the pneumatological pattern is well suited to express the plenitude of blessing and glory revealed by the Trinity in the economy of salvation and the breadth of human experience in the cosmos.

The pneumatological pattern is patient with the ordinary. It gathers up the language of the everyday, often meager and unpromising in itself, and transforms it into praise of the everlasting Trinity.

Furthermore, the pneumatological pattern is context-sensitive to a far greater degree than the other patterns we have examined. The theological pattern is inextricably from an ancient form of Jewish piety; the christological pattern remains more or less the same from culture to culture and age to age. In contrast, the pneumatological pattern adapts itself to the varying contours of time and place. It makes use of what is ready to hand. It insists on no single fixed vocabulary of its own, but unfolds the inexhaustible glory of the triune Name through the general forms of speech and possibilities of speech present in the discourse of all peoples, tribes, and nations.

While these considerations are substantial, I do not think they show that the pneumatological pattern is *the* most appropriate way of naming the persons of the Trinity. Rather, they suggest that it is *a* most appropriate way, by virtue of its special affinity with the Holy Spirit and the mystery of divine blessing and glory that radiates from the triune life.

Conclusion

The Most Appropriate Name of the Trinity

You, O Lord, are our Father;
our Redeemer from of old is your name.
—*Isaiah 63:16*

We believe in one God, the Father, the Almighty.
We believe in one Lord, Jesus Christ,
the only Son of God, eternally begotten of the Father,
Light from Light, true God from true God.
We believe in the Holy Spirit,
the Lord,
the giver of life,
who proceeds from the Father,
and who with the Father and Son is worshiped and glorified.
—*from the Nicene-Constantinopolitan Creed (381)*

What is the most appropriate way of naming the persons of the Trinity? Our journeys through Christian tradition and the Scriptures have taken different routes, but they have all led to the same conclusion: there are three such ways, each of which is most appropriate by virtue of its special affinity with one person of the Trinity in particular.

• One way of naming the persons of the Trinity is most appropriate by virtue of its affinity with the person of the Holy Spirit. To be sure, the Holy Spirit participates fully in every work of the Trinity in the economy of salvation, including the work whereby the Trinity is revealed in the sending of Christ and the outpouring of the Spirit. Still, as we have seen, it is characteristic of the Holy Spirit to participate in this work in a distinctive way, by bestowing the countless blessings of the divine life, and by awakening creation to receive those blessings and to bless God in return. The Holy Spirit comes always from the living God and bears the gift of new life, yet it does so in an endless variety of ways, now as a dove descending, now as the sound of wind roaring, now as tongues of fire dancing, now as the gift of speech in ecstasy. So too the name of the Trinity in a pneumatological key unites constancy and variety in the naming of the persons of the Trinity. It insists upon no fixed vocabulary of its own, but unfolds the inexhaustible glory of the triune life through the possibilities of speech present among all peoples, tribes, and nations, multiplying and varying the name of the Trinity without end.

- Another way of naming the persons of the Trinity is most appropriate by virtue of its affinity with the second person, revealed in the economy of salvation as the human being Jesus Christ. While the second person participates fully in every way the Trinity makes itself known, it is characteristic of the second person to do so in a way that enacts the mystery of divine presence at the heart of the divine life. Just as the incarnate Christ brings the mystery of divine presence into the world in the form of a single, finite, human life, so too the name of the Trinity in a christological key assumes a slender, limited linguistic shape, characterized by the kinship vocabulary of Father, Son, and Spirit. The name of the Trinity in a christological key brings the church's fragmentary knowledge of the mystery to brilliant, focused expression, like Jesus' shining raiment on the Mount of Transfiguration.
- Still another way of naming the persons of the Trinity is most appropriate by virtue of its affinity with the first person of the Trinity, revealed in the economy of salvation as the one to whom Jesus prays in the power of the Spirit. The first person, too, participates in every work of the Trinity creationward, just as the second and third persons do. Yet the first person also speaks in a special way, with a distinctive modulation of voice, keyed to the unfathomable, ineffable mystery of divine uniqueness at the source of the triune life. While the uniqueness of the first person can be represented by a variety of linguistic tokens (Father, Font of Divinity, etc.), there is only one of these whose role consists solely in *pointing*, in gesturing away from itself to the transcendent, unfathomable mystery of its bearer. That linguistic token is the first person's personal proper name, the Tetragrammaton. The theological pattern of naming consists in the hallowing of *this* name, a hallowing that takes place through its giving, receiving, and glorification. Moreover, it is of the essence of this pattern to indicate the divine name *obliquely*, in conformity with Jesus' own practice, thus pointing away from every speaker but the one who alone is competent to declare this name. The theological pattern glows like a dancing fire hidden by the billowing clouds of its ever-changing coverings.

Each of these ways of naming illuminates the mystery of the Holy Trinity as revealed in the economy of salvation centered in Jesus, but each does so in a distinctive way. Each pattern tells the truth, the whole truth, and nothing but the truth, but each does so from a different vantage point. Each is *a* most appropriate way of naming the Trinity, but most appropriate in a different respect. But if each is *a* most appropriate way of naming, is there really nothing that counts as *the* most appropriate way? Yes, there is. *The* most appropriate way of naming the persons of the Trinity consists precisely in the three patterns together, as mutually illuminating, nonidentical repetitions of each other. Because each pattern is most appropriate in a different way, it is the three together, in their reciprocal supplementation, overlaps, and differences, that most fully illuminate the mystery of the Trinity revealed in the man named "Jesus," who is the Lord, the Son of God, the Bright and Morning Star.

Notes

Epigraph

1. Clement of Alexandria, *Exhortation to the Greeks* 1, in *The Ante-Nicene Fathers*, ed. Alexander Roberts and James Donaldson (1867–73; repr., Edinburgh: T&T Clark, 1986–90), 2:171.

Introduction

1. Gregory the Great, *Moralia* 5.26.29.
2. William Shakespeare, *Romeo and Juliet*, Act 2, scene 2, 43–44. What Juliet actually said was "A rose by any other *word* would smell as sweet," but the paraphrase has long since eclipsed the original, as though to illustrate her point.
3. Goethe, *Faust*, Part 1, Great Books 47, ed. R. M. Hutchins (Chicago: Britannica, 1952), 84.
4. Cited in Oskar Grether, *Name und Wort Gottes im Alten Testament* (Giessen: Verlag von Alfred Töpelmann, 1934), 164.
5. Origen, *Contra Celsum* 1:24, trans. Henry Chadwick (Cambridge: Cambridge University Press, 1965), 23.
6. Ibid., 1:25, 25. The phrase "a deep and mysterious subject" is from the older English translation (ET) of *Contra Celsum*, by Frederick Crombie, in *The Ante-Nicene Fathers*, ed. Alexander Roberts and James Donaldson (1867–73; repr., Edinburgh: T&T Clark, 1986–90), 4:406.
7. J. R. Waton, *An Annotated Anthology of Hymns* (Oxford: Oxford University Press, 2003), 61.
8. Charles Wesley, *Hymns on the Trinity*, preface by S T Kimbrough Jr., introduction by Wilma J. Quantrille (Madison, NJ: The Charles Wesley Society, 1998), 102.

Chapter 1: Who Shall I Say Sent Me?

1. Gerald O'Collins, SJ, "The Holy Trinity: The State of the Questions" in *The Trinity: An Interdisciplinary Symposium on the Trinity*, ed. Stephen T. Davis and Daniel Kendall, S.J. (Oxford: Oxford University Press, 1999), 13.

2. For documentation, see Franklin Sherman, *Bridges: Documents of the Christian-Jewish Dialogue*, Vol. 1 *The Road to Reconciliation* (1945–1985) (New York: Paulist Press, forthcoming), and the forthcoming companion volume which will cover 1985 to the present.
3. Deborah Sontag and Alessandra Stanley, "Ending Pilgrimage, the Pope Asks God for Brotherhood," *The New York Times*, March 27, 2000.
4. Yehezekel Landau and Michael B. McGarry, *John Paul II in the Holy Land—in His Own Words: With Christian and Jewish Perspectives*, ed. Lawrence Boadt and Kevin di Camillo (Mahwah, NJ: Paulist Press, 2005), 121.
5. This impression is supported by John Paul II's remarks on other occasions during the same visit; see ibid., 64, 73.
6. To assist the reader in distinguishing God's reply in Exodus 3:14 from the reply of Exodus 3:15, I consistently render the former names using standard typeface (i.e., as "I am who I am" and "I am"), while retaining the traditional practice of using capital letters for the latter name (the Tetragrammaton, commonly represented in English by the surrogate LORD). Since ancient times Christians and Jews have accorded special orthographic treatment to the Tetragrammaton and its surrogates, as the following chapter shows. In contrast, the King James Version (1611) appears to have been the first translation to accord similar treatment to "I am who I am" and "I am" by rendering the words in all capital type, a practice subsequently followed by most other English translations, including the NRSV. While the precedent of the KJV is now hallowed by age, at least in the English speaking world, it easily contributes to the widespread but false impression that the names of Exodus 3:14 and 3:15 are identical and interchangeable. I therefore revert to the older and more universal Christian practice of leaving God's replies in Exod 3:14 unmarked by special orthography.
7. Among these authors' numerous publications, see especially Larry W. Hurtado, *Lord Jesus Christ: Devotion to Jesus in Earliest Christianity* (Grand Rapids: Wm. B. Eerdmans Publishing Co., 2003); Richard Bauckham, *Jesus and the God of Israel* (Grand Rapids: Wm. B. Eerdmans Publishing Co., 2008). Other authors who have enriched our understanding of this dimension of the New Testament include Gilles Quispel, Jean Daniélou, Richard Longenecker, Alan Segal, Christopher Rowland, Jarl E. Fossum, Charles A. Gieschen, Martin Hengel, Sean McDonough, C. Kavin Rowe, Dale C. Allison Jr., Christopher Seitz, Scot McKnight, Markus Bockmuehl, Carl Judson Davis, among others.
8. See Julius Boehmer, *Die Neutestamentliche Gotteschen und die ersten drei Bitten des Vaterunsers* (Halle: Richard Mühlmann Verlagsbuchhandlung, 1917), which includes an analysis and inventory (some eighty pages long) of every instance of speech shaped by name avoidance in the New Testament.
9. For the definition of supersessionism as a term of theological analysis, see the entries "Supersessionism" and "Replacement Theology" in *A Dictionary of Jewish-Christian Relations*, ed. Edward Kessler and Neil Wenborn (Cambridge: Cambridge University Press, 2005). For an overview of the emergence of the term in recent scholarship, see Terry Donaldson, "Supersessionism and Christian Self-Definition," in *Ambiguities, Complexities, and Half-Forgotten Adversaries: Crossing Boundaries in Ancient Judaism and Early Christianity*, ed. Kimberly Stratton and Andrea Lieber (Leiden: Brill, 2011).
10. Otto Weber, *Foundations of Dogmatics*, trans. Darrell L. Guder (Grand Rapids: Wm. B. Eerdmans Publishing Co., 1981–83), 1:418.

11. See Abhishiktananda, *Saccidananda: A Christian Approach to Advaitic Experience*, 2nd ed. (Delhi: ISPCK, 1984); Paul S. Chung, *Constructing Irregular Theology: Bamboo and Minjung in East Asian Perspective*, Studies in Systematic Theology 1 (Leiden: E. J. Brill, 2009), 85–91.
12. The in-text page numbers refer to Chung Hyun Kyung, "Come, Holy Spirit—Renew the Whole Creation," in *The Ecumenical Movement: An Anthology of Key Texts and Voices*, ed. Michael Kinnamon and Brian E. Cope (Geneva: WCC Publications, 1997), 231–38.
13. Responses to Chung Hyun Kyung are in ibid., 238.
14. Tertullian, *Treatise against Praxeas*, translation and commentary by Ernest Evans (London: SPCK, 1948), 139; cf. Tertullian, *Adversus Praxean* 2.34–35, in Corpus Christianorum: Series latina (Turnhout, Belgium: Typographi Brepols Editores Pontificii, 1954), 2:1161.
15. Basil the Great, of Caesarea, *On the Human Condition*, trans. Verna E. F. Harrison (Crestwood, NY: St. Vladimir's Seminary Press, 2005), 21.
16. Dale C. Allison Jr., *The Sermon on the Mount* (New York: Crossroad Publishing Co., 1999), 120–21.
17. On the broad scope of the term "name" in antiquity, see Richard J. Ketchum, "Names, Forms and Conventionalism: *Cratylus* 383–396," *Phronesis* 24 (1979): 133.
18. Lamin Sanneh, *Translating the Message* (Maryknoll, NY: Orbis Books, 1989), 3.
19. Elizabeth Cady Stanton, Susan B. Anthony, and Matilda Josyln Gage, eds., *History of Woman Suffrage*, 6 vols. (New York: Fowler & Wells, 1881; repr., New York: Arno Press, 1969), 1:796.
20. Mary McClintock Fulkerson, "Grace, Christian Controversy, and Tolerable Falsehoods," in *Grace upon Grace: Essays in Honor of Thomas A. Langford*, ed. Robert K. Johnston, L. Gregory Jones, and Jonathan R. Wilson (Nashville: Abingdon Press, 1999), 234.

Chapter 2: The Name of the Trinity in Early Christian Creeds

1. Jaroslav Pelikan, *Credo: Historical and Theological Guide to Creeds and Confessions of Faith in the Christian Tradition* (New Haven, CT: Yale University Press, 2003), 374.
2. My account of the *nomina sacra* draws especially on Larry W. Hurtado, *The Earliest Christian Artifacts: Manuscripts and Christian Origins* (Grand Rapids: Wm. B. Eerdmans Publishing Co., 2006); idem, "The Origin of the *Nomina Sacra*: A Proposal," *Journal of Biblical Literature* 117, no. 4 (1998): 655–73; Colin H. Roberts, "Nomina Sacra: Origins and Significance," in *Manuscript, Society, and Belief in Early Christian Egypt* (London: Oxford University Press, 1979); Schuyler Brown, "Concerning the Origin of the Nomina Sacra," *Studia papyrologica* 9, no. 1 (1970): 7–19.
3. For an overview of the manuscript evidence discussed in this section, see Hurtado, *Earliest Christian Artifacts*, 102–5. More comprehensive studies include Emanuel Tov, *Scribal Practices and Approaches Reflected in the Texts Found in the Judean Desert*, Studies on the Texts of the Desert of Judah 54 (Leiden: E. J. Brill, 2004); idem, "Scribal Features of Early Witnesses of Greek Scripture," in *The Old Greek Psalter: Studies in Honor of Albert Pietersma*, ed. Robert J. V. Hiebert, Claude E. Cox, and Peter J. Gentry, JSOTSup 332 (Sheffield: Sheffield Academic Press, 2001), 125–48.

4. C. H. Dodd, *The Bible and the Greeks* (London: Hodder & Stoughton, 1935), 4.
5. C. H. Roberts, "Nomina Sacra," 46.
6. Hurtado, "Origin of the *Nomina Sacra*," 672.
7. In what follows, I use the anachronistic and misleading monikers "Jewish" and "Christian" for purposes of simplicity and clarity. In reality, many early "Christian" scribes were likely to have been Jews who understood themselves and their Jesus-centered faith as a continuation of the same tradition represented by their non-Christian "Jewish" counterparts.
8. However expected by the habituated ear, the definite article (the) in the phrase "of the Lord" should be eliminated to give an accurate translation. In biblical usage where *kyrios* is used in place of the Tetragrammaton, it commonly appears in Greek without an article, which diverges from the conventions of extrabiblical speech and signals its function as a surrogate for a proper name. See Carl Judson Davis, *The Name and Way of the Lord: Old Testament Themes, New Testament Christology* (Sheffield: Sheffield Academic Press, 1996), 93.
9. Brown, "Concerning the Origin of the Nomina Sacra," 19.
10. George Howard, "Tetragrammaton in the New Testament," in *Anchor Bible Dictionary*, ed. David Noel Freedman (New York: Doubleday, 1992), 6:392–93.
11. George Howard, "The Tetragram and the New Testament," *Journal of Biblical Literature* 96, no. 1 (1977): 63.
12. Hurtado, "Origin of the *Nomina Sacra*," 663. Similarly Roberts, "Nomina Sacra," 48; J. Harold Greenlee, *Introduction to New Testament Textual Criticism* (Grand Rapids: Wm. B. Eerdmans Publishing Co., 1964), 30; Richard C. Nevius, *The Divine Names in St. Mark* (Salt Lake City: University of Utah Press, 1964), 6.
13. Brown, "Concerning the Origin of the Nomina Sacra," 15.
14. Some surviving fragments of Origen's Hexapla support the view that knowledgeable Christians would have understood the symbol $\overline{\mathrm{K}\Sigma}$ as an oblique reference to the Tetragrammaton. In the column for the LXX, we find the Tetragrammaton written in Hebrew, "significantly accompanied in a few passages by the *nomen sacrum* $\overline{\mathrm{K}\Sigma}$." The use of both scribal techniques for the same word indicates that whoever composed the manuscript was well aware that the two conventions were equivalent. Martin Hengel, *The Septuagint as Christian Scripture: Its Prehistory and the Problem of Its Canon*, trans. Mark E. Biddle (Edinburgh: T&T Clark, 2002), 14.
15. Ferdinand Hahn, "The Confession of the One God in the New Testament," in *Horizons in Biblical Theology: An International Dialogue*, no. 2 (1980): 72.
16. On 1 Cor. 8:6 and the Shema, see Erik Waaler, *The* Shema *and the First Commandment in First Corinthians*, WUNT, ser. 2 (Tübingen: Mohr Siebeck, 2008); also N. T. Wright, *The Climax of the Covenant* (Minneapolis: Fortress Press, 1992), 127–36; Richard B. Hays, *First Corinthians*, Interpretation: A Bible Commentary for Teaching and Preaching, ed. J. L. Mays, P. D. Miller, and P. J. Achtemeier (Louisville, KY: John Knox Press, 1997), 140.
17. I have modified the text slightly by supplying the omitted $\overline{\Theta\Sigma}$, which appears to have been left out by scribal error. In this I follow the emendation supplied by the editors of Codex Sinaiticus Project, who have produced an electronic version of Codex Sinaiticus, http://www.codexsinaiticus.org/en/. "Father" does not appear as a *nomen sacrum*, nor do "gods" or "lords" in the previous verse (1 Cor. 8:5). Larry Hurtado discusses 1 Cor. 8:6 as it appears in a different manuscript, Chester Beatty Pauline Codex P^{46}; Hurtado, *Earliest Christian*

Artifacts, 129–30. He notes that when *kyrios* is not used to refer to God or Christ, e.g., to master of a slave, "in these cases was not typically written as a *nomen sacrum*" (129–30). One can gain an overview of how other manuscripts handle the *nomina sacra* in this passage by consulting Reuben J. Swanson, *1 Corinthians: Variant Readings Arranged in Horizontal Lines against Codex Vaticanus*, New Testament Greek Manuscripts (Carol Stream, IL: Tyndale House Publishers, 2003).

18. For the following, see Hurtado, "Origin of the *Nomina Sacra*," 655.
19. George Herbert, second sonnet "The Holy Scriptures," in *The Works of George Herbert*, introduced by Tim Cook (Ware, Hertfordshire: Wordsworth Editions, 1994), 49.
20. On the Nicene Creed in historical context, see J. N. D. Kelly, *Early Christian Creeds*, 3rd ed. (Essex, UK: Longman, 1972); R. P. C. Hanson, *The Search for the Christian Doctrine of God: The Arian Controversy*, 318–81 (Edinburgh: T&T Clark, 1988); Lewis Ayres, *Nicaea and Its Legacy: An Approach to Fourth-Century Trinitarian Theology* (Oxford: Oxford University Press, 2004); Franz Dünzl, *A Brief History of the Doctrine of the Trinity in the Early Church*, trans. John Bowden (London: T&T Clark, 2007); Jaroslav Pelikan and Valerie Hotchkiss, *Creeds and Confessions of Faith in the Christian Tradition*, vol. 1 (New Haven, CT: Yale University Press, 2003). On the creed's relation to its literary antecedents, Dünzl writes, "[It] is now assumed that the Nicene Creed . . . was constructed on the 'building block' principle. In other words, the council fathers, or perhaps better a council commission which was to work out the creed, chose those theological 'building blocks' from earlier creeds which were undisputed and reformulated those at issue in the Arian dispute, namely, the statements about the pre-existence of the saviour." See Dünzl, *Brief History*, 55.
21. The confession of "one God" and "one Lord Jesus Christ" also formed the opening members of the creed of Caesarea, Palestine, presented by Eusebius to the council as evidence of his own orthodoxy. While Kelly, Dünzl, and others doubt Eusebius's claim that the Nicene Creed was modeled on that of his own home church, the correspondence between the creeds on this particular point is complete. Kelly himself judged that "the Palestinian traits in [the Nicene Creed] are unmistakable" (Kelly, *Early Christian Creeds*, 227), and conjectured that it was based—if not on Eusebius's creed—then still on "some local baptismal creed, of Syro-Palestinian provenance, into which the Nicene keywords were somewhat awkwardly interpolated" (Ibid., 229; cf. 182–230).
22. See ibid., 236–37.
23. Johannes Baptist Bauer, *Sacramentum Verbi: An Encyclopedia of Biblical Theology* (New York: Herder & Herder, 1970), 3:874.
24. Hanson points out that 1 Cor. 8:6 was "a favourite text [of the Arians] for proving that the Holy Spirit was not divine and was a creature," since Paul does not mention the Holy Spirit in that passage (Hanson, *The Search for the Christian Doctrine of God*, 840). To counter this argument, the bishops, in describing the Spirit, naturally turned precisely to the name that Paul uses to designate Christ's deity: "the Lord." Hanson is admittedly speaking of post-Nicene developments, but the trope itself may be older.

Chapter 3: The Name of the Trinity in Fourth-Century Theology

1. See J. N. D. Kelly, *Early Christian Creeds*, 3rd ed. (Essex, UK: Longman, 1972), 181–204.

2. Charles Gieschen, "The Divine Name in Ante-Nicene Christology," *Vigiliae christianae* 57, no. 2 (2003): 156. Gieschen's article is an excellent summary of evidence demonstrating the importance of the Tetragrammaton in early Christianity.
3. Eusebius of Caesarea, *Life of Constantine*, trans. Averil Cameron and Stuart G. Hall (Oxford: Clarendon Press, 1999), 128–29.
4. Jerome, "Ad Marcellam," Letter 25, in *Sancti Eusebii Hieronymi Epistulae*, ed. Isidorus Hillberg, in Corpus scriptorum ecclesiasticorum latinorum [CSEL] (Vindobonae: Verlag der Österreichischen Akademie der Wissenschaften, 1996), 54:219; Clement of Alexandria refers briefly and somewhat enigmatically to the Tetragrammaton: *Stromata* 5.6, 34 in Sources chrétiennes [SC] 278, ed. Alain Le Boulluec, trans. Pierre Voulet (Paris: Les Éditions du Cerf, 1981), 80–81; Origen discusses the Tetragrammaton in remarks about Ps. 2:2, in his *Selecta in Psalmos*, in Patrologiae cursus completus: Series graeca, ed. J. P. Migne (Paris: Imprimerie Catholique, 1857), 12:1104; cf. also in Origen's *Num. hom.* 14.1 (Die griechischen christlichen Schriftsteller der ersten [drei] Jahrhunderte [GCS] 7:121); ET in Origen, *Homilies on Numbers*, ed. Christopher A. Hall (Downers Grove, IL: InterVarsity Press, 2009), 80; for Eusebius, see G. W. H. Lampe, ed., *A Patristic Greek Lexicon* (Oxford: Clarendon Press, 1961), s.v. *anekphōnēton*. For further information on Jerome, see Ernst Würthwein, *The Text of the Old Testament: An Introduction to the Biblia Hebraica*, 2nd, rev. ed., trans. Erroll F. Rhodes (Grand Rapids: Wm. B. Eerdmans Publishing Co., 1995), 190. Irenaeus may refer to the Tetragrammaton on one occasion (*Against Heresies* 3.35.3), although it is unclear whether his remarks reflect a garbled understanding of the name or a lost interpretation of it; see A. Marmorstein, "Zur Erklärung der Gottesnamen bei Irenäus," *Zeitschrift für die neutestmentliche Wissenschaft und die Kunde der älteren Kirche* 25 (1926): 253–58.
5. My account of negative theology in pagan and Christian antiquity draws especially on Deirdre Carabine, *The Unknown God: Negative Theology in the Platonic Tradition; Plato to Eriugena*, Louvain Theological and Pastoral Monographs (Louvain: Peeters Press, 1995); Jaroslav Pelikan, *Christianity and Classical Culture: The Metamorphosis of Natural Theology in the Christian Encounter with Hellenism; Gifford Lectures, 1992–93* [hereafter *CCC*] (New Haven, CT: Yale University Press, 1993); Polymnia Athanassiadi and Michael Frede, *Pagan Monotheism in Late Antiquity* (Oxford: Oxford University Press, 1999); John Whittaker, *Studies in Platonism and Patristic Thought* (London: Variorum Reprints, 1984); Joseph C. McLelland, *God the Anonymous: A Study in Alexandrian Philosophical Theology*, Patristic Monograph Series (Cambridge, MA: The Philadelphia Patristic Foundation, 1976).
6. On Philo's knowledge of the Tetragrammaton, see James R. Royse, "Philo, Kyrios and the Tetragrammaton," in *The Studia Philonica Annual: Studies in Hellenistic Judaism*, ed. David T. Runia, vol. 2 (Atlanta: Scholars Press, 1991), 167–83.
7. Pelikan, *CCC*, 200. The Cappadocians did not lack a theory of personal proper names, but rather the notion that the Deity attested by Scripture had a proper name. See David G. Robertson, "A Patristic Theory of Proper Names," *Archiv für Geschichte der Philosophie* 84, no. 1 (2002): 1–17. On the theory of language that undergirded Gregory of Nyssa's conviction of divine namelessness, see Anthony Meredith, "The Language of God and Human Language," in *Gregory of Nyssa: Contra Eunomium II*, ed. Lenka Karfíková, Scot Douglass,

and Johannes Zachhuber, Supplements to Vigiliae christianae 82 (Leiden: E. J. Brill, 2007), 247–56.

8. Gregory of Nyssa, "An Answer to Ablabius: That We Should Not Think of Saying That There Are Three Gods," trans. Cyril C. Richardson, in *Christology of the Later Fathers*, ed. Edward R. Hardy, Library of Christian Classics 3 (Philadelphia: Westminster Press, 1954), 259; "Ad Ablabium: Quod non sint tres dei," in *Gregorii Nysseni opera dogmatica minora*, ed. F. Mueller, *Gregorii Nysseni opera* [hereafter *GNO*], vol. 3/1, ed. W. Jaeger (Leiden: E. J. Brill, 1958), 42–43.
9. Pelikan, *CCC*, 210–11; cf. 207–14.
10. Gregory of Nyssa, *Contra Eunomium* 3.6.8; *GNO* 2:188; ET, Pelikan, *CCC*, 214.
11. Gregory of Nazianzus, *Orations* 30.18; SC 250:264; ET, Frederick W. Norris, *Faith Gives Fullness to Reasoning: The Five Theological Orations of Gregory of Nazianzen* (Leiden: E. J. Brill, 1991), 274–5. The Cappadocians were not exceptional in this respect: as David Runia points out, the church fathers cite Exod. 3:14 on numerous occasions, but 3:15 receives almost no attention; cf. David T. Runia, *Philo in Early Christian Literature* (Minneapolis: Fortress Press, 1993), 329.
12. Gregory of Nyssa, *Contra Eunom.* 3.5.59; *GNO* 2:182.
13. Gregory of Nyssa, *Contra Eunom.* 3.9.31; *GNO* 2:279; ET, Pelikan, *CCC*, 213.
14. Gregory of Nyssa, *Contra Eunom.* 3.9.41; *GNO* 2:279; ET, Pelikan, *CCC*, 212.
15. Gregory of Nazianzus, *Or.* 30.17; cited in F. W. Norris, "The Tetragrammaton in Gregory Nazianzen *Or.* 30.17," *Vigiliae christianae* 43, no. 4 (December 1989): 339. Basil the Great makes a similar remark in *On the Holy Spirit* 44, in SC 17.2 (Paris: Cerf, 2002).
16. A. J. Mason, *The Five Theological Orations of Gregory Nazianzus*, Cambridge Patristic Texts (Cambridge: Cambridge University Press, 1899), 135; cited in Norris, "The Tetragrammaton," 339.
17. For more on Gregory's misapprehension, see Norris, *Faith Gives Fullness to Reasoning*, 177.
18. Pelikan, *CCC*, 29.
19. Cf. Gregory of Nyssa, "Ad Ablabium," in *GNO* 3/1:55.
20. Tertullian, *Treatise against Praxeas*, translation and commentary by Ernest Evans (London: SPCK, 1948), 139.
21. Clement of Alexandria, *Exhortation to the Heathen* 11, in *The Ante-Nicene Fathers*, ed. Alexander Roberts, James Donaldson, and A. Cleveland Coxe (repr., Grand Rapids: Wm. B. Eerdmans Publishing Co., 1971), 2:203.
22. Maximus of Tyre, *Philosophical Orations* 8.10; cited in Naomi Janowitz, *Icons of Power: Ritual Practices in Late Antiquity* (University Park: Pennsylvania State University Press, 2002), 38, along with several other classical and early Christian writers to similar effect.
23. Athanassiadi and Frede, *Pagan Monotheism*, 8; cf. 17, 81, 91. See also Günther Bader, "Gott nennen: Von Götternamen zu göttlichen Namen; Zur Vorgeschichte der Lehre von den göttlichen Eigenschaften," *Zeitschrift für Theologie und Kirche* 86 (1989): 306–54, esp. 340–54.
24. The Cappadocians did not only inherit presuppositions of non-Christian philosophy; they also actively transformed them to better express Christian truth; cf. Pelikan, *CCC*, 210–14; Andrew Radde-Gallwitz, *Basil of Caesarea, Gregory of Nyssa, and the Transformation of Divine Simplicity* (Oxford: Oxford University Press, 2009).

25. Athanassiadi and Frede, *Pagan Monotheism*, 8.
26. Origen, *Contra Celsum* 1.24–25, in *Contra Celsum*, trans. Henry Chadwick (Cambridge: Cambridge University Press, 1965).
27. Cited in Athanassiadi and Frede, *Pagan Monotheism*, 10–11.
28. Gregory of Nyssa, *Refutatio confessionis Eunomii*; *GNO*, 2:312–410; ET, *Against Eunomius*, trans. H. C. Ogle and H. A. Wilson, in *Nicene and Post-Nicene Fathers*, ser. 2 [*NPNF*[2]], ed. Philip Schaff and Henry Wace (Grand Rapids: Wm. B. Eerdmans Publishing Co., 1971), 5:101–34.
29. Gregory of Nyssa, *Refutatio* 17; *GNO* 2:312–13; *NPNF*[2] 5:101.
30. Gregory of Nyssa, *Refutatio* 17; *GNO* 2:314–5; *NPNF*[2] 5:102.
31. Gregory of Nyssa, *Refutatio* 17; *GNO* 2:314; *NPNF*[2] 5:102.
32. Gregory of Nyssa, *Refutatio* 17; *GNO* 2:317; *NPNF*[2] 5:103. I have altered the translation by substituting *hypostasis* and *hypostases* for "subsistence" and "subsistences."
33. See Gregory of Nyssa, *Contra Eunom.* 3.1, in *GNO* 2:48; *NPNF*[2] 5:150.
34. Ibid 3.9., in *GNO* 2:285; *NPNF*[2] 5:238. On the primacy of the names "Father," "Son," and "Holy Spirit" in Cappadocian theology, see James Le Grys, "Names for the Ineffable God: St. Gregory of Nyssa's Explanation," *The Thomist* 62 (1998): 333–54.
35. Gregory of Nyssa, *Refutatio* 17; *GNO* 2:318; *NPNF*[2] 5:102–3.
36. Ibid., in *GNO* 2:318; *NPNF*[2] 5:103.
37. Ibid., in *GNO* 2:331–32; *NPNF*[2] 5:108.
38. Ibid., in *GNO* 2:332–33; *NPNF*[2] 5:108.
39. Gregory of Nyssa, *Contra Eunom.* 3.9, in *GNO* 2:279; *NPNF*[2] 5:235.

Chapter 4: The Dionysian Tradition and the Transformation of Gentile Wisdom

1. Augustine of Hippo, *Confessions* 7.9–10.
2. Pseudo-Dionysius the Areopagite, *Divine Names* 2.3; the text is from *Pseudo-Dionysius: The Complete Works*, trans. Colm Luibheid; foreword, notes, and translation by Paul Rorem; preface by René Roques; introductions by Jaroslav Pelikan, Jean Leclercq, and Karlfried Froelich (New York: Paulist Press, 1987), 60. In this chapter, page numbers and citations of Dionysius's work are keyed to this volume. My brief discussion of Dionysius has been especially helped by Sarah Klitenic Wear and John M. Dillon, *Dionysius the Areopagite and the Neoplatonist Tradition: Despoiling the Hellenes* (Burlington, VT: Ashgate Publishing, 2007); John N. Jones, "The Status of the Trinity in Dionysian Thought," *Journal of Religion* 80, no. 4 (October 2000): 645–57; idem, "Sculpting God: The Logic of Dionysian Negative Theology," *Harvard Theological Review* 89, no. 4 (October 1996): 355–71; John D. Jones, "An Absolutely Simple God? Frameworks for Reading Pseudo-Dionysius Areopagite," *The Thomist*, no. 69 (2005): 371–406; Sarah Coakley and Charles M. Stang, *Re-Thinking Dionysius the Areopagite* (Oxford: Wiley-Blackwell, 2009); and Deirdre Carabine, *The Unknown God: Negative Theology in the Platonic Tradition; Plato to Eriugena*, Louvain Theological and Pastoral Monographs (Louvain: Peeters Press, 1995).
3. That divine names describe the simple being of God rather than composite attributes thereof was an axiom widely shared among Orthodox, Arian, and pagan theologians of the fourth century. It remains important today, for reasons articulated among others by David B. Hart. Dionysius "locates his discus-

sion of speech about God under topic of *names* of God, not under a discussion of the divine attributes. . . . The problem . . . with any practice of identifying the divine attributes univocally, as 'features' of the divine 'substance' in much the same way as they are features of created substances, . . . is that the God thus described is a logical nonsense: a being among beings, possessing the properties of his nature in a composite way, as aspects of his nature rather than as names ultimately convertible with one another in the simplicity of his transcendent essence." David B. Hart, *The Beauty of the Infinite: the Aesthetics of Christian Truth* (Grand Rapids: Wm. B. Eerdmans Publishing Co., 2004), 302.

4. Carabine, *Unknown God*, 282.
5. Ibid., 293.
6. John N. Jones, "Status of the Trinity," 645.
7. Some have argued that the apophatic trajectory of Dionysius's thought puts into question not only its Trinitarianism, but also its theistic character as such. See the provocative book by Thomas A. Carlson, *Indiscretion: Finitude and the Naming of God* (Chicago: University of Chicago Press, 1999), in which the author maintains a relation of "indiscretion" between Dionysian presence and Heideggerian absence, between superplenitude and the void.
8. Augustine of Hippo, *Trin.* 6.12, in *The Trinity*, vol. 1/5 of *The Works of Saint Augustine: A Translation for the Twenty-first Century*, trans. and ed. Edmund Hill, OP; ed. John E. Rotelle, OSA (Hyde Park, NY: New City Press, 1991), 213. My discussion of Augustine is limited to this work. In this chapter, page numbers and citations are keyed to this text. In addition to Hill's excellent introductory essay, I have been helped by Jean-Luc Marion, "Idipsum: The Name of God according to Augustine," in *Orthodox Readings of Augustine*, ed. George E. Demacopoulos and Aristotle Papanikolaou (Crestwood, NY: St. Vladimir's Seminary Press, 2008), 167–89; Roland Kany, *Augustins Trinitätsdenken: Bilanz, Kritik und Weiterführung der modernen Forschung zu "De Trinitate"* (Tübingen: Mohr Siebeck, 2007).
9. Hill, *The Trinity*, 50–51.
10. See Martin Rösel, *Adonaj—Warum Gott "Herr" gennant wird* (Tübingen: Mohr Siebeck, 2000), 6–7; Robert Hanhart, "Der Status confessionis Israels in hellenistischer Zeit," *Zeitschrift für Theologie und Kirche* 92 (1995): 315–28.
11. The exception that proves the rule is "YHWH Sabbaoth," a name of uncertain meaning commonly translated "YHWH of hosts."
12. Thomas Aquinas, *Summa contra Gentiles* 4.7. All references to Thomas's works, including the *Summa contra Gentiles* (hereafter *SCG*), will be incorporated in the text. See ET in Thomas Aquinas, *On the Truth of the Catholic Faith*, ed. and trans. A. C. Pegis (bk. 1), J. F. Anderson (bk. 2), V. J. Bourke (bk. 3), and C. J. O'Neil (bk. 4 in 2 vols.), 5 vols. (Garden City, NY: Hanover House, 1955–57; repr., Notre Dame, IN: University of Notre Dame Press, 1975).
13. The *Summa* is cited by part, question, and article, so that *ST* 1.33.1 ad 1 means pt. 1, question 33, art. 1, reply to objection 1. Unless otherwise noted, all citations of the *Summa* come from the Blackfriars edition, ed. T. Gilby and T. C. O'Brien, 61 vols. (New York: Oxford University Press, 1964).
14. My account of Thomas, his doctrine of the divine names, and the Trinity has been helped by the following works in particular: Gilles Emery, OP, *Trinity in Aquinas* (Ann Arbor, MI: Ave Maria University, 2006); Brian Davies, OP, *The Thought of Thomas Aquinas* (Oxford: Oxford University Press, 1994), 58–79; Matthew Levering, *Scripture and Metaphysics: Aquinas and the Renewal of*

Trinitarian Theology (Oxford: Blackwell, 2004); Gregory Rocca, OP, "Aquinas on God-Talk: Hovering over the Abyss," *Theological Studies* 54 (1993): 641–61; Mark F. Johnson, "Apophatic Knowledge's Cataphatic Dependencies," *The Thomist* 62 (1998): 519–31; Ralph McInerny, *Aquinas on Analogy* (Washington, DC: Catholic University of America Press, 1996); David B. Burrell, CSC, "From Analogy of 'Being' to the Analogy of Being," in *Recovering Nature: Essay in Natural Philosophy, Ethics, and Metaphysics in Honor of Ralph McInerny*, ed. John P. O'Callaghan and Thomas S. Hibbs (Notre Dame, IN: University of Notre Dame Press, 1999): 253–66. Also of great interest: Henk J. M. Schoot, *Christ the "Name" of God: Thomas Aquinas on Naming Christ* (Leuven: Peeters, 1993).

15. See John D. Jones, "An Absolutely Simple God?" 371.
16. See Emery, *Trinity in Aquinas*, 190.
17. Levering, *Scripture and Metaphysics*, 176.
18. Thomas hints that behind the plurality of personal names lie corresponding ways of speaking about the relations among the persons. For example, in his discussion of "Love" as a name of the Holy Spirit, Thomas suggests that "to speak" is a notional term that characterizes the first person's relation to the second with as much propriety as "to beget." "So far as these words ['love' and 'dilection'] are used to express the relation [of the Holy Spirit] to its principle of what proceeds by way of love, and *vice versa*, so that by 'love' is understood 'the love proceeding,' and by 'to love' is understood 'the spiration of the love proceeding,' in that sense 'love' is the name of the person, and 'to love' is a notional term, as are 'to speak' and 'to beget.'" *ST* 1:37.1.
19. The story of Thomas and the Tetragrammaton is wonderfully told by Armand Maurer, CSB, in "St. Thomas on the Sacred Name 'Tetragrammaton,'" in *Mediaeval Studies* 34 (Toronto: Pontifical Institute of Mediaeval Studies, 1972): 275–86; repr. in Armand Maurer's collection of essays *Being and Knowing: Studies in Thomas Aquinas and the Later Medieval Philosophers* (Toronto: Pontifical Institute of Mediaeval Studies, 1990), 59–70. I gratefully acknowledge my account's very heavy debt to his work. Apart from Maurer, the only older discussion known to me is that of Robert A. Herrera, "Saint Thomas and Maimonides on the Tetragrammaton: The 'Exodus' of Philosophy?" *The Modern Schoolman* 59 (March 1982): 179–93, who suggests that Thomas distinguishes between the names of Exod. 3:14 and 3:15 even more sharply than Maimonides (190–91). Recent discussions include Matthew Levering, *Scripture and Metaphysics: Aquinas and the Renewal of Trinitarian Theology* (Oxford: Blackwell, 2004), 57–74; Jean-Pierre Torrell, *Saint Thomas Aquinas: Spiritual Master* (Washington, DC: Catholic University of America, 2003); William W. Young III, *The Politics of Praise: Naming God and Friendship in Aquinas and Derrida* (Burlington, VT: Ashgate, 2007), 81–83. My grateful thanks to Matthew Levering, William Young III, and Matthew Tapie for helpful comments on earlier drafts of this chapter.
20. Here I follow the more literal translation by the Fathers of the English Dominican Province (1920). The Blackfriars translation inaccurately (albeit tellingly) recasts Thomas's remarks in the past tense, thereby blunting Thomas's startling remark.
21. Thomas, *ST* 1a 13.11 ad 1; ET in Maurer, "St. Thomas on the Sacred Name," 281. The original Latin reads, "Et adhuc magis proprium nomen est Tetragrammaton, quod est impositum ad significandam ipsam Dei substantiam incommunicabilem, et, ut sic liceat loqui, singularem."

22. Maurer notes that some information about the Tetragrammaton was available to Thomas from Jerome, who follows Jewish tradition in distinguishing between the Tetragrammaton and "He Who Is" in his "Letter to Marcella," "Ad Marcellam," Letter 25 in *Sancti Eusebii Hieronymi Epistulae*, ed. Isidorus Hillberg, Corpus scriptorum ecclesiasticorum latinorum [CSEL] (Vindobonae: Verlag der Österreichischen Akademie der Wissenschaften, 1996), 54:219. There Jerome says the Tetragrammaton is equivalent to Dominus in the LXX and that it applies properly to God.
23. Maimonides, *Dux seu Director dubitantium aut perplexorum* 1.60–62. The Latin version of this work was made about 1240 from the Hebrew translation of the Arabic original.
24. Étienne Gilson, *Elements of Christian Philosophy* (Garden City, NY: Doubleday, Catholic Textbook Division, 1960), 309n13, where Gilson largely repeats Thomas's own remarks without comment. In his essay "Maimonide et la Philosophie de l'Exode," *Mediaeval Studies* 13 (1951): 223–24, Gilson does not mention the Tetragrammaton at all. The "metaphysics of Exodus" that he describes is a metaphysics of Exod. 3:14, not of 3:14 and 3:15 together, despite the examples of Maimonides and Thomas themselves. This need not mean that the metaphysics of Exodus as understood by Gilson and others is unbiblical, unwarranted, or anything of the sort. It simply means that it is *incomplete*, by the logic of Thomas's own analysis. Since "He Who Is" and the Tetragrammaton *are two different kinds of names*, no amount of attention to the former—no matter how exemplary in itself—can take the place of comparable attention to the latter (YHWH), which after all is the more widely attested biblical name by several orders of magnitude. In this connection, I observe that my understanding of the relationship of the names is mischaracterized by Matthew Levering when he writes, "Soulen assumes that the ontological interpretation [of Exod. 3:14] belongs to the unwarranted philosophical displacement of YHWH" (*Scripture and Metaphysics: Aquinas and the Renewal of Trinitarian Theology* [Oxford: Blackwell, 2004], 57–74, 64–65). In the essay to which Levering refers, I defend the justifiability of interpreting Exod. 3:14 in ontological terms. My criticism of the tradition's handling of 3:14 is not directed against its ontological interpretation per se, but against the assumption that such interpretation provides *an equivalent substitute* for a comparable analysis of the Tetragrammaton and its place in the Old and New Testaments. See R. Kendall Soulen, "YHWH the Triune God," *Modern Theology* 15, no. 1 (January 1999): 25–54.
25. Curiously, Armand Maurer himself does not seem to grasp the full significance of Thomas's remarks. The Tetragrammaton, he declares, "finds small place in Thomas' writings" because it is "of so little use to a theologian who wishes to illumine the content of faith." But surely the fact that Thomas recognizes the name *at all* illumines the content of the faith in a most extraordinary way, if only by demonstrating the limited rather than all-encompassing validity of an approach to naming God that begins with creation.

Chapter 5: The Reformation Tradition and the Transformation of Jewish Wisdom

1. Martin Luther, *Lectures on Galatians* (1519), in *Luther's Works*, ed. Jaroslav Pelikan (St. Louis: Concordia Publishing House, 1964), 27:221.
2. My brief discussion of Kabbalah as a Jewish tradition draws especially on the excellent study Stephen G. Wald, *The Doctrine of the Divine Name: An*

Introduction to Classical Kabbalistic Theology, Brown Judaic Studies (Atlanta: Scholars Press, 1988). I have also relied on Gershom Scholem, *Kabbalah* (New York: New American Library, Meridian, 1978); Moshe [Mosheh] Hallamish, *An Introduction to the Kabbalah*, trans. R. Bar-Ilan and O. Wiskind-Elper (Albany: State University of New York Press, 1999); and Joseph Dan, *Kabbalah: A Very Short Introduction* (Oxford: Oxford University Press, 2006). My discussion of the Christian Kabbalah has been guided most especially by Joseph Dan, ed., *The Christian Kabbalah: Jewish Mystical Books and Their Christian Interpreters* (Cambridge, MA: Harvard College Library, 1997); Gershom Scholem, "The Beginnings of the Christian Kabbalah," in Dan, *Christian Kabbalah*, 17–51. In a still-valuable article of 1908, George F. Moore traces the "pre-history" of the Christian Kabbalah back to the early eleventh century. See George F. Moore, "Notes on the Name YHWH," *American Journal of Theology* 12, no. 1 (1908): 34–52.

3. Pico della Mirandola, "Oration on the Dignity of Man," in *The Renaissance Philosophy of Man*, ed. Ernst Cassirer, Paul Oskar Kristeller, and John Herman Randall (Chicago: University of Chicago Press, 1956), 252.
4. Dan, *Kabbalah: Introduction*, 66.
5. *De verbo mirifico* is available in a modern German and Latin edition in *Johannes Reuchlin: Sämtliche Werke*, ed. Widu-Wolfgang Ehlers, Hans-Gert Roloff, and Peter Schäfer, vol. 1, *De verbo mirifico* (1494; repr., Stuttgart: Frommann-Holzboog, 1996). Also notice the original of Reuchlin's *De verbo mirifico* (1494; facsimile repr., Stuttgart-Bad Cannstatt, 1964); and *De arte cabalistica* (1517; facsimile repr., Stuttgart-Bad Cannstatt, 1964). I have been helped by Charles Zika's discussion, "Reuchlin's *De verbo mirifico* and the Magic Debate of the Late Fifteenth Century," in *Exorcising Our Demons: Magic, Witchcraft and Visual Culture in Early Modern Europe* (Leiden: E. J. Brill, 2003), 21–68; and Christopher S. Celenza, "The Search for Ancient Wisdom in Early Modern Europe: Reuchlin and the Late Ancient Esoteric Paradigm," *Journal of Religious History* 25, no. 2 (June 2001): 115–33. For Luther's relation to the Christian kabbalists and to Reuchlin in particular, see Siegfried Raeder, *Grammatica theologica: Studien zu Luthers Operationes in Psalmos*, Beiträge zur historischen Theologie (Tübingen: J. C. B. Mohr [Paul Siebeck], 1977), 59–80.
6. Reuchlin, *De verbo mirifico*, sig. d 6^{v}; cited in Zika, "Reuchlin's *De verbo mirifico*," 52.
7. The idea rests on an artificial consonantal rendering of the name "Jesus" which some found dubious even in Reuchlin's time and is generally rejected by linguists today.
8. Reuchlin, *De verbo mirifico*, sig. g 2^{r}; cited in Zika, "Reuchlin's *De verbo mirifico*," 59; cf. 57–62. As Zika notes, Reuchlin's conviction that "Jesus" is the Tetragrammaton in its supplemented, transformed, and pronounceable form leads him to rail "against those modern [sic] grammarians who have mutilated this name into IHS" (ibid., 59). Reuchlin, it seems, is unaware of the latter symbol's character as a (sacred) abbreviation rooted in ancient Christian scribal practice, and instead interprets it as a (failed) modern effort to expose the name's etymological root, against which he pits his own quasi-etymological interpretation.
9. Johannes Reuchlin, *On the Art of the Kabbalah: De arte kabalistica*, trans. Martin and Sarah Goodman, with facsimile reprint of the 1517 edition on opposing pages (New York: Abaris Books, 1983), 339 (in bk. 3); cf. the Latin facsimile, 336.

10. The ambiguity of Reuchlin's interpretation is reflected in two divergent assessments of the Christian Kabbalah by Gershem Scholem and Joseph Dan respectively. Scholem has defined Christian Kabbalism as "the interpretation of Kabbalistic texts in the service of Christianity (or to be more precise, Catholicism); or the use of Kabbalistic concepts and methodology in support of Christian dogma" (Scholem, "Beginnings of the Christian Kabbalah," 17). Joseph Dan acknowledges the truth of Scholem's definition, but maintains that Christian Kabbalah was also "very nearly unique" in the history of Jewish-Christian relations in its maintenance of the belief that "Christianity itself has to be revitalized by a renewed understanding of its ancient origins that has become possible by the revelation of new sources [i.e., the Kabbalah]" (Dan, *Christian Kabbalah*, 56). Centuries before the Christian Kabbalah, the Jewish convert to Christianity Petrus Alphonsi (1062–ca. 1110) had argued that the Tetragrammaton was a mystic sign of the Trinity, a claim later taken up by Joachim of Fiore (ca. 1135–1202) and Raymond Martini (ca. 1220–85). See Petrus Alfonsi, *Dialogue against the Jews*, ed. Irven Michael Resnick, Fathers of the Church: Mediaeval Continuation 8 (Washington, DC: Catholic University of America Press, 2006), 172–73. On analogies between the doctrine of the Trinity and certain Zoharic teachings, see Scholem, "Beginnings of the Christian Kabbalah," 28–29; Elliot Wolfson, *Language, Eros, Being: Kabbalistic Hermeneutics and Poetic Imagination* (New York: Fordham University Press, 2005), esp. chap. 5.
11. Martin Luther, "[Digressio] De nomine dei Tetragrammaton," in *Operationes in Psalmos 1519–1521*, part 2, *Psalm 1 bis 10 (Vulgata)*, ed. Gerhard Hammer and Biersack, Archiv zur Weimarer Ausgabe der Werke Martin Luthers 2 (Cologne: Böhlau Verlag, 1981), 331–39. This volume is part of the critical revision of important texts that had already appeared in the Weimar edition. Subsequent references to this text cite the passage by page and line. I am grateful to my friend Nicholas Baechle of Hanover College for assistance with the translation from Latin, although all its deficiencies are my own. Discussions of the passage include Siegfried Raeder, *Grammatica theologica*, 63–68; Heinrich Assel, "Der Name Gottes bei Martin Luther: Trinität und Tetragramm—Ausgehend von Luthers Auslegung des Fünften Psalms," *Evangelische Theologie* 64, no. 5 (2004): 363–78.
12. Luther's disjunctive interpretation of the phrase "your name" (Ps. 5:11) might be compared to wanting to retain the sun's corona (name in the sense of God's reputation) while suppressing the star itself (name in the sense of God's personal proper name). The enterprise is quixotic at best, as even Luther's sympathetic commentator Siegfried Raeder notes in his remarks about this passage (Raeder, *Grammatica theologica*, 159, citing Ludwig Köhler and Walter Baumgartner, eds., *Lexicon in Veteris Testamenti libros* [Leiden: E. J. Brill, 1953], 368). Despite its implausibility, Luther's interpretive move has often been echoed, including by many who are presumably unaware of its origins in Luther's anti-Jewish polemic.
13. On Luther's relation to Dionysius, see Piotr J. Malysz, "Luther and Dionysius: Beyond Mere Negations," in *Rethinking Dionysius the Areopagite*, ed. Sarah Coakley and Charles M. Stand (Chichester, UK: Wiley-Blackwell, 2009), 137–48.
14. Martin Luther, "Preface to the Old Testament [1523]," trans. Charles M. Jacobs, in *Luther's Works*, ed. E. Theodore Bachmann and Helmut

T. Lehmann, vol. 35, *Word and Sacrament* (Philadelphia: Muhlenberg Press, 1960), 248–49.

15. On Luther's treatment of the divine names in translation, see Assel, "Der Name Gottes bei Martin Luther."
16. See Thomas Kaufmann, "Martin Luther and the Jews," in *Jews, Judaism, and the Reformation in Sixteenth-Century Germany*, ed. Dean Phillip Bell and Stephen G. Burnett (Leiden: E. J. Brill, 2006), 69–104.
17. Karl Barth, *The Doctrine of the Word of God*, vol. I of *Church Dogmatics* [*CD*], ed. Geoffrey William Bromiley and Thomas Forsyth Torrance, trans. Geoffrey William Bromiley, 2nd ed. (Edinburgh: T&T Clark, 1975), pt. 1:1 (*CD* I/1:1). References in the text are to this edition.
18. Karl Barth, *Die christliche Dogmatik im Entwurf*, vol. 1, *Die Lehre vom Worte Gottes: Prolegomena zur christlichen Dogmatik* [1927], ed. Gerhard Sauter, in Karl Barth, *Akademische Werke*, Gesamtausgabe 2 (Zurich: Theologischer Verlag, 1982). Page numbers in the text refer to this edition. The work has not been translated into English.
19. Barth summarizes these criticisms in *CD* I/1:299–300.
20. Barth, *CD* I/1:1 (first German ed., 1932; ET, 1936; ET, 2nd ed., 1975 [used here]).
21. So, e.g., Barth, *CD* I/1:400: "It cannot possibly have happened unawares and unintentionally that this word [*kyrios*] was at any rate used as well to translate [*übersetzte*] the Old Testament name of God Yahweh-Adonai, and was then applied to Jesus."
22. Barth seldom refers to the name in later writings, though when he does he continues to insist on its importance. Looking back on his early work as a "dialectical theologian," Barth in his essay "The Humanity of God" writes: "It is nevertheless true that it was pre-eminently the image and concept of a 'wholly other' that fascinated us and which we, though not without examination, had dared to identify with the deity of Him who in the Bible is called Yahweh-Kyrios." See Karl Barth, "The Humanity of God," in *The Humanity of God* (Richmond: John Knox Press, 1960), 44–45.
23. Barth introduces Yahweh as "Yahweh of Israel [*Jahwe Israels*]," an oddly unbiblical but revealing phrase, inasmuch as it may suggest that Yahweh is a function of Israel rather than vice versa!

Chapter 6: Traditions in Conflict

1. Mary McClintock Fulkerson, "Grace, Christian Controversy, and Tolerable Falsehoods," in *Grace upon Grace: Essays in Honor of Thomas A. Langford*, ed. Robert K. Johnston, L. Gregory Jones, and Jonathan R. Wilson (Nashville: Abingdon Press, 1999), 234.
2. Robert W. Jenson, *The Triune Identity: God according to the Gospel* (Philadelphia: Fortress Press, 1982). Subsequent page references in the text are to this volume. Criticisms of Jenson's thought in this chapter are based exclusively on this early work and are not intended to apply to Jenson's later and voluminous writings on the Trinity. For Jenson's more recent reflection on the Trinity and the Tetragrammaton, see, e.g., his *Systematic Theology* (New York: Oxford University Press, 1997), 1:44.
3. Elizabeth A. Johnson, *She Who Is: The Mystery of God in Feminist Theological Discourse* (New York: Crossroad, 1992). Page references in the text are to this volume. Since the publication of *She Who Is*, Johnson has continued to write on the Trinity, and my criticisms of *She Who Is* are not meant to be generalized

to these later works. In *Quest for the Living God: Mapping Frontiers in the Theology of God* (New York: Continuum, 2007), 215–16, Johnson employs an earlier version of the thesis advanced in this book in her own constructive work. The earlier version appears in R. Kendall Soulen, "Hallowed Be Thy Name! The Tetragrammaton and the Name of the Trinity" in *Jews and Christians: People of God*, ed. by Robert W. Jenson and Carl Braaten (Grand Rapids: Eerdmans, 2003): 14–41; "The Name of the Holy Trinity: a Triune Name" in *Theology Today*, vol. 59, no. 2 (July, 2002): 244–61.

4. Cf. John N. Jones, "The Status of the Trinity in Dionysian Thought," *Journal of Religion* 80, no. 4 (October 2000): 645–57, esp. 645. See chap. 4 above.

Chapter 7: "Well, What IS the Name, Then?"

1. Lewis Carroll, *Through the Looking Glass* (Ann Arbor, MI: University Microfilms, 1966), 175.

Part 2: Distinguishing the Voices

1. George Herbert, second sonnet titled "The Holy Scriptures," in *The Works of George Herbert*, introduced by Tim Cook (Ware, Hertfordshire: Wordsworth Editions, 1994), 49.
2. In addition to the model of theological exegesis offered by Hans Frei (especially *The Identity of Jesus Christ: The Hermeneutical Bases of Dogmatic Theology* (Philadelphia: Fortress Press, 1975), I have been particularly inspired by the work of Friedrich Mildenberger, *Biblische Dogmatik: Eine biblische Theologie in Dogmatischer Perspektive*, 3 vols. (Stuttgart: Verlag W. Kohlhammer, 1991–93), sadly a little-known work. For further on theological interpretation, see the entry under that name in Richard N. Soulen and R. Kendall Soulen, *Handbook of Biblical Criticism*, 4th ed. (Louisville, KY: Westminster John Knox Press, 2011); Charles M. Wood, *The Formation of Christian Understanding: An Essay in Theological Hermeneutics* (Philadelphia: Westminster Press, 1981); and Daniel J. Treier, *Introducing Theological Interpretation of Scripture: Recovering a Christian Practice* (Grand Rapids: Baker Academic, 2008). On the Trinity and theological interpretation, see Robert W. Jenson, "The Bible and the Trinity," *Pro ecclesia* 11 (2002): 329–39; C. Kavin Rowe, "Biblical Pressure and Trinitarian Hermeneutics," *Pro ecclesia* 11 (2002): 295–312; C. Clifton Black, "Trinity and Exegesis," *Pro ecclesia* 19, no. 2 (Spring 2010): 151–80.
3. Christian theologians commonly draw a distinction between the Trinity and the Trinity's works in the economy of salvation, or as is sometimes said, between the immanent and the economic Trinity. This distinction assumes that what the Trinity does in the economy of salvation (the so-called economic Trinity) reliably *reveals* who the Trinity eternally is (the so-called immanent Trinity), but what the Trinity does in time and space does not first *constitute* who the Trinity eternally is. Rather, who the Trinity eternally is would be just the same even if the cosmos had never been created and knowledge of the Trinity never revealed to creatures. Though the distinction is not without its critics, most theologians maintain, as I do, that it serves the indispensable purpose of guarding our understanding of the aseity, or self-sufficiency, of God and the gratuity and giftedness of the economy of salvation.

Chapter 8: Declaring the Name of LORD in the Old Testament I

1. I have adapted the helpful terminology of consistency and novelty from Richard Bauckham's important study "God Crucified: Monotheism and

Christology in the New Testament," in *Jesus and the God of Israel: God Crucified and Other Studies on the New Testament* (Grand Rapids: Wm. B. Eerdmans Publishing Co., 2008), esp. 53–57.

2. The emphasis is necessary to deflect any effort to split these apart, after the fashion of Luther and the Christian Kabbalah. See chap. 5 above.
3. Studies that I have found especially helpful for this chapter and the next are Walther Zimmerli, "'I Am Yahweh,'" in *I Am Yahweh*, ed. Walter Brueggemann, trans. Douglas W. Stott (Atlanta: John Knox Press, 1982); Rolf Rendtorff, *The Canonical Hebrew Bible: A Theology of the Old Testament*, trans. David E. Orton (Leiden: Deo Publishing, 2005); Michael Goldberg, *Jews and Christians, Getting Our Stories Straight: The Exodus and the Passion-Resurrection* (Philadelphia: Trinity Press International, 1991); Herbert Chanan Brichto, *The Names of God: Poetic Readings in Biblical Beginnings* (Oxford: Oxford University Press, 1998); R. W. L. Moberly, *The Old Testament of the Old Testament: Patriarchal Narratives and Mosaic Yahwism* (Minneapolis: Fortress Press, 1992); Christopher Seitz, *Word without End: The Old Testament as Abiding Theological Witness* (Grand Rapids: Wm. B. Eerdmans Publishing Co., 1998).
4. Zimmerli, *I Am Yahweh*, 1–2. Zimmerli goes on to memorably affirm, "The phrase 'I am Yahweh' carries all the weight and becomes the denominator upon which all else rests. Our interpretation may then assert that everything Yahweh has to announce to his people appears as an amplification of the fundamental statement 'I am Yahweh'" (9). "Virtually all the decisive elements of the revelation are already contained within Yahweh's revelation of his name" (13).
5. Rendtorff, *Canonical Hebrew Bible*, 605.
6. Ibid.
7. NRSV, with paragraph breaks drawn from NIV as printed in *The New Interpreters Bible*, with exception of "This is my name forever, this is my name for all generations," which follows paragraphing of NRSV.
8. That God's reply to Moses reaches its climax in the last of the three names is also affirmed by Rendtorff, *Canonical Hebrew Bible*, 546–47; Walter Brueggemann, "Exodus 3: Summons to Holy Transformation," in *The Theological Interpretation: Classic and Contemporary Readings*, ed. Stephen E. Fowl (Malden, MA: Blackwell, 1997), 155–77, esp. 164; Patrick D. Miller, *The Ten Commandments* (Louisville, KY: Westminster John Knox Press, 2009), 74.
9. Specifically, "I am who I am" and "I am" clearly comment or "play" on the name YHWH from a phonetic and semantic point of view, as puns do, but not so clearly from an *etymological* point of view, such as by purporting to provide the "original" or "true" meaning of the Tetragrammaton in a philological sense. The idea that YHWH is derived etymologically from the same root as "I am," and is to be interpreted accordingly to mean "He is," is (so far as I can see) a relatively modern hypothesis. If the etymological interpretation of the relationship of the names were widespread in earlier tradition, or manifestly operative in Exodus 3 or anywhere else in the Bible, it is hard to imagine how confusion and uncertainty concerning the pronunciation and pointing of the name could ever have arisen for YHWH, as it manifestly did among Jews such as Maimonides (see chap. 4 above). In my opinion, the contemporary popularity of etymological interpretations of the relationship of the names arises in part from a modern discomfort with the Tetragrammaton's character as an opaque proper name and a desire to resolve it into a meaning-bearing term that can then be ranged alongside other such terms, a desire that we saw already operative in the Reformation tradition influenced by the Christian

Kabbalah (see chap. 5 above.). Robert Jenson comes closer to the truth when he maintains (similarly to Joseph Ratzinger) that "I am who I am" is a word-play on the Tetragrammaton, whose "purpose is not to provide the 'meaning' of the name, but to rebuff curious inquiries into its meaning." See Robert W. Jenson, *The Triune Identity: God according to the Gospel* (Philadelphia: Fortress Press, 1982), 5.

10. See Jack R. Lundblum, "God's Use of the *Idem per Idem* to Terminate Debate," *Harvard Theological Review* 71: 3 / 4 (1978), 193–201; also Jochen Teuffel, *Mission als Namenszeugnis: eine Ideologiekritik in Sachen Religion* (Tübingen: Mohr Siebeck), 2009, 116.
11. In this respect, the names of Mount Horeb *taken together* simply transcend the unhappy paradox of Jacques Derrida: "Translate me, don't translate me. On the one hand, don't translate me, that is, respect me as a proper name. . . . And, on the other hand, translate me, that is understand me, preserve me within the universal language, follow my law, and so on." Jacques Derrida, *The Ear of the Other: Otobiography, Transference, Translation: Texts and Discussions with Jacques Derrida*, ed. Christie McDonald, trans. Peggy Kamuf (1985; repr., Lincoln: University of Nebraska Press, 1988), 102.
12. "God is not a member of any class." Thomas Aquinas, *Summa theologiae* 1.3.5.
13. *Epistle of Barnabas* 4, in *The Apostolic Fathers*, ed. and trans. Bart D. Ehrman, Loeb Classical Library 24–25 (Cambridge, MA: Harvard University Press, 2003), 2:23. About a generation later, Justin Martyr also famously refers to the golden calf incident in his *Dialogue with Trypho the Jew*, 18.2. Justin goes Barnabas one better (or worse) by interpreting God's written law as a mark, not of election, but of Israel's exceptional sinfulness. The two passages from Barnabas and Justin have a long afterlife and echo in Christian anti-Jewish rhetoric. Checking the index of a standard work (Heinz Schreckenberg, *Die christlichen Adversus-Judaeos-Texte und ihr literarisches und historisches Umfeld (1.–11. Jh.)* [Frankfurt: Peter Lang, 1982], 658), one sees that Exod. 32 is one of the most commonly cited texts in Christian anti-Jewish rhetoric during the first millennium.
14. See Augustine, *Letter 82*, to Jerome; Thomas Aquinas, *Summa theologiae* 1/2.103.4. On the teaching that Christ's coming renders the Mosaic law "dead and deadly," with special attention to its inevitably supersessionistic character, see Bruce D. Marshall, "*Quasi in Figura*: A Brief Reflection on Jewish Election, after Thomas Aquinas" *Nova et Vetera*, vol. 7:2 (2009): 477–84.

Chapter 9: Declaring the Name of Lord in the Old Testament II

1. On the important role of these sayings in the final canonical shaping of the Old Testament, see Rolf Rendtorff, *The Canonical Hebrew Bible: A Theology of the Old Testament*, trans. David E. Orton (Leiden: Deo Publishing, 2005), 606–7, 727–9. According to Rendtorff, the sayings unify the canon in light of "the fact that YHWH is God, and indeed uniquely and exclusively God," and that "it is *he* who acts and proves himself in what is announced" (606). See also C. H. Dodd, *The Interpretation of the Fourth Gospel* (Cambridge: Cambridge University Press, 1960), 93, where Dodd observes that to "'know the name'" of God, or to "'know that His name is YHWH' is an expression which sums up the ideal attitude of Israel (or of the individual Israelite) to YHWH. It is the vocation of the servant of God to 'declare His name' to other men (Ps. xxi. 23 [22:22]). In the good time coming the ideal relation of Israel to their God will be realized: 'My people shall know my name' (Isa. 52:6; cf. Jer. 16:21)."

2. As Walther Zimmerli observes: The "indefatigable repetition of *'ny yhwh* [I am YHWH] at the end of individual statements or smaller groups of statements in the legal offerings is not to be understood as thoughtlessly strewn decoration; rather, this repetition pushes these legal statements into the most central position from which the OT can make any statement. Each of these small groups of legal maxims thereby becomes a legal communication out of the heart of the OT revelation." See Zimmerli, "'I Am Yahweh,'" in *I Am Yahweh*, ed. Walter Brueggemann, trans. Douglas W. Stott (Atlanta: John Knox Press, 1982), 12.
3. So, e.g., Emil Brunner, *The Christian Doctrine of God*, trans. Olive Wyon, vol. 1 of *Dogmatics* (Philadelphia: Westminster Press, 1950), 119; Bruce M. Metzger, "To the Reader," in *The New Revised Standard Version*, Division of Christian Education of the National Council of the Churches of Christ in the United States of America (Nashville: Thomas Nelson, 1989).
4. See chap. 2 above.
5. Christopher Seitz, *Word without End: The Old Testament as Abiding Theological Witness* (Grand Rapids: Wm. B. Eerdmans Publishing Co., 1998), 254–56.
6. On this Psalm as a kind of epitome of the biblical witness as a whole, see Frans H. Breukelman, "Psalm 113 oder die Struktur der biblischen Theologie," *Texte und Kontexte* 53, no. 1 (1992): 2–32.
7. Dorothy Day cites this verse movingly in her autobiography, *The Long Loneliness* (New York: Harper, 1952), 286: "I found myself, a barren woman, the joyful mother of children." As Anne Astell writes, "Day's 'barrenness'—a condition associated with the traumatic abortion she had had in 1919—gave way not only to the birth of her child, Tamar, in 1927, but also to a spiritual rebirth in Day's own baptism and, not long afterward, in 1932, to her radical practice of welcoming the poor, unwanted, into the houses of hospitality that sprang up, one by one, during the Great Depression." Astell, "In the Bosom of Abraham," in *Crisis, Call, and Leadership in the Abrahamic Traditions* (New York: Palgrave Macmillan, 2009), 140.

Chapter 10: Declaring the Name of the Trinity in the New Testament I

1. I am grateful to the stimulation provided by the writings of Jeremy Begbie for this way of putting things, especially in his *Theology, Music, and Time* (Cambridge: Cambridge University Press, 2000).
2. In this chapter, I frequently use the terms "God," "Christ," and the "Spirit" to designate the first, second, and third persons of the Trinity respectively. I adopt this usage (1) for sake of simplicity and clarity of exposition, and (2) because it is consistent with the dominant usage of Scriptures, as rightly pointed out by Karl Rahner, "*Theos* in the New Testament," *Theological Investigations*, translated and introduced by Cornelius Ernst (Baltimore: Helicon Press, 1961), 1:79–148. I do not in any way mean thereby to deny that second and third persons may also rightly be called "God." The work of indicating the relationships among God, Christ, and the Spirit is accomplished by the different patterns of trinitarian naming—the theological, christological, and pneumatological patterns—more fully elaborated in subsequent chapters. In this chapter my reading of Scripture is informed by Joel Marcus, *The Way of the Lord* (New York: T&T Clark International, 2004); N. T. Wright, *Jesus and the Victory of God*, vol. 2 of *Christian Origins and the Question of God* (Minneapolis: Fortress Press, 1997); and perhaps most by the conversation that Wright's

work stimulated, especially the critical responses by Dale C. Allison Jr. and Richard B. Hays in *Jesus and the Restoration of Israel: A Critical Assessment of N. T. Wright's "Jesus and the Victory of God,"* ed. Carey C. Newman (Downers Grove, IL: InterVarsity Press, 1999).

3. On the concept of appropriation, see especially Bruce Marshall, *Trinity and Truth* (Cambridge: Cambridge University Press, 2000), 251–56, who in turn leans heavily on Thomas Aquinas.
4. In biblical usage *kyrios* as a surrogate for YHWH is frequently written without an article in the nominative case, which diverges from the conventions of extrabiblical speech. See Carl Judson Davis, *The Name and Way of the Lord: Old Testament Themes, New Testament Christology* (Sheffield: Sheffield Academic Press, 1996), 93; Martin Rösel, *Adonaj—Warum Gott "Herr" gennant wird* (Tübingen: Mohr Siebeck, 2000), 6–7; Albert Debrunner, "Zur Übersetzungstechnik der Septuaginta: Der Gebrauch des Artikels bei κύριος," in *Vom Alten Testament* [Festschrift for Karl Marti], ed. Karl Budde, BZAW 41 (Giessen: A. Töpelmann, 1925), 69–78.
5. Paul Ricoeur, "Naming God," in *Figuring the Sacred: Religion, Narrative, and Imagination* (Minneapolis: Fortress Press, 1995), 217–35, esp. 224.

Chapter 11: Declaring the Name of the Trinity in the New Testament II

1. Bruce Marshall, *Trinity and Truth* (Cambridge: Cambridge University Press, 2000), 254.
2. Ibid.
3. My reading of Rev. 1 has been especially aided by the fine work of Sean M. McDonough, *YHWH at Patmos: Rev. 1:4 in Its Hellenistic and Early Jewish Setting*, WUNT, ser. 2 (Tübingen: Mohr Siebeck, 1999); in addition to Otfried Hofius, "Das Zeugnis der Johannesoffenbarung von der Gottheit Jesu Christi," in *Geschichte—Tradition—Reflexion: Festschrift für Martin Hengel zum 70. Geburtstag*, vol. 3, *Frühes Christentum*, ed. Hermann Lichtenberger and Hubert Cancik (Tübingen: J. C. B. Mohr [Paul Siebeck], 1996), 511–28; Richard Bauckham, *The Theology of the Book of Revelation* (Cambridge: Cambridge University Press, 1993); idem, *The Climax of Prophecy: Studies on the Book of Revelation* (Edinburgh: T&T Clark, 1993); and Richard B. Hays, *The Moral Vision of the New Testament: Community, Cross, New Creation; A Contemporary Introduction to New Testament Ethics* (San Francisco: HarperSanFrancisco, 1996). Hays helpfully puts the book's images of divine violence into context by reminding us that the book of Revelation is above all a "political resistance document," written in the context of a hostile empire. "It refuses to acknowledge the legitimacy and authority of earthly rulers and looks defiantly to the future, when all things will be subjected to the authority of God" (Hays, *Moral Vision*, 170).
4. McDonough, *YHWH at Patmos*, 217–20; Bauckham, *Theology*, 27–28.
5. See McDonough, *YHWH at Patmos*, 49.
6. Ibid., 217. Notice that John evokes the name theophany of the burning bush in a way that is sensitive to the intricacies of the original context. God's initial reply to Moses ("I am who I am" [Exod. 3:14]) is an interpretative pun on the personal name that immediately follows (YHWH [3:15]), not a freestanding name in its own right. Similarly, John's improvisation on Exod. 3:14 represents and interprets the divine name of 3:15 without taking its place.

7. Stanley Grenz, *The Named God and the Question of Being: A Trinitarian Theo-Ontology* (Louisville, KY: Westminster John Knox Press, 2005), 234. See McDonough, *YHWH at Patmos*, 202, for discussion and literature.
8. Leon Morris, *Book of Revelation*, 49; quoted in Grenz, *The Named God*, 231.
9. Bauckham, *Theology of Revelation*, 113.
10. Ibid., 58. Hofius points out that commentators often fail to recognize the extraordinarily "high" character of John's Christology because they fail to recognize the role played by paraphrastic allusion to the Tetragrammaton, treating the words and phrases in question as nothing more than divine predicates and appellations. See Hofius, "Zeugnis der Johannesoffenbarung," 526.
11. My account of the compositional structure of Matt. 28:16–20 is especially informed by W. D. Davies and Dale C. Allison Jr., *A Critical and Exegetical Commentary on the Gospel according to Saint Matthew* (Edinburgh: T&T Clark, 1997), 3:676–90, although I do not mean to ascribe my reading to them, nor do I follow them at every point. I have also found the following works helpful: David D. Kupp, *Matthew's Emmanuel: Divine Presence and God's People in the First Gospel*, SNTSMS 90 (Cambridge: Cambridge University Press, 1996); Jane Schaberg, *The Father, the Son, and Holy Spirit: The Triadic Phrase in Matthew 28:19b*, SBLDS 61 (Chico, CA: Scholars Press, 1982); Otto Michel, "The Conclusion of Matthew's Gospel," in *The Interpretation of Matthew*, ed. Graham Stanton, 2nd ed. (Edinburgh: T&T Clark, 1995), 39–51; Jack Dean Kingsbury, "Composition and Christology of Matt 28:16–20," in *Journal of Biblical Literature* 93, no. 4 (1974): 573–84.
12. Following the suggestion of Dale C. Allison, I believe the reference to "the name" is best understood with reference to the personal name of God, which the first person has given to the second person and which is glorified by the third person; cf. Phil. 2. See Dale C. Allison Jr., *The Sermon on the Mount* (New York: Crossroad Publishing, 1999), 120–21.
13. My reading of Acts has been helped especially by Robert L. Mowery, "The Disappearance of the Father: The References to God the Father in Luke/Acts," *Encounter* 55, no. 4 (Autumn 1994): 353–58; Luke Timothy Johnson, *The Acts of the Apostles* (Collegeville, MN: Liturgical Press, 1992); Justo González, *Acts: Gospel of the Spirit* (New York: Orbis Books, 2001); and Beverly R. Gaventa, *The Acts of the Apostles* (Nashville: Abingdon Press, 2003).
14. Joseph Henry Thayer, *A Greek-English Lexicon of the New Testament* (New York: Harper & Brothers, 1889), 562.
15. On the special importance of Lord as a designation of God, Jesus, and their mutual relation in Luke–Acts, see C. Kavin Rowe, *Early Narrative Christology: The Lord in the Gospel of Luke*, BZNW 139 (New York: Walter de Gruyter, 2006); *World Upside Down: Reading Acts in the Graeco-Roman Age* (New York: Oxford University Press, 2010).

Interlude

1. Clement of Alexandria, *Exhortation to the Greeks* 11, in *The Ante-Nicene Fathers*, ed. Alexander Roberts, James Donaldson, and A. Cleveland Coxe (repr., Grand Rapids: Wm. B. Eerdmans Publishing Co., 1971), 2:172.

Chapter 12: Hallowed Be Your Name!

1. Brant Pelphrey, *Christ Our Mother: Julian of Norwich* (Wilmington, DE: Michael Glazier, 1989), 105.

2. Scholars who have increased our understanding of the important role played by reverence for the Tetragrammaton in Second Temple Judaism and early Christianity include Gilles Quispel, Jean Daniélou, Richard Longenecker, Alan Segal, Christopher Rowland, Jarl E. Fossum, Charles A. Gieschen, Martin Hengel, Sean McDonough, C. Kavin Rowe, Dale C. Allison, Scot McKnight, Markus Bockmuehl, Karl Judson Davis, and others. Although superseded by the wealth of twentieth-century manuscript discoveries, Gustaf Dalman's work *The Words of Jesus Considered in the Light of Post-Biblical Jewish Writings and the Aramaic Language*, trans. D. M. Kay (Edinburgh: T&T Clark, 1909) remains an excellent overview of this dimension of the New Testament witness to Jesus Christ's own speech. Julius Boehmer, *Die neutestamentliche Gottesscheu und die ersten drei Bitten des Vaterunsers* (Halle: Richard Mühlmann Verlagsbuchhandlung, 1917), provides an inventory of every word and phrase in the New Testament reflecting the impact of reserve before the name of God, totaling well over 2,000 instances in all. Sean M. McDonough, *YHWH at Patmos: Rev. 1:4 in Its Hellenistic and Early Jewish Setting*, WUNT, ser. 2 (Tübingen: Mohr Siebeck, 1999), offers an excellent contemporary overview of beliefs and practices connected with the divine name in Second Temple Judaism. General studies of the relevant material in the New Testament include Larry W. Hurtado, *Lord Jesus Christ: Devotion to Jesus in Earliest Christianity* (Grand Rapids: Wm. B. Eerdmans Publishing Co., 2003); Scot McKnight, *A New Vision for Israel: The Teachings of Jesus in National Context* (Grand Rapids: Wm. B. Eerdmans Publishing Co., 1999); Adelheid Ruck-Schroeder, *Der Name Gottes und der Name Jesu* (Neukirchen-Vluyn: Neukirchener Verlag, 1999); and Richard Bauckham, *Jesus and the God of Israel* (Grand Rapids: Wm. B. Eerdmans Publishing Co., 2008).
3. Ignatius of Antioch, *To the Ephesians*, 15.2.
4. See McDonough, *YHWH at Patmos*, 58–122.
5. Dalman, *Words of Jesus*, 196. Dalman drew attention to this and many other features of Jesus' speech that reflect reverence for the divine name, though with comparatively little effect on the world of systematic theology of subsequent generations. See also McDonough, *YHWH at Patmos*, 112.
6. Cf. Dalman, *Words of Jesus*, 196, 206.
7. Ibid., 226–29. The Synoptic Gospels record Jesus as saying "Amen" some 49 times, John some 25 times; cf. Hurtado, *Lord Jesus Christ*, 292. For further discussion and literature, see Bruce Chilton, "'Amen': An Approach through Syriac Gospels," in *Targumic Approaches to the Gospels: Essays in the Mutual Definition of Judaism and Christianity* (Lanham, MD: University Press of America, 1986), 15–23.
8. Dalman, *Words of Jesus*, 229.
9. On reference to the Tetragrammaton in the Lord's Prayer, with literature citations, see Ruck-Schroeder, *Der Name Gottes*, 149–50; also Boehmer, *Die neutestamentliche Gottesscheu*; Lyder Brun, "Der Name und die Königsherrschaft im Vaterunser," in *Harnack-Ehrung: Beiträge zur Kirchengeschichte, ihrem Lehrer Adolf von Harnack zu seinem 70. Geburtstage (7. Mai 1921) dargebracht von einer Reihe seiner Schüler* (Leipzig: J. C. Hinrichs, 1921), 22–31; Peter Stuhlmacher, *How to Do Biblical Theology* (Allison Park, PA: Pickwick Publications, 1995), 10.
10. On the divine passive in Jesus' speech, see Dalman, *Words of Jesus*, 224–24; McKnight, *New Vision for Israel*, 29–30; Hermann L. Strack and Paul

Billerbeck, *Kommentar zum Neuen Testament aus Talmud und Midrasch* (Munich: C. H. Beck, 1922), 1:330; Joachim Jeremias, *New Testament Theology: The Proclamation of Jesus*, trans. John Bowden (New York: Scribner, 1971), 9–14; Max Zerwick, *Biblical Greek: Illustrated from Examples*, ed. Joseph Smith (Rome: Pontifical Biblical Institute, 1963), 76; Neil Richardson, *God in the New Testament* (Peterborough, UK: Epworth Press, 1999), 28–30. Jeremias (*New Testament Theology*, 9–14) considers that the "'divine passive' occurs round about 100 times in the sayings of Jesus" alone. On the first petition of the Lord's Prayer as divine passive, see Boehmer, *Die neutestamentliche Gottesscheu*, 182–93; W. D. Davies and Dale C. Allison Jr., *A Critical and Exegetical Commentary on the Gospel according to Saint Matthew* (Edinburgh: T&T Clark, 1988), 1:602; Raymond E. Brown, "The Pater Noster as an Eschatological Prayer," in *New Testament Essays* (Garden City, NY: Doubleday, Image Books, 1968), 319. My thanks to Mark Kinzer for his helpful comments to me about Ezek. 36 and the first petition.

11. Otto Weber, *Foundations of Dogmatics*, trans. Darrell L. Guder (Grand Rapids: Wm. B. Eerdmans Publishing Co., 1981–83), 1:418. On Weber, see the discussion in chap. 1 above.
12. Jeremias (*New Testament Theology*), Richardson (*God in the New Testament*), and McKnight (*New Vision for Israel*) especially emphasize the future orientation of many divine passives in Jesus' speech.
13. My reading of Johannine references to the name of God is especially informed by Ruck-Schroeder, *Der Name Gottes*, 203–4; Raymond E. Brown, *The Gospel according to John*, Anchor Bible 29–29A (New York: Doubleday, 1966–70), 2 vols.; Franz Georg Untergassmair, *Im Name Jesu: Der Namensbegriff im Johannesevangelium; Eine exegetisch-religionsgeschichtliche Studie zu den johanneischen Namensaussagen* (Stuttgart: Verlag Katholisches Bibelwerk, 1974); Marianne Meye Thompson, *The God of the Gospel of John* (Grand Rapids: Wm. B. Eerdmans Publishing Co., 2001), 88–92. In my opinion, Charles Gieschen correctly suggests that "based upon the testimony in this prayer that the Son received the Father's glory before the foundation of the world (17:24), the giving of the Divine Name is probably also understood to have taken place before creation"; see Charles A. Gieschen, "The Divine Name in Ante-Nicene Christology," *Vigiliae christianae* 57, no. 2 (2003): 136.
14. In my discussion of the "I am" statements, I gratefully acknowledge indebtedness to Richard Bauckham, "Monotheism and Christology in the Gospel of John," in *Contours of Christology in the New Testament*, ed. Richard N. Longenecker (Grand Rapids: Wm. B. Eerdmans Publishing Co., 2005), 147–66. I have also been helped by Philip B. Harner, *The "I Am" of the Fourth Gospel: A Study in Johannine Usage and Thought* (Philadelphia: Fortress Press, 1970). On the connection between John 17 and the "I am" statements, see Brown, *Gospel according to John*, 2:754–56; C. H. Dodd, *The Interpretation of the Fourth Gospel* (London: Cambridge University Press, 1970), 417n2; Ben Witherington III and Laura Michaels Ice, *Shadow of the Almighty: Father, Son, and Spirit in Biblical Perspective* (Grand Rapids: Wm. B. Eerdmans Publishing Co., 2002), 93–94. For further discussion and literature, see Stanley Grenz, *The Named God and the Question of Being: A Trinitarian Theo-Ontology* (Louisville, KY: Westminster John Knox Press, 2005), 200, 209–20.
15. I have altered the NRSV translation where necessary for accuracy, e.g., by changing "I am he" to the more literal "I am."

16. Hurtado, *Lord Jesus Christ*, 370.
17. See Bauckham, "Monotheism and Christology," 157–60; Harner, *The "I Am" of the Fourth Gospel*, 8–18; Thompson, *The God of the Gospel of John*, 89–90. Rudolf Bultmann denied any connection between the "I am" statements and Exod. 3, prompting Harold Bloom to remark that New Testament scholarship "manifests a very impoverished notion as to just what literary allusion is or can be"; see Harold Bloom, *The Gospels* (New Haven, CT: Chelsea House, 1987), 295.
18. Cf. Gieschen, "The Divine Name," 141: "Although the EGŌ EIMI formula in John should not be understood as the Divine Name that Jesus is said to have been given (17:11), nevertheless these absolute sayings are very closely related to it and function as a way of indicating that Jesus is the possessor of the Divine Name." Rudolf Bultmann also articulates this view as a possible interpretation of the "I am" statements, with supporting literature, while rejecting it himself. See Bultmann, *The Gospel of John: A Commentary* (Philadelphia: Westminster Press, 1971), 327–28.
19. Bauckham, "Monotheism and Christology," 162.
20. While I agree wholeheartedly with N. T. Wright that the New Testament writers "can be shown to be expressing a fully . . . trinitarian theology, and to be doing so as a fresh and creative variation from within, not an abandonment of, their Second Temple Jewish god-view" (Nicholas T. Wright, "Jesus and the Identity of God," *Ex auditu* 14 [1998]: 46–47), I respectfully demur from his judgment that "the sanctifying of God's name, as in the clause 'Hallowed be your name' (Lk. 11:2//Matt. 6:9), is not a major theme in the Gospels"; see Nicholas T. Wright, "Lord's Prayer as Paradigm," in *Into God's Presence: Prayer in the New Testament*, ed. Richard N. Longenecker (Grand Rapids: Wm. B. Eerdmans Publishing Co., 2001), 134. To the contrary, I maintain that zeal for the hallowing of God's name is the principal font from which all the trinitarian theology of the New Testament flows, including that of the Gospels.
21. On this point, see chap. 10 above.
22. So the perennially popular Matthew Henry in his commentary on the passage. He writes, "The judgment of the great day will effectually convince unbelievers that would not now be convinced: 'Then you will say, *Blessed is He that cometh*,' that is, 'you will be glad to be among those that say so, and *will not see Me* to be the Messiah till then, when it is too late.'" See Matthew Henry, *The Comprehensive Commentary on the Holy Bible* (Brattleboro, VT: Fessenden & Co, 1836), 4:522. Later he amplifies, "Then the unbelieving Jews shall be convinced, when too late, that Jesus was the Messiah; they that would not see Him coming in the power of his grace to save, shall be made to see Him coming in the power of his wrath to destroy them; those that would not have Him to reign, shall have Him to triumph over them" (ibid., 573).
23. Further discussion is in Ruck-Schroeder, *Der Name Gottes*, 154–55; Mark Kinzer, *Postmissionary Messianic Judaism: Redefining Christian Engagement with the Jewish People* (Grand Rapids: Brazos Press, 2005), 105; Richard Bauckham, "The Restoration of Israel in Luke–Acts," in *Restoration: Old Testament, Jewish, and Christian Perspectives*, ed. James M. Scott (Leiden: E. J. Brill, 2001), 435–88.
24. The passage has attracted a vast amount of critical attention since the publication of Ralph P. Martin, *Carmen Christi: Philippians 2:5–11 in Recent*

Interpretation and in the Setting of Early Christian Worship, rev. ed. (Grand Rapids: Wm. B. Eerdmans Publishing Co., 1983). Representative views are collected in Ralph P. Martin and Brian J. Dodd, eds., *Where Christology Began: Essays on Philippians 2* (Louisville, KY: Westminster John Knox Press, 1998).

25. Richard Bauckham, *Jesus and the God of Israel: God Crucified and Other Studies on the New Testament's Christology of Divine Identity* (Grand Rapids: Wm. B. Eerdmans Publishing Co., 2008), 199.
26. George MacDonald, *The Princess and the Goblin*, Everyman's Library Children's Classics (New York: Alfred A. Knopf, 1993), 20.
27. The theological pattern of naming the persons of the Trinity described in this chapter coincides substantially, so far as its exegetical basis is concerned, with what Richard Bauckham has called a "christology of divine identity." See especially Bauckham, *Jesus and the God of Israel*, 1–59.

Chapter 13: Our Father in Heaven!

1. A highly simplified version appears already in the great liberal historian Adolf von Harnack's Berlin lectures of 1899–1900 on the essence of Christianity (*What Is Christianity?* [Minneapolis: Fortress Press, 1987], 63–70); we see more elaborate and robustly trinitarian versions in countless subsequent works including, e.g., Edward Schillebeeckx, *An Experiment in Christology* (New York: Seabury Press,1979), 256–71; Jürgen Moltmann, *The Trinity and the Kingdom*, trans. Margaret Kohl (Minneapolis: Fortress Press, 1993), 61–96.
2. On this point see, e.g., Marianne Meye Thompson, *The Promise of the Father: Jesus and God in the New Testament* (Louisville, KY: Westminster John Knox Press, 2000), 21–34; Scot McKnight, *A New Vision for Israel: The Teachings of Jesus in National Context* (Grand Rapids: Wm. B. Eerdmans Publishing Co., 1999), 15–70.
3. Gottlob Schrenk, "πατήρ," in *Theological Dictionary of the New Testament*, ed. Gerhard Kittel and Gerhard Friedrich (Grand Rapids: Wm. B. Eerdmans Publishing Co., 1967), 5:996–97.
4. George Tavard, *The Vision of the Trinity* (Washington, DC: University Press of America, 1981), 10–11. Quoted in Peter Toon, *Our Triune God: A Biblical Portrait of the Trinity* (Wheaton, IL: Victor Books, 1996), 157.
5. Jean Galot, SJ, *Abba, Father, We Long to See Your Face: Theological Insights into the First Person of the Trinity*, trans. M. Angeline Bouchard (New York: Alba House, 1992), 181.
6. T. F. Torrance, "The Christian Apprehension of God the Father," in *Speaking the Christian God: The Holy Trinity and the Challenge of Feminism*, ed. Alvin F. Kimel Jr. (Grand Rapids: Wm. B. Eerdmans Publishing Co., 1992), 131.
7. Claude Geffre, "Father as the Proper Name of God," in *God as Father?* ed. Johannes-Baptist Metz, Edward Schillebeeckx, and Marcus Lefébure (Edinburgh: T&T Clark; 1981), 44–45.
8. J. I. Packer, *Knowing God* (Downers Grove, IL: InterVarsity Press, 1973), 182–83; cited in Thompson, *Promise of the Father*, 11.
9. Jon D. Levenson, *The Death and Resurrection of the Beloved Son: The Transformation of Child Sacrifice in Judaism and Christianity* (New Haven, CT: Yale University Press, 1993).
10. Ibid., 141.
11. Schrenk, "πατήρ," 997.

12. See, e.g., Frederick Fyvie Bruce, *The Epistle to the Hebrews* (Grand Rapids: Wm. B. Eerdmans Publishing Co., 1990), 49n33.
13. So, e.g., Mary Rose D'Angelo: "It is clearly the case that 'father' increased in importance in early Christianity. It is placed on the lips of Jesus in Matthew and Luke, significantly more frequently than in Mark and Q. There can be little doubt that development of Christology was the most significant factor in the importance of "father" in Christian theology." See Mary Rose D'Angelo, "Abba and 'Father': Imperial Theology and the Jesus Traditions," *Journal of Biblical Literature* 111, no. 4 (Winter 1992): 622.
14. Thompson's book (*Promise of the Father*) is helpfully read in conjunction with Ben Witherington III and Laura Michaels Ice, *The Shadow of the Almighty: Father, Son, and Holy Spirit in Biblical Perspective* (Grand Rapids: Wm. B. Eerdmans Publishing Co., 2002).
15. Thompson, *Promise of the Father*, 66.
16. This striking point of literary composition is emphasized by, e.g., Karl Barth, *Church Dogmatics*, trans. Geoffrey W. Bromiley, vol. IV, *The Christian Life*, pt. 4, *Lecture Fragments* (Grand Rapids: Wm. B. Eerdmans Publishing Co., 1981), 67 (*CD* IV/4:67).
17. My observations in this section are especially informed by David D. Kupp, *Matthew's Emmanuel: Divine Presence and God's People in the First Gospel*, SNTSMS 90 (Cambridge: Cambridge University Press, 1996).
18. Robert L. Mowery, "The Disappearance of the Father: The References to God the Father in Luke/Acts," *Encounter* 55, no. 4 (Autumn 1994): 353–58. My remarks are indebted to his work.
19. Stanley Grenz, *The Named God and the Question of Being: A Trinitarian Theo-Ontology* (Louisville, KY: Westminster John Knox Press, 2005), 266n68.
20. That God's being is one of personal communion is an insight elaborated in, e.g., John D. Zizioulas, *Being as Communion: Studies in Personhood and the Church* (1985; repr., Crestwood, NY: St. Vladimir's Seminary Press, 1997); Christopher Morse, *Not Every Spirit: A Dogmatics of Christian Disbelief*, 2nd ed. (New York: Continuum, 2009), 113–38.
21. My reading is informed by Paul W. Meyer, "'The Father': The Presentation of God in the Fourth Gospel," in *Exploring the Gospel of John: In Honor of D. Moody Smith*, ed. R. Alan Culpepper and C. Clifton Black (Louisville, KY: Westminster John Knox Press, 1996), 255–73; Marianne Meye Thompson, *The God of the Gospel of John* (Grand Rapids: Wm. B. Eerdmans Publishing Co., 2001); idem, *The Promise of the Father*.
22. Robert W. Jenson, *The Triune Identity: God according to the Gospel* (Philadelphia: Fortress Press, 1982), 44.

Chapter 14: "Your Kingdom Come!"

1. Bruce M. Metzger, Michael David Coogan, eds. *The Oxford Companion to the Bible* (Oxford: Oxford University Press, 1993), 464.
2. Basil the Great, of Caesarea, *Exegetic Homilies*, 13.5, trans. Agnes Clare Way, Fathers of the Church 46 (Washington, DC: Catholic University Press, 1963), 204–5.
3. Origen, *Commentary on Matthew* 14.7, on Matt. 18:23 (in J.-P. Migne, ed., Patrologia graeca 13:1197).
4. My brief account of the diversity of the parables draws especially upon Charles W. Hedrick, *Parables as Poetic Fictions: The Creative Voice of Jesus* (Peabody,

MA: Hendrickson Publishers, 1994), 259–60. I have also been helped by C. H. Dodd, *The Parables of the Kingdom* (New York: Scribner, 1961); Norman Perrin, *Jesus and the Language of the Kingdom* (Philadelphia: Fortress Press, 1976); Paul Ricoeur, "The 'Kingdom' in the Parables of Jesus," *Anglican Journal of Theology* 63, no. 2 (1981): 165–69; Craig L. Blomberg, *Interpreting the Parables* (Downers Grove, IL: InterVarsity Press, 1990); Andrew Parker, *Painfully Clear: The Parables of Jesus* (Sheffield: Sheffield Academic Press, 1996); Ben Witherington III, *Jesus the Sage: The Pilgrimage of Wisdom* (Minneapolis: Augsburg Fortress, 2000).

5. Gabriel Bunge, *The Rublev Trinity: The Icon of the Trinity by the Monk-Painter Andrei Rublev* (Crestwood, NY: St. Vladimir's Seminary Press, 2007), 34.
6. Jerome, Letter 30, *Letters and Select Works*, in *The Nicene and Post-Nicene Fathers*, ser. 2, ed. Philip Schaff and Henry Wace (Peabody, MA: Hendrickson Publishers, 1995), 6:45.
7. Augustine, *Sermons on New Testament Lessons*, Sermon 55.4 in *The Nicene and Post-Nicene Fathers*, ser. 1, ed. Philip Schaff (Peabody, MA: Hendrickson Publishers, 1995), 6:431. I have modified the translation by rendering it in contemporary English. On the variety of medieval interpretations of this and other parables, see Stephen L. Wailes, *Medieval Allegories of Jesus' Parables* (Berkeley: University of California Press, 1987).
8. An adaptation of Mark 4:30–32.
9. My overview of the historical period in question draws in part on Perrin, *Jesus and the Language of the Kingdom*; Jacobus Liebenberg, *The Language of the Kingdom and Jesus: Parable, Aphorism, and Metaphor in the Sayings Material Common to the Synoptic Tradition and the Gospel of Thomas* (New York: Walter de Gruyter, 2001), 1–105.
10. Sallie McFague, *Speaking in Parables: A Study in Metaphor and Theology* (Philadelphia: Fortress Press, 1975; repr., London: SCM Press, 2002), esp. 32, 56, 62. Theological analyses of metaphor quite different in spirit from that of McFague include those of Janet Martin Soskice, *Metaphor and Religious Language* (Oxford: Oxford University Press, 1987); and Eberhard Jüngel, *God as the Mystery of the World: On the Foundation of the Theology of the Crucified One in the Dispute between Theism and Atheism* (Grand Rapids: Wm. B. Eerdmans Publishing Co., 1983; repr., Eugene, OR: Wipf & Stock Publishers, 2009).
11. Representative views on both sides of the debate can be found respectively in, e.g., Alvin Kimel Jr., ed., *Speaking the Christian God: The Holy Trinity and the Challenge of Feminism* (Grand Rapids: Wm. B. Eerdmans Publishing Co., 1992); and Sally McFague, *Models of God: Theology for an Ecological, Nuclear Age* (Philadelphia: Fortress Press, 1983). In the latter work, McFague seeks to "dethrone" the name "Father, Son, and Holy Spirit," while at the same time indicating that she has no interest in maintaining traditional claims for the doctrine of the Trinity. Laurel C. Schneider argues that a commitment to a metaphorical understanding of religious language leads beyond trinitarianism entirely to a "monistic polytheism," which is better able than alternatives to support the ethical concerns of feminism; see Schneider, *Re-Imagining the Divine: Confronting the Backlash against Feminist Theology* (Cleveland: Pilgrim Press, 1998).
12. See esp. Hans W. Frei, *Types of Christian Theology* (New Haven, CT: Yale University Press, 1994); idem, *The Identity of Jesus Christ: The Hermeneutical Bases of Dogmatic Theology* (Philadelphia: Fortress Press, 1975).

13. The final canonical shaping of the Old Testament serves to relativize the distinction between names and metaphors applied to God (e.g., "the LORD is a great God" [Pss. 95:3]; "the LORD is a stronghold for the oppressed" [9:9]). On the one hand, both "great God" and "stronghold for the oppressed" are marked off from YHWH, which is uniquely God's personal proper name. On the other, both are enlisted to declare *who* YHWH is, in ways that cannot be duplicated by the name YHWH itself. This lends some further support to the ancient Christian tradition of encompassing both kinds of terms under the category "names." For a valuable defense of this older tradition, by one who has done much to illuminate the religious importance of the concept "metaphor," see Janet Martin Soskice, "Naming God: A Study in Faith and Reason," in *Reason and the Reasons of Faith*, ed. Paul J. Griffiths and Reinhard Hütter (New York: T&T Clark International, 2005), 241–56.
14. On the name and names of God in the Old Testament, see Tryggve N. D. Mettinger, *In Search of God: The Meaning and Message of the Everlasting Names* (Philadelphia: Fortress Press, 1987); David Noel Freedman, "Divine Names and Titles in Early Hebrew Poetry," in *Pottery, Poetry, and Prophecy: Studies in Early Hebrew Poetry* (Winona Lake, IN: Eisenbrauns, 1980), 77–130, esp. 125–30. Arthur Marmorstein has counted over ninety names used in the Mishnah and other influential sources developed in the early rabbinic period; see Marmorstein, *The Old Rabbinic Doctrine of God* (1927; repr., New York: Ktav, 1968), 17–147.
15. Elizabeth A. Johnson, *She Who Is: The Mystery of God in Feminist Theological Discourse* (New York: Crossroad, 1992), 91–92.
16. In addition to the literature noted in the discussion of the absolute "I am" sayings in chap. 12 (above), see Harvey K. McArthur, "Christology in the Predicates of the Johannine *Egō Eimi* Sayings," in *Christology in Dialogue*, ed. Robert F. Berkey and Sarah A. Edwards (Cleveland: Pilgrim Press, 1993), 122–41; Hartwig Thyen, "Ich-bin-Worte," in *Reallexikon für Antike und Christentum*, ed. Ernst Dassmann et al. (Stuttgart: Anton Hiersemann, 1996), 147–213; idem, "Ich bin das Licht der Welt: Das Ich- and Ich-bin-Sagen Jesu im Johannesevangelium," *Jahrbuch für Antike und Christentum* 35 (Münster: Aschendorffsche Verlagsbuchhandlung, 1992), 19–46.
17. Rudolf Bultmann denied the existence of such a connection, maintaining that the two kinds of sayings have "nothing to do" with each other [Bultmann, *Das Evangelium des Johannes* (Göttingen: Vandenhoeck & Ruprecht, 1957), 248]. Implausible as it was, Bultmann's judgment was congenial to his theory of the gnostic origins of Johannine theology. Whereas the formula "I am + predicate nominative" was a standard trope of divine figures in the ancient world, Jesus' absolute "I am" sayings have few if any counterparts in the ancient world, with the exception of the Bible's own distinctive traditions surrounding God's name (e.g., Isa. 43:25 [LXX]; Exod. 3:14–15). By denying a connection between the two kinds of sayings, Bultmann sought to give plausibility to his thesis that the predicative sayings draw on an earlier Mandaean form of Gnosticism and thus to deprive them of their purchase in an antecedent biblical tradition.
18. Origen, *Contra Celsum*, trans. Henry Chadwick (Cambridge: Cambridge University Press, 1980), 115. For further discussion of this attractive aspect of Origen's Christology, see Tom Greggs, "The Many Names of Christ in Wisdom," *Journal of Scriptural Reasoning* (January 2008), http://etext.lib.virginia.edu/journals/ssr/issues/volume7/number1/ssr07_01_e05.html.

19. Reginald E. O. White, *The Stranger of Galilee: Meditations on the Life of Our Lord*, rev. ed. (Evesham, UK: Arthur James, 1978), 72.
20. I gratefully acknowledge my debt to Leander Keck, *A Future for the Historical Jesus: The Place of Jesus in Preaching and Theology* (Philadelphia: Fortress Press, 1981), 244, 246–47, for my observations in this paragraph, which closely follow Keck's own words. Keck was concerned with "the historical Jesus," but his remarks are equally apt with respect to Jesus Christ as portrayed in the Gospels as well. On the history of the theme "Jesus the parable of God," see Petr Pokorný, "Jesus als Gleichnis Gottes: Möglichkeiten und Grenzen einer These," *Evangelische Theologie* 57 (1997): 401–7.
21. John P. Meier, "Matthew, Gospel of," in *Anchor Bible Dictionary*, ed. David Noel Freedman (New York: Doubleday, 1992), 4:638. Larry W. Hurtado also emphasizes the enigmatic quality of the phrase "Son of Man" in *Lord Jesus Christ: Devotion to Jesus in Earliest Christianity* (Grand Rapids: Wm. B. Eerdmans Publishing Co., 2003), 290–306.
22. Although commentators sometimes notice that the Gospels depict Jesus as a stranger, the insight is not often developed in scholarly genres, whose business so often is to dispel the strange, but instead appears in sermons and meditations, e.g., Edmund A. Steimle, *God the Stranger: Reflections about the Resurrection* (Philadelphia: Fortress Press, 1979); R. E. O. White, *Stranger of Galilee*; Joseph G. Donders, *Jesus the Stranger: Reflections on the Gospels* (New York: Orbis Books, 1999); John Barton, *Love Unknown: Meditations on the Death and Resurrection of Jesus* (London: SPCK, 1990).
23. Hans Frei intended something along these lines, I think, when he observed, "A Christian case can be made that we have not met the textual Jesus until we have also met him, as Søren Kierkegaard said, in forgetfulness of himself or incognito in a crowd." Hans Frei, *Types of Christian Theology* (New Haven, CT: Yale University Press, 1994), 136.
24. Charles Wesley, "Come, O Thou Traveler Unknown," in S T Kimbrough Jr., *A Heart to Praise My God* (Nashville: Abingdon Press, 1996), 76–78, verses 1, 2, 4, 9.
25. "Odes of Solomon 19" in James H. Charlesworth, ed. and trans., *The Old Testament Pseudepigrapha* (New York: Doubleday, 1985) 2:752.
26. I am grateful to Jean Dudek, Mandy Sayers, and Cynthia Burkert for their cheerful help in compiling this list of names. I also thank Vigen Guroian for providing me with an unpublished copy of "Liturgical Canons and Hymns of the Armenian Eastern Church," from whose extraordinary wealth many of the ternaries in this paragraph are drawn.
27. Barth, *The Doctrine of the Word of God*, vol. I of *Church Dogmatics* [*CD*], ed. Geoffrey William Bromiley and Thomas Forsyth Torrance, trans. Geoffrey William Bromiley, 2nd ed. (Edinburgh: T&T Clark, 1975), pt. 1:340 (*CD* I/1:340). If Barth had taken this insight more seriously, he might have realized that by exploring this mode of naming the persons of the Trinity, the Christian tradition was *not* introducing a *second* root of the doctrine of the Trinity alongside the true root of revelation, but rather explicating *the one root of revelation* under a different aspect.

Index